NEW HAMPSHIRE
TRAIL GUIDE

5TH EDITION

**AMC'S COMPREHENSIVE RESOURCE FOR NEW HAMPSHIRE
HIKING TRAILS SOUTH OF THE WHITE MOUNTAINS,
FEATURING MOUNTS MONADNOCK AND CARDIGAN**

Compiled and edited by
Ken MacGray with Steven D. Smith

Appalachian Mountain Club Books
Boston, Massachusetts

AMC is a nonprofit organization, and sales of AMC Books fund our mission of protecting the Northeast outdoors. If you appreciate our efforts and would like to become a member or make a donation to AMC, visit outdoors.org, call 800-372-1758, or contact us at Appalachian Mountain Club, 10 City Square, Boston, MA 02129.

outdoors.org/books-maps

Distributed by National Book Network

Front cover photograph of Mt. Monadnock © breannesparta, Creative Commons on Flickr.

Back cover photograph of Mt. Monadnock © William Rogers, Creative Commons on Flickr.

Cartography by Larry Garland © Appalachian Mountain Club

Cover design by Kim Thornton

Interior design by Abigail Coyle

Library of Congress Cataloging-in-Publication Data

Names: MacGray, Ken, editor. | Smith, Steven D., 1953- editor. |
   Appalachian Mountain Club, issuing body.
Title: Southern New Hampshire trail guide : AMC's comprehensive resource
   for New Hampshire hiking trails south of the White Mountains, featuring
   Mounts Monadnock and Cardigan / compiled and edited by Ken MacGray with
   Steven D. Smith.
Description: 5th edition. | Boston : Appalachian Mountain Club Books, 2020.
   | Includes index. | Summary: "A comprehensive guide to hiking trails in
   southern New Hampshire, including Mounts Monadnock and Cardigan"—
   Provided by publisher.
Identifiers: LCCN 2020003854 | ISBN 9781628421156 (trade paperback) | ISBN
   9781628421354 (ebook) | ISBN 9781628421361 (mobi)
Subjects: LCSH: Hiking—New Hampshire—Guidebooks. | Trails—New
   Hampshire—Guidebooks. | New Hampshire—Guidebooks.
Classification: LCC GV199.42.N4 S68 2020 | DDC 796.5109742—dc23
LC record available at https://lccn.loc.gov/2020003854

The paper used in this publication meets the minimum requirements of the American National Standard for Information Sciences-Permanence of Paper for Printed Library Materials, ANSI Z39.48-1984. ∞

Interior pages and cover are printed on responsibly harvested paper stock certified by The Forest Stewardship Council®, an independent auditor of responsible forestry practices.

Printed in the United States of America, using vegetable-based inks.

MIX
Paper from
responsible sources
FSC
www.fsc.org
FSC® C005010

5 4 3 2 1   21 22 23 24 25

CONTENTS

KEY TO LOCATOR MAPS

The numbers in the boxes below and on the locator maps at the beginning of Sections 1, 2, and 4 indicate which pull-out maps cover that section. Trail descriptions are listed by the section in which the trailhead is located; parts of a trail may lie in another section or sections.

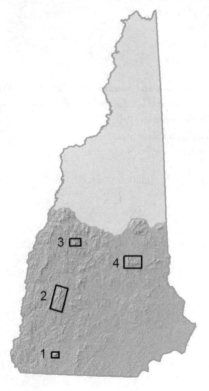

Map 1: Mt. Monadnock

Map 2: Mt. Sunapee and Pillsbury State Parks

Map 3: Mt. Cardigan

Map 4: Belknap Range

MAP INDEX

KEY TO MAP ICONS

The following icons are used in this guide's in-text and pull-out maps.

- Entrance or ranger station
- Visitor information
- Picnic area
- Parking
- Campground
- Shelter
- Tentsite
- Boat ramp
- Swimming area
- Observation/fire tower
- Cascade or waterfall
- Summit
- Gate
- Highway
- Improved road
- Unimproved road
- Trail
- Mountain bike trail
- Appalachian Trail

KEY TO HIKING ICONS

The following icons are used in this guide's suggested hikes and trail descriptions.

↕ Distance

↗ Elevation gain

○ Time

▒ Waterfall

● Pond, stream, spring, or other water feature

⚑ Exposed ledges (trail crosses an exposed ledge—a consideration in severe weather or in wet or icy conditions; hikes that end at a scenic ledge but do not cross an exposed ledge en route are not marked with this icon)

⚑ Steep or difficult terrain

⚑ Difficult brook crossings

◣ Shelter or hut

▲ Designated tentsite

⚑ Kid-friendly

⚑ Dog-friendly

⚑ Snowshoeing

⚑ Cross-country skiing

⚑ Scenic views

⚑ Fire tower (although some are more stable than others, all fire towers should be considered climb-at-your-own-risk)

ABBREVIATIONS AND ACRONYMS

The following abbreviations and acronyms are used in the book.

ACC   Ashland Conservation Commission

AMC   Appalachian Mountain Club

AMCBC   AMC's Berkshire Chapter

ASLPT   Ausbon Sargent Land Preservation Trust

Ave.   Avenue

BCC   Bradford Conservation Commission

BLT   Bedford Land Trust

Blvd.   Boulevard

BRATTS   Belknap Range Trail Tenders

CCC   Chesterfield Conservation Commission (*Note*: Not used in this book to represent the 1930s–40s public-works-based Civilian Conservation Corps)

CCCC   City of Concord's Conservation Commission

CHVTC   Cardigan Highlanders Volunteer Trail Crew

CMF   Crotched Mountain Foundation

Dr.   Drive

ECC   Epsom Conservation Commission

FCC   Francestown Conservation Commission

FOP   Friends of Pisgah

FOW   Friends of the Wapack

FRCT   Five Rivers Conservation Trust

ft.   foot, feet

GBRPP   Great Bay Resource Protection Partnership

GCC   Goffstown Conservation Commission

GPS   global positioning system

GSR   Griswold Scout Reservation

HCC   Hebron Conservation Commission

HCCE   Harris Center for Conservation Education

jct.   junction

LBWT   Land Bank of Wolfeboro-Tuftonboro

LCHIP   New Hampshire Land and Community Heritage Investment Program

LP   loop

LRCT   Lakes Region Conservation Trust

MC   Monadnock Conservancy

MCC   Milford Conservation Commission

mi.   mile(s)

min.   minute(s)

MSGTC   Monadnock–Sunapee Greenway Trail Club

Mt.	Mount
Mtn.	Mountain
Mtns.	Mountains
MVHC	Mountain View Hiking Club
NEFF	New England Forestry Foundation
NEMBA	New England Mountain Bike Association
NET	New England National Scenic Trail
NHA	New Hampshire Audubon
NHDFL	New Hampshire Division of Forests and Lands
NHDP	New Hampshire Division of Parks and Recreation
NHFG	New Hampshire Fish and Game Department
NLCC	New London Conservation Commission
NTC	Nelson Trails Committee
OW	one way
PCC	Plymouth Conservation Commission
Rd.	Road
rev.	reverse elevation
RT	round trip
SBFOE	Slim Baker Foundation for Outdoor Education
SCC	Swanzey Conservation Commission
SELT	Southeast Land Trust of New Hampshire
SLA	Squam Lakes Association
SLCS	Squam Lakes Conservation Society
SOSC	Swanzey Open Space Committee
SPNHF	Society for the Protection of New Hampshire Forests (Forest Society)
SRKG	Sunapee–Ragged–Kearsarge Greenway
SRKGC	Sunapee–Ragged–Kearsarge Greenway Coalition
St.	Street
TBCC	Town of Bedford's Conservation Commission
TNC	The Nature Conservancy
THCC	Town of Hooksett's Conservation Commission
TSCC	Town of Strafford's Conservation Commission
USGS	United States Geological Survey
WCC	Wolfeboro Conservation Commission
yd.	yard(s)

ACKNOWLEDGMENTS

Although only one name is listed as editor, this guide is the work of many people, including those who have contributed to the 30 editions of its forerunner, AMC's *White Mountain Guide*, since its inception in 1907. Guidebook editors must always keep in mind those who have built, maintained, walked, and described the trails over these many years, creating and carrying on the magnificent tradition of New Hampshire hiking. The first edition of AMC's *Southern New Hampshire Trail Guide* was created in 1998 by Jon Burroughs and Gene Daniell, and most of the descriptions in this fifth edition rely heavily on their initial field and editing work.

The current editor would first like to thank his loved ones, friends, family, and fellow hikers who have encouraged his obsession. Without their assistance and support, he would never have been able to give this book the time and energy it deserved. He also wants to especially thank his father, who first planted the seeds of walking in the woods by taking him out to explore the adjacent town forest when he was a child. Extra special thanks to Steve Smith, the former editor of this guide, a renowned authority on all things related to hiking in New Hampshire and the proprietor of The Mountain Wanderer in Lincoln, New Hampshire, for his support and help in putting together this edition, as well as his confidence in this editor to carry on Smith's good work.

Much gratitude is owed to AMC's cartographer, Larry Garland, whose trail maps are justly renowned for their clarity, accuracy, and ease of use. Many thanks go to the staff at AMC Books, including Tim Mudie, books project editor, who provided many helpful suggestions and much editorial guidance; Jennifer Wehunt, editorial director; Abigail Coyle, production manager; and interns.

For a book about trails spread far and wide and under many jurisdictions, an editor must rely heavily on the support of the dedicated staff and volunteers of the various agencies and organizations who maintain those trails. These folks have made innumerable contributions to this new edition. From the state of New Hampshire: Christina Barton, Tara Blaney, Patrick Hummel, Johanna Lyons, Ralph Newell, Greg Preville, Norma Reppucci, and Dave Richardson; New Hampshire Division of Parks and Recreation; and Chris Gamache, New Hampshire Bureau of Trails. From conservation organizations: Beth Fenstermacher, city of Concord; Leah Hart and Dave Mallard, Lakes Region Conservation Trust; Phil Brown, New Hampshire

Audubon; Carrie Deegan and Wendy Weisiger, Society for the Protection of New Hampshire Forests (Forest Society); Jason Morris, volunteer steward for the Forest Society's Moose Mountains Reservation, and Katri Gurney, Squam Lakes Association. From the volunteer trail organizations, whose dedication is truly inspiring: Craig Sanborn, Cardigan Highlanders Volunteer Trail Crew; Hal Graham and Steve Kidder, Belknap Range Trail Tenders; Gerry Gold and Brent Scudder, Sunapee–Ragged–Kearsarge Greenway Coalition; Rick Blanchette and Mike Przbyla, Friends of the Wapack; Tim Symonds, Monadnock–Sunapee Greenway Trail Club; John Herrick, John Hudachek, and K.R. Nilsen, Friends of Pisgah; Tom Duston, Chesterfield Conservation Commission; Ben Haubrich, Francestown Conservation Commission; and Bob Bulkeley, Camp Pasquaney.

Many valuable contributions were also made to this and previous editions of the guide by the hiking and trail volunteer community at large, including Ted Bonner, Weldon Bosworth, Scott Christensen, Jeremy Clark, Keith D'Alessandro, Mohamed Ellozy, Philip Forsyth, Joanne and Kevin Jones, Michelle Kingsbury, Mark and Marilyn Klim, Allen Koop, Ruth Doan MacDougall, Becca Munroe, Jon Niehof, Mike O'Brien, Kim Sharp, Fred Shirley, Steve and Christa Snyder, Dave Stinson, and William Ulwick. Special thanks to Clay Dingman for numerous contributions in the Cardigan area.

Any errors of commission or omission are the sole responsibility of the editor.

HOW TO USE THIS BOOK

In recent years there has been a spectacular growth in the number and variety of trails available in New Hampshire south of the White Mtns. Recognizing that our *White Mountain Guide* could afford the space for only a small fraction of these trails, the Appalachian Mountain Club began publishing a guide to trails in southern and central New Hampshire in the late 1990s (the first edition of this book). With the exception of the Appalachian Trail, the dividing line for the coverage of the two guides generally follows the route of NH 25. This guide cannot possibly include all of the hundreds of trails that exist in this region, but it provides complete coverage of the trails on Mt. Monadnock, Mt. Cardigan, and Mt. Kearsarge—the three most prominent peaks in the region—as well as an overview of the trail systems of the three largest state parks, Pisgah, Bear Brook, and Pawtuckaway. The guide also covers trails in a number of other state parks and forests and on a variety of privately owned conservation lands that are open to public recreation. Also described are sections of several long-distance trails in the region. Brief descriptions are included for several additional conservation areas that offer opportunities for somewhat less strenuous walks and hikes with an emphasis on nature; where available, links are provided for trail maps and more detailed descriptions. Many trails that could not be included in this fifth edition merit consideration for inclusion in future editions. We will gratefully accept such suggestions from our readers.

SUGGESTED HIKES

At the beginning of each section of this guide are a number of options for easy, moderate, and strenuous hikes within the region. These hikes have been selected for their viewpoints, diverse terrain, or natural geologic features—such as boulder fields or waterfalls. (See Key to Hiking Icons, p. vii.) In general, an easy hike can be completed in about 2 hours or less by an average hiker, a moderate hike in a half day, and a strenuous hike in a full day of 7 or 8 hours. Distance, elevation gain, and time are listed for each suggested hike; for more information on how to interpret these numbers, see "Distances, Times, and Elevation Gains," p. xiii. Unlike under "Trail Descriptions," in "Suggested Hikes," most distance, time, and elevation numbers represent round trip; "OW," "RT," and "LP," mean "one way," "round trip," and "loop," respectively. These time allowances are merely rough estimates—some parties will require more time, others less—and do not include stops to appreciate the scenery or to rest.

When choosing a hike, consider these elements—distance, elevation gain, and time—as well as special factors, such as brook crossings and rough footing. A 6-mi. hike on easy terrain will require considerably less effort, though perhaps more time, than a 3-mi. hike over rocky trails with 1,500 ft. of elevation gain. Tailor every hike to the amount of time (and daylight) you have available and to the experience, fitness, and ambition of the least experienced person in your group. Larger groups will generally move at a slower pace than smaller groups.

TRAIL DESCRIPTIONS

Trail descriptions are organized by the mountains or parks on/in which the trails are found, although some trails are not associated with a mountain. Each trail in this book is described individually, almost always in one direction only—usually ascending. In the parentheses next to the trail name, the acronym for the organization maintaining the trail (where known) appears first, followed by a reference to the map or maps that correspond to the trail. This list may name the AMC in-text map or pull-out map, a U.S. Geological Survey quad, a land management agency map available in print or online, or any combination thereof that best covers that particular trail.

A typical trail description first provides an overview of the trail, including its origin and destination and, if notable, its general character (gradient, roughness, etc.). Driving directions to the trailhead are then given, where appropriate, followed by concise directions for hiking the trail. The description notes important features, such as junctions, stream crossings, viewpoints, and any significant difficulties. The information given in parentheses above the table of distances, elevation gains, and times refers to the map(s) that covers the route of the trail.

When a hike uses a combination of trails, several descriptions must be consulted. For example, a popular route to Mt. Cardigan from AMC's Cardigan Lodge first follows Holt Trail, then Holt–Clark Cutoff, and finally Clark Trail.

DISTANCES, TIMES, AND ELEVATION GAINS

The distances, times, and elevation gains that appear in the tables before the trail descriptions are cumulative from the starting point at the head of each table. *Note*: These numbers represent one-way travel only—usually ascending the trail—unless specified otherwise. Elevation gains are given for the reverse direction only when they are significant, and they are not cumulative; they apply only to a single interval. The following example annotates how to read the table at the beginning of each trail description.

PUMPELLY TRAIL (NHDP; MAP 1: A5–D3)			
From Lake Rd. [starting point] (1,530 ft. [starting elevation]) to:	↓↥	↗	⟳
Cascade Link (2,650 ft.)	3.0 mi.	1,200 ft. (rev. 100 ft.)	2:50
destination (elevation)	*distance*	*elevation gain (reverse elevation gain)*	*time*

Most of the fully described trails in this book have been measured with a surveyor's wheel. Minor inconsistencies sometimes occur when measured distances are rounded, and the distances given may differ from those on trail signs. Elevation gains are estimated and rounded to the nearest 50 ft. Some elevation gains can be determined almost to the foot, while others (such as those with several minor ups and downs) are only roughly accurate. Elevations of places are estimated as closely as possible when not given precisely by USGS source maps or updated LiDAR data.

No reliable method exists for predicting how much time a particular hiker or group of hikers will actually take to complete a particular hike on a particular day. The factors that influence the speed of an individual hiker or hiking group are simply too numerous and complex. Most hikers will observe that their own individual speed varies from day to day, often by a significant amount, depending on a number of factors, many of which—such as fatigue, weight of pack, and weather conditions—are fairly easy to identify. Also, a given segment of trail will usually require more time at the end of a strenuous day compared with what it might require at the start of the day.

To give a rough basis for planning, however, we use the estimated "book time" formula of 30 min. for each mile of distance or 1,000 ft. of climbing. No attempt has been made to adjust these times for the difficulties of specific trails, since fine-tuning an inherently limited method would probably only lead to greater unjustified reliance on it. In many cases, as hikers gain experience, they find they require a fairly predictable percentage of book time to hike most trails but are also almost certain to encounter a significant exception. All hikers using this book, therefore, should be well aware of the limitations of the time-estimating formula; these times may be inadequate for steep or rough trails, for hikers with heavy packs, or for large groups, particularly those including inexperienced hikers. Average descent times vary even more greatly, with agility and the condition of a hiker's knees being the principal factors; this book gives times for descending only for segments of ridge-crest trails that have substantial descents in both directions. In winter, times are even less predictable: On a hard-packed dirt trail, travel may be faster than in summer, but with heavy backpacks or in deep snow, a hike may take two or three times the summer estimate.

MAPS AND NAVIGATION

Always carry a map and compass, and carefully keep track of your approximate location on the map. The pull-out maps included with this guide are topographic (maps with the shape of the terrain represented by contour lines). Maps for all parts of New Hampshire, including the areas not covered by our maps, are available from the USGS. They are published in standard-size rectangles called quadrangles ("quads"). All areas in the regions described in this guide are now covered by the recent, more detailed 7.5-minute quads (7.5 minutes of latitude by 7.5 minutes of longitude)—some in metric format—that have replaced the old 15-minute quads (15 minutes of latitude by 15 minutes of longitude). Most of the 7.5-minute quads were produced in the 1980s and 1990s. Although topography on the newer maps is excellent, some recent maps are very inaccurate in showing the locations of trails, and many trails are not shown at all. USGS maps can be obtained at a number of local outlets and from USGS Map Sales (see store.usgs.gov). Index maps showing the available USGS quads in any state and an informative pamphlet titled *Topographic Maps* are available free on request from the USGS. USGS maps are now also available online from a number of sources.

This guide features several maps that were designed on a computer, using a variety of digital data. The most valuable source of data was GPS technology. Every mile of trail on these maps was hiked and electronically recorded with GPS technology, which is then processed and edited using GIS (geographic information system) technology. The resulting maps accurately depict trail locations. Many previous maps, including USGS quadrangle maps, relied on less precise techniques to determine a trail's location. Latitude and longitude coordinates are included on the map sheets to facilitate the use of GPS receivers in the field. Although the original GPS data are exact, certain features (including roads, streams, and trails) may have been approximated and/or exaggerated to show their proper relationships at map scale.

Summit elevations in this edition have been revised based on recently released LiDAR data. LiDAR (Light Detection and Ranging) uses laser light pulses from airborne sensors to collect very dense and accurate information about surface characteristics of a regional landscape. Current technology allows LiDAR measurements to be accurate to approximately 4 in. of elevation. With a nominal pulse density of two or more laser pulses per square meter, the data are aggregated to produce an assigned elevation for ground areas that are typically less than a square meter in size. Waveform and intensity values of each laser-pulse return can differentiate between vegetation, buildings, cars, water, and bare earth; summit elevations used in this guide are based on bare earth values.

The vast majority of LiDAR-derived summit elevations are within 20 ft. of pre-LiDAR elevations—a typical contour line on a topographic map. Thus, estimated hiking times and elevation gains/losses are not significantly affected by these revisions. Trailheads and nonsummit elevations (e.g., viewpoints, cols, notches, etc.) have not been reevaluated in this edition.

The pull-out map sheet included with this guide covers Mt. Monadnock (Map 1), Mt. Sunapee and Pillsbury state parks (Map 2), Mt. Cardigan (Map 3), and the Belknap Range (Map 4). Interior maps include Pisgah, Bear Brook, and Pawtuckaway state parks; Mt. Kearsarge; and several other popular hiking destinations.

Waterproof Tyvek versions of the folded maps may be purchased at AMC's Pinkham Notch and Highland Center retail locations, online at outdoors.org/amcstore, or by calling 800-262-4455, as well as at bookstores and outdoor outfitters. Other trail maps (some with accompanying guidebooks) for specific areas are mentioned in the individual sections of this guide. These are particularly useful in places with extensive trail systems and for the several long-distance trails in the region.

The best compass for hiking is the protractor type: a circular, liquid-filled compass that turns on a rectangular base made of clear plastic. Excellent compasses of this type, with ample instructions for their use, are available for less than $20. Such a compass is easily set to the bearing you wish to follow, and then you simply keep the compass needle aligned to north and follow the arrow on the base. (More sophisticated and expensive compasses have features designed for special applications that are apt to cause confusion in an emergency situation.) The compass directions given in the text are based on true north instead of magnetic north, unless otherwise specified. Magnetic north changes over time, but there is currently a deviation (called declination) of 14 to 15 degress between true north and magnetic north in the southern half of New Hampshire. This means that true north will be about 14 to 15 degrees to the right of (clockwise from) the compass's north needle. If you take a bearing from a map of this region, you should check the map for the more specific declination and add the correct number of degrees to the bearing when you set your compass.

GPS units and GPS smartphone apps are becoming increasingly popular, but to use them effectively, hikers need to understand exactly what devices will and will not do. GPS reception can be poor, particularly in deep valleys and under heavy foliage. Furthermore, like all electronic devices, they are subject to damage, battery failure, and other problems that can render them useless. Anyone traveling through remote areas should not rely on a GPS unit or smartphone for orientation; do not consider it a satisfactory substitute for a map and compass. Without a good map and a regular compass, the usefulness of a GPS unit is very limited. In the field, it is difficult to obtain precise coordinates from a map, and it is equally difficult to determine an exact location on a map from the coordinates provided by the GPS. More sophisticated, pricier models allow you to purchase maps and download them to the device, but the usefulness of this feature is limited due to the small display area. If you plan to use a GPS unit or app, prepare a list of coordinates for a number of useful landmarks before heading out; this can be done easily by using one of the several versions of the USGS maps available online.

INTRODUCTION

The trails in southern New Hampshire offer great variety, from easy strolls along the seacoast to strenuous trips ascending the bare, rocky crests of Mt. Monadnock and Mt. Cardigan. Numerous relatively short, moderate trips lead to small, attractive mountains with good views. Some trails lead to ponds, wetlands, waterfalls, historical sites, and other interesting features. In areas with extensive trail networks—such as Mt. Monadnock; Mt. Cardigan; the Ossipee Range; the Belknap Range; and Pisgah, Bear Brook, and Pawtuckaway state parks—hikers can fashion all-day circuit hikes of more than 10 mi. Five long-distance trails are also in the region: Wapack Trail, Metacomet–Monadnock Trail, Monadnock–Sunapee Greenway, Sunapee–Ragged–Kearsarge Greenway, and Wantastiquet–Monadnock Trail.

Notable benefits of hiking the southern New Hampshire trails are their proximity to major population centers and their longer snowless season, relative to the higher and more northern ranges. We encourage you to take advantage of these great resources, some of which are little used by hikers, and we wish you many safe and enjoyable journeys.

TRIP PLANNING AND SAFETY

Hiking has a tradition of self-reliance that imposes an obligation on each of us: At any time, we may have to rely on our own ingenuity and judgment—aided by map and compass, and perhaps GPS—to reach our goals or even to make a timely exit from the woods. While the penalty for error rarely exceeds an unplanned and uncomfortable night outdoors, more serious consequences are possible. Most hikers find a high degree of satisfaction in obtaining the knowledge and skills that free them from blind dependence on the next blaze or sign and enable them to walk trails with confidence. Those who learn the skills of getting about in the woods, develop the habits of studious acquisition of information before a trip, and make careful observations while on a hike soon find that they have earned the freedom and independence that hiking provides.

Plan your trip with safety in mind. Consider your strength and the strength of your party, as well as the general strenuousness of the trip: the overall distance, the amount of climbing, and the roughness of the terrain. Get a weather report, but be aware that most forecasts are not intended to apply to high elevations; a day that is sunny and pleasant in the lowlands may well be inclement in the mountains. The National Weather Service in Gray, Maine, issues forecasts for all of southern New Hampshire (weather.gov/gyx). The Concord-area forecast is also carried on the National Weather Service telephone line (603-225-5191). White Mtns. weather information is available on the Mt. Washington Observatory website (mountwashington.org). Conditions on even the highest peaks of southern New Hampshire are usually considerably less severe than atop the White Mtns., but forecasts may suggest lesser, but still serious, weather problems that could occur elsewhere in the state.

Plan to finish your hike with daylight to spare and remember that days grow shorter rapidly in late summer and fall. Hiking after dark, even with flashlights or headlamps (which frequently fail), makes finding trails more difficult and crossing streams hazardous. Always let someone back home know where you will be hiking, when you'll be leaving and expect to return, where you'll be parking, and what route you plan to take. Do not let inexperienced hikers get separated from the group. Many unpaved roads are not plowed in winter nor passable during the spring mud season (which varies from place to place), so access to some trails may be much more difficult at certain times of the year. Always check for news of trail closures, reroutings, and updates before you head out. One good place to check is New England Trail Conditions, which provides crowdsourced information at newenglandtrailconditions.com. For more information, see "Following Trails," p. xx.

HIKESAFE HIKER RESPONSIBILITY CODE

The Hiker Responsibility Code was developed and is endorsed by the White Mountain National Forest and New Hampshire Fish and Game. You are responsible for yourself, so be prepared:

1. **With knowledge and gear.** Become self-reliant by learning about the terrain, conditions, local weather, and your equipment before you start.
2. **To leave your plans.** Tell someone where you are going, the trails you are hiking, when you will return, and your emergency plans.
3. **To stay together.** When you start as a group, hike as a group and end as a group. Pace your hike to the slowest person.
4. **To turn back.** Weather changes quickly in the mountains. Fatigue and unexpected conditions can also affect your hike. Know your limitations and when to postpone your hike. The mountains will be there another day.

5. **For emergencies.** Even if you are headed out for just an hour, an injury, severe weather, or a wrong turn could become life-threatening. Don't assume you will be rescued; know how to rescue yourself.

6. **To share the hiker code with others.** HikeSafe: It's your responsibility.

The state of New Hampshire introduced the Hike Safe Card in 2015. Hikers in possession of this card are not held liable for costs incurred, should they need to be rescued. They may be responsible for such expenses, however, if it is determined they acted recklessly or intentionally created a situation requiring an emergency response. Those who carry a current New Hampshire Fish and Game hunting or fishing license, or possess a valid registration for an off-road vehicle, snowmobile, or boat, also will not be held liable for costs incurred by rescue due to negligence.

As of 2020, the cost for the card is $25 per year for individuals and $35 per year for families. Aside from a small transaction fee, all revenues go toward New Hampshire Fish and Game's search-and-rescue fund. The card can be ordered online at hikesafe.com, where more information on the program is also available.

FOLLOWING TRAILS

In general, trails are maintained to provide a clear pathway while protecting the environment by minimizing erosion and other damage. Some may offer rough and difficult passage.

Most hiking trails are marked with paint (blazes) on trees or rocks; patterns and colors used by maintainers are mentioned throughout this book. In some areas, the color of blazing has no significance and may change without notice; therefore, blaze color is not always a reliable means of distinguishing particular trails from intersecting ones. Above timberline and in ledgy areas, cairns (piles of rocks) typically mark the trails, although sometimes signage or other markings are used.

Where hikers have trodden down the vegetation, the footway is usually visible, although at times it may be covered by snow or fallen leaves. In winter, blazes and signs at trailheads and intersections also may be covered by snow. Trails following or crossing logging roads require special attention at intersections to distinguish the trail from diverging roads, particularly since blazing is usually very sparse when the trail follows a road. Around shelters or campsites, beaten paths may lead in all directions, so look for signs and paint blazes.

Some trails in this book (as noted in descriptions) are far less easy to follow than others; the presence of signs and blazes varies, and some trails are too new to have a well-beaten footway, while others have received very little use. Inexperienced hikers should avoid trails that are described as being difficult to follow, and all trail users should observe and follow trail markings carefully.

Although trails vary greatly in the amount of use they receive and the ease with which they can be followed, almost any trail can close unexpectedly, turn hazardous under certain conditions, or become obscured (difficult to follow due to overgrowth, damage, faded markings, or lack of treadway due to light traffic). Trails can be rerouted, abandoned, or closed by landowners. Signs are stolen or fall from their posts. Storms may cause blowdowns or landslides, which can obliterate a trail for an entire hiking season or longer. Trails may not be cleared of fallen trees and brush until late summer, and not all trails are cleared every year. Logging operations can cover trails with debris and add a bewildering network of new roads.

Momentary inattention to trail markers (particularly arrows at sharp turns or signs at junctions) or misinterpretation of signs or guidebook descriptions could cause you to become separated from all but the most heavily traveled paths—or at least lead you onto what could be a much longer or more difficult route. Please remember that this book is an aid to planning, not a substitute for observation and judgment. All trail-maintaining organizations, including AMC, reserve the right to discontinue any trail without notice.

IF YOU'RE LOST

If you find yourself off-trail with no path visible on either side, usually the best idea is to immediately backtrack to the last landmark you recognize and begin looking for the trail from there; doing so will be much easier if get in the habit of noting each trail marker and tracking where and how long ago you saw the most recent one. Most cases in which a person has been lost for any length of time involve panic and aimless wandering, so the most important first steps are to stop and take a break, make an inventory of useful information, and then decide on a course of action and stick to it. (Caution against allowing inexperienced people to become separated from a group should be emphasized here, since they are most likely to panic and wander. Also make sure that all group members are familiar with your route and the names of the trails on that route, so that if they do become separated, they will have a better prospect of rejoining the group.)

If you cannot immediately find the trail, the situation is serious but not desperate. If you have tracked your location on a map, you'll likely be able to identify a nearby trail or road to which you can set a course using your compass. Most distances in southern New Hampshire are short enough that it's possible, in the absence of alternatives, to reach a highway in a half day, or at most a whole day, simply by going downhill, carefully avoiding any dangerous cliffs (typically found in areas where a map's contour lines are unusually close together), and following a rough compass course—particularly in relatively flat areas—to avoid going in circles. If you find a stream, follow it downward.

WHAT TO CARRY AND WEAR

Adequate equipment for a hike in the New Hampshire hills and forests varies greatly, depending on the length of the trip and the difficulty of getting to the nearest trailhead if trouble arises. For even short day hikes, AMC advocates preparedness. If you are going above treeline or on an exposed ridge and are not inclined to turn back at the first sign of questionable weather, you will need a pack filled with plenty of warm clothing and food for emergency use, along with the usual gear.

AMC recommends always carrying the Ten Essentials:

- guidebook (or pages of it, or photographs of pages) and maps
- waterproof matches/firestarter
- compass
- first-aid and repair kits
- warm clothing, including hat and mittens
- whistle
- rain/wind gear
- extra food (high-energy snacks) and water (3 liters per hiker, per day; always treat water sourced in the woods before drinking)
- pocketknife or multitool
- flashlight or headlamp, with extra batteries and a spare bulb

You might also bring:

- watch
- personal medications
- nylon cord
- trash bag
- toilet paper
- sunscreen and sunglasses or hat
- space blanket or bivy sack

Wear comfortable, broken-in hiking boots. Lightweight boots, which are sturdier than sneakers, provide ankle support on rough and rocky trails. Two pairs of socks are recommended: a lightweight, inner pair and a heavier, outer pair made at least partly of wool. Adjustable trekking poles offer many advantages to hikers, especially on descents and traverses and at stream crossings.

Jeans, sweatshirts, and other cotton clothes are not recommended; once they become wet, they dry very slowly. In adverse weather conditions, they seriously drain a cold and tired hiker's heat reserves. (Thus the hiker's maxim "cotton kills.") Synthetics and wool are superior materials for hiking apparel, especially for people who are planning to travel in adverse conditions, to remote places, or in exposed areas. Wool keeps much of its insulating value even when wet, and it (or one of several modern synthetic materials) is indispensable for hikers who choose especially remote locations with tough journeys home if conditions turn bad. Hats, gloves, and other such gear provide safety in adverse weather and allow one to enjoy the summits in comfort on crisp, clear days when the views are particularly fine.

PRIVATE PROPERTY AND TRAIL COURTESY

Most of the trails in this book are located in public parks and forests or in the reservations of conservation organizations, such as New Hampshire Audubon, Lakes Region Conservation Trust, and the Society for the Protection of New Hampshire Forests (the Forest Society). Others—most prominently the several long-distance trails in the region—lie mostly on private land but with the protection of formal agreements with landowners. On such trails, exercise care to observe regulations that have been designed to protect the land itself and the rights of landowners. A number of trails cross private land with no formal permission from the landowner; the existence of such trails is supported only by a long tradition of public use. Some of these trails are among the most popular in southern New Hampshire—the trails to Mt. Major from NH 11, for example—and despite many decades of public use and enjoyment, these trails are subject to closure at the will of the landowner. In recent years, irresponsible use has caused some land in southern New Hampshire to be posted against trespassing, so be particularly careful to respect the lands these trails pass over so as to avoid giving owners cause to close them.

Many trails in the three largest state parks—Pisgah, Bear Brook, and Pawtuckaway—are multiuse trails, open to mountain bikes in summer and snowmobiles in winter; in Pisgah, several trails are also open to ATVs in summer. Hikers, skiers, and snowshoers should be aware they will be sharing the trails and should be prepared to extend trail courtesies to other users.

Dog owners should have their pets under control at all times, preferably on a leash. *Note*: Dogs are prohibited in some hiking areas, including Mt. Monadnock.

CAMPING

With very few exceptions, as noted in individual descriptions, trailside camping (backpacking) is not permitted along the trails described in this book. In state parks, camping is allowed only in vehicle-accessible campgrounds. On private lands, including those owned by organizations, such as New Hampshire Audubon and the Forest Society, camping is permitted only with the permission of the landowner, which is very rarely given. Where overnight options exist, a short overview of campsites, shelters, cabins, and lodges near the trails are described in the respective section.

Never kindle wood campfires, even in places where others have obviously done so. Illegal camping and campfires are among the most common practices that cause landowners to close trails.

WINTER ACTIVITIES

This book describes trails in the snowless seasons, which can vary considerably from year to year; higher elevations have much shorter snowless seasons. Because snowshoeing and cross-country skiing on southern New Hampshire trails and peaks have become more popular in recent years, a few general considerations are given. No attempt is made to cover any kind of skiing (alpine, downhill, or cross-country), although several cross-country (ski-touring) trails are mentioned where they are open to hiking use in summer or happen to intersect hiking trails. For further reading, see AMC's *Best Backcountry Skiing in the Northeast,* by David Goodman.

Advances in clothing and equipment have made it possible for experienced winter travelers to enjoy great comfort and safety. Winter on the lower trails often requires only some warm clothing; snowshoes; traction devices, such as Microspikes; or skis. Even so, summer hiking boots are inadequate, flashlight batteries fail quickly (an LED headlamp works better), and drinking water freezes unless carried in an insulated container or wrapped in a sock or sweater. The winter hiker needs good physical conditioning from regular exercise and must dress carefully to avoid overheating and excessive perspiration, which soaks clothing and soon leads to chilling.

Avoid cotton clothes in winter; only wool and some synthetic fabrics retain their insulating values when wet. Increase your fluid intake, as dehydration can be a serious problem in the dry winter air.

Conditions vary greatly from day to day and from trail to trail. Therefore, much more experience is required to foresee and avoid dangerous situations in winter than in summer. Obtaining a current weather forecast is a critical component of trip planning in winter. Days are very short, particularly in early winter, when darkness falls shortly after 4 P.M. Deep snow makes trails frequently difficult or impossible to follow, and navigation skills are hard to use (or learn) in adverse weather conditions. (Thus, out-and-back hikes—where you retrace your tracks—are preferable to loop hikes in winter, where unknown conditions ahead could make completion of the trip much more difficult than anticipated.) Brook crossings can be difficult and potentially dangerous if the brooks are not well frozen.

Deep snow requires snowshoes or skis and the skill to use them efficiently, although popular trails may be packed out (meaning well-trod) through most of the winter. Breaking trail on snowshoes through new snow can be strenuous and exhausting. Trail courtesy suggests that winter hikers wear snowshoes when trails are not solidly packed out; "bare-booting" in soft snow is unnecessarily tiring and creates unpleasant and potentially dangerous "post holes" in the trail for those who follow.

When ice is present, as it often is in late fall and early spring and after winter thaw-freeze cycles, there is particular danger on mountains with steep open ledges, such as Mt. Monadnock, Mt. Cardigan, and Mt. Major. Accidents, some of them serious, are common on such lesser mountains when winter conditions prevail due to the ease of access for people who are unequipped and unprepared for the hazards they encounter. If icy trail conditions are expected, it is prudent to bring some type of traction footgear, such as Microspikes or crampons. Do not underestimate the difficulty of these small mountains in adverse cold-weather conditions; Mt. Monadnock and Mt. Cardigan, especially, are high enough to have severe weather. In spring, deep snowdrifts may remain on northern slopes, even at lower elevations, after all snow is gone on southern exposures.

To learn more about winter hiking, consult AMC's *Essential Guide to Winter Recreation,* by Andrew Vietze. If you are interested in extending your activities into the winter season, seek out organized parties led by those with extensive winter experience. AMC and several of its chapters sponsor numerous evening and weekend workshops, in addition to introductory winter hikes and regular winter schedules through which participants can gain experience.

BACKCOUNTRY HAZARDS

Safe hiking means knowing how to avoid dangerous situations, as well as being prepared to deal with problems when they do occur. AMC and many other outdoor organizations offer courses that teach the principles of backcountry safety, wilderness first aid, and incident management. For further reading on backcountry hazards, as well as advice on trip planning and instruction in backpacking skills, see *AMC's Mountain Skills Manual,* by Christian Bisson and Jamie Hannon. The following section outlines some common hazards encountered in the Northeastern outdoors and how to approach them.

SEARCH AND RESCUE

In emergencies, call 911 or the toll-free New Hampshire State Police number: 800-525-5555. Cell phone coverage in the backcountry can be very unreliable, particularly in deep valleys but also on some summits, and you have absolutely no assurance that a call will get through to authorities. Phones and their batteries can also fail, often at inconvenient times.

By state law, New Hampshire Fish and Game is responsible for search-and-rescue operations in the New Hampshire outdoors, with assistance from several volunteer search-and-rescue groups and local fire departments. It takes a fair amount of time to organize rescue parties, which normally require a minimum of 18 people for litter carries. In addition, an unnecessary rescue mission may leave no resources available if a real emergency occurs, so please make sure there really is an emergency before you call or go for help. All such operations are expensive, and they frequently put people at risk. Also, note that under New Hampshire law, hikers who require rescue due to negligent behavior may be billed by the state for the cost of their rescue.

Purchasing a Hike Safe Card, which is voluntary, indemnifies a hiker against the costs of potential rescue operations, unless the hiker's actions are deemed "reckless." Hikers who wish to make monetary contributions in support of New Hampshire search-and-rescue organizations may do so through the New Hampshire Outdoor Council.

FALLS AND INJURIES

The remoteness of the backcountry makes any injury a potentially serious matter. Be alert for places where the footing may be poor, especially in rainy weather or on steep, rough, or wet sections of trail. In fall, wet leaves and hidden ice are particular hazards. Remember that carrying a heavy pack can affect your balance.

In case of serious injury, apply first aid and keep the injured party warm and comfortable. Then take a minute to assess the situation before going or calling for help. Backcountry evacuation can take many hours, so don't rush. Write down your location, the condition of the injured person, and any other pertinent facts. If phone service is not available and you are hiking with a group, at least one person should stay with the injured hiker while two others go for help—hence the maxim that it is safest to hike in the backcountry in groups of four or more.

Hypothermia

Hypothermia, the most serious danger to hikers in the New Hampshire woods, is the loss of ability to preserve body heat due to injury, exhaustion, lack of sufficient food, or inadequate or wet clothing. Although the mountains in southern New Hampshire are not as high as those to the north, remember that weather conditions can change rapidly on exposed peaks. Be prepared to deal with varying conditions. Many cases of hypothermia occur in temperatures above freezing; the most dangerous weather conditions involve rain with wind, at temperatures below 50 degrees Fahrenheit.

Symptoms of moderate hypothermia include shivering, impaired speech and movement, lowered body temperature, and drowsiness. Be on the lookout for what current hypothermia education programs refer to as the "umbles"—stumbles, mumbles, and bumbles—which amount to a loss of agility, an inability to speak clearly, difficulty with knots and zippers, and similar issues that indicate loss of control over normal muscular and mental functions. A victim should be given dry clothing; placed in a sleeping bag, if available; and given quick-energy food to eat and something warm (not hot) to drink.

In cases of severe hypothermia, which occurs when a body's temperature has reached a point below 90 degrees Fahrenheit, shivering ceases, but the victim becomes afflicted by an obvious lack of coordination to the point that walking becomes impossible. Sure indicators are slurred speech, mental confusion, irrational behavior, disorientation, and unconsciousness. Only prompt evacuation to a hospital offers reasonable hope for recovery. Extreme care must be used in attempting to transport a person with severe hypothermia, as even a slight jar can bring on heart failure. Protect the victim from further heat loss as much as possible and handle with extreme gentleness; call trained rescue personnel for assistance.

Successful rescue of a profoundly hypothermic person from the back-country is difficult, so prevention or early detection is essential. The advent of hypothermia is usually fairly slow, so in cold or wet weather, all members of a hiking group must be aware of the signs of developing hypothermia and pay constant attention to the first appearance of such signs—which may be fairly subtle—in all group members.

Heat Exhaustion

Ironically, excessive heat can be a serious problem in the mountains, particularly in midsummer. Heat exhaustion, usually in a mild form, is quite common. The hiker feels tired, perhaps light-headed or nauseated, and may have cramps in large muscles. The principal cause is dehydration and loss of electrolytes (mostly salt) through perspiration, often combined with overexertion.

On a hot day, a hiker can be well along the way to serious dehydration before feeling thirsty. Provide yourself and your group with adequate access to water by carrying it or the means to treat or filter it. Drink copiously before thirst is evident. Treat heat exhaustion by providing adequate water and possibly salt (salt without adequate water will make the situation worse), helping the victim cool down as much as possible (which may be difficult), and minimizing further exertion.

Take heat exhaustion seriously; it can proceed to life-threatening cardiac problems or heatstroke, a medical emergency in which irreversible damage to the brain and other vital organs can quickly occur. This condition requires immediate cooling of the victim.

Lightning

Lightning is a serious hazard on any bare ridge or summit. Avoid these dangerous places when thunderstorms are likely, and look for shelter in thick woods as quickly as possible if an unexpected "thumper" occurs. Most thunderstorms form when a cold front passes or on very warm days; storms produced by cold fronts are typically sudden and violent. Weather forecasts that mention cold fronts or predict temperatures much above 80 degrees Fahrenheit in the lowlands and valleys should cause concern. Avoid exposed summits, such as those on Mt. Monadnock and Mt. Cardigan, at these times.

Wildlife

In recent years, there have been hundreds of collisions between automobiles and moose, most occurring in spring and early summer, although the possibility exists year-round. Motorists need to be aware of the potential severity, particularly at night when these huge, dark-colored animals are both active and very difficult to see. Instinct often causes them to face a vehicle rather than to run from it, and they are apt to cross the road unpredictably as a car approaches. Slower driving speeds and using high beams are recommended at night. Moose normally constitute little threat to hikers on foot, although it would be wise to give a wide berth to a cow with young or to a bull during the fall mating season (mid-September to mid-October).

Black bears are common but tend to keep well out of sight. Attacks on humans are very rare; nevertheless, the bear is a large and unpredictable animal that must be treated with respect. Several recent, serious incidents have been unnecessarily provoked by deliberately feeding bears and by pesky dogs leading to an attack on people nearby. Bears live mostly on nuts, berries, other plants, and dead animals. Since the closing of many town dumps in New Hampshire, where some bears routinely foraged for food, bears have become a nuisance and even a hazard at some popular campsites; any bear that has lost its natural fear of humans and gotten used to living off humans' trash is extremely dangerous. If you are confronted by a bear, try to seem as though you're neither threatened nor frightened, and back off slowly. Never run. Do not abandon food unless the bear appears irresistibly aggressive. A loud noise, such as one made by a whistle or by banging metal pots, is often useful. Careful protection of food—and scented items, such as toothpaste—at campsites is mandatory; these items must never be kept overnight in a tent but should be hung between trees well off the ground—at least 10 ft. high and 4 ft. away from the tree trunk.

Poisonous snakes are very rare in southern New Hampshire, and hikers are unlikely to encounter them.

Hunting Seasons

New Hampshire moose-hunting season runs mid- to late October; deer-hunting season (with rifles) is in November and early December, at which time you'll probably see many more hunters than deer. Muzzleloader and bow-and-arrow seasons extend from mid-October through mid-

December. Most hunters usually stay fairly close to roads; in general, the harder it would be to haul a deer out of a given area, the lower the probability that a hiker will encounter hunters there. In any case, avoid wearing brown or anything white that might give a hunter the impression of a white-tailed deer running away. Instead, wearing bright-orange clothing, as hunters often do, is strongly recommended. Be aware of the wild turkey gobbler season in May, when authorities advise against wearing red, white, blue, or black. For dates of New Hampshire hunting seasons, visit wildlife.state.nh.us or call 603-271-3211.

Mosquitoes, Blackflies, and Ticks

The woodland residents hikers most frequently encounter are mosquitoes and blackflies. Mosquitoes are worst throughout summer in low, wet areas, and blackflies are bloodthirstiest from mid-May through early July; at times these winged pests can make life in the woods virtually unbearable. Head nets can be useful. Consider using repellent made with 25 to 30 percent picaridin. While the same concentration of N,N-Diethyl-meta-toluamide (commonly known as DEET) is considered safe and also works, DEET can dissolve certain plastics and ruin waterproofing. Picaridin is a better choice for the backcountry. Apply repellents to clothing rather than to skin when possible and avoid using repellents with DEET on small children.

Ticks have been an increasing problem in recent years and are now common in woods and grassy or brushy areas at lower elevations, especially in oak forests. The most feared tick, the tiny, easily overlooked deer tick, is now fairly prevalent in southern New Hampshire, and its range seems to be steadily increasing. Deer ticks can transmit Lyme disease, a potentially very serious illness that can be difficult to diagnose if the characteristic "bull's-eye" rash does not develop. Most common is the larger wood tick (also known as the dog tick), which can also carry serious diseases, such as Rocky Mountain spotted fever. Countermeasures include using insect repellent, wearing light-colored long pants tucked into socks, and frequently checking clothing and skin. Ticks wander for several hours before settling on a spot to bite, so they can be removed easily if found promptly. Once a tick is embedded, take care to remove the whole animal; the head detaches easily and may remain in the skin, possibly producing infection.

Brook Crossings

Hikers often cross rivers and brooks without bridges, and it is usually possible to step from rock to rock (also known as rock-hopping). Trekking poles or a stick can be a great aid to balance. Use caution: Several fatalities have resulted in recent years when hikers, particularly solo hikers, have fallen on slippery rocks and suffered injuries that rendered them unconscious, causing them to drown in relatively shallow streams. If you need to wade across a stream (often safer than rock-hopping), wearing boots but not necessarily socks is recommended. If you suspect in advance that wading may be required, consider carrying lightweight sneakers or water footwear.

Many crossings that may be nuisances in summer can become serious obstacles in cold weather, when hikers need to keep their feet and boots dry. Another hazard of cold weather is that exposed rocks may bear a treacherous coating of ice. High waters, which can turn innocuous brooks into virtually uncrossable torrents, come in the spring as snow melts or may appear after heavy rainstorms, particularly in fall, when trees drop their leaves and take up less water. Avoid trails with potentially dangerous stream crossings during these high-water periods. If you are cut off from roads by swollen streams, it is better to make a long detour or even to hunker down and spend a night in the woods waiting for the water levels to drop. Rushing current can make wading extremely hazardous, even resulting in death. Floodwaters may subside within a few hours, especially in small brooks. It is particularly important not to camp on the far side of a brook, opposite your exit route, if the crossing is difficult and heavy rain is predicted.

USGS real-time water data (waterdata.usgs.gov) is useful for assessing current streamflow conditions for a number of rivers in southern New Hampshire.

Drinking Water

The pleasure of quaffing a cup of water fresh from a pure spring is one of the traditional attractions of the mountains. Unfortunately, the intestinal parasite *Giardia lamblia*, which causes a disease called giardiasis, is thought to be common in water sources, if difficult to prove. It is impossible to be sure whether a natural water source is safe; thus, all water sources in the southern half of New Hampshire should be regarded as contaminated, no matter how clear the water seems or how remote the location. The safest course is to carry your own water or to filter or treat any water taken directly from natural sources before drinking it. Options include boiling; iodine-based disinfectants (allow extra time and use twice as many tablets if the water is very cold); less-effective chlorine-based products; and a variety of types of filters; see *AMC's Mountain Skills Manual* or *Essential Guide to Winter Recreation* for more information.

Giardiasis's symptoms include severe intestinal distress and diarrhea, but such discomforts can have many other causes, making the disease difficult to accurately diagnose. This noxious ailment is likely spread by the careless disposal of human waste. Keep waste at least 200 ft. away from water sources. If no toilets are nearby, dig a hole 6 to 8 in. deep (but not below the organic layer of the soil) for a latrine, and cover the hole completely after use. The bacteria in the organic layer of the soil will decompose the waste naturally. Be scrupulous about washing or sanitizing your hands after answering calls of nature.

Break-ins
Vehicles parked at trailheads are frequent targets of break-ins, so never leave valuables or expensive equipment in cars while you are off hiking, particularly overnight.

STEWARDSHIP AND CONSERVATION
The trails we use and enjoy are only in part the product of government agencies and nonprofit organizations. Many trails are cared for by one dedicated person or a small group. Funds for trail work are scarce, and unless hikers contribute both time and money to maintenance, the diversity of trails available to the public is almost certain to decline. These trails are ours, and without our participation in their care, they will languish. For more information on volunteer trail-maintenance opportunities, visit outdoors.org/trails.

In recent years, AMC has worked cooperatively with New Hampshire Division of Parks and Recreation on an adopt-a-trail program. Another group active in trail maintenance in the southern half of New Hampshire is Trailwrights; other opportunities are offered by Lakes Region Conservation Trust, Monadnock–Sunapee Greenway Trail Club, Friends of the Wapack, Sunapee–Ragged–Kearsarge Greenway Coalition, AMC's Berkshire and New Hampshire chapters, Cardigan Highlanders Volunteer Trail Crew, Belknap Range Trail Tenders, Society for the Protection of New Hampshire Forests (the Forest Society), and New Hampshire Audubon.

LEAVE NO TRACE

AMC is a national educational partner of Leave No Trace, a nonprofit organization dedicated to promoting and inspiring responsible outdoor recreation through education, research, and partnerships. The Leave No Trace program seeks to develop wild land ethics—or ways people think and act in the outdoors to minimize their impact on the areas they visit and to protect our natural resources for future enjoyment. Leave No Trace unites four federal land management agencies—the United States Forest Service, National Park Service, Bureau of Land Management, and U.S. Fish and Wildlife Service—with manufacturers, outdoor retailers, user groups, educators, organizations such as AMC, and individuals.

The Leave No Trace ethic is guided by the following seven principles:

1. **Plan Ahead and Prepare.** Know the terrain and any regulations applicable to the area you're planning to visit, and be prepared for extreme weather or other emergencies. This will enhance your enjoyment and ensure that you've chosen an appropriate destination. Small groups have less impact on resources and on the experiences of other backcountry visitors.

2. **Travel and Camp on Durable Surfaces.** Travel and camp on established trails and campsites, rock, gravel, dry grasses, or snow. Good campsites are found, not made. Camp at least 200 ft. from lakes and streams, and focus activities on areas where vegetation is absent. In pristine areas, disperse use to prevent the creation of campsites and trails.

3. **Dispose of Waste Properly.** Pack it in, pack it out. Inspect your camp for trash or food scraps. Deposit solid human waste in catholes dug 6 to 8 in. deep, at least 200 ft. from water, camps, and trails. Pack out toilet paper and hygiene products. To wash yourself or your dishes, carry water 200 ft. from streams or lakes and use small amounts of biodegradable soap. Scatter strained dishwater.

4. **Leave What You Find.** Cultural or historical artifacts, as well as natural objects such as plants and rocks, should be left as found.

5. **Minimize Campfire Impacts.** Cook on a stove. Use established fire rings, fire pans, or mound fires. If you build a campfire, keep it small and use dead sticks found on the ground.

6. **Respect Wildlife.** Observe wildlife from a distance. Feeding animals alters their natural behavior. Protect wildlife from your food by storing rations and trash securely.

7. **Be Considerate of Other Visitors.** Be courteous, respect the quality of other visitors' backcountry experience, and let nature's sounds prevail.

AMC is a national provider of the Leave No Trace Master Educator course. AMC offers this five-day course, designed especially for outdoor professionals and land managers, as well as the shorter two-day Leave No Trace Trainer course, at locations throughout the Northeast.

For Leave No Trace information and materials, contact the Leave No Trace Center for Outdoor Ethics, P.O. Box 997, Boulder, CO 80306; 800-332-4100 or 302-442-8222; lnt.org. For a schedule of AMC Leave No Trace courses, see outdoors.org/education/lnt.

SECTION 1
MONADNOCK AND SOUTHWESTERN NEW HAMPSHIRE

2

SEC 1

INTRODUCTION

Mt. Monadnock is by far the best known and most popular peak in the southern part of western New Hampshire's hill country, although a number of other attractive peaks in this region have drawn increasing numbers of hikers in recent years. Other mountains and areas covered in this section include Bear's Den Natural Area in Gilsum, Wantastiquet Mtn., Mine Ledge, Daniels Mtn., Bear Mtn., and the adjacent Madame Sherri Forest in Hinsdale and Chesterfield; Honey Hill and Mt. Caesar in Swanzey; Crotched Mtn. in Francestown; Fox Forest in Hillsborough; Skatutakee Mtn., Thumb Mtn., and Kulish Ledges and Osgood Hill in Nelson; the Peirce Reservation and Hubbard and Jackson hills in Stoddard; the dePierrefeu–Willard Pond Wildlife Sanctuary in Antrim; Pillsbury State Park in Washington; and Mt. Sunapee in Newbury. Pisgah State Park in Chesterfield, Hinsdale, and Winchester, a relatively undeveloped park containing 13,500 acres, has a trail network of more than 60 mi., including several attractive small mountains and ponds. Much land in this region has been protected from development in recent years through the efforts of the Monadnock Conservancy and other local conservation groups.

Partial descriptions are also provided for three longer trails that are wholly or partly in this region. Metacomet–Monadnock Trail runs from Meriden, Connecticut, across Massachusetts to Mt. Monadnock, passing over Little Monadnock Mtn. and Gap Mtn. in its New Hampshire section; the Connecticut and Massachusetts portions of this trail are now part of the New England National Scenic Trail (NET).

Monadnock–Sunapee Greenway runs from Mt. Monadnock to Mt. Sunapee, passing over Pitcher Mtn., Hubbard Hill, Jackson Hill, Oak Hill and Lovewell Mtn. A complete description is given for Wapack Trail, which follows the ridge crest of the Wapack Range, including the Pack Monadnocks, Temple Mtn., the ridge of Barrett and Pratt Mtns., and Mt. Watatic. In 2018, the 50-mi. Wantastiquet–Monadnock Trail was completed between Brattleboro, Vermont, and Mt. Monadnock. A local conservation group is working to create a new hiking route connecting Crotched Mtn. with Temple Mtn.

A major ice storm in December 2008 severely damaged many of the trails in the southwestern part of New Hampshire. In ice-damaged areas, there is likely to be a profusion of undergrowth that may make some footways obscure, especially in late summer when shrubs and berry bushes reach their maximum growth.

SEC 1

OVERNIGHT OPTIONS

While primitive camping is not allowed in many areas in this region, several campgrounds make it possible to set up a base camp for multiple-day hikes, and a few overnight shelters are available for public use. Unless expressly noted, camping is not permitted.

Monadnock State Park has two campgrounds: one at the park headquarters, offering youth group camping in summer by reservation, with family camping available late October through early spring, first come, first served; and the newer Gilson Pond Campground, open early May through late October. For information, call 603-532-8862. Reservations for Gilson Pond Campground can be made through ReserveAmerica at reserveamerica.com or 877-647-2757. Pillsbury State Park and Mt. Sunapee State Park have campgrounds open from May through October. Reservations can be made through ReserveAmerica as noted above. For information on Pillsbury, call 603-863-2860; for Mt. Sunapee, call 603-763-5561.

Friends of Pisgah completed a three-sided lean-to just outside Pisgah State Park in late 2013. The shelter is open to the public and is available for overnight use on a first-come, first-served basis. Off Wapack Trail, two shelters in Windblown Ski Touring Center may be rented by reservation only (603-878-2869). There are five shelters and one tentsite along Monadnock–Sunapee Greenway; campfires are not allowed. For details, see Monadnock–Sunapee Greenway Trail Club's website (msgtc.org) or trail guide.

SUGGESTED HIKES

■ Easy Hikes

PITCHER MTN.

LP via Monadnock–Sunapee Greenway and blue-blazed trail	0.8 mi.	300 ft.	0:35

This small mountain features panoramic views in all directions from its bare summit and fire tower for little effort. To begin, see Pitcher Mtn. Trails, p. 118.

BURNS HILL

LP via white-blazed trail	1.4 mi.	260 ft.	0:50

This small hill offers good views west to the Wapack Range from a clearing just beyond the summit. To begin, see Burns Hill, p. 95.

HONEY HILL

RT via green-blazed connector and Blue Trail	3.4 mi.	430 ft.	1:05

A climb that is somewhat steep in places leads through pleasant forests to a partly open summit with views east toward Mt. Monadnock. To begin, see Honey Hill, p. 79.

BALD MTN.

LP via Tamposi Trail	2.3 mi.	900 ft.	1:35

This route to Bald Mtn. passes two fine viewpoints—one overlooking Willard Pond—on a loop hike over this peak within New Hampshire Audubon's dePierrefeu–Willard Pond Sanctuary. To begin, see Tamposi Trail, p. 113.

GAP MTN.

	⇅	↗	↺
RT via Metacomet–Monadnock Trail from the northern trailhead	2.8 mi.	750 ft.	1:45
RT via Metacomet–Monadnock Trail from the southern trailhead	2.6 mi.	700 ft.	1:40

The north summit of this ledgy peak has fine views of Mt. Monadnock and the Wapack Range and also features abundant blueberries in season. To begin, see Metacomet–Monadnock Trail, p. 39.

■ Moderate Hikes
KULISH LEDGES AND OSGOOD HILL

	⇅	↗	↺
RT via Kulish Ledges Trail and Holt Trail	4.4 mi.	820 ft.	2:35

This loop visits the scenic Kulish Ledges with their good views east and ascends to Osgood Hill, the highest point in Nelson. To begin, see Kulish Ledges and Osgood Hill, p. 109.

CROTCHED MTN.

	⇅	↗	↺
RT via Shannon's Trail	3.4 mi.	850 ft.	2:10

Shannon's Trail provides a scenic route from the Greenfield trailhead to the fine "picnic table" outlook just below the summit.

LP via Link Trail, Summit Trail, Upper Link, Shannon's Trail, Lower Link, and Summit Trail	7.2 mi.	1,350 ft.	4:15

This route makes for a longer and more challenging loop, with several viewpoints along the way. To begin, see Crotched Mtn., p. 96.

HUBBARD HILL AND JACKSON HILL

	⇅	↗	○
RT via Monadnock–Sunapee Greenway from Pitcher Mtn. trailhead	7.4 mi.	760 ft.	2:15

This route traverses a ridgeline to the scenic open summits of Hubbard and Jackson hills, north of Pitcher Mtn. Hungry hikers will appreciate snacking on plenty of blueberries on Hubbard Hill. To begin, see Hubbard Hill and Jackson Hill, p. 118.

PACK MONADNOCK

	⇅	↗	○
LP via Wapack Trail, Summit Loop Trail, Spruce Knoll Trail, and Marion Davis Trail	3.7 mi.	1,150 ft.	2:25

This route within Miller State Park provides a loop hike over a partly open summit, with a fire tower and several viewpoints, plus a circuit of Summit Loop Trail and an out-and-back to a fine eastern outlook on Spruce Knoll Trail. Dogs must be leashed at all times. To begin, see Wapack Trail, Section V, p. 88.

MT. MONADNOCK

	⇅	↗	○
LP via White Dot Trail and White Cross Trail	4.1. mi.	1,800 ft.	2:55

A nearly limitless variety of routes ascend this iconic southern New Hampshire peak with its extensive above-treeline views, but the most direct and most traveled route—also quite steep—leaves from the state park headquarters on the southeast side of the mountain. To begin, see White Dot Trail, p. 18.

RT via Marlboro Trail and Dublin Trail	4.2 mi.	1,850 ft.	3:00

These trails provide a steep and rugged approach from the west, followed by an open walk up the northern ridge to the summit. To begin, see Marlboro Trail, p. 24.

SEC 1

LOVEWELL MTN.

RT via Monadnock–Sunapee Greenway	4.6 mi.	950 ft.	2:45

The southern approach to this remote-feeling peak passes several view-points en route and presents a directional view from the summit. To begin, see Lovewell Mtn., p. 120.

SKATUTAKEE MTN. AND THUMB MTN.

LP via Harriskat Trail, Thumbs Up Trail, and Thumbs Down Trail	4.9 mi	900 ft.	2:55

This route forms a loop hike over these two ledgy, partly open peaks with good views of Mt. Monadnock. Dogs must be leashed at all times. To begin, see Harriskat Trail, p. 106.

BALD ROCK AND MONTE ROSA

LP via Old Toll Rd., Parker Trail, Cliff Walk, Smith Connecting Link, Amphitheatre Trail, Smith Summit Trail, Monte Rosa Trail, White Arrow Trail, and Old Half Way House Trail	5.0 mi.	1,550 ft.	3:15

A rugged and scenic loop with many excellent views along lesser used trails crosses these two bare subpeaks of Mt. Monadnock, starting from the parking area on the south side of the mountain. To begin, see Old Toll Rd. parking area, p. 11.

LAKE SOLITUDE AND WHITE LEDGE

RT via Newbury Trail and Solitude Trail	5.6 mi.	1,600 ft.	3:35

These trails lead to a picturesque pond below an expansive set of open ledges on the south ridge of Mt. Sunapee. To begin, see Newbury Trail, p. 126.

NORTH PACK MONADNOCK

🎖️ 🧗 🧍 🐕 🍃   ��   ↗   ○

| LP via Ted's Trail, Cliff Trail, and Carolyn's Trail | 5.7 mi. | 1,350 ft. | 3:30 |

These trails combine to make a loop, steep and rugged in places, over this fine peak, with a variety of open viewpoints on ledges, including the spectacular South Cliff on Cliff Trail. To begin, see Ted's Trail, p. 94.

■ Strenuous Hikes

PISGAH RIDGE LOOP

🌢 🐕 🍃   �↑   ↗   ○

LP via Kilburn Rd., Kilburn Loop, connecting path,	9.5 mi.	1,450 ft.	5:30
Pisgah Ridge Trail, Baker Pond Trail, Reservoir Trail,			
spur trail to North Round Pond, Pisgah Ridge Trail,			
connecting path, Kilburn Loop, and Kilburn Rd.			

This loop leads past some of the finest scenery in Pisgah State Park, including four viewpoints on Pisgah Ridge and side trips to Baker and North Round ponds. To begin, see Kilburn Rd., p. 64.

LUCIA'S LOOKOUT

🌢 ◣ 🐕 🍃   ↨↑   ↗   ○

| RT via Five Summers Trail, Bear Pond Trail, | 9.6 mi. | 1,450 ft. | 5:30 |
| and Monadnock-Sunapee Greenway | | | |

This extended backcountry trek within Pillsbury State Park leads to an excellent ridge-crest outlook with expansive views. To begin, see Five Summers Trail, p. 122.

PACK MONADNOCK AND NORTH PACK MONADNOCK TRAVERSE

🧗 🧍 🐕 🔭 🍃   ↨↑   ↗   ○

| RT via Wapack Trail, Cliff Trail, and Marion Davis Trail | 8.0 mi. | 2,450 ft. | 5:15 |
| from Miller State Park | | | |

This hike to both Pack Monadnocks, starting from the south, passes several excellent viewpoints on both peaks and includes a traverse along a beautiful wooded ridge. To begin, see Wapack Trail, Section V, p. 88.

MT. MONADNOCK

RT via Pumpelly Trail	8.8 mi.	2,150 ft.	5:30

This is the longest and most strenuous route up Mt. Monadnock but also the most scenic, with plenty of open ridge walking. To begin, see Pumpelly Trail, p. 17.

BARRETT MTN., NEW IPSWICH MTN., STONY TOP, AND PRATT MTN.

RT via Wapack Trail from NH 123/NH 124	9.2 mi.	1,950 ft.	5:35

Follow Wapack Trail south through Windblown Ski Touring Center and across these four peaks, enjoying a variety of ledgy viewpoints. Turn back at the Binney Pond/Mt. Watatic overlook, just beyond Pratt Mtn. To begin, see Wapack Trail, Section II, p. 85.

TRAIL DESCRIPTIONS

MT. MONADNOCK (3,170 FT.)

Mt. Monadnock, also called Grand Monadnock (and listed as Monadnock Mtn. on USGS maps), rises in the towns of Jaffrey and Dublin, about 10 mi. north of the New Hampshire–Massachusetts border. This isolated mountain towers 1,500 to 2,000 ft. above the surrounding country, visible from most of the prominent viewpoints in central New England. Monadnock is an Abenaki word thought to mean "mountain that stands alone," though its exact meaning—and spelling—has been the subject of some debate. As a result of the mountain's prominence and popularity, geologists use the term "monadnock" in a general sense to describe an isolated mountain that rises far above the surrounding terrain. (The Harvard geography professor William Morris Davis originally suggested this usage in 1894. Webster's International Dictionary accepted it in 1900, and the Encyclopedia Britannica did so in 1910.) The bedrock of Mt. Monadnock is primarily layered schist and quartzite—metamorphic rocks thought to be about 400 million years old. In some outcroppings, prominent folds are visible. These rocks are highly resistant to erosion. Many signs of glaciation can be seen on the mountain, including a number of glacial striae (scratches made in the bedrock as boulders were dragged along the base of the ice sheet).

The summit of Mt. Monadnock commands exceptionally extensive and distant views; Mt. Washington is sometimes visible on very clear days. Two prominent southern crags are noteworthy: Monte Rosa (2,515 ft.) on the southwest ridge and Bald Rock (2,626 ft.) on the south ridge. On the northeast side is the long Pumpelly Ridge.

Combining rugged mountain scenery, a relatively short and moderate ascent (compared with major peaks in the White Mtns.), and convenient access from the population centers of southern New England, Mt. Monadnock is reputedly the third most frequently climbed mountain in the world, after Tai Shan in China and Mt. Fuji in Japan; it is estimated that 100,000 people climb it each year, with the highest numbers coming during foliage season in October.

Despite the relative ease of access, do not underestimate Mt. Monadnock, particularly if you are unused to mountain trails. All routes of ascent involve at least 1,700 ft. of elevation gain, and many trails are rocky and rugged, with some ledge scrambling. The vast expanses of open ledge on the upper slopes, which provide the panoramic vistas that make this mountain so attractive to visitors, can also be very slippery in wet or icy conditions (and slick even when dry), and hazardous in thunderstorms. Above treeline, trails can be difficult to follow when clouds cover the mountain; at such times, hikers must follow markings carefully to avoid encountering dangerous cliffs in an attempt to descend off-trail. In any weather, descending hikers must take extra care to follow the correct trail or end up miles away from the intended trailhead. On the open ledges, trail names are painted on the rock at intersections. Many trails may be very icy in late fall, winter, and early spring (depending on weather), at which times traction devices are required for safe passage. Treat any water source before drinking.

Major trails reach the summit from several directions, and there is a network of connecting and secondary trails on the east, south, and west sides of the main peak. The most popular trailhead is at Monadnock State Park Headquarters, located at the end of Poole Rd., on the southeast side of the mountain. The headquarters also has large parking areas (open year-round), picnic grounds, restrooms, a park store, a small visitor center, and a campground. The park has an admission fee year-round. For driving directions, see the description for White Dot Trail, perhaps the busiest route on the mountain.

The network of trails on the southwest and south sides deteriorated badly after a fire in 1954 destroyed an old hotel called the Half Way House, where many amateur trail builders had their base of operations, but most of these trails have been restored by the dedicated efforts of state park personnel and volunteers. It is possible to ascend Mt. Monadnock in relative solitude on these attractive trails, particularly on weekdays. White Arrow Trail—the most direct route to the summit on this side—and many other trails, including attractive circuit trips, begin near the Half Way House Site, an open, grassy clearing on the west flank of Mt. Monadnock's south ridge at about 2,100 ft. Direct routes to this site are provided by a foot trail—Old Half Way House Trail—and by a former toll road, now closed to public vehicular use but open for hikers. (*Note*: Yield to vehicles approaching or leaving the private residence near the top.) The trail and road both leave a parking area (sign: "Old Toll Rd. parking, fee charged") on NH 124 near the height-of-land (the highest point on a given trail, ridge, or road), 5.3 mi. west of the major intersection in the center of Jaffrey and about 4 mi. east of Troy. (At the busiest times, on the weekends and during summer, this lot may be filled to capacity.) From the parking area, Old Toll Rd., a gravel road, climbs 1.2 mi. and 600 ft. in elevation to the old hotel site. Parker Trail joins the road at 0.6 mi., 1.5 mi. from its trailhead at the state park headquarters. The maintained part of the road ends at 1.1 mi., where a driveway diverges right to a private house; just beyond here, Old Half Way House Trail joins from the left. The final 0.1 mi. to the hotel site follows the eroded old roadbed.

SEC 1

The upper 500 ft. of the mountain is open ledge, bared by a series of forest fires. Early eyewitness reports from European settlers indicate that the summit of the mountain was heavily forested, with Bald Rock being the only prominent bare ledge. Farmers frequently set fires to clear the lower slopes for pasture, and around 1800 a major fire of unknown origin burned for about two weeks, greatly damaging the forests on the upper part of the mountain. A second major fire occurred around 1820 and lasted for a number of days, fanned by wind and drought conditions. It burned with an intensity that consumed even the soil, reducing the upper part of the mountain to bare, sterile rock. Since then, small subalpine plants, shrubs, and trees have lodged themselves in cracks and crannies, creating pockets of soil and beginning the process that, if left undisturbed, will restore the mountain forest in a few millennia. Many rare subalpine plants around the summit are found nowhere else south of the White Mtns.

The first English-language recorded ascent of the mountain was in 1725, when Captain Samuel Willard and a company of 14 rangers climbed it from the south and "campt on ye top." Visitors from outside the immediate vicinity began to arrive at about the same time as the last of the great fires, and by 1850 Mt. Monadnock was established as a major attraction for New Englanders. Due to the proximity of the mountain to Concord, Massachusetts, where the transcendentalist literary movement and its deep interest in nature developed around the writers Ralph Waldo Emerson and Henry David Thoreau, Mt. Monadnock attained an almost sacred status and was immortalized in the works of these notable writers and others. Mt. Monadnock probably bears more historical trails, former trails, ruins, and named minor features than any other mountain in New England, including Mt. Washington. Details about the mountain's storied history are found in *Annals of the Grand Monadnock,* by Allen Chamberlain (who served as both councillor of exploration and president of AMC in the early 1900s and edited earlier versions of the AMC Monadnock trail map), originally published in 1936. An interesting history is *Monadnock: More Than a Mountain,* by Craig Brandon, published by Surry Cottage Books. *The Monadnock Guide,* by Henry I. Baldwin, was originally published by the Forest Society and has been reissued by Surry Cottage Books. It provides historical background, as well as extensive information about the natural history of the mountain.

Land protection on Mt. Monadnock began in the 1880s, when the selectmen of the town of Jaffrey set aside a tract for public ownership and

SEC 1

protection. Over the years, local citizens and conservation groups, led by the Forest Society, have averted several development threats. In 1987, the mountain was designated a National Natural Landmark. The public reservation on the mountain now comprises more than 5,000 contiguous acres and includes conservation and public lands owned by the Forest Society; the towns of Dublin, Jaffrey, and Troy; the Monadnock Conservancy; The Nature Conservancy; the New England Forestry Foundation; and the New Hampshire Department of Resources and Economic Development. Recreation use is managed by the NHDP in conjunction with the Monadnock Advisory Commission.

Note: Camping is not permitted anywhere on Mt. Monadnock, except at the state park campgrounds. By New Hampshire state law, dogs or other pets are not allowed anywhere on the mountain, along the trails, or in the campgrounds.

The Mt. Monadnock trail system is shown on this book's *AMC Southern New Hampshire Trail Map* (Map 1), and Mt. Monadnock is covered by the USGS Monadnock Mtn., Troy, Dublin, and Marlborough quadrangles. Also shown on the AMC map are 25 points of interest—historical and natural features that can be seen along the trails—described below. On the state park's trail map, the following are designated as "main trails": Dublin, Pumpelly, Cascade Link, Birchtoft, Red Spot, White Dot, White Cross, Lost Farm, Parker, White Arrow, Old Half Way House, and Marlboro. These are well trod and, in general, well marked and easy to follow. The other trails described here are designated as "footpaths" on the state park map, and while some are well marked, they may require considerable care to follow.

OLD HALF WAY HOUSE TRAIL (NHDP; MAP 1: E4–D4)

From Old Toll Rd. parking area (1,490 ft.) to:	↻	↗	⟳
Half Way House Site (2,090 ft.)	1.3 mi.	600 ft.	0:55

This trail (despite the name, opened only in 1996) parallels the western side of Old Toll Rd. and provides an attractive, less traveled approach to the Half Way House Site from the Old Toll Rd. parking area (sign) on NH 124 near the height-of-land, 5.3 mi. west of the major intersection in the center of Jaffrey and about 4 mi. east of Troy. At the busiest times, on the weekends and during summer, this parking lot may be filled to capacity. Although not blazed, the trail is frequently hiked and easy to follow. Grades are easy to moderate.

The trail bears left off Old Toll Rd., just above the parking area, trail kiosk, and gate and parallels the road next to an old stone wall. It soon ascends a short distance away from the road, follows a long level section, then swings right and climbs moderately. At 1.1 mi. it ends at a junction with Cart Path, joining Old Toll Rd. near the beginning of that road's short, unmaintained upper section, less than 0.1 mi. below the Half Way House Site clearing.

WHITE ARROW TRAIL (NHDP; MAP 1: C4–B4)

From Half Way House Site (2,090 ft.) to:	↕	↗	↻
Mt. Monadnock summit (3,170 ft.)	1.1 mi.	1,050 ft.	1:50
From Old Toll Rd. parking area (1,490 ft.) to:			
Mt. Monadnock summit (3,170 ft.) via Old Half Way House Trail or Old Toll Rd. and White Arrow Trail	2.3 mi.	1,700 ft.	2:00

One of the oldest and most heavily used routes to the summit, this trail—marked by painted white arrows—continues along the north end of Old Toll Rd. from the site of the Half Way House, where numerous far less heavily used side trails also originate. The trail was first built around 1825. In 1861, the U.S. Coastal Survey widened the trail and built rock steps on its middle section; only a few of these steps survive today. Parts of this route are quite steep and rough.

White Arrow Trail begins at the Half Way House Site clearing, 1.2 mi. from the NH 124 parking area via Old Toll Rd. (From the south end of the Half Way House Site clearing, Hello Rock, Point Surprise, and Thoreau trails diverge to the right at a sign. At the north end of the clearing, Do Drop, Noble, and Side Foot trails leave on the right at a sign.) At the clearing, White Arrow Trail continues ahead on the old road, which soon ends at a small opening at 0.1 mi., where Royce Trail (Metacomet–Monadnock Trail, diverging sharply left and descending 1.3 mi. to NH 124) and Monte Rosa Trail (diverging left; the sign is 50 yd. up the trail) begin. From this point to the summit, White Arrow Trail is part of Metacomet–Monadnock Trail. It immediately begins to rise rather steeply through the woods. At 0.6 mi. it crosses Amphitheatre Trail; to the left this trail leads toward Smith Summit Trail, and to the right, it coincides with the upper part of Side Foot Trail for about 100 yd. White Arrow Trail continues upward and soon reaches treeline, where it bears left and ascends steep ledges in the open. After a short easier stretch, it climbs a very steep and rough pitch up a rocky gully between impressive crags and soon gains the summit plateau. Here, it meets Dublin Trail and turns sharply right, in company with this trail, to reach the summit in another 75 yd.

On the way down, note that White Arrow Trail descends northwest 75 yd. with Dublin and Marlboro trails then diverges sharply left (south) and drops off steeply; the name of the trail is painted on a ledge.

DUBLIN TRAIL
(NHDP; MAP 1: MONADNOCK AREA INSET MAP; A3–B4)

From Old Troy Rd. (1,480 ft.) to:	⇅	↗	⟳
Mt. Monadnock summit (3,159 ft.)	2.4 mi.	1,750 ft. (rev. 50 ft.)	2:50

This trail, dating to about 1840 or earlier, ascends Mt. Monadnock from the north; it is the southernmost section of Monadnock–Sunapee Greenway. Dublin Trail is considered one of the less challenging routes up the mountain. From the flagpole in the village of Dublin, go west on NH 101 (Main St.). At 0.4 mi. bear left on Lake Rd., which becomes Old Marlborough Rd. At 2.5 mi. go left downhill on gravel Old Troy Rd. and continue to the parking area on the right at 4.4 mi. (Beyond the houses at 3.4 mi., the road becomes narrow and rougher; it may be impassable when muddy and is often closed in spring.) The trail, marked with white rectangles (and white Ds on the upper part), leaves the west side of the parking area near a kiosk and swings left, immediately crossing Old Troy Rd. (The northbound Monadnock–Sunapee Greenway also leaves near the kiosk, diverging to the right.) The trail climbs briefly then descends gradually to cross a small brook. At 0.4 mi. it bears right onto a logging road, and in 150 yd. turns left off that road and ascends to join the original route of the trail at 0.8 mi. It then climbs more steeply to the tip of the ridge, passing an unreliable spring (may not always have water) at 1.2 mi. The path follows a ledgy ridge with occasional good views and short scrambles, passes another unreliable spring at the foot of a rock at 2.0 mi., and emerges above timberline. Marlboro Trail enters on the right at 2.2 mi. (sign: "Jim's Junction"), just beyond a prominent cap of rock on the left, a false summit called Dublin Peak. Dublin Trail continues upward at a moderate grade—in the open, amid interesting rock formations, with occasional short scrambles—to meet Smith Summit Trail and White Arrow Trail 75 yd. below the true summit.

Descending, Dublin Trail leaves the summit on the northwest side, continuing in that direction to a junction in 75 yd., where White Arrow

Trail diverges sharply left (south), and Smith Summit Trail diverges left
(west); look for white *D*s and *M*s and "Dublin Trail/Marlboro Tr," painted
on the ledges.

PUMPELLY TRAIL
(NHDP; MAP 1: MONADNOCK AREA INSET MAP; A6–B4)

Cumulative from Lake Rd. (1,530 ft.) to:	⇅	↗	↻
Cascade Link (2,650 ft.)	3.0 mi.	1,200 ft. (rev. 100 ft.)	2:05
Spellman Trail (2,785 ft.)	3.7 mi.	1,450 ft. (rev. 100 ft.)	2:35
Red Spot Trail (2,970 ft.)	4.0 mi.	1,650 ft.	2:50
Mt. Monadnock summit (3,170 ft.)	4.4 mi.	1,900 ft. (rev. 50 ft.)	3:10

This is the longest and most strenuous direct route to the summit of
Mt. Monadnock, but the upper half is very scenic. It was laid out in 1884
by Raphael Pumpelly, a professor, geologist, archaeologist, adventurer, and
summer resident of Dublin. Follow NH 101 (Main St.) west from the
flagpole in Dublin 0.4 mi. then turn left onto Lake Rd. (sign). The trail
turns left off the road in another 0.4 mi., opposite a log cabin on a pond and
75 yd. east of where Lake Rd. reaches the pond's shore; the trail sign is set
back in the woods. There is no designated parking area, and space is limited; hikers must park along the side of the road, observing posted parking
regulations and taking care not to block emergency-vehicle access. The
first 1.5 mi. of this trail is on private land with a trail easement.

The mostly unblazed (white where there are blazes) trail follows a
woods road for 120 yd., turns right onto a narrow path through a stone
wall (arrow), then turns left onto another woods road (in reverse: arrows)
at 0.2 mi. It crosses Oak Hill at 0.7 mi. and continues with gradual ups
and downs, becoming a footpath. At 1.8 mi. it turns sharply left and
begins the rather steep and rough ascent of the north end of Pumpelly
Ridge. The trail zigzags up and emerges on the first semi-open ledges on
the shoulder of the mountain at 2.2 mi., almost exactly halfway to the
summit. From here the trail is rugged and rocky, running near the ridge
crest with many minor ups and downs, but it offers excellent views from
bare ledges. At 3.0 mi. Cascade Link enters on the left, ascending from
the Monadnock State Park Headquarters trail network on the eastern
slopes. Stay on Pumpelly Trail to pass near the bare top of Town Line
Peak (2,884 ft.; near the boundary of Dublin and Jaffrey) and descend to
a junction at 3.7 mi., where steep Spellman Trail meets Pumpelly Trail on
the left. Just beyond this point, the trail climbs past the Sarcophagus, a

huge rectangular boulder on the right. From here the trail, marked by large cairns, runs mostly on open ledge, where many glacial striations are plainly visible. It soon passes a small alpine meadow and at 4.0 mi. reaches a junction with Red Spot Trail on the left (large cairn and sign). (Red Spot Trail connects Pumpelly Trail with Cascade Link on the lower east slope of the mountain.) Pumpelly Trail drops into a little gap with steep, ledgy walls then climbs out and comes completely into the open. It now takes a winding route over steep ledges to the summit at 4.4 mi., passing several small alpine pools; follow the cairns carefully in this section.

Descending, the trail runs nearly due east; look for a ledge with "Pumpelly Trail" and a large white arrow painted on it. A few cairns lie along the first 200 yd., and hikers must take care to locate the first one. Many of the cairns are rather small, and this trail could be quite difficult to follow down from the summit in the fog.

WHITE DOT TRAIL (NHDP; MAP 1: D6–B4)

Cumulative from Poole Rd. (1,380 ft.) to:	⇅	↗	↻
White Cross Trail, lower jct. (1,700 ft.)	0.5 mi.	300 ft.	0:25
Falcon Spring and Cascade Link (1,850 ft.)	0.7 mi.	450 ft.	0:35
White Cross Trail, upper jct. (2,870 ft.)	1.7 mi.	1,500 ft.	1:35
Mt. Monadnock summit (3,170 ft.)	2.0 mi.	1,800 ft.	1:55

This popular trail, marked with round white paint spots, starts at the parking area near the Monadnock State Park Headquarters at the west end of Poole Rd. It was blazed in 1900 by N.E. Paine, his three sons, and William Royce.

From the south, reach this major trailhead by following NH 124 west 2.3 mi. from its junction with NH 137 and US 202 in Jaffrey then turning right (north) on Dublin Rd. at a sign for Monadnock State Park. Drive 1.3 mi. on Dublin Rd. and turn left at the main state park entrance onto Poole Rd. Drive 0.7 mi. to the gatehouse and park in the parking lot on the left. The trail starts farther west along Poole Rd., diverging to the right at a prominent sign and passing to the left of a small visitor center. From the north, approach the trailhead from NH 101 in Dublin. From the flagpole in the village center, follow NH 101 west 0.3 mi. then turn left (south) onto Upper Jaffrey Rd. at a state park sign. Follow this road (which becomes Dublin Rd.) 5.1 mi., passing the Gilson Pond entrance on the right at 3.5 mi. from NH 101, and turn right onto Poole Rd. at the main state park entrance.

White Dot Trail directly ascends the mountain and is quite steep in its middle section and on the summit cone, with slippery ledges, some of which require scrambling. This is perhaps the most heavily used trail on Mt. Monadnock. It begins on a broad woods road, descends slightly, crosses a small brook, then ascends moderately. At 0.5 mi. White Cross Trail splits off to the left on a section that was formerly known as Spruce Link. White Cross and White Dot trails run roughly parallel from here and rejoin high up on the mountain; White Dot Trail is steeper but only 0.1 mi. shorter than White Cross.

White Dot Trail climbs gradually through the woods to a junction with Cascade Link (right) just above Falcon Spring (on the left via a short side loop path) at 0.7 mi. The section of White Cross Trail formerly leading to the left here has been closed. White Dot Trail goes straight at the junction just above Falcon Spring, ascends the steep ridge over rock steps and ledges that may be slippery when wet, and emerges at 1.1 mi. on the semi-open plateau near treeline. It passes Old Ski Path, which descends right (northeast) 0.2 mi. and 150 ft. to Red Spot Trail. White Dot Trail then climbs on ledges through meager evergreens. At 1.6 mi., on the flat southeast shoulder, White Dot Trail crosses the abandoned northern section of Smith Connecting Link. White Cross Trail rejoins on the left at 1.7 mi. White Dot Trail then dips into a spruce grove before continuing 0.3 mi. up steep, slanting ledges to the summit.

Descending, White Dot Trail drops off the summit to the southeast; look for "To State Park HQ" and a large white dot and cross painted on a ledge.

WHITE CROSS TRAIL (NHDP; MAP 1: C6–C4)

From lower jct. with White Dot Trail (1,700 ft.) to:	↥↧	↗	⟳
Upper jct. with White Dot Trail (2,870 ft.)	1.3 mi.	1,150 ft.	1:15
From Poole Rd. (1,380 ft.) to:			
Mt. Monadnock summit (3,170 ft.) via White Dot Trail, White Cross Trail, and White Dot Trail	2.1 mi.	1,800 ft.	1:55

This route, marked with painted white crosses, provides a less steep alternative to the middle section of White Dot Trail. It is typically used for descent; ascending this trail is not recommended during very busy days when most hikers are coming down the trail. Trail distances given below are from the state park parking area via White Dot Trail.

White Cross Trail diverges left from White Dot Trail 0.5 mi. from the parking area, following a section of trail formerly called Spruce Link. It heads west 0.1 mi., swings right (north), and climbs gradually. Then a relocated portion rises more steeply past the original section (now closed) on the right at 0.8 mi. White Cross Trail now ascends at moderate grades over boulders left by an old slide. It passes through an old burn with some views and finally reaches the flat southeastern shoulder, emerging from sparse evergreens on the ledges. Smith Connecting Link enters on the left at 1.7 mi., and White Cross Trail rejoins White Dot Trail at 1.8 mi. Follow White Dot Trail 0.3 mi. to the summit.

HINKLEY TRAIL (NHDP; MAP 1: D6–C7)

Cumulative from Poole Rd. (1,290 ft.) to:	↧↥	↗	↻
Harling Trail (1,385 ft.)	0.6 mi.	100 ft.	0:20
Birchtoft Trail (1,435 ft.)	1.2 mi.	200 ft.	0:40

This pleasant, lightly used trail, marked with yellow rectangles, leads from Poole Rd., 0.2 mi. east of the state park headquarters gatehouse entrance, to Birchtoft Trail, 0.9 mi. west of the Gilson Pond trailhead. Its northern section was recently extended to provide loop hike possibilities from the new campground at Gilson Pond. The trail sign is set back from the road, although a yellow blaze is visible. Because there is no parking at the start of the trail, hikers should leave their vehicles in the main lot in the state park and walk 0.2 mi. back down Poole Rd.

Once found, Hinkley Trail is easy to follow. From Poole Rd. it leads north at easy grades with minor ups and downs. At about 0.4 mi., it approaches small, attractive Ark Brook (also known as Poole Brook) on the right and follows the water, climbing gradually and swinging left to a junction with Harling Trail, which diverges on a woods road to the left at 0.6 mi. Here, Hinkley Trail turns right onto the woods road, crosses the brook on a culvert, and in 10 yd. turns left off the road. After another 50 yd., a ski trail diverges left at XC junction #18. Hinkley Trail descends gradually, crosses bridges over two small brooks, and ascends to meet Birchtoft Trail.

HARLING TRAIL (NHDP; MAP 1: C7–C6)

From Hinkley Trail (1,385 ft.) to:	↧↥	↗	↻
Cascade Link (1,840 ft.)	0.7 mi.	450 ft.	0:35

Lightly used, unblazed Harling Trail connects Hinkley Trail, 0.6 mi. north of Poole Rd., with Cascade Link 0.1 mi. north of its junction with White Dot Trail near Falcon Spring. Harling Trail was opened in 1914 by E.J. Harling, the second fire warden on the summit.

From Hinkley Trail, Harling Trail ascends gradually west on an old woods road, passing junctions with two ski trails on the left and then another on the right at 0.3 mi. It soon reaches another junction with a ski trail on the left (sign: "XC 14"). Here, Harling Trail turns right and in 20 yd. turns left and begins climbing steadily. The trail swings left as it reaches Cascade Link; from here, follow Cascade Link right for Red Spot, Spellman, and Pumpelly trails, or left for White Dot Trail and Falcon Spring.

CASCADE LINK (NHDP; MAP 1: C5–A5)

Cumulative from White Dot Trail (1,850 ft.) to:	↥↧	↗	↻
Red Spot Trail (2,110 ft.)	0.5 mi.	250 ft.	0:25
Spellman Trail (2,180 ft.)	0.7 mi.	350 ft.	0:30
Pumpelly Trail (2,650 ft.)	1.4 mi.	800 ft.	1:05

This trail, cut in 1921 by AMC's Worcester Chapter, runs between White Dot Trail near Falcon Spring and Pumpelly Trail, angling upward, south to north. Combined with Pumpelly Trail, it forms an interesting descent route from the summit to the state park headquarters. When adding either Spellman Trail or Red Spot Trail, it offers the most varied ascents from the east side of the mountain.

Cascade Link, marked with yellow disks, starts at White Dot Trail, just above the short side loop to Falcon Spring. It runs northeast, descends slightly, and rises to the junction with Harling Trail on the right at 0.1 mi. Then Cascade Link swings left and rises gently, but on rocky terrain, through hardwood forest. It passes a side path that leads 30 yd. right to a small cascade on Ark Brook (also known as Poole Brook), and at 0.3 mi. it crosses this mossy brook before climbing gradually over ledges in thick woods. At 0.5 mi. Cascade Link turns left as Birchtoft Trail enters on the right. In another 40 yd., Cascade Link turns right as Red Spot Trail continues ahead toward Pumpelly Ridge and Pumpelly Trail. Immediately after the right turn, Cascade Link crosses an old east–west stone wall then climbs moderately over ledges in spruce woods. At 0.7 mi., steep Spellman Trail leaves left, and Cascade Link climbs along the east bank of a small brook to a spot where the brook rises, close to the boundary between Dublin and Jaffrey. From there, prominent cairns mark Cascade Link over open ledges. Near the top of the ledges, the route passes a rock formation (somewhat obscured by trees) on the left known as the Imp, which resembles a human profile. Cascade Link then arrives at a saddle on Pumpelly Ridge before ending at Pumpelly Trail. (Pumpelly Trail is a scenic route to the summit with many outlooks and is marked with cairns.)

SPELLMAN TRAIL (NHDP; MAP 1: B6–B5)

From Cascade Link (2,180 ft.) to:	⇅	↗	⟳
Pumpelly Trail (2,785 ft.)	0.6 mi.	600 ft.	0:35

This trail leaves Cascade Link 0.7 mi. from White Dot Trail and in its middle section makes the steepest climb on the mountain, leading up to Pumpelly Trail just north of the rectangular boulder known as the Sarcophagus. (*Caution*: Spellman Trail is best used for ascent rather than descent and should be avoided in wet or icy conditions.)

Spellman Trail starts out at an easy grade and soon swings left before a short, steep pitch. From there, it runs along a clifftop across a small brook then swings right and eases again briefly. It then ascends very steeply over boulders and ledges that require a fair amount of scrambling and emerges in the open with excellent views back to the east, including the skyline of Boston on a clear day. White rectangles mark the route on the rocks, requiring some care to follow. At the top of the upper steep scramble the grade eases, and the path enters spruce woods and climbs at a moderate grade to Pumpelly Trail, where there are trail signs and trail names painted on the ledges.

RED SPOT TRAIL (NHDP; MAP 1: B6–B5)

From Cascade Link (2,110 ft.) to:	⇅	↗	⟳
Pumpelly Trail (2,970 ft.)	1.0 mi.	850 ft.	0:55

This trail, somewhat less challenging than Spellman Trail but still steep and rough in places, provides a scenic alternative to the more heavily used paths on the east side of the mountain. Marked with red paint spots inside white circles, it leaves Cascade Link 0.5 mi. from White Dot Trail, 40 yd. beyond Birchtoft Trail, and ascends on rocky terrain via long switchbacks, crossing two small brooks. At 0.4 mi. Old Ski Path leaves left. (Old Ski Path ascends southwest 0.2 mi. and 150 ft., providing a cutoff to White Dot Trail.) Red Spot Trail now climbs more steeply, with rough footing over boulders and several ledge scrambles. At 0.7 mi. it emerges on ledges with good views. After more steep climbing, the grade eases, and at 0.9 mi. the trail passes the abandoned northern end of Smith Connecting Link on the left. Red Spot Trail then swings right and climbs moderately across open ledges to Pumpelly Trail at a large cairn, 0.4 mi. below the summit.

BIRCHTOFT TRAIL
(NHDP; MAP 1: MONADNOCK AREA INSET MAP; C7–B6)

Cumulative from Gilson Pond parking area (1,260 ft.) to:	⬇⬆	↗	⟳
Hinkley Trail (1,435 ft.)	1.0 mi.	250 ft. (rev. 50 ft.)	0:35
Cascade Link (2,100 ft.)	2.0 mi.	900 ft.	1:25
Mt. Monadnock summit (3,170 ft.) via Cascade Link, Red Spot Trail, and Pumpelly Trail	3.4 mi.	2,000 ft. (rev. 50 ft.)	2:40

This trail, opened in 1966, begins near the state-owned Gilson Pond Area, on Dublin Rd. at the eastern base of Mt. Monadnock, and is marked with red rectangles. In combination with Cascade Link and Red Spot and Pumpelly trails, Birchtoft Trail provides a pleasant and less used route up the mountain from the east. A new campground opened at Gilson Pond in 2010.

From the north, approach the trailhead from NH 101 in Dublin. From the town center, follow NH 101 west 0.3 mi. then turn left (south) onto Upper Jaffrey Rd. at a state park sign. Follow this road (which becomes Dublin Rd.) 3.5 mi. to the Gilson Pond entrance on the right. To approach from the south, follow NH 124 west 2.3 mi. from its junction with NH 137 and US 202 in Jaffrey then turn right (north) onto Dublin Rd. at a sign for Monadnock State Park. Follow Dublin Rd. past the main state park entrance on the left at 1.3 mi. from NH 124 and continue to the Gilson Pond Area on the left at 2.9 mi. Drive to the tollbooth and park in the designated lot beyond on the right. (This parking lot is not plowed in winter; winter parking is available at a lot on the right before the tollbooth.)

From the south end of the summer parking lot, a connecting path (sign for Birchtoft Trail and Pond Loop Trail) descends 125 yd. through the woods to a gravel campground road. Birchtoft Trail begins at a kiosk across the road, at the left edge of a small field, while the north segment of Pond Loop Trail (marked with blue disks) begins at the right edge of the field. Birchtoft Trail descends to Gilson Pond and skirts the east and south shores; 100 yd. beyond the kiosk, side paths lead right to ledges with beautiful views across the pond to Mt. Monadnock. At 0.3 mi. the south segment of Pond Loop Trail diverges right (west).

(Pond Loop Trail is a path 0.8 mi. long that runs around Gilson Pond, passing several points with views across the pond. On the east side of the dam along the north segment of Pond Loop Trail, 0.2 mi. west of its eastern junction with Birchtoft Trail, lightly used Ravine Trail diverges right. Ravine Trail descends an overgrown bank to a sign, crosses a bridge over the pond's outlet brook, and follows the brook north through an attractive hemlock ravine. At 0.3 mi. from Pond Loop Trail, Ravine Trail ends at a T junction with a path that leads to remote park campsites.)

From this junction Birchtoft Trail swings left and ascends easily through several turns, crossing two ski trails. Hinkley Trail enters on the left from Poole Rd. at 1.0 mi. Birchtoft Trail soon begins to climb at moderate grades, crossing another ski trail at 1.2 mi., and continues ascending to Cascade Link, 0.5 mi. north of White Dot Trail and Falcon Spring. For the summit, follow Cascade Link 40 yd. and then continue ahead on Red Spot Trail where Cascade Link turns right.

MARLBORO TRAIL
(NHDP; MAP 1: MONADNOCK AREA INSET MAP; B3–B4)

Cumulative from parking area on Shaker Farm Rd. (1,320 ft.) to:	⇅	↗	○
Marian Trail (2,380 ft.)	1.3 mi.	1,050 ft.	1:10
Dublin Trail (3,010 ft.)	1.9 mi.	1,700 ft.	1:50
Mt. Monadnock summit (3,170 ft.) via Dublin Trail	2.1 mi.	1,850 ft.	2:00

This is one of the oldest trails to the summit, dating to about 1825. It is the only route up Mt. Monadnock from the west. Parts of it are quite steep and rough. Follow NH 124 west from the major intersection of US 202 and NH 137 in the center of Jaffrey. Pass Dublin Rd. (leading to the main entrance for Monadnock State Park) at 2.3 mi. and the Old Toll Rd. parking area at 5.3 mi. At 7.3 mi. turn right (north) on South Shaker Farm Rd., the first dirt road on the right past the Troy–Marlboro town line. Follow this road 0.7 mi. to a clearing on the left and an old cellar hole (parking). (This road is blocked about halfway along in winter, when hikers must walk down the unplowed road to the trailhead; it may be impassable during mud season.)

The white-blazed trail starts at a kiosk across the road from the parking area and briefly follows a woods road north at easy to moderate grades before swinging to the east. At 0.9 mi. it crosses a stone wall then ascends steeply up the nose of the ridge, crossing several open ledges with good views; on the ledges the trail is marked with cairns and white *M*s. At 1.3 mi. Marian Trail leaves Marlboro Trail on the right on a large open slab; the trail names are painted on the rock. Above this junction on the right is the formation known as the Rock House or Stone House, a natural shelter. Marlboro Trail continues briefly up open ledges, reenters the trees at a hairpin turn, and rises steeply at times, with rough footing and occasional views. It emerges from the woods; climbs a very steep, ledgy pitch; and at

1.9 mi. ends at the junction with Dublin Trail (sign: "Jim's Junction"), which comes up from the left and continues 0.2 mi. in the open, at moderate grades, to the summit.

Descending, look for white painted *D*s and *M*s leading northwest off the summit. After White Arrow Trail diverges left (south), continue northwest to a ledge with "Dublin Trail/Marlboro Tr" painted in white. Where Dublin and Marlboro trails diverge, arrows and *D* and *M* are painted on a ledge. Follow *M* to return to your starting point.

HALF WAY HOUSE SITE REGION PATHS

	↑↓	↗	↻
Hello Rock Trail, from Half Way House Site to Cliff Walk	0.4 mi.	100 ft. (rev. 50 ft.)	0:15
Point Surprise Trail, from Hello Rock Trail to Cliff Walk	0.3 mi.	150 ft. (rev. 50 ft.)	0:15
Thoreau Trail, from Hello Rock Trail to Cliff Walk	0.4 mi.	300 ft.	0:20
Side Foot Trail, from Half Way House Site to White Arrow Trail	0.7 mi.	650 ft.	0:40
Do Drop Trail, from Side Foot Trail to Cliff Walk	0.2 mi.	300 ft.	0:15
Noble Trail, from Side Foot Trail to Cliff Walk	0.3 mi.	250 ft.	0:15
Smith Connecting Link, from Cliff Walk to White Cross Trail	0.5 mi.	250 ft. (rev. 50 ft.)	0:20
Monte Rosa Trail, from White Arrow Trail to Monte Rosa summit	0.4 mi.	400 ft.	0:25
Smith Bypass, from Monte Rosa Trail to Smith Summit Trail	0.1 mi.	100 ft.	0:05
Fairy Spring Trail, from Monte Rosa Trail to Monte Rosa Trail	0.3 mi.	300 ft.	0:20
Amphitheatre Trail, from Smith Summit Trail to Smith Connecting Link	0.4 mi.	150 ft.	0:15
Cart Path, from Old Toll Rd. to Mossy Brook Trail	0.5 mi.	50 ft. (rev. 50 ft.)	0:15
Mossy Brook Trail, from Cart Path to Great Pasture Trail	0.3 mi.	150 ft.	0:15
Great Pasture Trail, from Marian/ Mossy Brook trails to Monte Rosa Trail	0.3 mi.	400 ft.	0:20
Marian Trail, from Mossy Brook/ Great Pasture trails to Marlboro Trail	0.6 mi.	250 ft.	0:25

Hikers can start an almost unlimited variety of enjoyable walks from the Half Way House Site, reached from the Old Toll Rd. parking area by traveling 1.2 mi. via either Old Half Way House Trail or Old Toll Rd. Guests staying at the Half Way House opened most of these paths in the late 1800s and early 1900s. Many rewarding loop trips are possible in this area, taking in viewpoints along Cliff Walk, Bald Rock, Monte Rosa, and the main summit, if desired. Coordinates given are for this book's *AMC Southern New Hampshire Trail Map 1: Mount Monadnock*, which shows all of these trails.

Several paths lead up to Cliff Walk from the Half Way House Site. Hello Rock Trail, Point Surprise Trail, and Thoreau Trail leave the Half Way House Site clearing at a sign at the southeast corner between Old Toll Rd. and Moses Spring.

Hello Rock Trail (NHDP). Hello Rock Trail (D4) ascends gradually through a fine forest to Cliff Walk near Hello Rock.

Point Surprise Trail (NHDP). At 80 yd. above the Half Way House Site on Hello Rock Trail, Point Surprise Trail (D4) diverges left and ascends to Cliff Walk behind the Point Surprise outlook.

Thoreau Trail (NHDP). Opposite the junction of Hello Rock Trail and Point Surprise Trail, Thoreau Trail (D4) diverges left, climbing moderately and then gradually through spruce woods to Cliff Walk a few yards above the ledge called Thoreau's Seat.

Side Foot Trail (NHDP). Side Foot Trail (C4–D4) is an excellent alternative to the lower part of White Arrow Trail and avoids much of the heavy traffic on that trail. Marked with white dots, it begins at a sign for Side Foot, Do Drop, and Noble trails at the northeast corner of the Half Way House Site clearing. Side Foot Trail leads into the woods, swings right, and at 0.1 mi. turns left at a junction; here steep and rough Do Drop Trail (D4) continues ahead. At 0.2 mi. on Side Foot Trail, Noble Trail (C4) diverges right. In a very short distance, Side Foot Trail passes a former junction with Hedgehog Trail (now closed) on the right. Side Foot Trail then climbs north through spruce woods at a moderate grade and meets yellow-blazed Amphitheatre Trail at 0.7 mi. Here, it turns left and, coinciding with Amphitheatre Trail (watch for white and yellow markings), soon turns right up a steep ledge and then left again, reaching White Arrow Trail in 40 yd. Here, Side Foot Trail ends, and Amphitheatre Trail continues ahead across White Arrow Trail. For the shortest route to the summit, turn right on White Arrow Trail for a steep climb of 0.5 mi.

Do Drop Trail (NHDP). Do Drop Trail (D4) begins on Side Foot Trail 0.1 mi. from the Half Way House Site and makes a rough and steep climb to Cliff Walk.

Noble Trail (NHDP). Noble Trail (C4) begins on Side Foot Trail 0.2 mi. from the Half Way House Site and ascends to Cliff Walk, about 0.1 mi. north of Do Drop Trail.

Smith Connecting Link (NHDP). The bare peak on Mt. Monadnock's south ridge at the upper terminus of Cliff Walk is Bald Rock; its high point is a sharp-sided boulder inscribed "Kiasticuticus Peak". From Bald Rock, Smith Connecting Link (C4), marked with yellow Ss, descends a short distance north over ledges, and at 0.2 mi. reaches Four Spots, a trail junction. (Here, the path that forks left is the eastern end of Amphitheatre Trail, described below, connecting with Side Foot, White Arrow, and Smith Summit trails.) Smith Connecting Link continues straight ahead at this junction and ascends moderately through woods and then over ledges to White Cross Trail, 0.1 mi. below its upper junction with White Dot Trail. (Smith Connecting Link once continued across White Dot Trail to Red Spot Trail, but that section is no longer maintained.)

Monte Rosa Trail (NHDP). Monte Rosa Trail (C4) leaves the west side of White Arrow Trail at a small opening just north of the Half Way House Site clearing; there are signs for Monte Rosa Trail and Fairy Spring Trail 50 yd. in from the junction. In a few steps Royce Trail (also known as Metacomet–Monadnock Trail) enters left from NH 124. Monte Rosa Trail crosses a bridge over Fassett Brook, and in 35 yd. Fairy Spring Trail diverges right. Monte Rosa Trail continues ahead and climbs steadily to a junction at 0.3 mi. where Fairy Spring Trail reenters on the right. A few steps above this junction, Monte Rosa Trail bears left (right is yellow-blazed Smith Bypass [C4]) and climbs to the top of Monte Rosa, a lower subpeak of Mt. Monadnock. To the left are the open south knob and a weather vane; a few yards ahead are open ledges on the north knob, the true summit. From here Smith Summit Trail descends northeast off the summit, and Great Pasture Trail descends to the west.

Fairy Spring Trail (NHDP). Fairy Spring Trail (C4), marked with small yellow rectangles, leaves the east side of Monte Rosa Trail just beyond the bridge over Fassett Brook. It runs 35 yd. northeast on a relocated section, turns left back onto the original route, and ascends past the foundation of Fassett's Mountain House (sign) on the left. It then climbs, steeply at times, across Fairy Brook at Fairy Spring and rejoins Monte Rosa Trail.

Amphitheatre Trail (NHDP). Scenic, yellow-blazed Amphitheatre Trail (C4) leaves Smith Summit Trail on the right (east) 0.3 mi. above Monte Rosa and climbs to open ledges at the top of Black Precipice at 0.1 mi., where there are wide views south over a ravine called the Amphitheatre.

The trail swings left and climbs steeply then turns right and runs across ledges at easier grades. It descends to cross White Arrow Trail at 0.3 mi., coincides with white-dotted Side Foot Trail for 100 yd., continues ahead when Side Foot Trail diverges right, and finally descends to Smith Connecting Link at 0.4 mi., at the junction known as Four Spots.

Cart Path (NHDP). Cart Path (D3–C3), marked with yellow rectangles, leads west from Old Toll Rd. about 0.1 mi. below the Half Way House Site, descending gradually and crossing Old Half Way House Trail, Royce Trail (Metacomet–Monadnock Trail), Fassett Brook, and another small brook. It then runs at easy grades northwest through hardwood forest, ascends briefly, and ends abruptly at 0.5 mi., at a junction with Mossy Brook Trail, where there are signs for both trails.

Mossy Brook Trail (NHDP). Where Cart Path ends, Mossy Brook Trail (C3) continues, also marked with yellow rectangles. It swings right (north) into spruce woods and soon comes beside Mossy Brook on the left. The path climbs alongside the brook and then crosses the water shortly before ending at 0.3 mi., at a junction with Great Pasture Trail (right) and Marian Trail (left).

Great Pasture Trail (NHDP). Great Pasture Trail (C3–C4) is also marked with yellow rectangles, though it is blazed only for the ascent. The trail leaves the junction of Marian and Mossy Brook trails, crosses Mossy Brook, and ascends to the summit of Monte Rosa and Monte Rosa Trail at 0.3 mi., emerging on ledges near the top.

Marian Trail (NHDP). Lightly used Marian Trail (C3–B3), marked with yellow disks, begins at the junction with Mossy Brook and Great Pasture trails, turns sharply right in 60 yd., and ascends north through spruce woods, with occasional short descents. At 0.2 mi. it crosses a ledge with a view west. It continues up through the woods, crosses a small brook, and then climbs by switchbacks through a rough, rocky area, emerging on open ledges before reaching Marlboro Trail at 0.6 mi. by the Rock House.

SMITH SUMMIT TRAIL (NHDP; MAP 1: C4–B4)

From Monte Rosa summit (2,515 ft.) to:	⇅	↗	◯
Mt. Monadnock summit (3,170 ft.)	0.7 mi.	700 ft. (rev. 50 ft.)	0:40

This lightly used trail, opened by Scott A. Smith in 1898, ascends from Monte Rosa to Mt. Monadnock's main summit, following a winding route on the southwest side of the cone. The path is steep in places but affords many fine views. It is marked with white dots and *S*s, which must be followed carefully on the upper ledges.

From the summit of Monte Rosa, Smith Summit Trail makes a short, steep descent to the Tooth, a prominent pointed ledge on the right with a scenic view, where Smith Bypass (a yellow-blazed connector, 0.1 mi. long, from Monte Rosa Trail) enters on the right. Smith Summit Trail bears left and winds up over ledges and through scrub to the junction with Amphitheatre Trail on the right (signs) at 0.3 mi. It ascends moderately through spruce woods, and then at 0.4 mi. it begins to climb up steep ledges, with occasional scrambles and excellent views south and west. At 0.6 mi. the trail swings right (east) and soon scrambles up a narrow gully. (At the bottom of this pitch, ledges 20 yd. to the right of the trail provide a good view of the Billings Fold—layers of rock that were pressed or "folded" up against each other when the mountain was formed—on a cliff.) The route meets White Arrow and Dublin trails just below the summit.

Descending, look for "Smith Summit Trail" painted in white on the rock just below where White Arrow Trail diverges to the left.

CLIFF WALK (NHDP; MAP 1: D4–C4)

Cumulative from Parker Trail (1,750 ft.) to:	⇅	↗	↺
Hello Rock (2,150 ft.)	0.6 mi.	450 ft. (rev. 50 ft.)	0:30
Lost Farm Trail (2,340 ft.)	1.0 mi.	700 ft. (rev. 50 ft.)	0:50
Bald Rock (2,626 ft.)	1.4 mi.	1,000 ft.	1:10

This is one of the finest scenic trails on Mt. Monadnock, leading from Parker Trail, 0.3 mi. east of Old Toll Rd., to Bald Rock. It runs along the south and east edges of the south ridge, passing several splendid viewpoints and historical points of interest. Cliff Walk is marked with white diamonds on the trees and white *C*s on the rocks, and in places it is steep and rough. Cut in the 1890s, it was a popular route for guests staying at the Half Way House.

From Parker Trail, Cliff Walk ascends briefly northeast then swings left and climbs a steep pitch (with a ladder). It ascends moderately, with some steep pitches and occasional short descents, west and north through woods to Hello Rock on the right at 0.6 mi., where there is a good view east. The path drops into a wooded col, where Hello Rock Trail (sign) diverges left, and then it climbs northeast, reaching the fine outlook known as Point Surprise at 0.7 mi. At the spot where Point Surprise Trail (sign) departs on the left, Cliff Walk dips into the woods behind the outlook and continues across the flank of the mountain past a side path on the right (sign) at 0.8 mi. that leads 20 yd. to the viewpoint known as What Cheer Point. Cliff

Walk then descends briefly to Black-Throated Blue Point (another outlook) before climbing to the viewpoint called Ainsworth's Seat. Past this site, the route descends slightly to a junction at 1.0 mi., where Lost Farm Trail joins from the right. (An excellent viewpoint sits 15 yd. down this trail.) Here, Cliff Walk swings left and climbs steeply to the ledge known as Thoreau's Seat (sign and view). Just beyond, Thoreau Trail (sign) leaves on the left. Cliff Walk soon turns left (west) again by the wooded ledge called Emerson's Seat. It dips and then climbs rough ledges, passing Do Drop Trail (sign) on the left at 1.2 mi. Then it swings north and crosses an outcropping with a view south. In another 60 yd., Noble Trail (sign) diverges left. (Hikers can reach a ledge with good views west and up to the summit of Mt. Monadnock by following this trail for 40 yd.) Cliff Walk continues north, climbing past a short side path on the left that leads to the boulders and crevices of the geologic feature known as the Wolf's Den (see p. 37), and then past another path leading to the Graphite Mine (see p. 37). The trail then climbs steeply up ledges to the summit of Bald Rock, where Smith Connecting Link continues ahead (north). (Hedgehog Trail, which used to diverge left here, is now closed.) Visitors can see fine views in all directions here, including the summit of Mt. Monadnock to the north.

PARKER TRAIL (NHDP; MAP 1: D6–D4)

Cumulative from bridge below spillway of Poole Reservoir (1,370 ft.) to:	�	↗	○
Lost Farm Trail (1,570 ft.)	0.6 mi.	200 ft.	0:25
Cliff Walk (1,750 ft.)	1.2 mi.	400 ft.	0:50
Old Toll Rd. (1,810 ft.)	1.5 mi.	500 ft. (rev. 50 ft.)	1:00

Parker Trail, opened in 1911 by Mr. and Mrs. G.H. Parker, begins at the bridge over the outlet brook below the spillway at the south end of Poole Reservoir, near the picnic area at Monadnock State Park Headquarters. It heads west across the south slope of the mountain to Old Toll Rd. and connects numerous loop hikes. Blazed with yellow rectangles, Parker Trail maintains a mostly gentle grade and provides easy walking through mature woods.

To reach the east end of the route, follow signs for Parker Trail along an access road leading 0.1 mi. south from a pavilion near the park headquarters to the picnic area on the east side of the reservoir. Turn right here and follow a grassy road along a fence at the south end of the reservoir, passing a trail sign, and descend to a bridge over the outlet brook below the dam and spillway. Mileages begin here.

The trail ascends moderately, crossing over two stone walls, and then becomes nearly level. At 0.6 mi. Lost Farm Trail diverges right for the upper part of Cliff Walk. Parker Trail continues at mostly easy grades, paralleling a stone wall on the left for some distance. It loops briefly out to the right past a large boulder to cross Ainsworth Brook on a new bridge, crosses two more stone walls, and then passes Hunter's Rock, another large boulder, on the right at 1.0 mi. At 1.2 mi. Cliff Walk diverges right (sign). Parker Trail continues a gradual ascent, passes through a small wooded pass called the Notch, bears right where an obscure path to a viewpoint on Little Mtn. diverges left, and descends slightly to join Old Toll Rd. 0.6 mi. above NH 124 and 0.6 mi. below the Half Way House Site.

LOST FARM TRAIL (NHDP; MAP 1: D5–D4)

From Parker Trail (1,570 ft.) to:	⮯⮭	⬈	⟳
Cliff Walk (2,340 ft.)	1.1 mi.	800 ft. (rev. 50 ft.)	0:55

This white-blazed trail branches right (north) from Parker Trail 0.6 mi. from the bridge at Poole Reservoir in Monadnock State Park. It ascends gradually 0.1 mi. along a stone wall, dips to cross a small brook, and then ascends moderately through hardwood forest. At 0.5 mi., with a stone wall on the right, the trail turns left and climbs northwest across the slope. It then swings more to the southwest, angling up across the side of the ridge on rocky terrain. The path alternately follows the contour of the steep slope and climbs along it then passes a fine outlook ledge on the left just before ending at its junction with Cliff Walk at 1.1 mi., a short distance below Thoreau's Seat.

Points of Interest on Mt. Monadnock

Described briefly on the following pages are some of the numerous historical and natural points of interest on Mt. Monadnock. Coordinates given correspond with this book's *AMC Southern New Hampshire Trail Map 1: Mount Monadnock*. Most of these features are easily seen along the mountain's trails; some are identified by signs.

1. Mt. Monadnock Summit (B4). Much of interest surrounds this bare rock summit. Evidence of survey work is prominent on the ledges. In 1861, the U.S. Coastal Survey established a station at the summit for several weeks. Workers carved a triangle into the rock around a drill hole, with five lines radiating from it—representing the triangulation stations (reference points used for surveying and mapping) at Gunstock Mtn. and South

Uncanoonuc Mtn. in New Hampshire, Wachusett Mtn. and Mt. Tom in Massachusetts, and Bald Hill in Union, Connecticut. These inscriptions are easily visible today. Close by is a brass disk placed in 1931 by the USGS that established the summit elevation at 3,165 ft.—just a foot lower than the 3,166 ft. published on the first USGS map of the mountain in 1898. The most recent USGS map (the metric-based Monadnock Mtn. quadrangle, 1984) does not give an exact elevation. Based on the 2019 New Hampshire LiDAR survey, the elevation listed in this guidebook is 3,170 ft. The USGS has placed other brass disks around the summit as reference marks, and arrows chiseled by Coastal Survey workers point toward the main triangulation marker. Also seen on the ledges is a bewildering array of initials, names, dates, and symbols carved into the rock by early visitors—a practice noted disapprovingly by the writer Henry David Thoreau. (Chiseling into the rocks on Mt. Monadnock is now illegal.)

Various small structures have been placed on the summit over the years. In the 1860s, the Coastal Survey erected a prominent tripod with a pole, which was later replaced by a large flagpole. In 1910, members of the Monadnock Mountain Association from the Half Way House built a crude stone shelter against a cliff on the south side of the summit, but a hurricane blew the roof off in 1938, and the structure was dismantled. In 1912, the New Hampshire Forestry Commission built a small wooden lookout cabin on the summit, which became known as the Pill Box or Tip Top House. It was just 6 ft. square and was chained to the rocks. In 1928, the Pill Box was moved down onto Pumpelly Trail as a refuge shelter. It was replaced by a stone lookout station with a metal roof and windows on all sides. The structure was set down in a depression on the south side of the summit. (Hikers often use the depression, informally called "the cellar," to get out of the wind.) The lookout station was staffed until 1948. After that it was used as a refreshment stand, but this was discontinued in 1969, and the building was removed in 1972. No structures have stood on the summit since then.

The expansive view from the summit has long been heralded as among the best in New England. On clear days hikers may see Mt. Washington 105 mi. to the north; the southern Green Mtns. to the west and northwest; Mt. Greylock to the west-southwest; and the Clarendon (formerly John Hancock) and Prudential towers and financial district skyline in Boston, 65 mi. to the southeast. Edward G. Chamberlain crafted a masterful panorama of the view for AMC that was published in the November 1920 issue of *Appalachia*. A more recent panorama appears in *Scudder's White Mountain Viewing Guide* (High Top Press, 2005).

2. Billings Fold (B4). On a prominent cliff southwest of the summit, between White Arrow and Smith Summit trails, is a dramatic example of the folding in the mountain's schist and quartzite bedrock. (These metamorphic rocks formed when layered sedimentary rocks were subjected to intense heat and pressure and were folded in the process.) This feature was named for geologists Katherine Fowler-Billings and Marland Billings. Katherine Fowler-Billings performed the first comprehensive research on the geology of Mt. Monadnock, and in 1949 she wrote *Geology of the Monadnock Quadrangle, New Hampshire.* Marland Billings, her husband, wrote a well-known textbook called *Structural Geology.* The best vantage point for seeing the fold is a ledgy outcropping a few yards to the right of Smith Summit Trail, just before that trail scrambles up a narrow gully below its junction with Dublin Trail.

3. Falcon Spring (C5). This reliable water source (always treat sourced water) is on a loop side path on the west side of White Dot Trail just below its junction with Cascade Link. The name refers to William M. Falconer, who manned a forest fire lookout station on Mt. Monadnock starting in 1913. A log cabin built for him near the spring was soon named the Falcon Hut. Before long, the spring—for the previous 10 years known as Bubbling Spring—was rechristened Falcon Spring. In 1995, the Jaffrey Boy Scouts rebuilt the spring enclosure and made other improvements to the site. The spring issues from a pipe, and benches nearby beckon hikers to take a break.

4. Hunter's Rock (D4). This large glacial erratic (a boulder dragged along by a continental glacier and deposited in place) sits along the north side of Parker Trail 0.2 mi. east of its junction with Cliff Walk. Situated in a hardwood forest, with a stone wall running along its base, the boulder reputedly has been used as a deer stand by past hunters (hunting is not currently allowed within Monadnock State Park).

5. Hello Rock (D4). Guests staying at the nearby Half Way House used to stand on this ledge and shout, "Hello!" to visitors ascending Old Toll Rd. The open ledge, along the east side of Cliff Walk just below its junction with Hello Rock Trail, provides an expansive view east and south. Half Way House guest Scott A. Smith built Hello Rock Trail in 1896.

6. Point Surprise (D4). Half Way House guests named this spacious open ledge along Cliff Walk for the wide eastern and southern views it suddenly reveals when the hiker emerges from a dense stand of spruce forest. Scott A. Smith built Point Surprise Trail, which joins Cliff Walk behind the outlook, in 1894.

7. What Cheer Point (D4). Another of the ledges along Cliff Walk, located 130 yd. above Point Surprise, this fairly small outlook is on a short side path, marked by a sign. Half Way House guests from Providence, Rhode Island, were the primary trail builders in this area. To name this outlook, they borrowed an expression from early Rhode Island history. When Roger Williams, the state's first governor, initially landed at Providence, lore has it the Narragansett gave him a greeting that resembled "what cheer netop."

8. Black-Throated Blue Point (D4). This fine open ledge (no sign) on Cliff Walk, about 0.1 mi. above What Cheer Point, got its name from the black-throated blue warblers seen from there by Dr. Leon Augustus Hausman, a professor at Rutgers University who was a frequent guest at Half Way House. Dr. Hausman wrote an essay on the birdlife of Mt. Monadnock for the November 1935 issue of *Appalachia*. "To the student of bird life," he wrote, "Monadnock affords a region rich in interest of an unusual sort." *The Monadnock Guide* (Surry Cottage Books, 2010) notes that 150 species of birds have been identified on the mountain, with as many as 75 species nesting there.

9. Ainsworth's Seat (D4). On the east side of Cliff Walk, just below the junction with Lost Farm Trail, this open, rocky viewpoint was named for Rev. Laban Ainsworth (Jaffrey's first minister), who settled in the town in 1784. At that time he acquired ownership of two lots high up on the mountain, property that later became the route of White Arrow Trail. Ainsworth's land holdings became important in 1865 when the owners of the Half Way House placed a claim on ownership of the summit of Mt. Monadnock and the land crossed by White Arrow Trail. If the claim had gone unchallenged for 20 years, the hotel would have obtained full ownership of the tract. In 1884, however, the selectmen of Jaffrey, wishing to see public ownership of the upper mountain, contested the claim, and with the cooperation of Ainsworth's heirs, ownership of the land was transferred to the town. This is said to have been the first time in post-Columbian history that a municipality acquired land for the sole purpose of preserving it.

10. Thoreau's Seat (D4). The famous philosopher and naturalist Henry David Thoreau visited Mt. Monadnock four times (in 1844, 1852, 1858, and 1860) and rambled across its slopes, making detailed natural history observations in his journal. This hogback-shaped ledge, on Cliff Walk just below the junction with Thoreau Trail, was named in his honor, although it is uncertain whether he actually sat there. The view is good but partly restricted. During his 1860 visit, Thoreau noted 40 people on the summit at one time and about 500 people over a six-day period, indicating that crowds are nothing new on Mt. Monadnock. Thoreau Bog, another Mt. Monadnock feature named for him, is a large, high-elevation bog at the head of Mountain Brook, northeast of the summit.

11. Emerson's Seat (D4). Mt. Monadnock was an iconic mountain for the transcendentalist philosopher Ralph Waldo Emerson. He may have visited Mt. Monadnock in 1845, although there is considerable doubt about this. In any case, in 1846 he published a long poem, *Monadnoc*, that brought the mountain to the attention of the literary world. Emerson did climb Mt. Monadnock in June 1866, when he was a guest at Half Way House (then called the Monadnock Mountain House). At the top he marveled at the view: "The country below was a vast campaign—half cleared, half forest—with 40 ponds in sight, studded with villages and farmhouses and all around the horizon, closed with mountain ranges." He had planned to camp near the summit with his son, daughter, and friends, but a heavy rainstorm drove him and several of the would-be campers back down White Arrow Trail to the hotel. The next day, with better weather, he went back to the peak to take in the scenery again. It's uncertain whether he ever stopped at Emerson's Seat, a ledge along Cliff Walk a short distance above Thoreau's Seat, but summer resident and trail builder Scott A. Smith named it in his honor. The view from this ledge, however, is now overgrown.

12. Half Way House Site (C4). A clearing at the top of Old Toll Rd. marks the site of Half Way House, a Mt. Monadnock landmark. The grassy space is a pleasant rest spot, with a peek up at the summit of Mt. Monadnock and a distant view west. Several primitive lodgings had been developed at various locations on the mountain, starting in 1823, but it was not until Moses Cudworth of Rindge, New Hampshire, built a barn and wagon shed in 1860 and a two-story house the following year—at the top of the wagon road that went halfway up the south side of the mountain—that a more comfortable style of lodging was available to Mt. Monadnock visitors. (Work on this road, which later became known as Old Toll Rd., began as early as 1779.) The hostelry was first known as the Monadnock Mountain House, or simply the Mountain House.

In 1863, George and Abbie Rice purchased the property and expanded the operation, building a three-and-a-half-story resort hotel that opened in June 1866. Boarding rates were $8 to $14 weekly, with children staying at half price. The new hotel burned down shortly after closing for the winter. George Rice built a smaller hotel on the site the following spring, but in 1868 he sold the property to Philip S. and Stephen Batcheller and Charles Newton, residents of Fitzwilliam, New Hampshire. They constructed a larger hotel, and over the years it expanded; by 1885 it could accommodate 100 guests. The property had its own reservoir, expansive yards, a spacious porch, and several guest cottages.

The hotel continued to operate well into the 1900s under the Batcheller heirs. Many guests returned year after year, building numerous paths around the mountain. In 1916, the name was officially changed to Half Way House. The property came into public ownership in 1947, when local residents formed the Association to Protect Mt. Monadnock in response to a proposal to build a radio tower on the summit. The hotel continued to operate until it burned in 1954. For the next 15 years volunteers ran a refreshment stand at the site, but in 1969 Old Toll Rd. was closed to public motor vehicle traffic, and the refreshment stand was dismantled. Today, little remains of the hotel, save for Moses Spring, where a hole was drilled and a basin sculpted in the rock behind the hotel. A memorial inscription (now covered in moss) is on a rock face in the woods just to the left of the entrance to Thoreau, Point Surprise, and Hello Rock trails.

A once popular picnic grove a short distance northwest of Half Way House is now quite overgrown. In this place, local farmer Joseph Fassett, who operated Fassett's Mountain House nearby during the 1850s, built an outdoor bowling alley for the amusement of his guests. Here, Monte Rosa and Royce trails diverge from White Arrow Trail.

13. Fassett House Site (C4). In 1854, local farmer Joseph Fassett built a small frame cabin with a stone foundation on the west side of Fairy Spring Trail, a short distance above that path's junction with Monte Rosa Trail. The building was only about 25 feet square. It burned in 1856 but was soon rebuilt as the Mountain House. Fassett developed a wagon road (the upper part of what is now known as Old Toll Rd.) to provide access to his hostelry. He is also credited with opening a trail up the valley of what is now known as Fassett Brook and with improving White Arrow Trail to the summit. He dammed a nearby brook to provide a water source for the Mountain House. In 1857, some 700 visitors signed his guest book. Thoreau passed by the house in 1858, noting in his journal that Fassett was "so busily at work inside that he did not see us." Fassett died later that year, and the Mountain House ceased operations after 1860. Today visitors can see a large overturned rock at the site that bears the inscription "MOUNTAIN HOUSE JF 1857."

14. Fairy Spring (C4). On Fairy Spring Trail between the Half Way House Site and Monte Rosa, there is a pool amid the moss-covered rocks of Fairy Brook, and a small spring issues from a crack in a ledge. The fanciful name was presumably bestowed by Half Way House guests. Joseph Fassett opened the steep trail that ascends past the spring in the 1850s.

15. Wolf's Den (C4). These crevices amid ledges and boulders along the west side of Cliff Walk, just below Bald Rock and the Graphite Mine, were named by guests of Half Way House, who imagined that wolves could find refuge there. In fact, settlers had exterminated wolves in the area by about 1820. A sign marks a short side trail that leads to the rocks.

16. Graphite Mine (C4). This old mine site is on the west side of Cliff Walk just south of and below Bald Rock. A sign marks a side path that scrambles up and over a ledge to the base of the outcropping; just below, broken rocks were lined up and stacked to make a primitive causeway. Dr. Jeremy Belknap noted the presence of "black lead" (as graphite was called, distinguishing it from metallic lead) on Mt. Monadnock in his *History of New Hampshire* (1792). His information may have come through a letter from Reverend Laban Ainsworth, who owned the lot on which the mine was later developed. From about 1847 to 1850, David Harvey Gilmore, a Jaffrey resident, and an unnamed partner operated a graphite mine here. Supposedly the two men packed the excavated graphite into kegs and rolled them partway down the mountain on a crude path from which the rocks had been cleared. A pair of oxen helped move the rock along the road that led down from what later became the site of Half Way House. The mine no longer contains any graphite.

17. Bald Rock (C4). According to D.B. Cutter's 1881 history of Jaffrey, this prominent 2,626-ft. spur peak south of Mt. Monadnock's summit was the only area of bare ledge on the mountain before the fires in the early 1800s. At that time it was known as Bald Rocks. Several trails allow access to the site, which offers views in all directions, including an impressive look up to the summit of Mt. Monadnock itself. On the northeast side is a large boulder inscribed "Kiasticuticus Peak." This unusual name is thought to derive from a Greek word meaning "bald" or, literally, "skinhead." The sharp-edged rock supposedly resembles a monster from Greek mythology.

18. Four Spots (C4). The east end of Amphitheatre Trail meets Smith Connecting Link at this historical trail junction. In earlier days there were several trails in this area, all now abandoned, including Dingle Dell Trail (named for the valley between Bald Rock and White Cross Trail), Teapot Trail, and Inspiration Rock Trail, which led to an eponymous viewpoint.

19. Black Precipice (C4). Located northeast of Monte Rosa, this impressive rock face (no sign) is reportedly the largest cliff on Mt. Monadnock. It was named for its dark color and the shadows created by its overhang. Folds in the schist and quartzite are evident near the top of the cliff. Rock climbers occasionally use the anchors bolted into the rock. Amphitheatre Trail runs along the open ledges at the top of Black Precipice, providing panoramic southern views and a peek down into the ravine known as the Amphitheatre. The trail was built in 1897 by Half Way House guest Scott A. Smith. Interesting distant views of Black Precipice can be seen from the west side of Bald Rock and from an outlook near the top of Noble Trail.

20. The Tooth (C4). This prominent fang-like pointed ledge is just northeast of Monte Rosa, near the junction of Smith Summit Trail and Smith Bypass. Scott A. Smith built Smith Summit Trail in 1898. The top of the Tooth is a fine and easily reachable viewpoint.

21. Monte Rosa (C4). This 2,515-ft. knob southwest of the main summit of Mt. Monadnock can be seen from the Half Way House Site and was named by Scott A. Smith for its rosy hue at sunset. (It was formerly known as Newton's Peak.) Open knobs sit on its north and south sides, with a slight drop between. Several trails reach the area, including Monte Rosa Trail, which Smith opened in 1895. Atop the south knob is a prominent metal weather vane, a replica of one that stood there in earlier days so that guests sitting on the piazza of Half Way House could tell which direction the wind was blowing.

22. Rock House (B3). This natural rock shelter is a prominent landmark for hikers ascending the Marlboro Trail. It lies on the southeast side of the junction of Marlboro and Marian trails. In the 1920s, this prominent feature helped trail workers locate and reopen Marlboro Trail, which had fallen into disrepair.

23. Thoreau's 1860 Campsite (C4). In August 1860, Henry David Thoreau made the last of his four visits to Mt. Monadnock in the company of poet and fellow Concord, Massachusetts, resident William Ellery Channing. After camping the first two nights at a location Thoreau had used in 1858, the pair relocated to a new campsite on a high plateau east of the summit. Here, they built a substantial camp from spruce trees and limbs cut on the site. (Leave No Trace principles had not yet been written in 1860!) The shelter backed up to a small cliff and looked out on a commanding view to the south. Thoreau and Channing spent three nights here while exploring the mountain. Channing used the campsite several times in ensuing years and wrote a poem about the "fortress" he and Thoreau had built. Thoreau was planning a book about Mt. Monadnock and made extensive notes planning his next Monadnock trip during this visit. But his health deteriorated over the next year and he died on May 6, 1862, of tuberculosis.

In 1918, Mt. Monadnock historian Allen Chamberlain and Thoreau researcher Herbert W. Gleason searched the area for the site of the long-forgotten 1860 camp. On the second day, Gleason found it, identifying it by the ledge on the back side and the two old spruces on which the shelter had been framed. He also found stones placed on the floor to level the sleeping surface, and a long-disused fire ring in front. The view was as expansive as Thoreau had described. The site of the 1860 camp is well off the trails, south of the junction of White Cross Trail and Smith Connecting Link. In 2003, seven members of the Thoreau Society found the site of Thoreau's 1858 campsite to the west of Smith Connecting Link.

24. The Imp (A5). This interesting rock formation is on the southwest side of Cascade Link shortly before it reaches its junction with Pumpelly Trail on Pumpelly Ridge. From the trail the formation resembles the profile of a humanlike face, with a sharp nose and jutting chin. In recent years, however, tree growth has begun obscuring the view.

25. The Sarcophagus (B5). This massive glacial boulder is perched on the ledges near the west side of Pumpelly Trail, just above the junction with Spellman Trail. When seen from the trail, the boulder resembles a burial coffin, or sarcophagus. In earlier times it was called Bible Rock and the Boat.

METACOMET–MONADNOCK TRAIL (AMCBC) AND VICINITY

Metacomet–Monadnock Trail begins in the Hanging Hills of Meriden, Connecticut, and runs north along the traprock ridge that borders the Connecticut River. It traverses Mt. Tom and the Holyoke Range and passes over the Northfield Hills and Mt. Grace. In Connecticut (in combination with the Mattabesett and Menunkatuck trails) and Massachusetts, Metacomet–Monadnock Trail (M–M Trail) has been designated a National Scenic Trail now known as the New England Trail, a 215-mi. route. The New Hampshire section retains the Metacomet–Monadnock name. This section, 18.5 mi. long, includes Little Monadnock Mtn. and Gap Mtn. and terminates at Mt. Monadnock. (Before this section, the trail parallels the state line for some distance and runs briefly just inside the New Hampshire border.) The trail is maintained by AMC's Berkshire

Chapter and the Forest Society and is clearly marked by white rectangular paint blazes. Described below are two of its more important features: Gap Mtn. (south peak, 1,901 ft.; north peak, 1,840 ft.) and Little Monadnock Mtn. (1,890 ft.).

An online map is available at newenglandtrail.org. The *New England Trail Map & Guide* by AMC and the Connecticut Forest & Park Association (AMC Books, 2015) follows the entirety of the designated New England Trail and many adjoining trails from the Massachusetts–New Hampshire border through Connecticut. AMC's *Massachusetts Trail Guide* provides a detailed description of the entire length of the trail in Massachusetts.

GAP MTN. (1,901 FT.)

This small mountain (south peak, 1,901 ft.; north peak, 1,840 ft.) in the town of Troy is named for the space between its double-humped summit, which is a prominent feature of the view south from Mt. Monadnock. Most of the mountain is in the Forest Society's Gap Mtn. Reservation. Metacomet–Monadnock Trail crosses it, with trailheads providing easy access from north or south. (No pedestrian route connects the two trailheads other than the climb over the mountain.) The open ledges of the north peak provide excellent views in several directions, with an especially fine perspective on Mt. Monadnock. The higher south peak, reached by an obscure, little-used side path, affords a restricted view to the northeast. The trails are shown on the in-text map in this guide, and a trail map is available at forestsociety.org. Also, refer to the USGS Troy quadrangle.

GAP MTN. NORTH APPROACH
(NHDP; AMC GAP MTN. MAP; USGS TROY QUAD)

From trailhead on Bullard Rd. (1,190 ft.) to:	⇅	↗	↻
North peak of Gap Mtn. (1,840 ft.)	1.4 mi.	700 ft. (rev. 50 ft.)	1:05

From NH 124, 0.8 mi. west of the Old Toll Rd. parking area for Mt. Monadnock and 0.5 mi. east of the junction with Jaffrey Rd., turn south onto Bullard Rd. (formerly Old County Rd.). The trailhead is on a short side road to the left, 0.5 mi. from NH 124. The trail passes a kiosk and in 60 yd. meets white-blazed Metacomet–Monadnock Trail (M–M Trail) and turns right onto it. (Returning, be sure to turn left here to reach the trailhead.) At 0.1 mi. the route crosses a stone wall and turns left up the slope (in the reverse direction, watch carefully for this turn), bears right through another

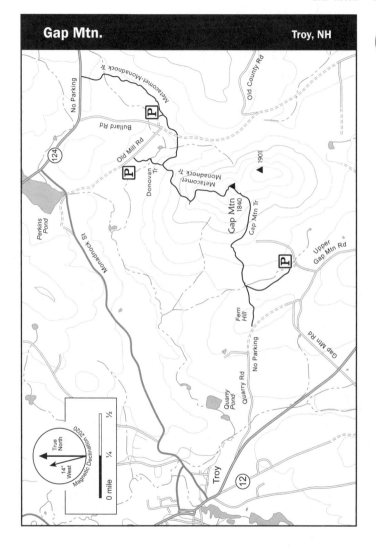

Gap Mtn.

Troy, NH

stone wall (follow blazes carefully), and then descends to cross a woods road. (Avoid a path that forks left on the far side.) It crosses Quarry Brook at 0.3 mi. then soon passes through a stone wall and turns sharply right to follow it. At 0.5 mi., where blue-blazed Donovan Trail diverges right (leading 0.3 mi. to Old Mill Rd. and another 0.5 mi. to a small parking area on Monadnock St. opposite Perkins Pond), Metacomet–Monadnock Trail bears left (sign: "Royce Trail") and climbs steadily by switchbacks to a left turn at 0.8 mi., where a short spur leads right to a viewpoint. The main trail ascends into an area of low growth, with increasing views north to Mt. Monadnock. It crosses a ledgy false summit with views, dips to a minor saddle, and ascends a short distance to the open, true north peak. (*Note*: In some descriptions the false summit is called the north peak, and the higher open summit is called the middle peak.)

GAP MTN. SOUTH APPROACH
(NHDP; AMC GAP MTN. MAP; USGS TROY QUAD)
From trailhead on Gap Mtn. Rd. (1,250 ft.) to:

	⇅	↗	↺
North peak of Gap Mtn. (1,840 ft.)	1.3 mi.	650 ft. (rev. 50 ft.)	1:00

From NH 12, 1.5 mi. south of the Troy town center, turn left (north) onto Gap Mtn. Rd. In 0.4 mi. this road bears right at a fork, and at 0.8 mi. from NH 12 it turns left and reaches trailhead parking on the left in another 0.1 mi. (*Note*: Do not use the paved road that continues ahead from the trailhead; this former access is private property, and trespassing is forbidden.)

The yellow-blazed connecting trail passes a kiosk and runs nearly level, then gradually downhill, to meet white-blazed Metacomet–Monadnock Trail at 0.4 mi. (Descending, be sure to bear left on the yellow-blazed trail immediately after crossing the brook.) The route to Gap Mtn. turns right here, crosses Tyler Brook, and ascends through hemlocks and pines, crossing two stone walls. At 0.7 mi. it turns left across a stone wall on a relocated section. It soon swings right and ascends at easy to moderate grades through pines and old overgrown pastures. At 1.1 mi. it crosses a brushy opening, turns left, and begins a steeper ascent. In another 0.1 mi. it climbs steeply up ledges, passing an obscure side path on the right that leads about 0.2 mi. to the mostly wooded south peak (1,901 ft.). Passing this side path, the main trail continues up steeply then runs at easier grades through low growth to the open north peak.

LITTLE MONADNOCK MTN. (1,890 FT.)

This small mountain in the town of Fitzwilliam offers good views to the north from its northern ridge. Ascend it on Metacomet–Monadnock Trail from the north or the south, or on a path that rises from Rhododendron State Park in Fitzwilliam. Refer to the USGS Troy quadrangle.

SEC 1

LITTLE MONADNOCK MTN. TRAILS (NHDP; USGS TROY QUAD)

Cumulative from Rhododendron State Park (1,200 ft.) to:	↧↥	↗	↺
Metacomet–Monadnock Trail (1,780 ft.)	1.1 mi.	600 ft.	0:50
Little Monadnock Mtn. summit (1,890 ft.)	1.4 mi.	690 ft.	1:00

In addition to Little Monadnock, this park features a 16-acre stand of Rhododendron maximum, the largest stand in northern New England and a designated National Natural Landmark. A loop hike of 0.6 mi. cuts through the stand via Rhododendron Loop Trail; peak blooming season is in July. Find information and a trail map for the park at nhstateparks.org. To reach Rhododendron State Park, follow NH 119 west for 0.9 mi. from its junction with NH 12 in Fitzwilliam then turn right onto Rhododendron Rd. In another 2.1 mi. turn right into Rhododendron State Park.

From the parking area, walk between granite posts and follow the eastern section of Rhododendron Loop Trail 0.2 mi., passing a junction on the left with Laurel Trail. Bear right on yellow-blazed Little Monadnock Trail, as Rhododendron Loop Trail bears left. Little Monadnock Trail ascends moderately, with one short steep section, to meet white-blazed Metacomet–Monadnock Trail at 1.1 mi., 0.3 mi. north of the summit of Little Monadnock. A restricted view of Mt. Monadnock appears here, and an additional outlook lies 0.2 mi. gently downhill (to the right) from this junction along Metacomet–Monadnock Trail at an open ledgy area called North Meadows. (To return to the park trailhead from this viewpoint, you must retrace your steps back to the junction and descend the way you came via Little Monadnock and Rhododendron Loop trails.) For the summit (no views), turn left at the junction and follow Metacomet–Monadnock Trail south 0.3 mi. (*Note*: Leashed pets are allowed up Little Monadnock but are not permitted on the trails within the rhododendron stand.)

WANTASTIQUET MTN. (1,384 FT.) AREA

Wantastiquet Mtn. is a bluff 0.6 mi. from the Connecticut River, directly across from Brattleboro, Vermont. Refer to the USGS Brattleboro quadrangle. Excellent views stretch across the Connecticut River Valley from the flat summit of this mountain, which stands on the Chesterfield–Hinsdale town line about 3 mi. west of Pisgah State Park. Local legend states that the mountain is the lair of many rattlesnakes; this may have been true at one time, but no reliable sightings of venomous reptiles have been made for many years, and they are now officially considered to have been extirpated from the area.

The northeast slopes are part of the Forest Society's 513-acre Madame Sherri Forest, named for the theatrical costume designer who once owned this land and built a castle (now in ruins) on it. (For more information on Madame Sherri Forest, visit forestsociety.org.) The summit and western slopes of the mountain are in the state of New Hampshire's Wantastiquet Mtn. Natural Area. These parcels, along with the smaller James O'Neil Sr. Town Forest to the east, represent more than 1,000 contiguous acres of conservation land. A network of trails provides access to Mine Ledge (1,365 ft.), East Hill (1,115 ft.), Daniels Mtn. (1,221 ft.), and Bear Mtn. (1,270 ft.) to the east of Wantastiquet. Parts of these trails are used for the western section of Wantastiquet–Monadnock Trail from Brattleboro to Mt. Monadnock. The routes described here are covered on the Wantastiquet Mtn. trail map, p. 45. Maps of the trails in this area may also be found online at chesterfieldoutdoors.com, the website of the Chesterfield Conservation Commission. CCC and the Friends of Pisgah maintain several of the trails in this area.

WANTASTIQUET MTN. TRAIL (NHDFL; AMC WANTASTIQUET MTN. MAP, CCC TRAIL MAP, USGS BRATTLEBORO QUAD)

From parking area on Mountain Rd. (280 ft.) to:	⇅	↗	○
Viewpoint near Wantastiquet Mtn. summit (1,384 ft.)	2.0 mi.	1,100 ft.	1:35

For most of its length, this trail is a gravel road that was cut to serve the quarries on the mountain. It is also a segment of Wantastiquet–Monadnock Trail. The route begins on Mountain Rd., which leaves the north side of NH 119 just east of the bridge over the Connecticut River leading to Vermont; this is about 7 mi. west of the junction of NH 119 with NH 63 in Hinsdale. Parking is on the right about 0.2 mi. from NH 119. The

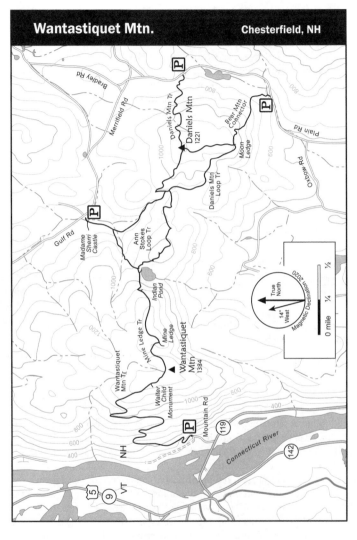

Wantastiquet Mtn.

Chesterfield, NH

trail passes between a pair of granite posts and ascends. (Avoid a lower road to the left that has a green gate.) Almost immediately the path passes through an orange gate, with a waterfall on a small stream to the right; don't take the multiple side paths (except to view the waterfall or explore). The trail ascends past two switchbacks to another orange gate, followed by a view to the west, and then climbs by seven more switchbacks to a point where a side path turns right and rises the last 50 yd. to a prominent rock outcropping with an excellent view, marked by a monument to Walter H. Child. The route continues 0.1 mi. to a clearing (no view) near the communications tower at the main summit. Here, Mine Ledge Trail (left arrow) runs east to a side path to Mine Ledge and continues to Ann Stokes Loop at Indian Pond.

ANN STOKES LOOP
(CCC/FOP/SPNHF; AMC WANTASTIQUET MTN. MAP, CCC TRAIL MAP, USGS BRATTLEBORO QUAD)

Cumulative from parking area on Gulf Rd. (640 ft.) to:	⇅	↗	⟳
Mine Ledge Trail and Indian Pond (915 ft.)	0.6 mi.	300 ft.	0:25
Daniels Mtn. Loop, south branch (900 ft.)	1.6 mi.	550 ft. (rev. 250 ft.)	1:05
Complete loop	2.4 mi.	550 ft. (rev. 250 ft.)	1:30

This trail, named for the landowner who donated this parcel of conservation land, provides a loop hike in Madame Sherri Forest to secluded Indian Pond and two fine viewpoints on East Hill. It also offers access to Mine Ledge Trail, which leads to Wantastiquet Mtn. and Daniels Mtn. Loop over Daniels Mtn. The southern section of this loop is also a segment of Wantastiquet–Monadnock Trail. From the intersection of NH 9 and NH 63 in Chesterfield, follow NH 63 south 1.6 mi. and turn right onto Stage Rd.; bear left onto Castle Rd. at 1.8 mi. At 2.8 mi. turn left onto Gulf Rd. and follow it to trailhead parking for Madame Sherri Forest on the left at 4.7 mi. If approaching from the west on NH 9, turn right onto Mountain Rd. 0.4 mi. east of US 5 then quickly bear left onto Gulf Rd. and follow it 2.2 mi. to the trailhead on the right.

Ann Stokes Loop, marked by white diamonds, crosses a bridge over the outlet from a small pond and reaches a fork in 60 yd. The right fork leads 90 yd. uphill to the ruins of Madame Sherri Castle. The left fork is the main trail, which runs along the shore of a marshy pond and reaches the loop junction at 0.2 mi. The loop is described in the counterclockwise direction. Turning right at the junction, the west branch of the loop climbs moderately to the junction with Mine Ledge Trail near the shore of Indian Pond at 0.6 mi. (To find the best viewpoint at the pond, follow blue-blazed Mine Ledge Trail 70 yd. to the right then take a side path 50 yd. farther along on the left down to the shore.) Ann Stokes Loop turns left at the junction, skirts the shrubby shore of the pond, and climbs steeply to a ledge overlooking the pond and Wantastiquet Mtn. at 0.8 mi. In another 0.1 mi., the trail reaches the summit of East Hill; here a short side path leads left to a ledge with a northeastern view toward the hills of Pisgah State Park. The trail then descends to a low area with many large hemlocks, ascends easily, turns left just before reaching a ledge, runs over a knoll, and descends to its junction with the south branch of Daniels Mtn. Loop on the right at 1.6 mi. Here, Ann Stokes Loop turns sharply left and descends 50 yd. to a junction with the north branch of Daniels Mtn. Loop, also on the right. Ann Stokes Loop again bears left and descends at mostly easy grades before returning to the loop junction at 2.2 mi. Continue straight to return to the trailhead.

MINE LEDGE TRAIL (CCC/FOP; AMC WANTASTIQUET MTN. MAP, CCC TRAIL MAP, USGS BRATTLEBORO QUAD)

From Ann Stokes Loop (915 ft.) to:	⇅	↗	↻
Viewpoint near Wantastiquet Mtn. summit (1,368 ft.)	1.2 mi.	600 ft. (rev. 150 ft.)	0:55

This trail provides a route from Ann Stokes Loop and Madame Sherri Forest to Mine Ledge—a prominent outcropping with a good view—and Wantastiquet Mtn. It is also a segment of Wantastiquet–Monadnock Trail. Marked with blue diamonds, Mine Ledge Trail diverges right (sign) from the west branch of Ann Stokes Loop, 0.6 mi. from the parking area on Gulf Rd. In 70 yd. a side path leads 50 yd. left to the shore of Indian Pond. The main trail ascends steeply to a ledge overlooking the pond at 0.2 mi. It continues up through an oak forest then meanders along a ridge crest with minor ups and downs. At 0.7 mi. Mine Ledge Trail turns right. (Here, a side path continues ahead 70 yd. to a ledge with a view west then bears left and runs 80 yd. along a cliff edge—use caution!—to the best viewpoint at Mine Ledge, with vistas south and east.) The trail descends steeply to a saddle; a short distance down to the left (south), at the base of Mine Ledge, are several interesting ice caves. The route climbs over a knoll and descends into a gully then ascends briefly to a clearing near the main summit of Wantastiquet Mtn., just north of a communications tower, at 1.1

mi. To reach the viewpoint at the west end of the summit area, follow an obvious old road 0.1 mi. west from the clearing, descending slightly, and then take a side path on the left 50 yd. to the ledge and Walter H. Child monument. In the reverse direction, Mine Ledge Trail (sign) leaves the northeast side of the clearing near the communications tower.

DANIELS MTN. LOOP (CCC/FOP/MC; AMC WANTASTIQUET MTN. MAP, CCC TRAIL MAP, USGS BRATTLEBORO QUAD)

Cumulative from southern jct. with Ann Stokes Loop (900 ft.) to:	⇅	↗	↻
Moon Ledge and Bear Mtn. Connector (1,175 ft.)	0.8 mi.	300 ft.	0:35
Daniels Mtn. summit (1,221 ft.)	1.2 mi	390 ft. (rev. 50 ft.)	0:45
Northern jct. with Ann Stokes Loop (900 ft.)	1.8 mi.	400 ft. (rev. 350 ft.)	1:05
Total circuit of Ann Stokes Loop and Daniels Mtn. Loop	4.2 mi.	950 ft.	2:35

This trail loops over the wooded summit of Daniels Mtn., passing two fine viewpoints, and is a segment of Wantastiquet–Monadnock Trail. It may be reached from Gulf Rd. to the north via Ann Stokes Loop or from Plain Rd. to the east via Daniels Mtn. Trail or Bear Mtn. Connector. Daniels Mtn. Loop, marked by blue diamonds, is described here starting at its southern junction with Ann Stokes Loop (1.6 mi. from Gulf Rd. via the west branch of Ann Stokes Loop) and running in the counterclockwise direction.

From its southern junction with Ann Stokes Loop, the south branch of Daniels Mtn. Loop leads south on an old road, crosses a wet area, and descends gently, passing an older road that joins from the right (in the reverse direction, bear right here). Daniels Mtn. Loop diverges left off the road at 0.3 mi. and climbs to a small saddle at 0.4 mi., where it then swings right across a streambed and climbs along a slope of hemlocks. After a slight descent, the trail climbs easily to a left turn at 0.8 mi., where a side path leads 20 yd. right to Moon Ledge, with an excellent view south over North Hinsdale and the Connecticut River. Here, Bear Mtn. Connector goes straight. Stay on Daniels Mtn. Loop as it turns left and climbs north. The loop crosses the south knob of Daniels Mtn., descends to a saddle, and ascends rather steeply to the wooded true summit at 1.2 mi., where Daniels Mtn. Trail joins from the right. Here, the loop turns sharply left and descends moderately, passing a side path on the left that leads to a limited view. It climbs over a knoll and swings left, then right, to the O'Neil Ledges at 1.6 mi., where there is a view west to East Hill and

Wantastiquet Mtn. The trail descends steeply from the outlook, turns sharply left onto an old road, and reaches its northern junction with Ann Stokes Loop at 1.8 mi. The junction with the south branch of Daniels Mtn. Loop is 50 yd. to the left. To the right, the east branch of Ann Stokes Loop leads 0.8 mi. to the Gulf Rd. parking area.

SEC 1

DANIELS MTN. TRAIL (CCC/FOP; AMC WANTASTIQUET MTN. MAP, CCC TRAIL MAP, USGS BRATTLEBORO QUAD)

From Plain Rd.
(700 ft.) to:

	⇅	↗	◔
Daniels Mtn. summit (1,221 ft.)	0.8 mi.	540 ft.	0:40

This lightly used trail ascends Daniels Mtn. from the east, meeting Daniels Mtn. Loop at the wooded summit. From NH 119 in Hinsdale, follow Plain Rd. north, passing the parking area for Bear Mtn. Trail and Bear Mtn. Connector at 4.6 mi. The trail (small sign) begins on the left at 5.6 mi.; there is limited parking in a pulloff on the opposite side of the road, just uphill from the trailhead (on some maps, Town Line Loop Trail is indicated as leaving south from this trailhead; it is not an actual trail but simply a walk along Plain Rd.). Marked by orange diamonds, Daniels Mtn. Trail descends 25 yd. to cross a brook, climbs alongside a stone wall for 65 yd., turns sharply right onto an old road, and then turns left off the road after another 70 yd. It climbs steeply, swings right along another stone wall at 0.2 mi. and levels; then it bears left again to climb steadily by switchbacks. The route passes through a scenic mossy area and to the right of a rocky knoll at 0.5 mi., eases briefly again, and then climbs through a ferny area to the summit and the junction with Daniels Mtn. Loop.

BEAR MTN. TRAIL (CCC/FOP; AMC WANTASTIQUET MTN. MAP, CCC TRAIL MAP, USGS HINSDALE AND BRATTLEBORO QUADS)

Cumulative from NH 63
(1,080 ft.) to:

	⇅	↗	◔
High point on Bear Mtn. (1,270 ft.)	0.8 mi.	200 ft.	0:30
Plain Rd. (560 ft.)	1.6 mi.	200 ft. (rev. 700 ft.)	0:55

This trail is a segment of Wantastiquet–Monadnock Trail and is marked with white diamonds. It is described from east to west, the most common direction of travel. Bear Mtn. Trail leaves the west side of NH 63 on an old road about 150 yd. north of the entrance road to the Kilburn Rd. trailhead in Pisgah State Park (4.6 mi. south of NH 9 in Chesterfield and 3.9 mi. north of NH 119 in Hinsdale), where there is ample parking. It bears right as it ascends through an old logged area then descends briefly and continues west, crossing a small stream and then a snowmobile trail at 0.3 mi. (In the reverse direction, watch for a sharp downhill right turn.)

After crossing another stream, the trail turns left off the old road and ascends into Bear Mtn. State Forest, passing a western outlook at 0.5 mi. It climbs south along the ridge then descends into a ravine. The route follows the ravine left (south) and then climbs right (west) out of it, reaching the trail's high point on the wooded Bear Mtn. ridge at 0.8 mi. The trail then descends northwest, gradually at first and then more steeply, into a ravine. It turns left at the top of a steep, rocky drop, descends into a second ravine, crosses a stream, and turns right onto an old road. The route then descends moderately, recrossing the stream, and at 1.3 mi., shortly after another stream crossing, the path turns sharply left and descends by switchbacks to a crossing of a larger stream. It turns left onto an old road and then bears right and descends to Plain Rd. at 1.6 mi. Bear Mtn. Connector leaves from the west side of the road, where there is parking for several cars.

BEAR MTN. CONNECTOR (CCC/FOP; AMC WANTASTIQUET MTN. MAP, CCC TRAIL MAP, USGS BRATTLEBORO QUAD)

From Plain Rd.
(560 ft.) to:

	⇅	↗	○
Daniels Mtn. Loop (1,175 ft.)	0.7 mi.	600 ft.	0:40

Bear Mtn. Connector links Daniels Mtn. Loop to Bear Mtn. Trail at Plain Rd. and is a segment of Wantastiquet–Monadnock Trail. It passes through a dry oak forest, which is unusual in the Appalachian region. These forests are more common in Pennsylvania and West Virginia. Bear Mtn. Connector is most often used as the shortest access to the views at Moon Ledge and is described in that direction. Reach the trailhead on Plain Rd. by following Plain Rd. north 4.6 mi. from the blinking light on NH 119 just west of Hinsdale Center. From the west, follow Gulf Rd., Merriman Rd., Bradley Rd., and Plain Rd. 2.6 mi. beyond the Madame Sherri Forest trailhead. The trailhead can also be reached from NH 63 via North Hinsdale Rd. and Plain Rd. Parking for several cars is available off the west side of Plain Rd. (On some maps, Town Line Loop Trail is indicated as leaving north from this trailhead; it is not an actual trail but simply a walk along Plain Rd.)

Leaving Plain Rd., Bear Mtn. Connector, marked by white diamonds, ascends north to an old road at 0.1 mi., turns right onto it and then immediately turns left off it, and climbs through a logged area. It swings west (left) and ascends, steeply at times, to the left of cliffs. At 0.3 mi. a switchback around a rock outcropping requires caution. At 0.5 mi. the grade eases briefly but then becomes steep again to a shoulder of Daniels Mtn. A short walk through a grassy scrub oak area leads to Daniels Mtn. Loop; the viewpoint at Moon Ledge is a short distance to the left.

WANTASTIQUET–MONADNOCK TRAIL (CCC/FOP/MC/SPNHF; CCC TRAIL MAPS, SPNHF TRAIL MAPS)

This 50-mi. trail, completed in 2018, connects Brattleboro, Vermont, and Wantastiquet Mtn. with Mt. Monadnock. Some of the route described below can be followed on the in-text maps for Wantastiquet Mtn. and Pisgah State Park. Maps of the trail segments are available at chesterfieldoutdoors.com and forestsociety.org. From Troy to its eastern terminus at Mt. Monadnock, Wantastiquet–Monadnock Trail (WMT) is part of Metacomet–Monadnock Trail. Further information and maps for that section are available at nhmmtrail.org.

As of 2020, overnight options for backpackers are still being developed, but a few currently exist. Just outside Pisgah State Park in Chesterfield is a shelter built by Friends of Pisgah, with access by side paths off of Davis Hill Trail and Hubbard Hill Trail. Other accommodations include various inns and hotels in Keene, and Inn at East Hill Farm in Troy (603-242-6495).

Although the western end of this trail officially starts at Brattleboro Food Co-Op on Main St. in Brattleboro, Vermont, parking there is reserved for customers only. Secure parking is available at the Brattleboro Transportation Center parking garage, 77 Flat St., 0.2 mi. northwest of the co-op. For information on long-term rates, call 802-257-2305. Additional parking is at the Wantastiquet Mtn. trailhead in Hinsdale, New Hampshire, on the opposite side of the Connecticut River. From the co-op, follow VT/NH 119 east across the bridge over the river 0.4 mi. then turn left onto Mountain Rd. and continue 0.1 mi. to a small parking area on the right. Parking at the eastern end of the trail is available (for a fee) at Monadnock State Park on Poole Rd. in Jaffrey. Various other parking areas are located along the trail; see the maps referenced above for details. In the future, a new automobile bridge will be constructed over the Connecticut River, and the current bridges will become the start of the trail.

From the Mountain Rd. trailhead, WMT, marked by blue diamonds for its entire length, follows Wantastiquet Mtn. Trail to the summit of Wantastiquet Mtn. at 2.7 mi. Then it follows Mine Ledge Trail, the southern section of Ann Stokes Loop, and the northern section of Daniels Mtn. Loop, reaching Moon Ledge at 5.8 mi. Here, the route turns left onto Bear Mtn. Connector, crosses Plain Rd. at 6.5 mi., and then follows Bear Mtn. Trail over Bear Mtn. to the west side of NH 63 at 8.1 mi. WMT follows NH 63 south 150 yd. to the Kilburn Rd. trailhead at Pisgah State Park and turns left onto Davis Hill Trail in the park, following Davis Hill Trail for 2.2 mi., Baker Pond Trail for 0.8 mi., Reservoir Trail for 0.7 mi., North Ponds Trail for 1.1 mi., Old Chesterfield Rd. for 1.1 mi., Nash Trail for 1.2 mi., Fullam Pond Trail for 0.6 mi., and Beal's Rd. for 1.1 mi., reaching the Beal's Rd. trailhead on Stones Mill Rd. at 16.7 mi. from Brattleboro.

From here, Keene Connector leads about 8 mi. northeast to the trailhead parking area for Horatio Colony Nature Preserve on Daniels Hill Rd. in Keene. This section is remote for much of its length and is suitable for experienced hikers only. Parts of it are marked with yellow blazes, or red and yellow blazes, in addition to blue diamonds. The first 4.2 mi. of this section—from the trailhead on Stones Mill Rd. to the 645-acre Horatio Colony Nature Preserve—follow a series of old roads, segments of foot trail, and occasional stretches of gravel road, with several stream crossings and a number of turns that must be followed carefully. The last 3.7 mi. are on the blazed trails of Horatio Colony Nature Preserve; a map of these trails is available at horatiocolonymuseum.org. To reach this trailhead from Keene, start at the intersection of NH 9 with NH 10 and NH 12 south of Keene and drive 1.1 mi. west on NH 9. Then turn left onto Daniels Hill Rd. The parking area for the preserve is on the left, 0.2 mi. from NH 9.

From the Horatio Colony parking lot, turn left on Daniels Hill Rd. and continue 0.2 mi. then turn right onto Whitcomb's Mill Rd. and continue 0.1 mi. Carefully cross busy NH 9, and in 0.2 mi. turn right onto Cheshire Rail Trail (limited parking is available here), which WMT follows for the next 12.4 mi. Continue on Cheshire Rail Trail through downtown Keene. (*Note*: In 2019, a detour led to Eastern Ave. and Marlborough St., crossed NH 101, and rejoined Cheshire Rail Trail at the historic Stone Arch Bridge. The parallel section of rail trail is expected to open in 2020.) Ascend gradually along the old rail bed to Troy Depot, where Metacomet–Monadnock Trail joins from the right, 7.0 mi. from the Stone Arch Bridge. From this point both trails run together to the summit of Mt. Monadnock.

The trails turn left on Water St. and continue 0.1 mi., immediately before the depot building. Now blazed with white rectangles and blue diamonds, WMT turns right onto NH 12 south through Troy and then turns left onto Quarry Rd. in 0.4. mi. The trail follows Quarry Rd. as it becomes gravel and then continues straight on an abandoned section of road at 0.7 mi. from NH 12, where the gravel road bears left onto private property. (Very limited roadside parking is available here, but do not block the private road.) Water is available from a spring house (a small one-room building constructed over a spring) on the right. At 1.5 mi. from Troy Depot, near the summit of Fern Hill, the abandoned road bears right. Turn left to stay on WMT as it enters the woods, descends to a rocky area, and then ascends to Gap Mtn. and its ledgy views. From Gap Mtn. to the summit of Mt. Monadnock, WMT continues to follow Metacomet–Monadnock Trail via Royce Trail and White Arrow Trail. Refer to the Gap Mtn. and Mt. Monadnock sections of this guide for details.

CHESTERFIELD GORGE NATURAL AREA

This small state park in Chesterfield offers a scenic 0.7-mi. loop hike with 200-ft. elevation gain through hemlock forest and past several waterfalls and rock formations in Chesterfield Gorge. Bridges cross Wilde Brook at both ends of the gorge. Refer to the USGS Spofford quadrangle. A map of the trail is available at chesterfieldoutdoors.com.

In the late 1800s, the gorge was marketed to tourists as the area's Grand Canyon. The land around the gorge was protected in 1936 by a local farmer, George White, who sold it to the Forest Society. It was then donated to the state. The park is open year-round to the public at no charge. In summer and fall a volunteer-run information center may be open. Chesterfield Gorge Natural Area is on the north side of NH 9, 3.2 mi. east of its junction with NH 63 and 5.7 mi. west of its southern junction with NH 12.

PISGAH STATE PARK

Pisgah State Park—in the southwest corner of New Hampshire, in the towns of Chesterfield, Winchester, and Hinsdale—is the largest state park in New Hampshire, covering approximately 13,500 acres. It is largely undeveloped but has a network of about 60 mi. of multiuse trails. The park in general receives few visitors and is consequently a wilder place than might be expected—but also more satisfying for those looking for adventure and solitude. Significant hills accessible by trails include a southwestern spur (1,328 ft.) of Hubbard Hill, with a restricted view to the west, and the wooded Mt. Pisgah (1,329 ft.), which has three fine east-facing viewpoints on its north ridge and another on its south ridge. Other interesting features include several scenic ponds and wetlands, fine hemlock forests

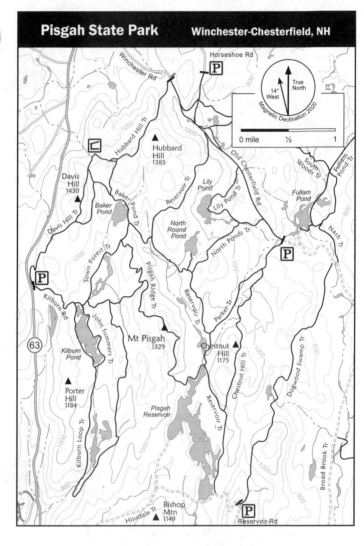

Pisgah State Park   Winchester-Chesterfield, NH

(including several old-growth stands), and a number of historical sites. (*Note*: Some trails are obscure and require care to follow.)

The park has six trailheads; driving directions are included in individual trail descriptions. Several parking areas have trailhead boxes, known as "iron rangers," for donations: Fullam Pond, Old Chesterfield Rd. Visitor Center, NH 119 parking lot, Kilburn Rd. trailhead, and Horseshoe trailhead. The park does not charge an entrance fee, so donations are welcomed and appreciated. Most of the trails are covered by the in-text Pisgah State Park map (see p. 54). Winter and summer trail maps are available from the New Hampshire Division of Parks and Recreation at some park trailheads and at nhstateparks.org. Also, refer to the USGS Hinsdale and Spofford quadrangles. In summer, several trails that follow gravel roads are open to motorized (ATV) use, with a few more open to mountain biking; the remainder are reserved for pedestrian use. In winter, most of the trails are open to snowmobiling. All major trails in the park have been updated with white diamond blazes with trail names on them, and both signage and bridges have been improved. Interpretive services and trail maintenance are provided by the volunteer Friends of Pisgah in cooperation with NHDP. In 2013, FOP also constructed a shelter just outside the park, with access by side paths off Davis Hill Trail and Hubbard Hill Trail. Camping elsewhere is prohibited.

A management plan completed in 2011 could potentially result in some changes to the trail system. Logging may occasionally disrupt some trails in the northern and eastern parts of the park. For updates, check with NHDP or FOP.

OLD HORSESHOE RD.
(NHDP/FOP; AMC PISGAH STATE PARK MAP)

From Horseshoe Rd. trailhead
(1,060 ft.) to:

	⇅	↗	↻
Old Chesterfield Rd./Winchester Rd. (910 ft.)	0.5 mi.	0 ft. (rev. 150 ft.)	0:15

The trailhead for this historical dirt road provides the major northern access to Pisgah State Park. Located at the birthplace of Harlan Fiske Stone (1872–1946), former U.S. attorney general and associate justice of the Supreme Court of the United States, the trailhead sits on a scenic bluff overlooking the valleys and ridges of the park to the south. Ample parking and a kiosk with maps are available. Take Old Chesterfield Rd. 0.3 mi. east from NH 63 in Chesterfield then turn right onto Horseshoe Rd. (sign) and follow it 1.4 mi. southeast to the parking area.

The old road, lined with stone walls, descends past an orange gate. At 0.3 mi., Old Horseshoe Rd. Connector follows the trail as it curves right and reaches Winchester Rd. in an additional 0.3 mi.; here the trail bears left onto a grassy road. Soon the northwest fork of South Woods Trail leaves on the left. Old Horseshoe Rd. continues south, passes a wetland on the right, and at 0.5 mi. reaches a junction with Old Chesterfield Rd. (left) and Winchester Rd. (right) in a wet area.

WINCHESTER RD. (NHDP/FOP; AMC PISGAH STATE PARK MAP)

From gate and jct. with Hubbard Hill Trail (980 ft.) to:	⬆⬇	⬈	↻
Old Chesterfield Rd. and Old Horseshoe Rd. (910 ft.)	0.6 mi.	0 ft. (rev. 50 ft.)	0:20

This historical dirt road was once part of a highway that connected the towns of Chesterfield and Winchester. It provides opportunities to create various loops through the northwest section of Pisgah State Park. No parking is available at this trailhead, which is at a locked gate on Winchester Rd. 1.3 mi. southeast of NH 63 in Chesterfield. For hikes in this area, use the Old Horseshoe Rd. trailhead with its large parking area.

At the gate, Hubbard Hill Trail diverges to the southwest. From the gate and junction, Winchester Rd. descends, lined with stone walls. At 0.2 mi., Old Horseshoe Rd. Connector follows the main trail as it curves left and reaches Old Horseshoe Rd. in an additional 0.3 mi., while Winchester Rd. bears right onto an old woods road and continues to descend then enters a wet area and meets Old Chesterfield Rd. (straight ahead) and Old Horseshoe Rd. (left) at a well-marked junction.

DOGWOOD SWAMP TRAIL
(NHDP/FOP; AMC PISGAH STATE PARK MAP)

Cumulative from Reservoir Rd. trailhead (620 ft.) to:	⬆⬇	⬈	↻
First height-of-land (920 ft.)	0.8 mi.	300 ft.	0:35
Last height-of-land (1,000 ft.)	2.1 mi.	500 ft. (rev. 100 ft.)	1:20
Old Chesterfield Rd. (680 ft.)	3.3 mi.	500 ft. (rev. 300 ft.)	1:55

This trail connects Reservoir Rd. with Old Chesterfield Rd. near Fullam Pond and requires care to follow. The trail begins on Reservoir Rd. at a small parking area 1.6 mi. north of its junction with NH 119. This point can be reached on foot from a designated parking area for Pisgah State Park on NH 119 (2.2 mi. east of Hinsdale) by following an access trail and then Reservoir Rd. itself (total distance: 1.4 mi.).

From the Reservoir Rd. parking area, Dogwood Swamp Trail ascends northeast on an old woods road up a prominent ridge. It swings right and at 0.8 mi. reaches the first of several heights-of-land, beginning a series of undulating descents and ascents along the ridge. At 1.3 mi. it passes an open marsh on the left, crosses a bridge over a brook near another marsh, and descends gradually. After passing another marshy area, the trail swings right and then sharply left (follow arrows and white blazes) in a hemlock forest. (*Note*: Do not descend on an old logging road that continues straight ahead.)

Almost immediately the trail crosses a bridge over a brook and swings left near a large marsh on the left. It follows this open area along an undulating ridge and reaches the final height-of-land at 2.1 mi., where it begins the long descent toward Fullam Pond, passing through a wet area and crossing several minor streams. After the trail crosses a bridge over a stream, the grade eases, and the path passes through an obscure section with numerous blowdowns. It leads through several wet, bouldery areas, joins a road coming from the left, and soon reaches Old Chesterfield Rd. at a point 1.1 mi. north of Broad Brook Rd. and 0.8 mi. east of Chestnut Hill Trail and an adjacent parking area.

RESERVOIR TRAIL (NHDP/FOP; AMC PISGAH STATE PARK MAP)

Cumulative from Dogwood Swamp Trail parking area on Reservoir Rd. (620 ft.) to:	↥↧	↗	◯
Start of Reservoir Trail (940 ft.) via Reservoir Rd.	0.5 mi.	300 ft.	0:25
Chestnut Hill Trail (940 ft.)	1.4 mi.	300 ft.	0:50
Pisgah Ridge Trail (910 ft.)	2.0 mi.	300 ft. (rev. 50 ft.)	1:10
Parker Trail (940 ft.)	2.4 mi.	400 ft. (rev. 50 ft.)	1:25
North Ponds Trail (1,120 ft.)	3.1 mi.	600 ft.	1:50
Baker Pond Trail (1,030 ft.)	3.8 mi.	600 ft. (rev. 100 ft.)	2:10
Old Chesterfield Rd. (910 ft.)	5.3 mi.	750 ft. (rev. 250 ft.)	3:00

This old woods road connects Reservoir Rd. from the south with Old Chesterfield Rd. to the north, forming a major artery through the center of Pisgah State Park. Part of this route is also a segment of Wantastiquet–Monadnock Trail. It intersects with many trails entering from the east and west, allowing for numerous loops. Reservoir Trail begins on Reservoir Rd., 0.5 mi. north of the gate at the Dogwood Swamp Trail parking area; the ascent from the parking area to the start of Reservoir Trail is 300 ft. Distances are given from the parking area.

The trail follows the eastern shore of Pisgah Reservoir, with several unmarked paths leading left to the attractive shoreline. It swings right at an intersection (sign), passes through several wet areas, and at 1.4 mi. from the parking area reaches Chestnut Hill Trail on the right. Passing by this trail, Reservoir Trail continues to parallel the eastern shore but at a greater distance, and at 2.0 mi. it reaches the northeast corner of the reservoir, where Pisgah Ridge Trail leaves left across a small bridge. Reservoir Trail swings right (arrow), crosses a bridge over a brook, and passes a small beaver pond on the left, which can be reached by a short side path at 2.2 mi. After crossing another bridge, the trail swings right, then left, and at 2.4 mi. reaches Parker Trail on the right. Reservoir Trail then swings left (arrows), crosses a bridge over a brook, and begins a gradual ascent, crossing several small bridges. After reaching a small rocky ridge, it swings right, and at 3.1 mi. North Ponds Trail leaves right.

Reservoir Trail swings left and descends, and in less than 0.1 mi. a yellow-blazed spur (sign) leaves right and runs 0.2 mi. (0 ft., rev. 50 ft.) to the southwest shore of secluded North Round Pond. The main trail continues to descend by switchbacks, crosses two bridges, and at 3.8 mi. reaches Baker Pond Trail (left). Reservoir Trail now ascends steadily, crossing a small stream several times. It reaches the height-of-land and begins a long gradual descent, passing through a clearing with a view northeast toward Mt. Monadnock. The trail descends past ledges, crosses several small streams, swings right, and then swings left. At 5.3 mi. it reaches Old Chesterfield Rd. just past an orange gate. From here it is 0.1 mi. north (left) on Old Chesterfield Rd. to the junction with Winchester Rd. and Old Horseshoe Rd.

CHESTNUT HILL TRAIL
(NHDP/FOP; AMC PISGAH STATE PARK MAP)
From Old Chesterfield Rd.
(690 ft.) to:

	⇅	⬈	↻
Reservoir Trail (950 ft.)	2.2 mi.	450 ft. (rev. 200 ft.)	1:20

This route follows a woods road and connects Old Chesterfield Rd. at a gate and parking area southwest of Fullam Pond with Reservoir Trail at a point 0.9 mi. north of Reservoir Rd. Chestnut Hill Trail crosses a ridge that runs south to north through the middle of Pisgah State Park. The gate and parking area are located 3.1 mi. north of the south gate on Old Chesterfield Rd. and 1.5 mi. south of the junction with Winchester Rd., Old Chesterfield Rd., and Old Horseshoe Rd. This trailhead, the northernmost point to which vehicles are permitted to drive on Old Chesterfield Rd., can usually be reached from the south by motorized vehicles from late spring through fall.

The trail ascends gradually south past an orange gate. After several stream crossings, Parker Trail leaves right at 0.4 mi. for Reservoir Trail. Chestnut Hill Trail swings left and ascends gradually to a small ridge. The route continues to ascend by switchbacks, descends briefly to a bridge over a small stream, and then ascends again to the height-of-land. It descends to Reservoir Trail at a point 0.9 mi. north of Reservoir Rd. and 0.6 mi. south of Pisgah Ridge Trail.

PARKER TRAIL
(NHDP/FOP; AMC PISGAH STATE PARK MAP)

From Chestnut Hill Trail (750 ft.) to:	⇅	↗	◔
Reservoir Trail (920 ft.)	0.9 mi.	150 ft.	0:35

This trail connects Chestnut Hill Trail with Reservoir Trail. It ascends a ridge that runs south to north through the center of Pisgah State Park and meets Reservoir Trail south of its height-of-land on this ridge.

Parker Trail turns right (southwest) onto an old woods road off Chestnut Hill Trail, 0.4 mi. south of Old Chesterfield Rd., and ascends gradually 0.2 mi. After crossing a log bridge over a stream, the route narrows to a footpath that soon ascends through a shallow gully then crosses a seasonal stream and passes a marsh on the left. At 0.9 mi. the trail reaches the height-of-land and descends gradually to Reservoir Trail at a point 0.4 mi. north of Pisgah Ridge Trail and 0.7 mi. south of North Ponds Trail.

NORTH PONDS TRAIL
(NHDP/FOP; AMC PISGAH STATE PARK MAP)

From Old Chesterfield Rd. (690 ft.) to:	⇅	↗	◔
Reservoir Trail (1,120 ft.)	1.1 mi.	450 ft.	0:45

This route follows an old woods road and connects Old Chesterfield Rd. with Reservoir Trail near its height-of-land on a long ridge. It is also a segment of Wantastiquet–Monadnock Trail and provides access to Lily Pond via Lily Pond Trail and to North Round Pond via Reservoir Trail and a short spur path. It leaves Old Chesterfield Rd. 0.3 mi. north of the gate and parking area at the north end of Chestnut Hill Trail and 1.2 mi. south of the junction with Winchester Rd. and Old Horseshoe Rd.

The trail ascends gradually, passing the Chesterfield–Winchester town line before crossing a small stream. At 0.3 mi. Lily Pond Trail leaves to the right, just before a bridge over a brook. North Ponds Trail continues across the bridge, swings left and then right, and ascends a broad ridge. It crosses a small stream, reaches the height-of-land, and descends gradually to Reservoir Trail. From here it is 0.3 mi. north to North Round Pond by Reservoir Trail and a spur path, 0.7 mi. north to Baker Pond Trail, and 2.6 mi. south to Reservoir Rd.

BAKER POND TRAIL
(NHDP/FOP; AMC PISGAH STATE PARK MAP)

Cumulative from Davis Hill Trail and Hubbard Hill Trail (1,200 ft.) to:	⇅	↗	⟳
Pisgah Ridge Trail (1,150 ft.)	0.4 mi.	0 ft. (rev. 50 ft.)	0:10
Reservoir Trail (1,030 ft.)	0.8 mi.	0 ft. (rev. 100 ft.)	0:25

This route connects Davis Hill Trail and Hubbard Hill Trail with Reservoir Trail, passing by scenic Baker Pond. Part of Baker Pond Trail is also a segment of Wantastiquet–Monadnock Trail. From the junction with Davis Hill Trail and Hubbard Hill Trail, Baker Pond Trail descends gradually and at 0.1 mi. swings left along the north shore of Baker Pond, where an unmarked path leads right 50 yd. to a fine outlook across the water. Baker Pond Trail crosses a bridge over an inlet brook and swings right (south) along the eastern shore of the pond. Another unmarked path on the right leads to an outlook across the pond toward Davis Hill. At 0.4 mi. Pisgah Ridge Trail diverges right in a small clearing. At 0.7 mi. Baker Pond Trail turns sharply left (northeast) onto an old woods road and descends gradually to Reservoir Trail at a point 0.7 mi. north of North Ponds Trail and 1.5 mi. south of Old Chesterfield Rd.

HUBBARD HILL TRAIL
(NHDP/FOP; AMC PISGAH STATE PARK MAP)

Cumulative from Winchester Rd. (980 ft.) to:	⇅	↗	⟳
Viewpoint loop path (1,310 ft.)	1.2 mi.	350 ft.	0:45
Davis Hill Trail and Baker Pond Trail (1,200 ft.)	1.6 mi.	350 ft. (rev. 100 ft.)	1:00

This trail ascends from Winchester Rd. along a ridge to a spur of Hubbard Hill, where there is a restricted view west, then descends to meet Baker Pond Trail and Davis Hill Trail just above Baker Pond. No parking is available at the Winchester Rd. trailhead, 1.3 mi. southeast of NH 63 in

Chesterfield. If entering Pisgah State Park from the northwest, park at the Old Horseshoe Rd. trailhead. The northern end of Hubbard Hill Trail is 0.8 mi. away via Old Horseshoe Rd., Old Horseshoe Rd. Connector, and Winchester Rd.

Leaving the west side of Winchester Rd., Hubbard Hill Trail follows an old woods road, ascending gradually. It swings left (south) past an old cellar hole on the left and then passes through the site of an old farm. The road ascends sharply past two stone walls then more gradually along a wooded ridge. After passing a spring on the left, the road makes one long switchback up to the crest of a ridge at 1.2 mi. Here, the north leg of a short loop path leads right 0.1 mi. to the spur of Hubbard Hill, where there is a bench with a restricted view of the southern Green Mtns. From the south side of the outlook a spur path descends 0.2 mi. and 150 ft. west to a shelter built by Friends of Pisgah (first come, first served) just outside the park boundary. The loop continues ahead 0.1 mi. back to the main trail, about 70 yd. south of its north end. From the south loop junction, the old road descends gradually along a switchback, and at 1.6 mi. Hubbard Hill Trail ends at the junction with Davis Hill Trail and Baker Pond Trail.

DAVIS HILL TRAIL
(NHDP/FOP; AMC PISGAH STATE PARK MAP)

Cumulative from Kilburn Rd. trailhead (1,060 ft.) to:	↾⇂	↗	⟳
Southern junction with Old Davis Hill Trail (1,330 ft.)	1.1 mi.	270 ft.	0:40
Height-of-land on Davis Hill (1,400 ft.)	1.3 mi.	340 ft.	0:50
FOP Shelter spur (1,240 ft.)	1.7 mi.	340 ft. (rev. 160 ft.)	1:00
Northern junction with Old Davis Hill Trail (1,210 ft.)	2.0 mi.	340 ft.	1:10
Jct. of Hubbard Hill Trail and Baker Pond Trail (1,200 ft.)	2.2 mi.	340 ft.	1:15

This route connects NH 63 at the Kilburn Rd. trailhead with Hubbard Hill Trail and Baker Pond Trail just north of Baker Pond, making possible a number of attractive loop hikes. It is also a segment of Wantastiquet–Monadnock Trail and provides access (via a side path) to a shelter built by Friends of Pisgah (first come, first served) on the west slope of Hubbard Hill, just outside Pisgah State Park. The Kilburn Rd. trailhead is on NH 63, 4.6 mi. south of NH 9 in Chesterfield and 3.9 mi. north of NH 119 in Hinsdale. The site includes ample parking and an information kiosk.

Davis Hill Trail (sign) follows an old woods road north from a point back near the entrance from NH 63. At 0.2 mi. it turns right onto a snowmobile trail, which it follows the rest of the way. The trail ascends by several switchbacks, bears right at a fork, and descends to cross a bridge over a stream. It then ascends again, passing blue-blazed boundary markers at 0.9 mi. that indicate the Pisgah State Park–Winchester Town Forest boundary. At 1.1 mi. it bears left at a fork where Old Davis Hill Trail diverges right, and ascends gradually to the height-of-land on Davis Hill, just east of the true summit. The trail descends, passes a cleared outlook and bench on the left, then turns sharply right at a hairpin turn at 1.7 mi. where a spur trail to FOP Shelter (sign) leaves on the left (this spur path descends for 0.1 mi. then turns right onto a woods road and reaches the shelter at 0.2 mi. from the main trail; note signage in this area as various paths intersect). From the hairpin turn, Davis Hill Trail descends at gentle grades, passes its northern junction with Old Davis Hill Trail on the right at 2.0 mi., then ends at a junction with Hubbard Hill Trail (left) and Baker Pond Trail (straight ahead), just north of Baker Pond and 0.4 mi. south of the western outlook on Hubbard Hill.

OLD DAVIS HILL TRAIL (NHDP/FOP; AMC PISGAH STATE PARK MAP)

From southern junction with Davis Hill Trail (1,330 ft.) to:	↕	↗	↻
Northern junction with Davis Hill Trail (1,210 ft.)	0.6 mi.	0 ft. (rev. 120 ft.)	0:20

This loop trail, a former section of Davis Hill Trail, provides a bypass around the summit area of Davis Hill. From Davis Hill Trail, 1.1 mi. from the Kilburn Rd. trailhead, the trail diverges right at a fork and descends moderately. It slowly curves left and then makes a gradual descent along the eastern base of Davis Hill, reaching its northern junction with Davis Hill Trail at 0.6 mi.

PISGAH RIDGE TRAIL (NHDP/FOP; AMC PISGAH STATE PARK MAP)

Cumulative from Reservoir Trail (910 ft.) to:	↕	↗	↻
Mt. Pisgah summit (1,329 ft.)	1.2 mi.	450 ft. (rev. 50 ft.)	0:50
Connecting path to Kilburn Loop (1,170 ft.)	2.0 mi.	600 ft. (rev. 300 ft.)	1:20
Baker Pond Trail (1,150 ft.)	3.1 mi.	750 ft. (rev. 150 ft.)	1:55

A ridge of small, craggy, wooded peaks forms the backbone of Pisgah State Park, running south to north from Pisgah Reservoir to Baker Pond. Some of these hills offer excellent views of Mt. Monadnock to the east and the southern Green Mtns. to the west. Pisgah Ridge Trail, one of the most interesting and scenic routes in the park, runs from the northern shore of Pisgah Reservoir over this chain, connecting with Kilburn Loop (via a link path) and Baker Pond Trail.

Pisgah Ridge Trail leaves Reservoir Trail at the northeast corner of Pisgah Reservoir, 1.5 mi. north of Reservoir Rd. It crosses a bridge over a brook and skirts the northern shore of the reservoir. At 0.3 mi. it swings away from the reservoir and ascends a boulder-strewn slope alongside a mossy stream. It veers away from the stream and bears left, heading north onto the spine of the hemlock-wooded ridge. At 1.0 mi., after a short descent, the trail turns left, and a side path descends 30 yd. ahead to Parker's Perch, a ledgy outlook with views toward Mt. Monadnock and back toward the southern end of the reservoir. Soon Pisgah Ridge Trail descends into a small gully and then ascends toward Mt. Pisgah (1,329 ft.), reaching the wooded summit at 1.2 mi.

The trail descends to a small stream then ascends scattered ledges, emerging onto an open crag with pines at 1.7 mi. (sign: "Mt. Pisgah vista"), where there is a fine view of Mt. Monadnock to the east and toward southern Vermont to the west. The trail descends steadily into a hemlock glen then swings left into a small gully at 2.0 mi. Here, an unnamed, yellow-blazed connecting path (sign: "To Kilburn Loop") diverges left. (The connecting path descends to a swamp then ascends slightly and crosses several small streams on bridges. After passing a beaver bog on the left, it reaches Kilburn Loop, 0.5 mi. from Pisgah Ridge Trail [ascent 50 ft.; rev. 100 ft.]. Turn right to reach Kilburn Rd. in 0.3 mi. and the trailhead on NH 63 in 1.1 mi.)

From the junction with the connecting path, Pisgah Ridge Trail climbs out of the gully, ascends gradually north on a small ridge, and then descends gradually by switchbacks into a rocky hemlock grove. It ascends again (more switchbacks), this time onto a ridge with an eastern viewpoint (Little's Lookout) on semi-open ledges. Then the trail swings left past a cellar hole on the right and at 2.6 mi. emerges onto an open ledge (Baker's Point) with a good view of Mt. Monadnock and nearby hills to the east. The path descends to a junction with Town Forest Trail on the left at 2.9 mi. Here, Pisgah Ridge Trail turns right and descends to a small clearing and a junction with Baker Pond Trail, which leads left to Baker Pond and right to Reservoir Trail.

TOWN FOREST TRAIL
(NHDP/FOP; AMC PISGAH STATE PARK MAP)
From Kilburn Loop
(1,050 ft.) to: ⇅ ↗ ↻

Baker Pond Trail/Pisgah Ridge Trail (1,150 ft.)	1.2 mi.	100 ft.	0:40

This formerly abandoned trail, recleared and reopened by Friends of Pisgah in 2018, connects the Kilburn and Baker Pond areas. Grades are mostly gentle and footing is good. To reach the start of the trail from the Kilburn Rd. trailhead, follow Kilburn Rd. east 0.7 mi. to its junction with Kilburn Loop. Bear left and follow Kilburn Loop 0.2 mi. to a junction where it turns sharply right, and Town Forest Trail continues straight. The mileages begin at this point.

Town Forest Trail takes a long, mostly level ramble along a woods road. At 0.2 mi. it passes concrete structures on the right that were used for munitions testing in the 1950s and 1960s. The path continues smoothly, bearing left at a fork at 0.6 mi. before swinging first left and then right through a wet area, where new footbridges have been constructed. It then curves left and ascends gently alongside a brook that drains Baker Pond, passing the foundation of a nineteenth-century sawmill on the left at 1.0 mi. Climbing becomes more moderate as the trail reaches the height-of-land and descends along a slope high above the pond on the left to a low spot. An easier climb leads to a three-way junction at 1.2 mi. with Baker Pond Trail and Pisgah Ridge Trail.

KILBURN LOOP (NHDP/FOP; AMC PISGAH STATE PARK MAP)
Cumulative from Kilburn Rd.
trailhead (1,060 ft.) to: ⇅ ↗ ↻

Western end of Kilburn Loop (1,040 ft.)	0.6 mi.	100 ft. (rev. 100 ft.)	0:20
Southern end of Kilburn Loop (980 ft.)	2.7 mi.	150 ft. (rev. 100 ft.)	1:25
Connecting path to Pisgah Ridge Trail (1,080 ft.)	5.2 mi.	250 ft.	2:40
Eastern end of Kilburn Loop (1,050 ft.)	5.5 mi.	250 ft. (rev. 50 ft.)	2:50
Kilburn Rd. trailhead (1,060 ft.) via complete loop	6.3 mi.	350 ft.	3:20

One of the most popular hiking routes in Pisgah State Park, Kilburn Loop provides an attractive overview of the area from an easy-to-reach trailhead. The trail passes Kilburn Pond and its outlet brook, several wetlands, and attractive hemlock forests. It is ideal for a half-day family hike. The trailhead, shared with Davis Hill Trail, is on NH 63, 4.6 mi. south of NH 9 in

Chesterfield and 3.9 mi. north of NH 119 in Hinsdale. Ample parking and an information kiosk are available at the trailhead.

SEC 1

At first, the route follows Kilburn Rd., an old gravel road that heads east from the parking area through two gateposts and past a mailbox on the right. It ascends gradually, swings right, begins a gentle descent, and turns right onto the west end of Kilburn Loop at 0.6 mi. The loop is described here in a counterclockwise direction. It follows an old woods road south, almost immediately passing within sight of Kilburn Pond, an attractive body of water lined with rocky outcroppings and hemlocks. The trail follows the western shore, passing several unmarked paths on the left that lead to viewpoints overlooking the pond. At 1.3 mi. (0.7 mi. from Kilburn Rd.) John Summers Trail, opened in 2018, diverges left, providing a shorter loop hike around the pond. At 1.4 mi. Kilburn Loop reaches the southwestern corner of the pond, where an old woods road leaves left. The trail bears right here, however, avoiding another old woods road on the right and descending parallel to a large outlet brook on the left, crossing several small streams along the way.

At 1.9 mi. there are views to the left through the trees to a smaller pond. Kilburn Loop passes this pond then descends in earnest, crossing the outlet brook and a tributary stream on bridges. At the south end of the loop, the trail turns sharply left where an old woods road leaves right to exit the park, and then at 2.7 mi. the trail begins the northward climb to complete the loop. The route passes another small pond (seen through the trees on the left) and shortly reaches red blazes marking the Hinsdale–Winchester town line. After bearing left across a bridge over a brook, Kilburn Loop leaves the old road it was on and becomes a footpath in a hemlock forest.

The footpath passes another pond on the left and ascends gradually. At 4.4 mi. the trail reaches its high point on a small ridge then descends gradually by switchbacks. At 5.2 mi. an unnamed connecting path on the right ascends 0.5 mi. and 100 ft. to Pisgah Ridge Trail. At this junction, Kilburn Loop merges with an old woods road coming from the left. The trail descends and turns sharply left (avoid a false path ahead by making sure to follow the white blazes) then climbs over a rise. It bears right twice, passes the junction with the north end of John Summers Trail on the left, crosses a bridge over a large brook, and soon turns left (west) onto Kilburn Rd. at 5.5 mi. (In the reverse direction, turn sharply right here onto the east end of Kilburn Loop. The woods road ahead, shown as Town Forest Trail on the state park website map, was recleared, partly relocated, and reopened to the public in 2018 after years of abandonment. It leads 1.2 mi. to Pisgah Ridge Trail [or Baker Pond Trail].) Now following Kilburn Rd., Kilburn

Loop swings around the north shore of Kilburn Pond, passing a side path that leads 100 yd. left to a view over the north part of the pond. The main trail then ascends gradually and at 5.7 mi. reaches the west end of Kilburn Loop on the left, completing the circuit around Kilburn Pond. Continue ahead (west) 0.6 mi. to return to the trailhead.

JOHN SUMMERS TRAIL
(NHDP/FOP; AMC PISGAH STATE PARK MAP)

Cumulative from Kilburn Loop (eastern section) (1,080 ft.) to:	⇅	↗	⟳
Kilburn Loop (western section) (1,060 ft.)	1.1 mi.	130 ft.	0:35
Complete loop using Kilburn Rd., Kilburn Loop, and John Summers Trail	3.5 mi.	280 ft.	1:55

This new trail, opened in 2018, connects both sides of Kilburn Loop to create a shorter loop hike option around Kilburn Pond. The new route mostly follows an older informal path along the eastern shore of the pond. The trail is easy to follow, but watch for unmarked intersecting paths. Grades are easy or level overall, with many short ascents and descents, and footing is generally good. The northern end of the trail is 0.3 mi. east along Kilburn Loop from its junction with Kilburn Rd. (0.9 mi. from the trailhead). The southern end is 0.7 mi. south along the western section of Kilburn Loop from its junction with Kilburn Rd. (1.3 mi. from the trailhead). The route is described here from north to south.

From its northern junction with Kilburn Loop, the trail bears right (south) and descends easily to briefly run alongside the inlet brook for Kilburn Pond then ascends easily away from it, passing a large glacial boulder on the left at 0.2 mi. Opposite the boulder, a side path leads 15 yd. to ledges at the shore of the pond that are perfect for sitting on and taking a break. At 0.4 mi. the trail turns left at Whale Rock, a rounded granite ledge that falls 15 ft. into the pond. The trail continues, with many twists and turns, swinging around another large glacial boulder on the left, informally called Fox Den Rock, and then dipping to cross a footbridge over a beaver pond outlet at 0.8 mi. At 1.0 mi. it descends a short, steep pitch to cross a footbridge at the base of a dam, at the south end of the pond. Past the dam, the trail swings right (west) to join the western section of Kilburn Loop at 1.1 mi.

SOUTH WOODS TRAIL
(NHDP/FOP; AMC PISGAH STATE PARK MAP)
Cumulative from jct. of Old Chesterfield Rd.
and Old Horseshoe Rd. (910 ft.)
via southwest fork to:

	⇅	↗	⟳
Jct. with northwest fork (840 ft.)	0.5 mi.	0 ft. (rev. 50 ft.)	0:15
Fullam Pond Trail (690 ft.)	1.9 mi.	0 ft. (rev. 150 ft.)	0:55

This trail connects Old Horseshoe Rd. and Old Chesterfield Rd. with Fullam Pond Trail. Parts of the route may require care to follow. The western end has two paths from separate entrances that come together after 0.5 mi. The southwest fork passes a beaver pond where water may flood the trail.

The northwest fork (the least wet approach) leaves Old Horseshoe Rd. from an overgrown clearing, 0.3 mi. south of the Horseshoe Rd. trailhead and 0.2 mi. north of the junction of Old Chesterfield Rd. and Winchester Rd. It enters the woods, passes a stone wall, and descends to the point where the southwest fork comes in on the right at 0.5 mi.

The southwest fork leaves Old Chesterfield Rd. just south of the convergence of Old Horseshoe Rd. and Winchester Rd. It descends gradually on an old woods road, crosses two culverted brooks, and at 0.1 mi. makes a left onto an old grassy road. It follows this road to the southern shore of a large beaver pond and heads into the woods, bearing right onto another old woods road. This section is extremely wet. The southwest fork descends gradually past a stone wall and meets the northwest fork on the left at 0.5 mi.

South Woods Trail turns right (east) at this junction (or continues straight if you are coming in on the northwest fork) and enters a short relocated section that avoided a former deteriorated bridge (since removed) via a new bridge constructed in 2018. (A new wildlife viewing platform was also built along the old route of the trail, which is still open to the public.) From here the route narrows from a road to a footpath and may be difficult to follow. It bypasses a small bog on the left, crosses several small streams, and then turns right onto a different old woods road. It skirts to the right of an open wetland, reenters the woods, and climbs a rise into a hemlock forest, where it crosses a bridge over a large brook. The old road follows the north bank of this brook downstream, recrosses the bridge over the brook, and at 1.6 mi. reaches a junction where the route forks again. South Woods Trail bears left and ascends gradually to Fullam Pond Trail at a point just south of that trail's junction with Nash Trail. The former southeast fork (right at the jct. noted above) of the trail has been abandoned.

OLD CHESTERFIELD RD. (NHDP/FOP; NHDP PISGAH STATE PARK MAP, AMC PISGAH STATE PARK MAP)

Cumulative from southern
trailhead (880 ft.) to:

	⤵⤴	↗	◔
Broad Brook Rd. (710 ft.)	1.5 mi.	50 ft. (rev. 200 ft.)	0:45
Nash Trail (660 ft.)	2.5 mi.	150 ft. (rev. 150 ft.)	1:20
Chestnut Hill Trail and locked gate (680 ft.)	3.3 mi.	150 ft.	1:45
Winchester Rd. and Old Horseshoe Rd. (910 ft.)	4.8 mi.	400 ft.	2:35

Once the highway between Winchester and Chesterfield, this historical road is now the southeast-to-northwest artery through Pisgah State Park. Motorized vehicles may generally use the southern 3.3-mi. section from late spring through fall. It is gated the remainder of the year. Part of this road is also a segment of Wantastiquet–Monadnock Trail.

A small parking area sits at the southern trailhead, 2.8 mi. northwest of the village of Winchester (via Elm St. and Old Chesterfield Rd.). Old Chesterfield Rd. heads north, and in 0.2 mi. it passes an orange gate (locked during winter and early spring) and descends gradually on a gravel roadway, passing the park's visitor center and office on the left. It then passes several historical sites; at the second of these (0.4 mi.), Doolittle Trail diverges left. At 1.1 mi. Old Chesterfield Rd. reaches a second orange gate that is locked during winter and early spring. Here, Jon Hill Rd. leaves right and runs to Old Spofford Rd. At 1.5 mi. Broad Brook Rd. diverges sharply left, and at 1.7 mi. Snow Brook Trail diverges right at an orange gatepost. At 2.5 mi. Old Chesterfield Rd. meets Nash Trail on the right at a small parking area. It then swings left (west), crosses a bridge over Broad Brook, and shortly passes Dogwood Swamp Trail on the left in a small clearing. The road curves several times through an open bog and at 3.1 mi. arrives at the road that leads 0.2 mi. to the Fullam Pond parking area on the right. At 3.3 mi. it reaches Chestnut Hill Trail on the left at a small parking area.

The road now becomes a woods road and ascends gradually past a locked orange gate, passes the Winchester–Chesterfield boundary, and at 3.6 mi. reaches North Ponds Trail on the left. After a gradual descent, at 4.2 mi. the road arrives at the northern terminus of Lily Pond Trail on the left. At 4.4 mi. the route passes an unmarked woods road on the right that leads 0.3 mi. to meet South Woods Trail near a beaver pond. Old Chesterfield Rd. descends gradually to Reservoir Trail, which comes in on the left at an orange gate at 4.7 mi., and at 4.8 mi. the road reaches the southwest terminus of South Woods Trail on the right. Old Chesterfield Rd. ends just beyond, at an area of beaver activity. Here, Winchester Rd. leads straight uphill 0.6 mi. to the Winchester Rd. trailhead (no parking), and Old Horseshoe Rd. leaves right uphill 0.5 mi. to the Horseshoe Rd. parking area.

LILY POND TRAIL (NHDP/FOP); AMC PISGAH STATE PARK MAP)

Cumulative from Old Chesterfield Rd. (820 ft.) to:	⥮	⤴	⟳
Lily Pond (960 ft.)	0.5 mi.	150 ft.	0:20
North Ponds Trail (690 ft.)	1.1 mi.	150 ft. (rev. 250 ft.)	0:40
Starting point (820 ft.) via jct. of North Ponds Trail and Old Chesterfield Rd.	1.9 mi.	300 ft.	1:05

This lightly used trail provides access from Old Chesterfield Rd. or North Ponds Trail to attractive Lily Pond. The north end of the route leaves Old Chesterfield Rd. 0.9 mi. north of the Fullam Pond gate and parking area, and 0.6 mi. south of the junction with Winchester Rd. and Old Horseshoe Rd.

Leaving from Old Chesterfield Rd., Lily Pond Trail first follows an old woods road through hemlocks to a small beaver pond on the left. The obscure route skirts to the right of the pond and bears right uphill on another old woods road, crossing a small stream and ascending to a flat area, where the trail swings left by the northeast corner of Lily Pond at 0.5 mi. From here it leads south along the eastern shore and then swings left, away from Lily Pond, and descends. At the southeast corner of a beaver pond, the trail ends at North Ponds Trail (no sign), 0.3 mi. west of Old Chesterfield Rd. (To reach Old Chesterfield Rd., turn left. Turn left again onto Old Chesterfield Rd. to reach the north end of Lily Pond Trail in 0.5 mi.)

DOOLITTLE TRAIL (NHDP/FOP; AMC PISGAH STATE PARK MAP)

Cumulative from Old Chesterfield Rd. (910 ft.) to:	⥮	⤴	⟳
Broad Brook Rd. (590 ft.)	1.1 mi.	50 ft. (rev. 350 ft.)	0:35
Complete loop via Doolittle Trail, Broad Brook Rd., and Old Chesterfield Rd.	3.2 mi.	400 ft. (rev. 50 ft.)	1:50

This short trail connects Old Chesterfield Rd. with Broad Brook Rd., descending into the Broad Brook valley through the remains of an early New Hampshire farming and industrial community. Hikers can make an interesting loop using Doolittle Trail, Broad Brook Rd., and Old Chesterfield Rd.

Doolittle Trail leaves Old Chesterfield Rd. via an old grassy road, 0.4 mi. north of the Old Chesterfield Rd. trailhead and 0.7 mi. south of Jon Hill Rd. It leads through an old orchard and overgrown field, passing several stone walls, and then bears right off the old road into the forest (no sign). The trail turns left onto a footpath (sign) and ascends a small hill. Follow this section with care, as the footpath is faint. The route swings right and then left before descending gradually and turning left onto an old woods road (sign). From here on, the route is easier to follow. It passes over a small hill, descends to Old Broad Brook Meadow (left) at 0.7 mi., then swings right (north) and ascends. It crosses a bridge over a stream and follows Broad Brook upstream, passes the Water Mill Dam Site (left) at 0.9 mi., and then swings left (west) and crosses Broad Brook and a tributary stream on bridges. Soon the trail meets Broad Brook Rd., 1.0 mi. south of Old Chesterfield Rd. and 1.9 mi. north of the South Link trail.

BROAD BROOK RD. (NHDP/FOP; NHDP PISGAH STATE PARK MAP, AMC PISGAH STATE PARK MAP)

Cumulative from designated Reservoir Rd. trailhead on NH 119 (390 ft.) to:	⬍	↗	⟳
Broad Brook Rd. (560 ft.) via jct. of Connector Trail and South Link	1.1 mi.	200 ft. (rev. 50 ft.)	0:40
Historical sites parking area (590 ft.)	2.9 mi.	250 ft.	1:30
Old Chesterfield Rd. (710 ft.)	4.0 mi.	350 ft.	2:10

This scenic and historical walk through the valley of Broad Brook was once the location of a thriving nineteenth-century farming and industrial community. The southern section of the road (which is open to ATV riders as well as hikers and mountain bikers) passes through attractive open marshes. The northern mile passes numerous historical sites. Motorized vehicles are allowed through this northern section (via Old Chesterfield Rd.) from late spring through fall.

The best access from the south is via the designated Reservoir Rd. trailhead (on NH 119, 2.2 mi. east of Hinsdale). The access route follows a woods road that leads uphill past an orange gate and crosses a power-line clearing. At 0.2 mi. the route turns right and follows Connector Trail, a snowmobile trail that passes through a pine grove and reaches Reservoir Rd. at 0.4 mi. A short distance downhill to the right from here, at 0.5 mi., South Link leaves on the left and ascends on an old woods road then descends to meet Broad Brook Rd. at 1.1 mi. from the parking area on NH 119. This is 0.6 mi. north of where Broad Brook Rd. leaves NH 119 (at a point 3.2 mi. east of Hinsdale; parking very limited) and 0.1 mi. north of the locked south gate where Broad Brook Rd. enters Pisgah State Park (parking very limited here also). Distances given below are from the designated Reservoir Rd. trailhead.

From the junction with South Link, Broad Brook Rd. leads gradually uphill past an open marsh on the right and finally runs alongside Broad Brook itself, keeping the brook on the right. At 2.9 mi. it reaches the historical sites parking area and turnaround on the left, which is the southern limit for motorized vehicle travel during the summer season. From here the route parallels Broad Brook through the remains of the early settlement, with more than a dozen historical exhibits (from when this area contained farmsteads and mills) on either side of the road. At 3.0 mi. the road reaches the western terminus of Doolittle Trail on the right, which provides access to several other historical sites. In another 0.5 mi., the road crosses Broad Brook next to a mill site and ascends gradually away from the brook, passing several additional historical sites before reaching Old Chesterfield Rd., 0.4 mi. north of Jon Hill Rd. and 1.8 mi. south of the Chestnut Hill Trail parking area.

SNOW BROOK TRAIL
(NHDP/FOP; NHDP PISGAH STATE PARK MAP)

Cumulative from Old Spofford Rd. trailhead (920 ft.) to:	⬇⬆	↗	⟳
Orchard Trail (850 ft.)	0.9 mi.	0 ft. (rev. 50 ft.)	0:25
Old Chesterfield Rd. (720 ft.)	1.8 mi.	0 ft. (rev. 150 ft.)	0:55

This trail meanders westward from Old Spofford Rd. to Old Chesterfield Rd., following an old woods road along Snow Brook and beside open marshlands. The eastern trailhead is on Old Spofford Rd. From NH 10 in Winchester, turn northwest onto Elm St. Turn right onto Howard St. at 0.1 mi. and right again onto Old Westport Rd. at 0.8 mi. At 1.0 mi. bear left onto Old Spofford Rd. and follow it past Jon Hill Rd. on the left at 4.5 mi. to the trailhead on the left (4.7 mi.), where there is ample parking.

The route leads past an orange gate and through several turns before crossing a bridge over Snow Brook. It then swings left and recrosses Snow Brook on another bridge, and at 0.9 mi. passes a closed and posted section of Orchard Trail on the right. A short distance beyond, Orchard Trail leaves left for Jon Hill Rd. Snow Brook Trail swings right, however, and crosses a bridge over Snow Brook, ascends away from the brook, and skirts a large open marsh. It enters a pine forest and ascends to Old Chesterfield Rd., 0.2 mi. north of Broad Brook Rd. and 1.6 mi. south of the Chestnut Hill Trail parking area.

JON HILL RD. (NHDP/FOP; NHDP PISGAH STATE PARK MAP)

Cumulative from
Old Spofford Rd. (920 ft.) to:

	⬇⬆	↗	⟳
Orchard Trail (900 ft.)	0.6 mi.	0 ft.	0:20
Old Chesterfield Rd. (750 ft.)	1.2 mi.	0 ft. (rev. 150 ft.)	0:35

This partly paved, partly gravel road connects Old Spofford Rd. with Old Chesterfield Rd. It is used by hikers, ATV riders, and snowmobilers and is gated on both ends. Jon Hill Rd. leaves Old Spofford Rd. 0.2 mi. south of the trailhead for Snow Brook Trail and 4.5 mi. north of Winchester. Visitors find ample space to park at the trailhead for Snow Brook Trail. Jon Hill Rd. descends through a gate past a beaver pond on the left and then ascends to the height-of-land at 0.4 mi. Here, it swings right and descends. At 0.6 mi. an unmarked woods road (Orchard Trail) leaves right (north). After passing another old road and a small clearing with utility lines on the right, Jon Hill Rd. swings left and descends to Old Chesterfield Rd. at an orange gate, 0.4 mi. south of Broad Brook Rd. and 1.1 mi. north of the southern trailhead.

ORCHARD TRAIL (NHDP/FOP; NHDP PISGAH STATE PARK MAP)

From Jon Hill Rd.
(900 ft.) to:

	⬇⬆	↗	⟳
Snow Brook Trail (850 ft.)	0.6 mi.	0 ft. (rev. 50 ft.)	0:20

This white-blazed (though somewhat ill-defined) trail connects Jon Hill Rd. to Snow Brook Trail. A former section of the route north of Snow Brook Trail has been abandoned and posted against trespassing. The southern trailhead is on Jon Hill Rd. at a point 0.6 mi. west of Old Spofford Rd. and 0.6 mi. east of Old Chesterfield Rd.

The route starts as an unmarked dirt road that almost immediately reaches a turnaround, where Orchard Trail bears right onto an old woods road (sign) and enters the woods. It passes two stone walls, descends gradually to a beaver bog, passes another stone wall, crosses a small stream, and at 0.6 mi. ends at Snow Brook Trail.

RESERVOIR RD. (NHDP/FOP; NHDP PISGAH STATE PARK MAP, AMC PISGAH STATE PARK MAP)

Cumulative from designated
Reservoir Rd. trailhead on NH 119 (390 ft.) to:

	⬇⬆	↗	⟳
Reservoir Rd. (560 ft.)	0.5 mi.	150 ft.	0:20
Dogwood Swamp Trail (620 ft.)	1.4 mi.	250 ft.	0:50

| Reservoir Trail (940 ft.) | 1.9 mi. | 550 ft. | 1:15 |
| Spillway at southern end of Pisgah Reservoir (890 ft.) | 2.1 mi. | 550 ft. (rev. 50 ft.) | 1:20 |

This trail from NH 119 to the south shore of Pisgah Reservoir uses a gravel road—open seasonally for motor vehicles up to the Dogwood Swamp Trail parking area—for most of its length. Views from the reservoir's shore are excellent.

Reservoir Rd. has two approaches: One follows an access route from the designated trailhead and parking area, 2.2 mi. east of Hinsdale on NH 119, and meets Reservoir Rd. The other, a gravel road, follows the first part of Reservoir Rd. (no parking here), which begins 0.3 mi. east of the designated trailhead. Both are described below.

From the designated trailhead, the access route, a woods road marked by blue diamonds, ascends past an orange gate and through a power-line clearing. At 0.2 mi. Connector Trail, a snowmobile trail, leaves right uphill and runs 0.2 mi. through a pine grove to Reservoir Rd. The access route, however, continues straight uphill on an old woods road then quickly fades to a footpath and reaches Reservoir Rd. at 0.5 mi. Turn left here for Pisgah Reservoir (no sign).

From the base of Reservoir Rd. at NH 119 (no parking), the gravel road ascends past an orange gate and immediately enters Pisgah State Park (signs). At 0.4 mi. the road reaches South Link on the right, which leads 0.6 mi. to Broad Brook Rd. at a point 0.1 mi. north of that road's southern gate. Reservoir Rd. continues straight 0.1 mi. to Connector Trail on the left. In another 0.2 mi. the access route enters on the left (sign). Mileages given below are from the designated trailhead.

Beyond the junction with the access route, Reservoir Rd. crosses a brook, passes two beaver ponds, and at 1.4 mi. reaches Dogwood Swamp Trail on the right, across from a small parking area. The road swings left here, passes an orange gate with a mailbox on the left, and begins a series of switchbacks up the side of a ridge. After a moderate climb, the grade eases, and Reservoir Rd. descends gradually to Reservoir Trail on the right, which serves as one of the major north–south arteries in the park. The road swings left around the south end of Pisgah Reservoir, passing several unmarked paths on the right that lead to the reservoir's shore. At 2.1 mi. the road reaches a spillway at the southern end of the reservoir, where there are views north over the water toward Mt. Pisgah. On the other side of the spillway, Reservoir Rd. continues as Hinsdale Snowmobile Trail, which leads 2.8 mi. down to NH 63. Use caution if you cross the spillway. (*Note*:

If the spillway cannot be crossed due to high water or winds, an unmarked bypass road to the left avoids the spillway and dam area.)

HINSDALE SNOWMOBILE TRAIL (NHDP/FOP; NHDP PISGAH STATE PARK MAP, AMC PISGAH STATE PARK MAP)

Cumulative from Pisgah Reservoir spillway and Reservoir Rd. (890 ft.) to:	⇅	↗	↺
Spur trail to western cove of Pisgah Reservoir (890 ft.)	0.7 mi.	0 ft.	0:20
Western cove of Pisgah Reservoir (890 ft.) via spur trail	1.1 mi.	0 ft.	0:35
NH 63 (330 ft.)	2.8 mi.	0 ft. (rev. 550 ft.)	1:25

This woods road is actively used in winter as part of a major snowmobile corridor through Pisgah State Park. For hikers, its primary attraction is that it can be followed 0.7 mi. west from the spillway at the south end of Pisgah Reservoir, crossing several bridges over streams, to a spur road that leads right (north) 0.4 mi. over a small, rocky ridge to a beautiful cove on the western arm of the reservoir. From the junction with this spur road, Hinsdale Snowmobile Trail turns left and runs southwest, leaving the park at 1.5 mi. It reaches NH 63 at a point 0.6 mi. north of Hinsdale (no parking here) and 2.8 mi. from the spillway. This route has few trail markings, with the exception of snowmobile signs at major intersections.

Use caution if you cross the spillway. (*Note*: If the spillway cannot be crossed due to high water or winds, an unmarked bypass road to the left avoids the spillway and dam area.)

NASH TRAIL (NHDP/FOP; AMC PISGAH STATE PARK MAP)

Cumulative from Old Chesterfield Rd. (660 ft.) to:	⇅	↗	↺
Nash Trail Spur (690 ft.)	0.5 mi.	50 ft.	0:15
Jct. of Fullam Pond Trail and South Woods Trail (690 ft.)	1.2 mi.	50 ft.	0:40

This route connects Old Chesterfield Rd., 2.5 mi. from its southern trail-head, with Fullam Pond Trail and is also a segment of Wantastiquet–Monadnock Trail. It parallels the eastern shore of Fullam Pond with a connecting spur that leads down to the Fullam Pond Dam and the southern terminus of Fullam Pond Trail. It is well marked and easy to follow.

Leaving Old Chesterfield Rd. from a small parking area just south of the bridge over Broad Brook, the trail follows an old grassy road north. After a short distance, Broad Brook is visible on the left. At 0.4 mi. the route passes from Winchester into Chesterfield and swings right. Soon a connecting path (Nash Trail Spur) leaves to the left downhill on an old grassy road and in 0.1 mi. reaches the southern terminus of Fullam Pond Trail. It crosses Fullam Pond Dam on a grated walkway and ends 0.1 mi. beyond at the eastern shore of Fullam Pond.

The main trail swings right and then left, passes a stone wall, crosses a bridge over a stream, swings left again, and ends at Fullam Pond Trail just north of South Woods Trail. From here it is 0.6 mi. south to the Fullam Pond Dam by Fullam Pond Trail, 0.6 mi. north to Beal's Rd. by Fullam Pond Trail, and 2.2 mi. northwest to the Horseshoe Rd. trailhead via South Woods Trail and Old Horseshoe Rd.

FULLAM POND TRAIL (NHDP/FOP; NHDP PISGAH STATE PARK MAP, AMC PISGAH STATE PARK MAP)

Cumulative from Old Swanzey Rd.
(1,030 ft.) to:

	⇅	↗	↺
Beal's Rd. (790 ft.)	1.6 mi.	50 ft. (rev. 300 ft.)	0:50
Nash Trail and South Woods Trail (690 ft.)	2.2 mi.	50 ft. (rev. 100 ft.)	1:10
Nash Trail Spur, just east of Fullam Pond Dam (680 ft.)	2.8 mi.	50 ft.	1:25

This trail on an old road runs south from Old Swanzey Rd. to Fullam Pond, 50 yd. east of the Fullam Pond Dam at Nash Trail Spur. Although the path is wide and easy to follow, the northern end has few markings. Fullam Pond Trail (no signs) leaves Old Swanzey Rd. 1.2 mi. southeast of Tuttle Rd. via an unmarked woods road with a chain-link gate, located between a large white house on the right and a log cabin on the left. Request permission from the owners of the white house before leaving cars here. Part of this route is also a segment of Wantastiquet–Monadnock Trail.

The trail follows the old road south into Pisgah State Park (signs) at 0.2 mi. It swings left then right at an unmarked intersection; take care not to turn left onto one of several other old roads. The route ascends gradually to the height-of-land at 0.8 mi. and then descends gradually, following a stream and crossing it several times. Shortly after crossing a bridge over this stream, Fullam Pond Trail reaches Beal's Rd. on the left at 1.6 mi.

The trail continues to descend, crossing the stream several more times. Pass Nash Trail on the left and South Woods Trail on the right at 2.2 mi. Shortly after crossing another bridge, Fullam Pond Trail reaches the abandoned southeast fork of South Woods Trail on the right. Bypassing this fork, Fullam Pond Trail now follows a large brook south as it enters the northern cove of Fullam Pond. At 2.5 mi. the trail crosses the northeast corner of Fullam Pond on a causeway with a small spillway in the center (use caution when crossing). The trail then reenters the woods, with several unmarked paths on the right leading to the eastern shore of Fullam Pond, and ends at unmarked Nash Trail Spur, 0.1 mi. west of Nash Trail and 50 yd. east of the Fullam Pond Dam and the pond's eastern shore.

BEAL'S RD. (NHDP/FOP; NHDP PISGAH STATE PARK MAP)

Cumulative from Beal's Rd. trailhead (990 ft.) to:	⇅	↗	◔
Beal's Knob Trail, upper jct. (1,080 ft.)	0.4 mi.	100 ft.	0:15
Fullam Pond Trail (790 ft.)	1.1 mi.	100 ft. (rev. 300 ft.)	0:35

This historical route ascends from the Beal's Rd. trailhead along the southern side of Beal's Knob then descends past an eighteenth-century graveyard on its way to Fullam Pond Trail. Part of this road is also a segment of Wantastiquet–Monadnock Trail. It is well signed at its trailhead and easy to follow; however, it is unsigned at its junction with Fullam Pond Trail. To reach Beal's Rd., turn south onto Old Chesterfield Rd. from NH 9, 2.1 mi. east of its junction with NH 63. In less than 0.1 mi. turn left onto Tuttle Rd., and in another 0.3 mi. turn right onto Old Swanzey Rd. At 1.8 mi. from Tuttle Rd., turn right onto gravel Stones Mill Rd. and follow it 0.6 mi. south to a small clearing with trail signs and very limited parking. (*Note*: Do not block the gate or driveways.)

From the trailhead, the route passes an orange gate and follows an old grassy road, almost immediately arriving at the lower junction with Beal's Knob Trail on the right. Both trails are marked with blue diamond blazes as part of Beal's Knob Cross-Country Ski Loop over the summit of Beal's Knob. Beal's Rd. passes a beaver pond on the left and ascends 0.4 mi. to the height-of-land and the upper junction with Beal's Knob Trail on the right, which leads in 0.4 mi. to the summit, where there is a restricted view of Mt. Monadnock.

No longer marked by blue blazes, Beal's Rd. descends into the forest and passes the Latham Beal Cemetery (est. 1790) at 0.7 mi. It swings right and descends gradually to Fullam Pond Trail, 1.6 mi. south of Old Swanzey Rd. and 1.2 mi. north of the Fullam Pond Dam.

BEAL'S KNOB TRAIL
(NHDP/FOP; NHDP PISGAH STATE PARK MAP)

Cumulative from Beal's Rd. trailhead (990 ft.) to:	⇅	↗	◔
Spur path to Beal's Knob summit (1,100 ft.)	0.4 mi.	100 ft.	0:15
Beal's Knob summit via spur path (1,180 ft.)	0.6 mi.	200 ft.	0:25

Beal's Rd. at height-of-land (1,080 ft.)	0.6 mi.	100 ft.	0:20
Complete loop to Beal's Knob summit via Beal's Knob Trail, spur path, and Beal's Rd.	1.4 mi.	200 ft.	0:50

This trail, marked with blue diamond blazes as part of Beal's Knob Cross-Country Ski Loop, ascends Beal's Knob, which has a restricted view east toward Mt. Monadnock. It leaves Beal's Rd. just beyond the orange gate at the Beal's Rd. trailhead and ascends a grassy road around the north side of Beal's Knob. At 0.3 mi. the route swings left (south) and reaches a three-way junction, where a spur path leads left 0.2 mi. to the summit of Beal's Knob. The main trail bears right, passes a stone wall, swings left onto an old road, passes two more stone walls, and ascends gradually to Beal's Rd. at its height-of-land. From here it is 0.7 mi. right (west) to Fullam Pond Trail and 0.4 mi. left (east) back downhill to the Beal's Rd. trailhead.

CARROLL'S HILL OUTLOOK (885 FT.)

This open viewpoint provides a vista east to Mt. Monadnock from the eastern slope of Carroll's Hill in Swanzey, located at the northern end of the Franconia Mtn. Range, a chain of small hills extending between Swanzey and Richmond. Carroll's Hill Trail climbs through attractive hemlock and hardwood groves on its way to the outlook and is on private property protected by a conservation easement held by the Monadnock Conservancy and maintained by the Swanzey Open Space Committee. Foot traffic is welcomed and encouraged, but please stay on the trail and obey all posted signage. A trail map and guide is available at swanzeynh.gov.

To reach the trailhead from NH 101 in Keene, take NH 12 South 0.8 mi. then turn right onto NH 32 South. In 6.6 mi. bear right onto Westbrook Court and continue 0.4 mi. to a large grassy field on the right. Follow signs into the field to a parking area on the left edge.

CARROLL'S HILL TRAIL (SOSC/MC; MC MAP)

From Westbrook Court (550 ft.) to:	↓↑	↗	↺
Carroll's Hill Outlook (885 ft.)	1.1 mi.	400 ft. (rev. 50 ft.)	0:45

This trail follows a series of three woods roads and a section of footpath to the viewpoint at Carroll's Hill Outlook. Grades are easy to moderate, with one steeper section, and footing is generally good. The route has no blazes, but junctions are well marked with signs and arrows.

From the parking area on Westbrook Court, the trail enters the woods at the left corner of the field (sign, map box) and ascends easily along an old woods road next to a small brook. At 0.2 mi. it bears left (in the reverse direction, bear right at the arrow) onto Old Calvin Curtiss Rd., a route that once connected various small farms between East Swanzey and Richmond. It then passes around a gate and begins a steady ascent up the wide road. At 0.5 mi. the trail bears left at a fork, and at 0.6 mi. it turns left onto a lesser woods road. Climbing here is moderate, with one steeper section, and the footing is slightly rougher. At 0.9 mi. the trail turns left off the woods road onto a footpath (sign: "View"). It quickly bears right at a fork, swings left through an area of interesting high rock faces on the left, and then descends easily to the outlook and a log bench at 1.1 mi.

HEWES HILL (940 FT.)

This small mountain in Swanzey offers easy hiking and natural features that include Tippin Rock, a large glacial boulder that can be made to sway slightly; a southwest-facing open ledge with good views; and impressive cliffs. It is on property protected by a conservation easement held by the Monadnock Conservancy and maintained by the Swanzey Open Space Committee. From the junction of NH 101 and NH 12 in Keene, take NH 12 South for 0.9 mi. Turn right onto NH 32 South, follow it 6.4 mi., and then turn right onto Warmac Rd. and drive 0.5 mi. to the trailhead on the left. Look for the gated entrance to a field across from Chebaco Kennel. As of 2018, there was no property sign. Limited roadside parking is available; do not block the gate. A trail map is available at town.swanzeynh.gov.

TIPPIN ROCK FARM TRAIL
(SOSC/MC; MC MAP, USGS KEENE QUAD)

Cumulative from Warmac Rd. (530 ft.) to:	⇅	↗	○
Tippin Rock (850 ft.)	0.7 mi.	320 ft.	0:30
Ledge Overlook (885 ft.)	1.0 mi.	355 ft.	0:40
Hewes Hill summit (940 ft.)	1.1 mi.	415 ft.	0:45

This trail, a combination of a woods road and sections of footpath, provides a direct route to Tippin Rock and the ledge outlook just below the summit of Hewes Hill. Grades are generally easy, and footing is excellent. From the parking area gate, head southwest across the field along a beaten grassy path 130 yd. to enter the woods, where the trail officially begins (sign). The blue-blazed trail proceeds generally level 0.2 mi. and then turns sharply left onto a woods road. (In the reverse direction, watch carefully for a blue arrow on a stump indicating a right turn off the road; there is also a large boulder at this junction.) The route climbs easily along the road up the north slope of Hewes Hill, turns left off the road at 0.6 mi., and then descends slightly to Tippin Rock on the left at 0.7 mi. The trail swings right (northwest), descends gradually, and then rises gently to a spur path on the left at 1.0 mi. The path leads 25 yd. to Ledge Overlook, offering views south and southwest to nearby hills in Winchester. The main trail ascends more moderately to traverse the top of a large cliff that is sometimes used by rock climbers; a short side path on the left leads to the cliff's base. The blue blazes end atop the cliff, but the trail swings right and continues an easy ascent to the wooded summit of Hewes Hill at 1.1 mi.

HONEY HILL (865 FT.)

Honey Hill in Swanzey offers good views east from its partly open summit. The first portion of the route described below is on town-owned land managed by the Swanzey Conservation Commission. The remaining section is on private property, but hikers are welcomed by the landowner as long as they stay on the marked trail and obey all posted signs. From NH 101 in Keene, take NH 12 South for 0.8 mi. and then turn right onto NH 32 South. Continue 4.9 mi. to a small parking area on the right (sign).

BLUE TRAIL (SCC; USGS KEENE QUAD)

From trailhead (500 ft.) to:	↕↑	↗	↻
Honey Hill summit (865 ft.)	1.7 mi.	430 ft. (rev. 120 ft.)	1:00

From the parking area, cross the edge of the field on a grassy easement between two private residences and enter the woods (sign). A green-blazed connecting path meets Blue Trail at 0.1 mi. Bear left onto blue-blazed Blue Trail, which follows an old woods road. Footing is wet and muddy to start but improves quickly. The old road ascends moderately at first and then more easily as it makes its way to a junction at 0.6 mi., where the road continues ahead and deteriorates.

   Blue Trail, now a footpath (but still blazed blue), turns left off the old road to enter private property (sign). It descends briefly and then runs at easy grades through mixed forest and areas of regrowth. At 1.0 mi. the path swings left and descends to a low point between Honey Hill and an unnamed bump to the north. At 1.1 mi. Blue Trail reaches the lower junction with Yellow Trail on the right. (Yellow Trail, a 0.6-mi. yellow-blazed loop trail, offers a lightly used, wilder, and somewhat steeper alternative to Blue Trail, rejoining that trail 0.2 mi. below the summit.)

Blue Trail begins the first of a series of switchbacks at 1.3 mi. Avoid the beaten path that continues ahead and turn sharply left. At the second switchback, a high ledge wall looms on the left. At 1.5 mi. the trail passes the upper junction with Yellow Trail on the right and turns sharply left again at another switchback. It then twists and turns up the steep-sided summit cone through woods and over ledges to reach Honey Hill's summit and a clearing at 1.7 mi. A bench here offers a good resting spot and a view of Mt. Monadnock to the east, 9 mi. away.

MT. CAESAR (964 FT.)

Mt. Caesar, in Swanzey, was once used as a lookout by American Indians. Its partly open, ledgy summit features excellent views south and southwest to hills in Winchester, to Swanzey Lake, and to Pisgah State Park in Chesterfield. An FAA beacon for nearby Dillant-Hopkins Airport is also at the summit.

From NH 101 in Keene, take NH 12 South 0.8 mi. and then turn right onto NH 32 South. Continue 3.1 mi. to Swanzey Center. Turn right into Mt. Caesar Cemetery. Follow the cemetery road 0.1 mi. and then turn right (sign for parking) onto a side road. Parking is on the right.

MT. CAESAR PATHS (SCC; USGS KEENE QUAD)

From Mt. Caesar Cemetery (530 ft.) to:	↥↧	↗	↻
Mt. Caesar summit (964 ft.)	1.1 mi.	435 ft.	0:45

No formal trail to the summit exists, but a combination of paths and woods roads lead the way up. In early 2019, this route was not blazed and was potentially confusing to navigate at its start, where other paths and roads intersect. The land is managed by the Swanzey Conservation Commission. Refer to the USGS Keene quadrangle.

From the parking area, a short footpath leads to the cemetery. Follow the northern edge of the cemetery to a break in the stone wall 130 yd. from the parking area. Turn right to pass through the break in the wall and then immediately turn left onto a wide cart path. At 0.1 mi. bear right at a fork and ascend easily beside a logged area. Turn right onto a woods road (in the reverse direction, bear left at this junction instead of continuing straight) and at 0.3 mi. turn left at a large clearing (in the reverse direction, turn right out of the clearing).

Ascend along an eroded logging road, wet and muddy at times, to a fork at 0.6 mi. Bear left at the fork onto a woods road (sign for peak on right), which climbs steadily. At 0.8 mi. bear left where an unmarked path joins from the right (bear right at this fork when descending; marked by a small arrow) and continue a moderate ascent to reach the summit ledges at 1.1 mi. From the summit, a side path (sign: "To View") descends easily 75 yd. to the clifftop outlook. The vista here is similar to that of the summit but includes a view east to Mt. Monadnock.

BEAR'S DEN NATURAL AREA

This natural geologic area in Gilsum is a state forest of almost 100 acres and contains numerous natural features, including cliffs, potholes, and boulder caves. A marked hiking trail leads to the main caves. The trailhead and a parking area are located along NH 10 in Gilsum, 4.1 mi. north of NH 9. Refer to the USGS Gilsum quadrangle.

ORANGE TRAIL (NHDP; USGS GILSUM QUAD)

From NH 10 (1,110 ft.) to:	⇕	↗	⟳
Boulder caves at end of trail (1,180 ft.)	0.5 mi.	120 ft. (rev. 50 ft.)	0:20

From the parking area, enter the woods and bear left onto this orange-blazed trail, which ascends moderately with several minor descents to the saddle between the twin summits of Bingham Hill at 0.2 mi. The trail then bears left onto a woods road (in the reverse direction, bear right here at a double blaze), descending steeply at first then easily. At 0.4 mi. it dips to cross a seasonal drainage, clambers up the other side, and then continues an undulating route with numerous small ups and downs. At 0.5 mi. Orange Trail reaches a junction on the left with an informal, unmaintained path, but Orange Trail continues ahead several yards, descending to an area of boulder caves in a natural rocky amphitheater.

WAPACK TRAIL AND VICINITY

Wapack Trail follows the ridge of the Wapack Range, running mostly along the skyline more than 21 mi. from Mt. Watatic in Ashburnham, Massachusetts, to Pratt, New Ipswich, Barrett, and Temple mtns. and Pack Monadnock and North Pack Monadnock in New Hampshire. Many open ledges offer fine views, and the spruce forest in several places is similar to that of a more northern region. Refer to the USGS Ashburnham, Peterborough South, Peterborough North, and Greenfield quadrangles. Section V of Wapack Trail and the intersecting trails on Pack Monadnock and North Pack Monadnock are covered on the in-text map in this guide. Wapack Trail is blazed with yellow triangles and marked by cairns on open ledges. The organization Friends of the Wapack protects and

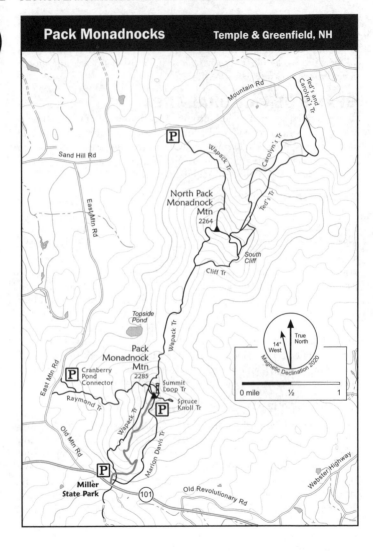

maintains the trail; this group publishes a detailed guidebook and map to Wapack Trail. Several side trails maintained by FOW provide access to summits on or near Wapack Trail; most of these are described separately in this guide. Camping is not allowed on Wapack Trail except at two year-round shelters in Windblown Ski Touring Center (by reservation only, 603-878-2869).

In 2007, the state of New Hampshire purchased the former Temple Mtn. Ski Area, creating the 352-acre Temple Mtn. State Reservation. It includes a section of Wapack Trail and the new Beebe Trail. A long-term goal for the Monadnock Conservancy and several partners is the creation of the 15-mi. Temple-to-Crotched Community Conservation Corridor, which would link conservation lands on Temple and Crotched mtns. with a network of conservation-easement-protected lands in Greenfield, Peterborough, and Sharon.

WAPACK TRAIL (FOW; FOW WAPACK TRAIL GUIDE MAP, AMC PACK MONADNOCK AND NORTH PACK MONADNOCK MAP, AND USGS ASHBURNHAM, PETERBOROUGH SOUTH, PETERBOROUGH NORTH, AND GREENFIELD QUADS)

Cumulative from MA 119 (1,250 ft.) to:	↓↥	⟋	○
Mt. Watatic summit (1,836 ft.)	1.2 mi.	600 ft.	0:55
Binney Hill Rd. near Binney Pond (1,360 ft.)	3.7 mi.	800 ft. (rev. 700 ft.)	2:15
Pratt Mtn. (1,826 ft.)	5.1 mi.	1,360 ft. (rev. 100 ft.)	3:15
Barrett Mtn. (1,847 ft.)	7.5 mi.	1,900 ft. (rev. 500 ft.)	4:40
NH 123/NH 124 (1,450 ft.)	9.5 mi.	2,050 ft. (rev. 550 ft.)	5:45
Beletette parking area (1,330 ft.)	12.2 mi.	2,300 ft. (rev. 350 ft.)	7:15
Temple Mtn., main summit (aka Holt Peak, 2,059 ft.)	14.6 mi.	3,220 ft. (rev. 200 ft.)	8:55
NH 101 (1,480 ft.)	16.5 mi.	3,350 ft. (rev. 700 ft.)	9:55
Pack Monadnock summit (2,285 ft.)	17.9 mi.	4,200 ft. (rev. 50 ft.)	11:05
Cliff Trail, southern jct. (1,880 ft.)	19.6 mi.	4,450 ft. (rev. 650 ft.)	12:00
North Pack Monadnock summit (2,264 ft.)	20.3 mi.	4,840 ft.	12:35
Parking area off Mountain Rd. (1,310 ft.)	21.9 mi.	4,850 ft. (rev. 950 ft.)	13:25

Section I. Mt. Watatic. The southern end of Wapack Trail begins in a small parking area off MA 119, 1.4 mi. west of its junction with MA 101, northeast of Ashburnham, Massachusetts, and 1.5 mi. east of the

Massachusetts–New Hampshire border. The route coincides with Mid-state Trail up to the New Hampshire state line. It passes a small pond and ascends to a junction at 0.3 mi., where it turns right. Here, blue-blazed State Line Trail continues straight for 1.0 mi. and rejoins Midstate Trail at the state line, making possible a loop hike over Mt. Watatic.

Wapack Trail crosses a small brook and climbs, steeply at times, past two viewpoints, before it swings left for the final approach to the summit. Just before the summit, at 1.2 mi., northbound Wapack Trail turns sharply left; watch carefully for signs and blazes, as there are several unofficial beaten paths in the summit area. A short distance ahead is the summit of Mt. Watatic (1,836 ft.) and the site of a former fire tower, where there is a sweeping view. Additional views are available from a bare subpeak just to the southeast, reached by a side path 130 yd. long. From the junction just below the main summit, northbound Wapack Trail descends a short distance to the left of a dirt road and then continues to descend northwest through woods that are a state bird sanctuary. It descends to a saddle and then makes a short climb to the Nutting Ledges on Nutting Hill, with views south, at 2.0 mi. The trail then descends to cellar holes that are obscured by bushes. These mark the Nutting Place, settled by James Spaulding just before the American Revolution and continued by his son-in-law, Jonas Nutting, until about 1840.

At the Nutting Place, an old cart path enters from the left and leads 0.1 mi. to State Line Trail, which can be followed 0.7 mi. back to the parking lot on MA 119. From the Nutting Place junction, Wapack Trail continues north on a long-abandoned road, and at 2.4 mi. it crosses a stone wall that runs from east to west on the Massachusetts–New Hampshire border. Here, Midstate Trail diverges left (west) and follows the stone wall about 80 yd. to State Line Trail; the junction of Midstate and State Line trails marks the northern terminus for both. Between these two junctions, close to the wall, are two stone survey monuments, one marking the boundary between Ashburnham and Ashby, Massachusetts, and the other erected in 1834 by Simeon Borden as part of the first statewide survey done in the United States.

The next section of Wapack Trail, from the Massachusetts–New Hampshire border to Binney Hill Rd., now known as Binney Hill Preserve, is currently owned and permanently protected as "forever wild" by a partnership between the Northeast Wilderness Trust and Friends of the Wapack. Due to this designation, motorized and wheeled vehicles are not allowed in the preserve. Two gates are now on Wapack Trail in this area: one at the southern end of the preserve (a short distance north of the state line) and one where Wapack Trail meets Binney Hill Rd.

Wapack Trail continues north from the state line past the old woods roads and cellar holes of long-deserted farms. At 0.7 mi. north of the Massachusetts–New Hampshire border, white-blazed Frank Robbins Trail, opened in 2018, turns sharply left off Wapack Trail and follows a grassy, brushy logging road at easy grades. It heads southeast at first and then loops back to rejoin Wapack Trail at 1.1 mi. (This trail provides an alternate route around the logged area described next.)

From the southern junction with Frank Robbins Trail, Wapack Trail follows logging roads through an extensively cleared area where the yellow triangle markings must be followed with care. It reaches Binney Hill Rd. at 3.5 mi. This part of Binney Hill Rd. is not maintained, and it is no longer possible to drive in from NH 119 due to beaver dam flooding and a lack of parking near private residences. The trail turns left (west) on this road and follows it 0.2 mi. to the point where the Pratt Mtn. to Barrett Mtn. section of Wapack Trail turns to the right off the road.

Section II. Pratt Mtn. to Barrett Mtn. This section of Wapack Trail runs from Binney Hill Rd. to the entrance of Windblown Ski Touring Center on NH 123/NH 124. It traverses a ridge nearly 3 mi. long, with four summits and numerous outlooks. Shortly after leaving Binney Hill Rd. at 3.7 mi., the trail crosses a small brook then skirts Binney Pond near its western shore; this is part of the state-owned Binney Pond Natural Area. (Flooding from beaver dams may require a detour here.)

At the north end of the pond, the trail crosses a brook and then ascends steadily up the south slope of Pratt Mtn., passing a side path (sign) on the right at 4.9 mi. that descends 35 yd. to an open ledge with a beautiful view of Binney Pond and Mt. Watatic. Wapack Trail continues up through grassy oak forest to the ledgy summit of Pratt Mtn. (1,826 ft.) at 5.1 mi., where there are outlooks east and west.

The trail descends the ledgy ridge (follow the yellow triangle blazes and cairns carefully), passing a view of Pratt Pond on the right at 5.4 mi., and then ascends slightly to the partly open summit of Stony Top (1,765 ft.) at 5.6 mi. On the summit ledge, there is a view west, and up to the left of the trail, plaques mark the 1,400-acre Wapack Wilderness, conserved by Northeast Wilderness Trust and Hampshire Country School. In another 125 yd. the trail swings right on a ledge with a fine view of Mt. Monadnock. Then it bears left past a side path leading 30 yd. left to a ledgy area with wide views west and south.

Wapack Trail now drops over ledges to a col, where it passes private Pratt Pond Trail on the right and then ascends over ledges with a view back to Stony Top and Pratt Mtn. It continues up through woods, turns right through a stone wall, and then turns left, reaching the partly open but viewless summit of New Ipswich Mtn. (1,881 ft.) at 6.1 mi. It descends easily across viewless ledges and through woods and at 6.5 mi. passes a ledge 25 yd. to the left with a view west—the last open viewpoint in this section.

The trail descends with a glimpse ahead to Temple Mtn. and Pack Monadnock, bears left at a fork where an ATV trail diverges right, and at 6.9 mi. reaches the deep saddle between New Ipswich and Barrett mtns. Here, the trail crosses Boston Rd. Built in 1753, it is one of the oldest roads from Massachusetts to the hill towns. The trail climbs over a knob and then ascends to the wooded summit of Barrett Mtn. (1,847 ft.) at 7.5 mi. It runs at easy grades through a beautiful spruce forest and at 7.8 mi. enters Windblown Ski Touring Center. Visitors must purchase a trail pass during winter when the ski area is open; it is closed during spring mud season.

Here, Wapack Trail bears left at a fork (the right fork leads to a shelter and cross-country ski trails) and descends steadily, passing through semi-open woods carpeted with ferns. It bears left at a junction with a trail to another shelter, and at 8.2 mi. it turns left onto Back Forty ski trail. The grade soon eases as Wapack Trail continues on the ski trail, passing several other ski trails that diverge to the right. Hiking is permitted only on the ski and snowshoe trails followed by Wapack Trail; the route is clearly marked with signs and yellow triangles. At 8.5 mi. Wapack Trail angles to the right across a power-line clearing and bears left at another junction.

Now following Stagecoach Rd. ski trail, the route crosses a low point over a brook and ascends gradually. It travels under the power line again at 9.2 mi., soon merges left onto a gravel road, passes to the left of the Windblown lodge, and descends on the gravel driveway to the Windblown entrance on NH 123/NH 124 at 9.5 mi. Wapack Trail turns right and follows the south shoulder of NH 123/NH 124 0.1 mi. to Wapack Rd. on the right. Trailhead parking is available in a new parking area (sign: "Wapack Parking") across the highway from the entrance to Windblown (the former roadside parking area has now been posted no parking and hikers are not permitted to park on Windblown property). From this new parking area, a new connector trail, Wapack Link, ascends easily for 0.3 mi. to meet Wapack Trail. At Wapack Rd. the trail crosses NH 123/NH 124; use caution on this busy road.

Section III. Kidder Mtn. Wapack Trail next crosses the lower western slopes of Kidder Mtn. (1,816 ft.). From the north side of NH 123/NH 124, the trail follows Old Rindge Rd. for several yards, quickly bears left into the woods, passes close to a private residence, and then crosses an open field, site of a former downhill ski area. At 10.1 mi. Wapack Trail turns left on an old grassy road bordered by stone walls and crosses under a power line 150 yd. beyond. Here, blue-blazed Kidder Mtn. Trail (described below) diverges right, leading 0.9 mi. to the open summit of Kidder Mtn. Meanwhile, Wapack Trail descends to a junction with a gravel road from the left at a pond on the right. Here, the trail turns right onto a woods road, crosses the pond outlet, and ascends gradually to the Wildcat Hill–Conant Hill saddle, where there is an old homestead site to the right. The route descends gradually, still on the old woods road, and crosses the outlet of a beaver pond on the right. It then bears left where Todd Rd. diverges right at 11.4 mi. and continues to Nashua Rd. (the road from Temple to Jaffrey) at 11.8 mi.

Section IV. Temple Mtn. Wapack Trail crosses Nashua Rd. and continues straight ahead along Temple Rd. 0.4 mi., bears right at a fork where Greenleaf Rd. diverges left, and then turns right in 30 yd. to begin climbing the south ridge of Temple Mtn. Trailhead parking is available 0.3 mi. from NH 123 via Greenleaf Rd. at the Belletette parking area, across the street from where the trail leaves Temple Rd. From this point north, Wapack Trail passes through private conservation land managed by the New England Forestry Foundation. Please observe the posted rules about no fires and no smoking.

The trail ascends moderately up the south end of Temple Mtn., which boasts several summits. This part of the trail has been named the Cabot Skyline in honor of longtime conservationist (and past AMC president) Tom Cabot. At 12.6 mi. a side path (sign) descends 40 yd. to Roger Myrick Outlook on the Sharon Ledges, with a view southeast and south. The grade eases on the main trail, and at 12.7 mi. another side path leads 40 yd. right to a southeast outlook. At 13.5 mi. blue-blazed Berry Pasture Trail (FOW) leaves left and descends 0.9 mi. and 750 ft. through blueberry pastures and down an old woods road. It ends at Mountain Rd., 0.6 mi. northeast of the Sharon Arts Center on NH 123. (About halfway down this trail, views west were opened with a large clear-cut during a timber harvest.) Wapack Trail, however, ascends steadily to Burton Peak (2,014 ft.) at 13.6 mi., where a short, blue-blazed loop trail on the left leads past good views west (also opened by the timber harvest). From here north, stone monuments mark the Sharon–Temple town line, which also follows this ridge.

Wapack Trail continues north along the ridge, crossing a knob with views east and west at 14.0 mi. It descends to a saddle and then ascends steeply to wooded and viewless Holt Peak (2,059 ft.), the highest point on Temple Mtn., at 14.6 mi. (A side path on the left leads to the true summit.) The trail descends to a col and then ascends easily to the Temple Mtn. Ledges at 15.1 mi., where there are cairns and views to the left. The trail once again descends and then ascends easily, passing just to the west of Temple Mtn.'s north summit. Wapack Trail then swings left past a communications tower on the right. At 15.7 mi., 50 yd. beyond the tower, white-blazed Beebe Trail joins from the right, making a loop hike possible from NH 101.

Wapack Trail descends along the tower-access dirt road through the former Temple Mtn. Ski Area (now part of Temple Mtn. State Reservation), with views of Pack Monadnock from ski trail openings. At 16.3 mi. a connecting path diverges right and descends 130 yd. to Beebe Trail.

At the base of the descent through the former ski area, just before a steel gate and a right turn, Wapack Trail turns left off the access road. (The access road continues ahead 0.1 mi. to the lower terminus of Beebe Trail on the right and then another 80 yd. to a large parking area off NH 101 at the base of the old ski area, 0.1 mi. east of the entrance to Miller State Park. This is the best trailhead parking for Temple Mtn.) Wapack Trail passes through a brushy area and two gravel areas and reaches NH 101 in Peterborough Gap at 16.5 mi., a few yards east of the road up Pack Monadnock. (*Caution*: Take extreme care when crossing NH 101, as sight distances are limited and automobile speeds are high.)

Section V. Pack Monadnock and North Pack Monadnock. This extended ridge culminates in two open peaks: Pack Monadnock (2,285 ft.) and North Pack Monadnock (2,264 ft.). (*Pack* is an American Indian word meaning "little.") The mountains stand between the towns of Peterborough and Temple and are well-known landmarks in southern New Hampshire and eastern Massachusetts. The summit and most of the southern slopes of Pack Monadnock are in a small state reservation, General James Miller Park. The entrance to the park (sign) is just off NH 101, 0.1 mi. west of the Temple Mtn. parking area. An admission fee is required. The road is gated when the park is closed; see nhstateparks.org for current fees and operating hours.

Wapack Trail crosses NH 101 just east of the state park sign, enters the woods, and reaches a trail junction 25 yd. east of the state park parking area (sign at the east end of the parking area: "foot trails"). The blue-blazed trail on the right is the former route of Wapack Trail and is now Marion Davis Trail (described below). Wapack Trail is more scenic but also somewhat more difficult than Marion Davis Trail, particularly for descent.

Wapack Trail continues north (left) from the trail junction near the parking area; crosses the automobile road in 0.1 mi.; and immediately scrambles up a steep, rocky pitch. Turning northwest, it skirts the crest of ledges with views southwest and passes two crevice caves. The trail turns briefly east, leading through woods and over ledges before crossing a hollow at 17.2 mi. It then runs north, angling upward parallel to the automobile road through a beautiful spruce forest. At 17.8 mi Wapack Trail reaches a junction with red-blazed Summit Loop Trail (also known as Red Dot Trail or Red Circle Trail; described below), which leads to the right and continues straight ahead. Wapack Trail turns sharply right here and ascends, coinciding with Summit Loop Trail, to a parking area and fire tower on the summit of Pack Monadnock at 17.9 mi. (*Note*: Because several trails leave from the summit area, look carefully for the yellow triangles when descending to make sure you are on your intended route.)

Wapack Trail continues north from the north end of the summit road, to the left of a stone lean-to (sign: "Wapack"), following a gravel path at first and then descending gradually over ledges. About 0.1 mi. from the summit, at an open ledge and picnic area with a fine view north and west, Raymond Trail (described below) diverges on the left. (The sign for this trail is a short distance downhill to the left, where Raymond Trail crosses Summit Loop Trail.) Wapack Trail bears right, soon crosses Summit Loop Trail, and descends over ledges. At 18.1 mi., at a left turn, a side path (sign: "Joanne Bass Bross Memorial Scenic Outlook") leads 35 yd. right to a viewpoint east and northeast. Wapack Trail moderately descends the wooded north slope past a spring and crosses a col at 18.6 mi. In 0.1 mi. it passes briefly through The Nature Conservancy's Joanne Bass Bross Preserve (sign), and in 100 yd. it enters the 1,672-acre Wapack National Wildlife Refuge (sign). Wapack Trail crosses another col and ascends through fine spruce woods over a knoll (sometimes called Middle Peak) at 19.2 mi. At 19.6 mi. it reaches the junction with Cliff Trail on the right. (Cliff Trail, described below, is a longer and rougher but more scenic alternate route from here to the summit of North Pack Monadnock.)

From its southern junction with Cliff Trail, Wapack Trail continues north along the ridge then swings right and ascends fairly steeply to the summit of North Pack Monadnock, marked by a large cairn, at 20.3 mi.; Cliff Trail rejoins from the right. (In the reverse direction, look carefully for yellow blazes where Wapack Trail descends southwest off the summit, to the left of a southwest outlook.) Ledges around the summit area provide partial views in several directions; the best views are at 0.2 mi. and 0.5 mi. down Cliff Trail.

From the summit, Wapack Trail descends generally north at a moderate grade through spruce forest, with occasional steeper pitches. (Ledges in this section may be slippery when wet and are often icy in late fall and spring.) The trail continues down through an area of overgrown pastures with occasional views north, passing the last view at 21.0 mi. (In this area, take care to follow blazes in order to distinguish the trail from other paths.) In another 0.1 mi. Wapack Trail descends a steep, rocky pitch and swings left at an easier grade. It traverses a flat area and crosses a brook at 21.6 mi. At 21.8 mi. a spur path leads 0.1 mi. left to a trailhead parking area on Mountain Rd., while the original route continues ahead, descending to Mountain Rd. in 100 yd.

To reach the trailhead parking area by car, from NH 31 at the blinking light in Greenfield go south 2.8 mi. and turn right (west) onto Russell Station Rd. In 0.8 mi. turn right onto Mountain Rd. At 2.7 mi. from NH 31, just beyond the older trailhead, the parking area is on the left.

KIDDER MTN. TRAIL (FOW; FOW WAPACK TRAIL GUIDE MAP)
From Wapack Trail
(1,530 ft.) to:

	⇅	◢	○
Kidder Mtn. summit (1,816 ft.)	0.9 mi.	310 ft.	0:35

This blue-blazed trail diverges east from Wapack Trail 0.6 mi. north of NH 123/NH 124. It follows a road along the right side of a power-line clearing, crosses a small brook at 0.1 mi., and then turns left under the power line and enters the woods. It ascends moderately to the northeast, passes through two logged areas well up on the mountain, and swings right and then left, reaching the open summit of Kidder Mtn., with good views east and south, at 0.9 mi. from Wapack Trail.

BEEBE TRAIL (FOW)
From Temple Mtn. parking area off NH 101
(1,470 ft.) to:

	⇅	◢	○
Wapack Trail near Temple Mtn. north summit (1,880 ft.)	0.8 mi.	400 ft.	0:35

This white-blazed trail, opened by Friends of the Wapack in 2014, ascends to the north end of Temple Mtn. and makes a loop hike possible when combined with that section of Wapack Trail. It was named for Charlie and

Lucie Beebe, who founded the former Temple Mtn. Ski Area on this property in 1937 and maintained Wapack Trail along the Temple Mtn. ridge for many years. In 2019, the trail was improved with new bog bridges and water bars in wet areas. From the south end of the large parking area on the south side of NH 101 at the base of the old ski area, 0.1 mi. east of the entrance to Miller State Park, follow a dirt access road 80 yd. and turn left at a sign for Beebe Trail. (Ahead, the access road joins Wapack Trail in 0.1 mi.) In 70 yd. a connecting path (sign) diverges right, ascending 130 yd. to Wapack Trail. Beebe Trail continues ahead across an open area then bears left and makes a winding ascent, crossing or following a number of old alpine and nordic ski trails; look for several turns marked by signs. Near the top there is a good view north toward Pack Monadnock. Beebe Trail joins Wapack Trail near the north summit of Temple Mtn., 50 yd. west of a communications tower.

SUMMIT LOOP TRAIL (NHDP; AMC PACK MONADNOCK AND NORTH PACK MONADNOCK MAP, FOW WAPACK TRAIL GUIDE MAP)

From Pack Monadnock summit (2,285 ft.) to:	⬇⬆	↗	⟳
Starting point via complete loop	0.4 mi.	100 ft.	0:15

This short trail (also known as Red Dot Trail or Red Circle Trail), marked with red spots, makes an interesting circuit around the summit of Pack Monadnock. From the summit's high point on the west side of the fire tower, the trail crosses the automobile road and descends into the woods to the left of a shed. (Marion Davis Trail leaves the summit to the right of this shed.) Summit Loop Trail descends 35 yd. to a sign ("Boston View"), an eastern viewpoint a short distance to the right. Here, the trail bears left, descends, and circles around the north side of the summit. It ascends and crosses northbound Wapack Trail and then Raymond Trail, continuing 50 yd. across ledges to meet Wapack Trail coming up from the south. Summit Loop Trail coincides with Wapack Trail back to the top of the summit road, completing its loop.

SPRUCE KNOLL TRAIL (FOW; AMC PACK MONADNOCK AND NORTH PACK MONADNOCK MAP, FOW WAPACK TRAIL GUIDE MAP)

From Boston View (2,285 ft.) to:	⬇⬆	↗	⟳
Spruce Knoll viewpoint (2,185 ft.)	0.3 mi.	0 ft. (rev. 100 ft.)	0:10

This short spur path marked by The Nature Conservancy descends east from the Boston View area near the summit. In 0.1 mi. it reaches a junction where branches of the path fork left and right. The two branches rejoin in 125 yd., and the path continues to a fine eastern outlook at 0.3 mi. from the Boston View area. This viewpoint is part of TNC's Joanne Bass Bross Preserve on the east side of the mountain.

MARION DAVIS TRAIL (FOW; AMC PACK MONADNOCK AND NORTH PACK MONADNOCK MAP, FOW WAPACK TRAIL GUIDE MAP)

From trailhead parking at Miller State Park
(1,480 ft.) to:

	⇅	↗	↻
Pack Monadnock summit (2,285 ft.)	1.3 mi.	900 ft. (rev. 100 ft.)	1:05

Use this blue-blazed trail to make an attractive loop hike over Pack Monadnock from the Miller State Park trailhead in combination with Wapack Trail. From the signed trail junction east of the parking area, Marion Davis Trail angles up the east side of the mountain through hardwood forest, with occasional short descents, crossing several small brooks. It passes under an impressive cliff and then swings left at 0.8 mi. and climbs moderately, with occasional steeper pitches, passing through part of TNC's Joanne Bass Bross Preserve. It reenters the state park and in another 0.1 mi. reaches the automobile road at the summit across from the fire tower. Descending, the trail (sign) begins on the east side of the road, to the right of a shed.

RAYMOND TRAIL (FOW; AMC PACK MONADNOCK AND NORTH PACK MONADNOCK MAP, WAPACK TRAIL GUIDE MAP)

From East Mtn. Rd.
(1,330 ft.) to:

	⇅	↗	↻
Pack Monadnock summit (2,285 ft.)	1.6 mi.	1,050 ft. (rev. 100 ft.)	1:20

This attractive, white-blazed trail ascends the west slope of Pack Monadnock from East Mtn. Rd.; on its upper section are several steep, rocky pitches. To reach this trailhead, follow NH 101 0.4 mi. west from the entrance to Miller State Park. Turn right onto Old Mtn. Rd., and at 1.0 mi. turn right again onto East Mtn. Rd. The trailhead, with parking space for several cars, is on the right at 1.2 mi. from the park entrance. A new, larger parking area, signed for Cranberry Meadow Pond Trail, is 0.2 mi. farther along the road, also on the right. A 0.2-mi. connecting path leads from here to Raymond Trail.

From its trailhead, Raymond Trail climbs over a small ridge and then ascends to a junction with the spur from Cranberry Meadow Pond Trail on the left at 0.3 mi. It continues straight and descends briefly to cross a brook at 0.6 mi. and then dips to a side path on the right at 0.8 mi. that descends 15 yd. to a view of a cascade. Raymond Trail ascends along the brook; turns left away from it; crosses a plateau; and climbs a steep, rocky pitch to a restricted outlook west at 1.3 mi. Then it continues up through woods, steeply at times, and emerges on ledges. Raymond Trail crosses Summit Loop Trail at 1.5 mi. and in a few steps ends at Wapack Trail, 0.1 mi. below the summit of Pack Monadnock.

CLIFF TRAIL (FOW; AMC PACK MONADNOCK AND NORTH PACK MONADNOCK MAP, FOW WAPACK TRAIL GUIDE MAP)

From southern jct. with Wapack Trail (1,880 ft.) to:	⇅	↗	↺
North Pack Monadnock summit (2,264 ft.)	1.1 mi.	590 ft. (rev. 200 ft.)	0:50

This blue-blazed trail, steep and rough in places, offers some of the finest views in the Monadnock region. Use it and Wapack Trail to loop over the south side of North Pack Monadnock.

Cliff Trail diverges east from Wapack Trail 0.6 mi. south of the summit of North Pack Monadnock in a small, ledgy opening (the trail name is painted on a rock). It descends 0.2 mi., crosses a small brook, climbs briefly, and descends again to cross another brook. Then it swings left and ascends steeply to a ledgy area with restricted views. It reenters the woods, winds through some ledges, and then turns left at a ledge to climb steeply past a talus slope, swinging left higher up to the top of the South Cliff (the best viewpoint) at 0.7 mi. Here, Cliff Trail bears left at the junction with Ted's Trail on the right (sign). In another 15 yd. Cliff Trail swings right; an unmarked path leads 30 yd. left to the widest views atop the South Cliff. The grade eases as Cliff Trail ascends north and then northwest along an undulating ridge with several ledgy knobs. At 1.0 mi., at the top of a steep pitch, Cliff Trail passes a signed junction with yellow-blazed Carolyn's Trail on the right. Open ledges 20 yd. down Carolyn's Trail provide excellent views north and east. Cliff Trail itself continues to climb easily and rejoins yellow-triangle-blazed Wapack Trail at the summit of North Pack Monadnock, at 1.1 mi.

In the reverse direction, at the summit of North Pack Monadnock, Cliff Trail diverges left (southeast) from Wapack Trail at a signed junction and a rock with "Cliff Trail" painted in blue.

TED'S TRAIL (MVHC; AMC PACK MONADNOCK AND NORTH PACK MONADNOCK MAP, USGS GREENFIELD QUAD)

Cumulative from Mountain Rd.
(950 ft.) to:

	⮃	↗	◯
Cliff Trail (2,200 ft.)	2.6 mi.	1,250 ft.	1:55
North Pack Monadnock summit (2,264 ft.) via Cliff Trail	3.1 mi.	1,340 ft.	2:15

This trail provides a relatively long but scenic route to North Pack Monadnock from the north. From NH 31 at the blinking light in Greenfield, go south 2.8 mi. and turn right (west) onto Russell Station Rd. In 0.8 mi. turn right onto Mountain Rd. At 0.6 mi. from Russell Station Rd. the trail (sign for Ted's Trail/Carolyn's Trail, yellow blazes) begins on the left, with parking for a few cars on the right.

Ted's Trail runs concurrently with Carolyn's Trail level through a wet area, crosses a bridge over a brook at 0.2 mi., and ascends easily to a junction (small sign) at 0.5 mi., where Carolyn's Trail diverges right. Ted's Trail bears left, crosses a skid road and a bridge over a brook, and meanders through a beautiful stand of red pine. It swings right and crosses two small brooks then crosses a bridge over a larger brook at the foot of a waterfall at 1.0 mi. It turns sharply left and climbs to the top of the waterfall, where a signed connector trail diverges right, leading 0.2 mi. to Carolyn's Trail. Ted's Trail climbs alongside the brook, passing several more waterfalls and skirting a logged area. At 1.5 mi. it enters Wapack National Wildlife Refuge, and at 1.8 mi. it swings to the right, up the slope and away from the brook. In 200 yd. the route passes through a stone wall and turns sharply left then ascends through spruces and ledgy areas, passing a view back to the north at 2.2 mi. In another 120 yd. the trail turns left where a connecting path ascends 0.1 mi. right to Carolyn's Trail.

At 2.4 mi. Ted's Trail turns sharply right on a ledge with a view east and climbs over ledges with occasional views southeast toward the Boston skyline. It turns right again and traverses an open area to end at a junction with Cliff Trail at 2.6 mi. at the top of the South Cliff, which offers a 180-degree panorama—the best view on the mountain. From the junction, continue on Cliff Trail 15 yd. and then follow an unmarked side path straight ahead to the widest viewpoint atop the cliffs, just past where Cliff Trail turns right. From this turn, Cliff Trail ascends easily over ledges and reaches the summit of North Pack Monadnock in 0.5 mi. Ledges around the summit area provide partial views in several directions.

Descending, there is a sign for Ted's Trail where it diverges left from Cliff Trail, which turns right and descends alongside the cliffs.

CAROLYN'S TRAIL (MVHC; AMC PACK MONADNOCK AND NORTH PACK MONADNOCK MAP, USGS GREENFIELD QUAD)

Cumulative from Mountain Rd. (950 ft.) to:	↧↥	↗	↺
Cliff Trail (2,210 ft.)	2.3 mi.	1,260 ft.	1:45
Complete loop of North Pack Monadnock (2,264 ft.) via Ted's Trail, Cliff Trail, and Carolyn's Trail, including side trip to the South Cliff	5.7 mi.	1,340 ft.	3:30

This yellow-blazed trail links Ted's Trail and Cliff Trail, providing a more direct route to North Pack Monadnock. The first 0.5 mi. runs concurrently with Ted's Trail to a junction where Carolyn's Trail diverges right. At 0.6 mi. Carolyn's Trail bears left where an alternate route (sign: "Dry Season Trail") bears right to run alongside a swamp, quickly rejoining the main route, and at 0.7 mi. it turns right where a connecting path diverges left, leading 0.2 mi. over a low ridge to Ted's Trail. Carolyn's Trail ascends at easy grades, passing through a stone wall at 0.9 mi. At 1.5 mi. the grade increases, and at 1.8 mi. the trail enters a beautiful spruce forest. At 2.1 mi. a connecting path diverges left, descending 0.1 mi. to Ted's Trail. Carolyn's Trail continues ahead and climbs up open ledges to a junction with Cliff Trail at 2.3 mi., 0.3 mi. below the summit of North Pack Monadnock.

BURNS HILL (741 FT.)

This small hill in Milford offers good views west to the Wapack Range from near Burns's summit and tasty blueberries in season. A white-blazed trail maintained by the Milford Conservation Commission makes a loop over the summit; part of the route lies within Hitchiner Town Forest. Grades are easy to moderate, and footing is good. A trail map is available at milfordnh.info.

To reach the trailhead from NH 101, take NH 13 south and immediately turn right onto Armory Rd. and drive 1.0 mi. Take the second left onto Osgood Rd. and drive 1.1 mi. Then turn right onto Mullen Rd. (gravel road; hiker symbol) and continue 0.2 mi. to a parking area at the end of the road.

WHITE TRAIL (MCC; MCC MAP)
From Mullen Rd.
(490 ft.) to:

	⇅	↗	↻
Burns Hill summit (741 ft.)	1.4 mi.	260 ft. (rev. 260 ft.)	0:50

The loop is described here in the steeper, counterclockwise direction. The white-blazed trail heads west from the parking area and bears left where a blue-blazed connecting trail continues straight. White Trail ascends easily to a junction at 0.3 mi. where the other end of the blue-blazed trail leaves on the left. White Trail bears left and then right almost immediately (sign: "East Summit Trail") and angles up a steep slope. It swings right, passing a different blue-blazed trail on the left, and then ascends easily to the summit at 0.6 mi. Beaten paths lead 25 yd. ahead to an open clearing with good views toward the Wapack Range.

From the summit, White Trail swings left and descends easily over rocky terrain to a junction at 0.9 mi., where a yellow-blazed trail leaves to the right. White Trail turns left onto an old woods road and runs mostly level, bearing right at a fork at 1.1 mi. and then descending easily back to the trailhead at 1.4 mi.

CROTCHED MTN. (2,062 FT.)

Crotched Mtn. is in Francestown and Bennington, with a south spur in Greenfield. Refer to the USGS Greenfield and Peterborough North quadrangles. Excellent views extend from various ledges along the ridge crest, although there are none at the summit itself, where there are communications towers and related buildings. The ski trails of the Crotched Mtn. Ski Area are on the north slopes of the mountain. This extensive trail system has a major trailhead in the 900-acre Crotched Mtn. Town Forest (CMTF) in Francestown, which includes the southeastern slopes of the mountain. In addition to the in-text maps for Crotched Mtn. and Francestown in this guide, trail maps are available on the town of Francestown website (francestownnh.org).

The southwestern slopes of the mountain are the property of the Crotched Mountain Foundation, which manages the Crotched Mountain Rehabilitation Center, at the southern base in Greenfield. In 2011 CMF opened two universally accessible hiking trails on the lower slopes: Gregg Trail and Dutton Brook Trail. These are the longest accessible trails in a mountainside environment in the United States. Gregg Trail ascends 0.8 mi. and 200 ft. to a knoll with fine views from an observation platform. Dutton Brook Trail is a 2-mi. loop around a beaver wetland. Information

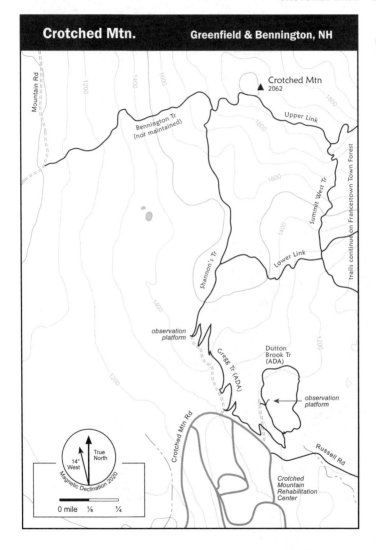

Crotched Mtn.   Greenfield & Bennington, NH

Mountain Rd

Bennington Tr
(not maintained)

Crotched Mtn
2062

Upper Link

Summit West Tr

trails continue on Francestown Town Forest

1800

1600

1400

1200

Shannon's Tr

Lower Link

observation
platform

Gregg Tr (ADA)

Dutton
Brook Tr
(ADA)

observation
platform

Crotched Mtn Rd

Russell Rd

Crotched
Mountain
Rehabilitation
Center

True
North
14°
West
Magnetic Declination 2020

0 mile   ⅛   ¼

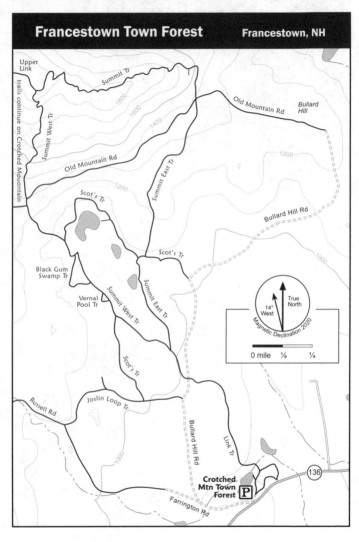

and maps are available at cmf.org. (*Note*: These trails may be closed at times when weather conditions make them too soft.)

SHANNON'S TRAIL (CMF; AMC CROTCHED MTN. MAP, FCC TRAIL MAP, USGS GREENFIELD AND PETERBOROUGH NORTH QUADS)

Cumulative from parking area off Crotched Mtn. Rd. (1,300 ft.) to:	↰↱	↗	○
Grassy knoll (1,510 ft.)	0.4 mi.	200 ft.	0:20
Upper Link at open ledge near summit (2,040 ft.)	1.7 mi.	800 ft. (rev. 50 ft.)	1:15

The lower part of this trail from the southern trailhead near the Crotched Mtn. Rehabilitation Center has been relocated, as part of its route has been superseded by universally accessible Gregg Trail. From NH 31 0.9 mi. north of Greenfield, turn north onto Crotched Mtn. Rd. Pass Gilbert Verney Dr. on the right 1.4 mi. from NH 31, and in another 0.1 mi. turn left onto a gravel road (sign) and quickly left again into the trailhead parking area. Gregg and Dutton Brook trails diverge right (east) from the entrance road to the parking area, while yellow-blazed Shannon's Trail (no sign) follows the gravel road ahead past a gate. The entirety of Shannon's Trail is on CMF property.

Shannon's Trail ascends easily up the gravel road to an open grassy knoll at 0.4 mi., where a viewing platform on the left provides restricted views. (Here, Gregg Trail comes in from the right and ends.) The next section of Shannon's Trail is poorly marked and overgrown; follow it with care. It continues straight on the remnants of an old service road and then keeps straight ahead on a footpath as the old road bends to the left at 0.5 mi. The path passes through a short section of woods, crosses a stone wall, and then crosses a large blueberry pasture reclamation area. It enters the woods at the upper right (northeast) corner of the pasture area, and just beyond, at 0.7 mi., Lower Link diverges right. Shannon's Trail descends slightly, follows the contour of the slope, and crosses a brook at 1.1 mi. It ascends moderately, and at 1.3 mi. it turns right where a remnant of the former Greenfield Trail may be seen to the left. From this junction Shannon's Trail climbs steeply over ledges and is joined by Bennington Trail on the left at 1.4 mi. It ascends across two ledges with good views south and scrambles up the left side of a large open ledge just below the summit, with excellent views south and west. The trail ends behind the top of the ledge, where it meets Upper Link coming in from the right. From here a rough path climbs 125 yd. to the viewless summit. As of 2019, the USGS benchmark was missing.

BENNINGTON TRAIL (AMC CROTCHED MTN. MAP, FCC TRAIL MAP, USGS GREENFIELD AND PETERBOROUGH NORTH QUADS)

Cumulative from trailhead on dirt road (1,000 ft.) to:	↕	↗	○
Shannon's Trail (1,750 ft.)	1.2 mi.	750 ft.	1:00
Open ledge near Crotched Mtn. summit and jct. with Upper Link (2,040 ft.) via Shannon's Trail	1.5 mi.	1,050 ft.	1:15

This orange-blazed trail, not officially maintained, ascends Crotched Mtn. from the west. Much of the route is on private land; higher up it enters Crotched Mtn. Town Forest. The uppermost section of the trail has been abandoned. From NH 31, 1.6 mi. south of the flashing light in Bennington, turn east onto Mountain Rd. (sign: "Bennington Trail"). At 0.4 mi. from NH 31, bear to the far right onto a dirt road at a three-way fork. The trail (sign) begins on the right 0.2 mi. up this somewhat rough road. Parking is limited at the trailhead; there is also parking beside the road on the left, just beyond the last house.

The trail turns sharply right off the dirt road and follows an old woods road to a sign, where Bennington Trail turns left. Follow with care. It crosses several brooks, passes a spring, and then begins to climb more steeply to a junction with a remnant of the old Greenfield Trail on the right and the abandoned upper section of Bennington Trail on the left at 1.2 mi. Bennington Trail ends 80 yd. ahead at Shannon's Trail. Turn left to reach the large open ledge and the junction with Upper Link at the upper terminus of Shannon's Trail in 0.3 mi.

SUMMIT TRAIL (FCC; AMC FRANCESTOWN TOWN FOREST MAP, AMC CROTCHED MTN. MAP, FCC TRAIL MAP, USGS GREENFIELD QUAD)

Cumulative from Crotched Mtn. Town Forest parking area (915 ft.) to:	↕	↗	○
Beginning of Summit Trail (960 ft.) via Link Trail	0.7 mi.	50 ft.	0:25
Jct. with Upper Link (1,970 ft.) via east loop of Summit Trail	3.3 mi.	1,200 ft. (rev. 150 ft.)	2:15
Loop back to parking area via west loop of Summit Trail and Link Trail	5.8 mi.	1,200 ft.	3:30

This trail makes a loop over the eastern half of Crotched Mtn.'s ridge crest (although it does not go to the true summit), offering views from a number of ledges. From NH 136, 1.9 mi. north of Greenfield and 2.5 mi. south of

Francestown, turn west onto Farrington Rd. and immediately bear right into the parking area for Crotched Mtn. Town Forest, where there is a kiosk with a trail map.

Follow yellow-blazed Link Trail to the left of the kiosk. This connecting path bears left at 0.1 mi., crosses a footbridge over a flooded area, and runs at easy grades through logged areas to Bullard Hill Rd. (a gravel road on which vehicle access is restricted) at 0.7 mi. Summit Trail (sign) starts across the road. (*Note*: Various segments of Summit Trail were previously known as Miki's Trail, Cindy's Trail, and Randy's Trail; these names may still appear on some old maps.) Mileages given below include the approach on Link Trail.

From Bullard Hill Rd., yellow-blazed Summit Trail (sign) soon bears right and comes to a fork at 0.8 mi. The loop is described in the counter-clockwise direction, taking the right fork (Summit East Trail) for the ascent. The trail crosses a brook at 1.2 mi. and skirts the edge of a beaver pond with a viewing blind on the left. It then runs along the left edge of a field 75 yd. and reenters the woods, with white-blazed Scot's Trail joining from the left. In a short distance, Summit East Trail turns left, as Scot's Trail diverges right. Summit East Trail runs along the edge of a beaver swamp, climbs through a grove of large pines and hemlocks, and at 2.1 mi. crosses a woods road (sign: "Old Mt. Road").

Now Summit Trail climbs steeply along the base of a talus slope and at 2.3 mi. swings left to ascend the ridge. After a short, steep climb, a side path leads 50 yd. left to a ledge with a view east. The main trail ascends past another outlook and reaches open ledges with views south at 2.6 mi. It meanders along the crest with minor ups and downs, soon crossing a ledge with a view north. At 2.9 mi. it emerges on a rocky knob with more views and then descends to a col and makes a winding climb to the next knob. It descends past a southeast viewpoint to a junction at 3.3 mi. Here, blue-blazed Upper Link bears right and leads 0.5 mi. to the large open ledge and the upper end of Shannon's Trail near the true summit, while yellow-blazed Summit West Trail continues left and makes a steep, rough descent 0.2 mi., passing a cut view toward Mt. Monadnock.

Follow Summit West Trail (yellow blazes) down at a moderate grade, passing a junction on the left with Old Mt. Rd. and then on the right with Lower Link at 4.0 mi. At 4.2 mi. white-blazed Scot's Trail rejoins from the left just before a brook crossing; Summit West Trail and Scot's Trail coincide for the next 0.4 mi. Soon Black Gum Swamp Trail diverges right. Summit West Trail passes a marsh with a view up to Crotched Mtn. Black Gum Swamp Trail rejoins from the right, and then Vernal Pool Trail diverges and shortly rejoins from the right. At 4.6 mi. Scot's Trail diverges right, and Summit West Trail reaches the loop junction at 5.0 mi. Bear right to reach Bullard Hill Rd. in 0.1 mi. and the parking area via Link Trail in another 0.7 mi.

UPPER LINK (FCC; AMC FRANCESTOWN TOWN FOREST MAP, AMC CROTCHED MTN. MAP, FCC TRAIL MAP, USGS GREENFIELD QUAD)

From Summit Trail (1,970 ft.) to:	⇅	↗	↺
Shannon's Trail (2,040 ft.)	0.5 mi.	150 ft. (rev. 100 ft.)	0:20

This short blue-blazed trail provides a link between Summit Trail, at the point where its western loop descends off the ridge crest, and Shannon's Trail, at the outlook ledge just below Crotched Mtn.'s true summit. Leaving Summit Trail, it runs westward along the south side of the ridge crest, descends, and then climbs along the base of wooded ledges to meet Shannon's Trail at the back of the outlook ledge.

LOWER LINK (CMF; AMC FRANCESTOWN TOWN FOREST MAP, AMC CROTCHED MTN. MAP, FCC TRAIL MAP, USGS GREENFIELD QUAD)

From west loop of Summit Trail (1,200 ft.) to:	⇅	↗	↺
Shannon's Trail (1,600 ft.)	0.6 mi.	400 ft.	0:30
From Crotched Mtn. Town Forest parking area (915 ft.) to:			
Complete loop over Crotched Mtn. ridge via Link Trail, east loop of Summit Trail, Upper Link, Shannon's Trail, Lower Link, and west loop of Summit Trail	7.2 mi.	1,350 ft.	4:15

This blue-blazed trail runs along the southern base of the mountain, linking Shannon's Trail with the west loop of Summit Trail (Summit West Trail) and making various loop hikes possible. At its east end, it leaves the west loop of Summit Trail 1.8 mi. from the parking area. It crosses a brook, switchbacks up the side of a ridge, and then turns left at a cairn and meanders across the flat crest to meet Shannon's Trail at 0.6 mi.

BRADFORD BOG

The town of Bradford acquired this unique ecosystem in 1971 from the New England Floral Society, which had purchased it to protect a tract of Atlantic white cedar swamp, a natural community rare in New Hampshire, usually found in freshwater coastal environments, containing trees capable of living for up to 300 years. The bog itself also features a variety of wild

SEC 1

plants, such as rhodora, sheep laurel, bog rosemary, pitcher plant, and mountain holly, all identified by signs. An elevated observation deck at the end of the trail provides views of the bog and the surrounding peaks of Lovewell Mtn., Avery Hill, Haystack Mtn., and Pickett Hill. The bog is on property protected under a conservation easement held by Ausbon Sargent Land Preservation Trust. A guide to the bog is available at bradfordnh.org, and printed versions are available at the trailhead.

From NH 103, 0.2 mi. west of NH 114, take Center Rd. for 2.3 mi. (bearing right at the fork at 0.3 mi.). Turn right onto West Rd. and drive 1.8 mi. Turn left onto East Washington Rd. and continue 3.2 mi. to the trailhead on the left. Roadside parking is available in pull-offs just north and south of this point.

BRADFORD BOG TRAIL (BCC/ASLPT; ASLPT MAP)
From East Washington Rd.
(895 ft.) to:

	↧↥	◥	↻
Observation deck (895 ft.)	0.4 mi.	0 ft.	0:10

Bradford Bog Trail runs level along bog bridges its entire distance. Use caution during times of high water, however, because the bridges can be wet and slippery. The trail first passes through a striking narrow corridor of Atlantic white cedar that towers over a bed of lush sphagnum moss and blooming rhodora. At 0.3 mi. the trail turns left to enter the bog proper, where an abandoned section continues ahead. The route winds through a narrow passage of wild plants and shrubs to reach the observation deck at 0.4 mi.

THE CAROLINE A. FOX RESEARCH AND DEMONSTRATION FOREST, AKA FOX FOREST

This 1,455-acre preserve in the town of Hillsborough, managed by the New Hampshire Division of Forests and Lands, features a network of about 20 mi. of nature and multiuse trails leading to a variety of natural and historical features, including stands of old-growth hemlock and beech forest. An informational brochure with a map of the trail system can usually be obtained at the forest's headquarters. Though not described in depth in this guide, the trails are shown on the in-text map on p. 104. Refer to the USGS Hillsboro Upper Village and Hillsboro quadrangles.

From West Main St. in Hillsborough, turn northwest onto School St., which soon becomes Center Rd., and follow it 1.9 mi. to the headquarters and parking on the right. Center Rd. divides the forest in half.

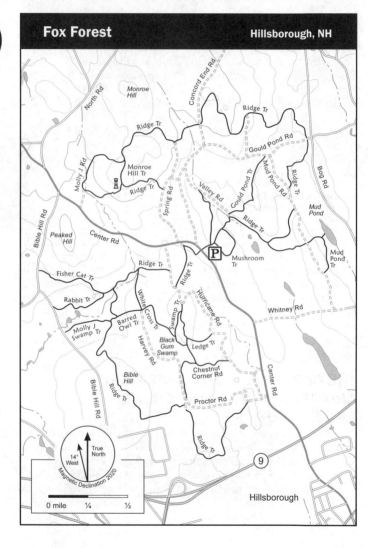

No distant views exist here, except for a very limited cleared view south to Mt. Monadnock from a small observation tower on the side of Monroe Hill, but there are possibilities for many short, medium, and even long woods walks. Ridge Trail, 10.0 mi. long, is the central artery through the forest, connecting with most of the other trails. Short nature walks are available on the popular Tree I.D. Trail and Mushroom Trail, while Black Gum Swamp and Mud Pond offer somewhat longer walks. Black Gum Swamp, which supports a stand of black gum (tupelo) trees—quite rare in New Hampshire—is of particular interest. A brochure with map describing a 2-mi. round-trip hike to the Black Gum Swamp via Ridge Trail and Swamp Trail, published by the New Hampshire Natural Heritage Bureau, can be viewed at nhdfl.org. Mud Pond, whose name fails to suggest the beauty of this small pond surrounded by a quaking bog with many notable plant species, is the jewel of the area. It can be reached from the headquarters via a round trip of about 2 mi. on Ridge Trail and Mud Pond Trail. A stand of old-growth forest is near the junction of these trails.

SKATUTAKEE MTN. (1,999 FT.) AND THUMB MTN. (1,989 FT.)

Skatutakee Mtn. and Thumb Mtn., in the town of Hancock, offer scenic views, particularly to the south, from their open ledges. Refer to the USGS Dublin quadrangle. The trails on these mountains, as well as a number of other trails nearby, are maintained by the Harris Center for Conservation Education, the focal point of a 12,500-acre "super sanctuary" of connected conservation land maintained primarily as wildlife habitat by the cooperative efforts of the HCCE, New Hampshire Audubon, the SPNHF (Forest Society), the New Hampshire Fish and Game Department, the town of Hancock, and a number of private landowners. The HCCE also maintains a network of easier trails on the east side of King's Highway. To reach the Harris Center, follow NH 123 west from its junction with NH 137 for 2.2 mi.; turn left at a small Harris Center sign and follow Hunts Pond Rd. 0.4 mi.; then turn left onto King's Highway and follow it another 0.5 mi. to the Harris Center's parking lot.

The trails to Skatutakee Mtn. and Thumb Mtn. are covered by the in-text map in this guide. Trail maps are usually available at the Harris Center's entryway; they are also posted at the trailhead kiosks and can be found at harriscenter.org. From the Harris Center, Harriskat Trail leads west to the summit of Skatutakee Mtn., which has the best views; to make a returning

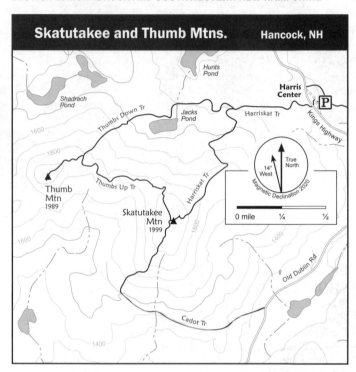

loop hike, take Thumbs Up Trail from Skatutakee Mtn. to Thumb Mtn. and then descend to the parking lot via Thumbs Down Trail. Cadot Trail (formerly Bee Line Trail) ascends Skatutakee Mtn. from the south. Finding the correct trail when descending from the summit of Skatutakee requires a bit of care. (*Note*: Dogs are welcome but must be leashed at all times.)

HARRISKAT TRAIL (HCCE; AMC SKATUTAKEE AND THUMB MTNS. MAP, HCCE TRAIL MAP, USGS DUBLIN QUAD)

Cumulative from King's Highway (1,290 ft.) to:	⇅	↗	○
Thumbs Down Trail (1,400 ft.)	0.6 mi.	100 ft.	0:20

Skatutakee Mtn. summit (1,999 ft.)	1.6 mi.	700 ft.	1:10
Complete loop via Harriskat Trail, Thumbs Up Trail, and Thumbs Down Trail	4.9 mi.	900 ft.	2:55

This trail, marked with white rectangles, begins on King's Highway (sign) opposite the main building of the Harris Center, just northwest of a sign for Briggs Preserve. In 2019, the trail was reported as being lightly maintained and difficult to follow. The route ascends on a switchback, crosses a wet area with several large boulders, and at 0.6 mi. reaches the junction on the right with Thumbs Down Trail to Thumb Mtn. Harriskat Trail bears left uphill and soon swings left onto a broad ridge and climbs across a stone wall, ascending with alternating moderate climbs and nearly level sections on the contour. At 0.9 mi. the trail runs level across a small boulder field, and at 1.2 mi. it makes a sharp right turn. Harriskat Trail now runs mostly through stands of conifers and high up it passes a narrow outlook on the left with a view through trees to Crotched Mtn. It climbs on ledges, runs level across more ledges, and reaches the summit of Skatutakee Mtn., which is the highest of several jumbled ledges in an extensive open area. Views of Crotched Mtn., the Wapack Range, and Mt. Monadnock can be seen from here. In 2019, this outlook was recleared by volunteers. A short distance beyond the highest ledge, Harriskat Trail ends at a three-way junction with Cadot Trail on the left and Thumbs Up Trail to Thumb Mtn. on the right.

THUMBS UP TRAIL (HCCE; AMC SKATUTAKEE AND THUMB MTNS. MAP, HCCE TRAIL MAP, USGS DUBLIN QUAD)

Cumulative from Skatutakee Mtn. summit (1,999 ft.) to:	⮐	↗	⟳
Jct. with Thumbs Down Trail (1,820 ft.)	1.0 mi.	50 ft. (rev. 250 ft.)	0:30
Thumb Mtn. summit (1,989 ft.)	1.3 mi.	210 ft.	0:45

This trail connects the summits of Skatutakee Mtn. and Thumb Mtn. The route is well marked with white plastic triangles, although the footway is not always well beaten. From the three-way junction with Cadot Trail and Harriskat Trail at the summit of Skatutakee Mtn., Thumbs Up Trail leaves northwest (sign: "Mt. Thumb"). The trail descends through a dark coniferous forest and makes a very sharp left turn at the foot of the descent from Skatutakee Mtn. at 0.3 mi. After leaving the coniferous forest, it winds about a great deal on a fairly level ridge. At 1.0 mi. Thumbs Down Trail (yellow plastic rectangles) enters on the right. At this junction, Thumbs Up Trail turns left and ascends steeply to the summit of the first knob of

Thumb Mtn., where it levels, descends slightly, crosses a stone wall, and resumes a moderate ascent to the wooded summit of Thumb Mtn. at 1.3 mi. The trail continues 50 yd. to a ledge with excellent views to Mt. Monadnock and the Wapack Range.

THUMBS DOWN TRAIL (HCCE; AMC SKATUTAKEE AND THUMB MTNS. MAP, HCCE TRAIL MAP, USGS DUBLIN QUAD)

From jct. with Thumbs Up Trail
(1,820 ft.) to:

Jct. with Harriskat Trail (1,400 ft.)	1.1 mi.	0 ft. (rev. 400 ft.)	0:35

This trail descends from Thumbs Up Trail at a junction 0.3 mi. east of the summit of Thumb Mtn., completing the Skatutakee–Thumb loop. Since the loop is described in this guide in the clockwise direction, Thumbs Down Trail is used for the descent. In 2019, this trail was reported as being lightly maintained and difficult to follow. Marked by yellow plastic rectangles, it descends from the junction at the foot of Thumb Mtn. across several stone walls and reaches the north shore of Jacks Pond at 0.6 mi. Here, a side path descends to the right 20 yd. to the edge of the pond. In another 100 yd. Thumbs Down Trail makes a 90-degree turn to the left and follows a woods road downhill, crossing the outlet brook from Jacks Pond. At 1.0 mi. the trail bears right, leaving the road, and crosses a brook, then runs to the junction with Harriskat Trail 0.6 mi. from the Harris Center; go left to return to the center. If you are ascending by Thumbs Down Trail, go right (slightly downhill) at this junction.

CADOT TRAIL (HCCE; AMC SKATUTAKEE AND THUMB MTNS. MAP, HCCE TRAIL MAP, USGS DUBLIN QUAD)

From Old Dublin Rd.
(1,160 ft.) to:

Skatutakee Mtn. summit (1,999 ft.)	1.5 mi.	850 ft.	1:10

This trail (formerly Bee Line Trail) ascends Skatutakee Mtn. from the south. In 2019, it was reported as being lightly maintained and difficult to follow. The trailhead (parking in roadside pull-off) is on the west side of Old Dublin Rd., 1.1 mi. southwest of its junction with King's Highway. (This junction is 0.7 mi. southeast of the Harris Center.) Loop hikes can be made in combination with the direct trails from the Harris Center by means of the 1.8-mi. walk along King's Highway and Old Dublin Rd., both country gravel roads with little traffic.

Cadot Trail (poorly marked with infrequent and very faded blue blazes for the first 0.9 mi.) starts at a gate (sign: "Cadot Trail") and ascends moderately on an old woods road lined with stone walls and furnished with rock culverts. At 0.3 mi. the trail levels and then climbs at easy grades. At 0.9 mi., now marked with white plastic disks, it turns to the right off the road into an overgrown pasture and descends slightly to cross the bed of a small brook. It then begins a fairly steep ascent and passes through a stone wall. The grade becomes moderate, and the trail passes boulders where there is a limited outlook. The terrain becomes ledgy, and at one ledge—where there is a 5-ft.-high conical boulder about 10 yd. ahead in a level section—there is a restricted view of Mt. Monadnock, framed by trees, in the downhill direction. At 1.4 mi. Cadot Trail passes through a stone wall on a ledge, and the grade becomes easy as the trail wanders around the summit ledges to a three-way junction with Thumbs Up and Harriskat trails. Follow Harriskat Trail a short distance right to the summit ledge, where there are good views of Crotched Mtn., the Wapack Range, and Mt. Monadnock.

KULISH LEDGES (2,080 FT.)
AND OSGOOD HILL (2,240 FT.)

Kulish Ledges are a scenic viewpoint on the eastern shoulder of Osgood Hill, the highest point in Nelson and second highest point in Cheshire County. A multiuse trail system managed by the Nelson Trails Committee (opened in 2019) covers the peak within Partridge Woods, a 588-acre tract owned by the Town of Nelson and protected by a conservation easement held by the Harris Center for Conservation Education. Partridge Woods is part of the Harris Center's larger 36,000-acre SuperSanctuary, a series of connected protected lands in the Monadnock Region of southwest New Hampshire. Maps of Kulish Ledges Trail and Bailey Brook Trail are available at harriscenter.org. At the time of this book's publication, there was no map for Holt Trail, and maps of the other trails were partially depicted at trailfinder.info.

Three trailheads with parking provide access to the trail network. The northern trailhead (yellow-and-black "bug" sign) are on the south side of Old Stoddard Rd. in Nelson, 1.4 mi. southwest from its junction with NH 123 in Stoddard (where Old Stoddard Rd. is called Bailey Brook Rd.). A western trailhead (sign for Partridge Woods) is located on Homestead Ln. Follow the directions above for the northern trailhead but continue on Old Stoddard Rd. At 2.5 mi. from NH 123, turn left onto Homestead Ln. for 0.4 mi. to the trailhead (this parking area is closed from December 1 to May 15, and parking is prohibited along the road at all times). The southern trailhead (sign for Partridge Woods) is located on Brickyard Rd. From

Nelson Village, follow Nelson Rd. south for 0.2 mi., then turn left onto Tolman Pond Rd. In 1.4 mi., bear left onto Brickyard Rd. and continue 0.4 mi. to the trailhead on the left.

KULISH LEDGES TRAIL (HCCE/NTC; HARRIS CENTER MAP)
Cumulative from Old Stoddard Rd.
(1,380 ft.) to:

	↧↥	↗	○
East Pinnacle viewpoint (1,850 ft.)	1.2 mi.	470 ft.	0:50
Kulish Ledges viewpoint (2,080 ft.)	1.4 mi.	700 ft.	1:05
Osgood Hill Link Trail (2,150 ft.)	1.8 mi.	730 ft.	1:15
Osgood Hill summit (2,240 ft.)	2.1 mi.	820 ft.	1:25
Starting point by loop via Kulish Ledges Trail, Holt Trail	4.4 mi	820 ft. (rev 820 ft.)	2:35

This yellow-blazed trail provides a direct route to two ledge outlooks. In conjunction with Holt Trail, it can also be used to make a loop over Osgood Hill. It begins at the Old Stoddard Rd. trailhead. Kulish Ledges Trail heads south along a woods road, coinciding with Bailey Brook Trail, and at 0.1 mi. turns right off the road onto a footpath where Bailey Brook Trail continues ahead. It swings left to cross a footbridge over Bailey Brook, passes a large beaver dam and pond, then turns left away from the pond at a junction at 0.4 mi. where Holt Trail diverges right. It ascends gradually, turns left through a stone wall and traverses a rocky area, then crosses a small brook. Past the brook, the trail passes a nineteenth-century cast iron stove at 0.8 mi., the relic of a former cabin at this location.

At 1.2 mi. the trail reaches the East Pinnacle viewpoint, an outlook over Spoonwood Pond and Nubanusit Lake to Skatutakee and Thumb Mtns. with North Pack Monadnock and Crotched Mtn. beyond. From this viewpoint, the trail climbs more steeply to a side path on the right which descends 20 yd. to a cleared view northeast to Mt. Sunapee. Kulish Ledges Trail now zigzags moderately up a wooded ridge and reaches a junction at 1.5 mi. where a short spur path diverges left for a few yd. to the main ledges and good views east. The main trail continues straight ahead, passes a junction with Osgood Hill Link Trail at 1.8 mi., and continues up to the summit of Osgood Hill and junction with Holt Trail at 2.1 mi.

BAILEY BROOK TRAIL (HCCE/NTC; HCCE MAP)
From Old Stoddard Rd. trailhead
(1,380 ft.) to:

Starting point by loop	1.1 mi.	140 ft. (rev. 140 ft.)	0:35

This trail makes a short loop along Bailey Brook, visiting a small waterfall and the remnants of a nineteenth-century mill. Blazed in yellow, Bailey Brook Trail turns right out of the Old Stoddard Rd. parking lot and follows the road downhill for 0.2 mi., then turns right into the woods onto a footpath. It passes a cascade and pool on the left, then joins alongside the brook and rises easily to the falls and site of Osborn Sawmill at 0.8 mi. The trail climbs up along the left side of the mill ruins, turns right then left, and crosses a woods road. At 0.9 mi. it turns right onto another old road, then quickly turns left onto yet another (a few yd. right of this junction is the Osborn Homestead cellar hole). It follows this road, passes a junction with Kulish Ledges Trail on the left, and returns to the parking area at 1.1 mi.

HOLT TRAIL (HCCE/NTC)
Cumulative from Kulish Ledges Trail
(1,560 ft.) to:

Osgood Hill summit (2,240 ft.)	1.9 mi.	700 ft.	1:20
Starting point by loop via Kulish Ledges Trail	3.6 mi.	700 ft. (rev. 700 ft.)	2:10

This blue-blazed trail ascends directly to the summit of Osgood Hill and, in combination with Kulish Ledges Trail, can be used to make a loop hike. It begins 0.4 mi. up Kulish Ledges Trail from the Old Stoddard Rd. trailhead. Holt Trail heads west along the shore of a beaver pond, swings away from it and ascends via numerous switchbacks, then climbs over the shoulder of a ridge in an area crisscrossed by old stone walls. As it meanders up, it passes three cellar holes (signs), remnants of the area's farming past. The trail continues a gentle ascent, passes a junction with an unsigned orange-blazed trail and ends at the summit of Osgood Hill and junction with Kulish Ledges Trail at 1.9 mi.

WHEELER TRAIL (HCCE/NTC; TRAILFINDER MAP)
Cumulative from Homestead Ln. trailhead
(1,980 ft.) to:

Ethan's Way (2,030 ft.)	0.9 mi.	100 ft. (rev. 80 ft.)	0:30
Osgood Hill Link Trail (1,940 ft.)	1.3 mi.	140 ft. (rev. 120 ft.)	0:45
Brickyard Rd. (1,810 ft.)	1.6 mi.	140 ft. (rev. 130 ft.)	0:50

This trail provides access into Partridge Woods from the west via the Homestead Ln. trailhead. Wheeler Trail continues up the private section of Homestead Ln. and at 0.2 mi. continues straight past a driveway and gate onto the abandoned portion of the road (yellow blazing begins here). At 0.8 mi. it crosses an unsigned orange-blazed trail (turn left here onto this trail for an alternate 0.5 mi. ascent to Osgood Hill), then reaches a junction with Ethan's Way at 0.9 mi., directly opposite the Wheeler Homestead site. Wheeler Trail continues ahead, bears right at a junction with Osgood Hill Link Trail at 1.3 mi. (this short connector, blazed in blue, turns left here and ascends 0.3 mi. and 210 ft. to meet Kulish Ledges Trail near the summit of Osgood Hill) and descends to Brickyard Rd. (no parking) at 1.6 mi.

ETHAN'S WAY (HCCE/NTC; TRAILFINDER MAP)
From Brickyard Rd. trailhead
(1,540 ft.) to:

Wheeler Trail (2,030 ft.)	1.1 mi.	490 ft.	0:45

This trail is the main route into Partridge Woods from the Brickyard Rd. trailhead. Blazed in blue, it leaves the north end of the parking lot and follows an abandoned woods road steadily uphill with one minor descent and ends at the Wheeler Homestead site and Wheeler Trail at 1.1 mi., 0.9 mi. east of the Homestead Ln. trailhead.

PEIRCE RESERVATION
The Charles L. Peirce Wildlife and Forest Reservation comprises more than 3,500 acres in Stoddard and Windsor owned by the SPNHF. Refer to the USGS Stoddard quadrangle.

TROUT-N-BACON TRAIL (SPNHF; USGS STODDARD QUAD)
From Old Antrim Rd.
(1,340 ft.) to:

Bacon Ledge (1,959 ft.)	1.2 mi.	600 ft.	0:50

Trout-n-Bacon Trail provides access to good views from Bacon Ledge; beyond the ledge it is somewhat difficult to follow in places as it leads to secluded Trout Pond. Follow NH 123 north for 1.7 mi. from its junction with NH 9 to Mill Village. To reach the trailhead for Bacon Ledge, follow Old Antrim Rd. (a gravel road, also called Barrett Pond Rd.) 0.9 mi. east from Mill Village to the start of the trail, which is marked by a yellow blaze and small arrow sign; there is limited roadside parking. The last 0.4 mi. of this road may be rough, in which case it may be better to park in a pulloff on the right 0.5 mi. from NH 123.

The yellow-blazed trail leaves from the north side of Old Antrim Rd. and almost immediately turns right onto a woods road. At a fork at 0.7 mi., a cross-country ski trail bears left and continues on the road, bypassing

Bacon Ledge and Round Mtn., while Trout-n-Bacon Trail leaves the road on the right and goes uphill, finally scrambling to the top of Bacon Ledge (1,959 ft.) at 1.2 mi., where there are good views. (A short side path on the left can be used to avoid the scramble up the ledge in adverse conditions.) Past Bacon Ledge, the lightly-used trail is obscure in places and is best suited for experienced hikers only. It leads over Round Mtn. to a clear-cut area above the shore of Trout Pond at 2.7 mi. and then continues on snow-mobile trails to Shedd Hill Rd., 0.8 mi. north of Mill Village, at 4.3 mi. From here Shedd Hill Rd. and Old Antrim Rd. can then be followed back to the trailhead at 6.0 mi.

DEPIERREFEU–WILLARD POND WILDLIFE SANCTUARY

This nearly 1,700-acre New Hampshire Audubon sanctuary in the towns of Antrim and Hancock contains the shoreline of Willard Pond (though not the pond itself) and Bald Mtn., which has two good outlook ledges. Several trails provide options for loop hikes over Bald Mtn. Refer to the in-text map in this guide and the USGS Stoddard quadrangle; for more information see nhaudubon.org.

Follow NH 123 north from Hancock for 3.7 mi. or south from NH 9 for 3.3 mi., and then turn east onto Willard Pond Rd. and follow it for 1.6 mi., bearing left at two forks, to a parking area and information kiosk on the left.

TAMPOSI TRAIL (NHA; AMC DEPIERREFEU WILDLIFE SANCTUARY MAP, USGS STODDARD QUAD)

Cumulative from parking area on Willard Pond Rd. (1,160 ft.) to:	↥↧	↗	↻
Loop jct. (1,500 ft.)	0.5 mi.	350 ft.	0:25
Bald Mtn. summit (2,034 ft.) via east loop	1.2 mi.	900 ft.	1:05
Complete loop	2.3 mi.	900 ft.	1:35

Tamposi Trail makes a loop over Bald Mtn. that includes two excellent viewpoints on the mountain. The yellow-blazed trail leaves from the left side of the trailhead parking area and climbs through a rocky section, with occasional minor descents, to the loop junction at 0.5 mi. The loop is described in the counterclockwise direction, taking the right (east) fork for the ascent. The east loop follows the contour of the ledgy slope, then swings left and climbs to an outlook with a fine view over Willard Pond and the mountains beyond at 0.8 mi., where it turns left and continues to climb. At

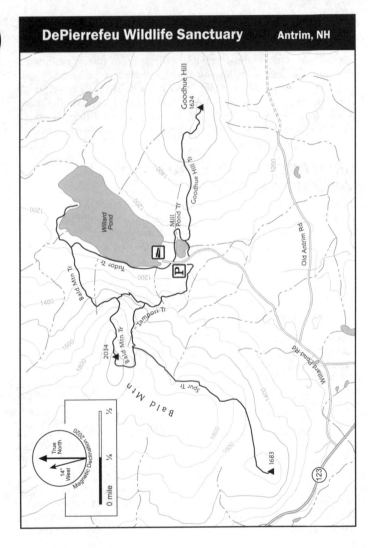

0.9 mi. red-blazed Bald Mtn. Trail enters on the right, and the trails coincide and turn left, ascending to an excellent south outlook at 1.0 mi. On the ledges above the outlook, the trails turn left into the woods and climb to a small clearing at the wooded, viewless summit at 1.2 mi. Here, Bald Mtn. Trail ends, and the west loop of Tamposi Trail continues ahead for the descent. It soon bears left and descends steadily through spruces. It bears left again, passes a cleared view southeast, and winds down through selectively logged hardwood forest. Tamposi Trail passes a junction on the right with lightly used, blue-blazed Spur Trail at about 1.5 mi. and continues down to the loop junction at 1.8 mi. Turn right to return to the parking area.

TUDOR TRAIL (NHA; AMC DEPIERREFEU WILDLIFE SANCTUARY MAP, USGS STODDARD QUAD)

Cumulative from parking area on Willard Pond Rd. (1,160 ft.) to:	↓↑	↗	⟳
Bald Mtn. Trail (1,160 ft.)	0.7 mi.	0 ft.	0:20
Pine Point (1,160 ft.)	1.0 mi.	0 ft.	0:30

This easy, yellow-blazed trail runs along the shore of Willard Pond and provides access to Bald Mtn. Trail. It leaves Willard Pond Rd. on the left (sign), 140 yd. beyond the trailhead parking area, and runs along the west shore of the pond, passing through a small boulder field and crossing several small brooks. At 0.7 mi. red-blazed Bald Mtn. Trail diverges left. Tudor Trail bears right and continues through large white pines to Pine Point, where there is a fine view of the pond.

BALD MTN. TRAIL (NHA; AMC DEPIERREFEU WILDLIFE SANCTUARY MAP, USGS STODDARD QUAD)

From Tudor Trail (1,160 ft.) to:	↓↑	↗	⟳
Bald Mtn. summit (2,034 ft.)	0.8 mi.	900 ft.	0:50

This red-blazed trail ascends Bald Mtn. from Tudor Trail on the shore of Willard Pond. It diverges left from Tudor Trail 0.7 mi. from the parking area and ascends gradually at first, passing through an area of glacial boulders, then rises more steeply. At 0.5 mi. the east loop of yellow-blazed Tamposi Trail joins from the left, and the two trails coincide, climbing to a fine south outlook at 0.6 mi. On the ledges above the outlook, the trails turn left into the woods and climb to a small clearing at the wooded, viewless summit at 0.8 mi. Here, Bald Mtn. Trail ends, and the west loop of Tamposi Trail continues ahead for the descent.

MILL POND TRAIL (NHA; AMC DEPIERREFEU WILDLIFE SANCTUARY MAP, USGS STODDARD QUAD)

From Willard Pond Rd.
(1,160 ft.) to:

Willard Pond Rd. (1,160 ft.)	0.4 mi.	0 ft.	0:10

From the east side of Willard Pond Rd., yellow-blazed Mill Pond Trail makes an easy 0.4-mi. loop around Hatch Mill Pond, a shallow pond where the remains of a sawmill can be seen. One end of the loop leaves the road about 70 yd. south of the parking area, while the other end leaves the road about 100 yd. north of the parking area.

GOODHUE HILL TRAIL (NHA; AMC DEPIERREFEU WILDLIFE SANCTUARY MAP, USGS STODDARD QUAD)

From Mill Pond Trail
(1,170 ft.) to:

Goodhue Hill summit (1,624 ft.)	0.9 mi.	450 ft.	0:40

Red-blazed Goodhue Hill Trail leaves the south end of Mill Pond Trail 0.1 mi. from Willard Pond Rd. and ascends steadily east for 0.7 mi. to a brushy clearing near Goodhue Hill's summit, where there are views of Mt. Monadnock, Skatutakee Mtn., Thumb Mtn., Bald Mtn., and summits to the north. (*Note*: This section of the trail is unmarked and takes careful attention to follow through the clearing.) The route continues through an open area where nest boxes and acres of shrubby habitat are maintained for wildlife food and cover, and then it leads briefly through woods (this section is poorly marked) before reaching a rocky area adjacent to the high point at 0.9 mi. This spot offers a fine view of Mt. Monadnock and other points to the southeast.

SPUR TRAIL (NHA; AMC DEPIERREFEU WILDLIFE SANCTUARY MAP, USGS STODDARD QUAD)

From Tamposi Trail
(1,820 ft.) to:

Complete loop at end of trail (1,683 ft.)	1.3 mi.	200 ft. (rev. 300 ft.)	0:45

Lightly used and maintained Spur Trail traverses the 376-acre Tamposi parcel, protected and managed by New Hampshire Audubon, with help from the Forest Legacy program. This trail was reported as overgrown and very difficult to follow in 2019, with no discernible footbed and few visible blazes, and it is recommended for experienced hikers only. The blue-blazed trail leaves the west loop of Tamposi Trail about 0.3 mi. above the loop junction. It descends south along a logging road through early successional forest with excellent possibilities for wildlife viewing, then bears right off the road and ascends gradually. Spur Trail skirts the southern spur of Bald Mtn. through recently logged areas, passes through an old apple orchard being maintained for wildlife, descends to a stream in a col, and then climbs to the top of a lower knob (1,683 ft.), where a loop leads past clearings with restricted views northwest and southeast.

MONADNOCK–SUNAPEE GREENWAY

Monadnock–Sunapee Greenway, 49 mi. long, extends north from Mt. Monadnock to Mt. Sunapee. The SPNHF and AMC cooperatively built this white-blazed trail, which runs mostly over hills and along ridges between these two major peaks in southwestern New Hampshire. Volunteer maintenance and other support of this trail are coordinated by the Monadnock–Sunapee Greenway Trail Club.

Because a large part of this trail is on private property, users should be particularly aware of their status as guests and avoid thoughtless behavior that could jeopardize this privilege. Camping is permitted at designated sites only. Space constraints prevent full and detailed coverage of the Greenway in this guide, but the following are descriptions of a few of its more important features (in addition to Mt. Monadnock and Mt. Sunapee): Pitcher Mtn. (2,163 ft.), Hubbard Hill (1,892 ft.), Jackson Hill (2,061 ft.), Oak Hill (1,960 ft.) and Lovewell Mtn. (2,477 ft.). The *Monadnock–Sunapee Greenway Trail Guide*, 8th edition (2019), along with the GPS-surveyed, waterproof Greenway SuperMap (updated in 2015), provides detailed coverage of the entire route and also includes several side trails in the Mt. Sunapee area; both the guide and map are available from the MSGTC (see Appendix). Recent trail updates are available at msgtc.org.

PITCHER MTN. (2,163 FT.)

This small mountain in the town of Stoddard has an open summit and a fire tower that offers fine views in all directions for little effort. The peak is also an excellent choice for sunrises and sunsets. Refer to the USGS Marlow quadrangle and the Monadnock–Sunapee Greenway map. The parking lot is on the northeast side of NH 123, 4.5 mi. north of its junction with NH 9 and 3.1 mi. south of its junction with NH 10.

PITCHER MTN. TRAILS
(MSGTC; MSGTC MAP, USGS MARLOW QUAD)

Cumulative from NH 123
(1,870 ft.) to:

	⇅	⬈	◯
Pitcher Mtn. summit (2,163 ft.) by either path	0.4 mi.	300 ft.	0:20
Starting point via complete loop	0.8 mi.	300 ft.	0:35

About 70 yd. above the parking area, two hiking trails divide; the left-hand trail (blue blazes) is the shorter, steeper path, while the right-hand trail (white blazes) is the less steep Monadnock–Sunapee Greenway, which follows the fire tower access road. The two trails rejoin about 70 yd. north of the summit.

■ HUBBARD HILL (1,892 FT.) AND JACKSON HILL (2,061 FT.)

Hubbard Hill and Jackson Hill, both in the town of Stoddard and crossed by Monadnock–Sunapee Greenway, offer expansive views from their open, shrubby summits, especially to the west and southwest. The summit of Hubbard Hill is covered in extensive blueberry fields, ripe for picking in season. Access to both summits involves first hiking up to Pitcher Mtn. (see Pitcher Mtn. trail description for driving directions and hiking details) and then traversing north across the ridge. Footing is generally good, and grades are easy to moderate. The route described here begins at the Pitcher Mtn. summit.

MONADNOCK–SUNAPEE GREENWAY
(MSGTC; MSGTC MAP; USGS MARLOW QUAD)

Cumulative from Pitcher Mtn. summit
(2,163 ft.) to:

	⇅	⬈	◯
Hubbard Hill summit (1,892 ft.)	2.3 mi.	280 ft. (rev. 400 ft.)	1:15
Spur trail to Fox Brook Campsite (1,700 ft.)	2.9 mi.	280 ft. (rev. 190 ft.)	1:35
Jackson Hill summit (2,061 ft.)	3.7 mi.	760 ft. (rev. 120 ft.)	2:15

From the fire tower on Pitcher Mtn., descend easily north along white-blazed Monadnock–Sunapee Greenway through low scrub and blueberry bushes, quickly passing a blue-blazed side trail that comes from the parking area on the left. Pass through a narrow corridor with several viewpoints on the left (west) to reenter the woods at 0.3 mi. (Follow the blazes on the ledges carefully to avoid the many intersecting paths used for berry picking.) The trail descends easily along an old woods road, turns sharply right just before reaching gravel Hubbard Hill Rd., and then descends easily again to cross that same gravel road at 0.5 mi. The trail descends briefly, climbs easily and then moderately over a wooded hump, drops over a mossy ledge (use caution if wet), and descends to an old woods road. The route turns left onto the old road and immediately turns right to climb a small ledge (avoid the worn path that continues straight). It descends easily to the junction with Hubbard Hill Rd. at 1.2 mi. Here, the trail turns left and follows the wide gravel road at easy grades, slowly heading west to a large clearing used by berry pickers. At the north end of the clearing, the trail enters the blueberry fields. Passing the halfway point along Monadnock–Sunapee Greenway (sign), it continues to the flat, shrubby summit (sign and cairn) of Hubbard Hill at 2.3 mi., which offers wide views west and southwest, and also back to the fire tower on Pitcher Mtn.

The trail travels northwest and then northeast from the summit through the blueberry fields (avoid side paths used by berry pickers). It then enters the woods and descends easily through the deep, dark Andorra Forest, where footing becomes a bit rougher, to the junction with a spur path on the right at 2.9 mi. This path leads 25 yd. to Fox Brook Campsite, a tent platform with a small brook just beyond it for a water source.

The trail passes through a stone wall and then descends easily to cross the brook near the campsite and then larger Fox Brook (potentially difficult in high water). It continues straight through a four-way junction with an old woods road at 3.0 mi. The trail then begins a moderate climb up the southern slope of Jackson Hill, heading slightly northwest. It turns sharply left onto an old woods road at 3.4 mi. and continues to make a moderate ascent to the open summit of Jackson Hill at 3.7 mi., where there are views in most directions.

■ OAK HILL (IN WASHINGTON; 1,960 FT.)

This small peak along Monadnock–Sunapee Greenway provides good views from its partly open summit. The best vista is to the southwest looking out to Mt. Ascutney and other peaks in southern Vermont. To reach the trailhead from NH 31 in Washington Village, follow Faxon Hill Rd. southwest for 1.6 mi. to a white-blazed wooden gate on the left (southeast) side of the road. There is limited room to park along the road here; do not block the gate. Just before reaching this gate is a small pull-off at the junction with Pine Point Rd. that provides better parking. In winter, parking may be nonexistent at either of these locations.

MONADNOCK–SUNAPEE GREENWAY (MSGTC; MSGTC MAP)

From gate on Faxon Hill Rd. (1,630 ft.) to:	⇕	↗	↻
Oak Hill summit (1,960 ft.)	0.7 mi.	360 ft. (rev. 50 ft.)	0:30

The route to Oak Hill uses a short section of Monadnock–Sunapee Greenway and is blazed in white. Grades are easy except for one steep push near the summit and footing is generally good. From the gate, Monadnock–Sunapee Greenway descends easily along an old logging road, passing an abandoned house on the left. In a little more than 0.1 mi. the trail turns left off the road onto a footpath, passes through a stone wall then turns right to enter the New England Forestry Foundation's Clark Robinson Memorial Forest (sign). It crosses a small brook on step stones and begins ascending at easy to moderate grades. At 0.6 the trail suddenly becomes steeper and rougher, quickly jogs left then right, scrambles up a small ledge and continues easily to the summit at 0.7 mi., marked by large cairn and sign.

■ LOVEWELL MTN. (2,477 FT.)

This mountain, in the village of Washington and crossed by Monadnock–Sunapee Greenway, offers interesting views from a number of scattered ledges. It is covered by this book's *AMC Southern New Hampshire Trail Map: Mount Sunapee and Pillsbury State Parks* (Map 2). Also, refer to the USGS Washington quadrangle. The summit of Lovewell Mtn. and much of this segment of the Greenway are within Pillsbury State Park.

From Washington on NH 31, follow gravel Halfmoon Pond Rd. southeast from the village church and school for 0.5 mi. and then turn sharply left and continue on Halfmoon Pond Rd. past Halfmoon Pond. (*Note*: The best parking may be at the Halfmoon Pond boat launch at 1.4 mi. from NH 31.) At 1.9 mi. turn right onto Lovewell Mtn. Rd., a rough woods road (limited parking; sign: "Greenway—do not block the road"). As this woods road is not passable for the vast majority of vehicles, the trail description begins here (alternate limited roadside parking for the loop hike described below is also available at the driveable end of Halfmoon Pond Rd. at the junction with Martin Rd. on the right, 3.2 mi. north of NH 31; do not park in the turnaround).

MONADNOCK–SUNAPEE GREENWAY (MSGTC; MAP 2: H1–H2)

Cumulative from jct. of Halfmoon Pond Rd. and Lovewell Mtn. Rd. (1,540 ft.) to:	↧↥	↗	○
Lovewell Mtn. summit (2,477 ft.)	2.3 mi.	950 ft.	1:40
Crossing of Halfmoon Pond Rd. (1,610 ft.)	4.6 mi.	1,200 ft. (rev. 1,100 ft.)	2:55
Starting point via Halfmoon Pond Rd.	6.5 mi.	1,300 ft. (rev. 150 ft.)	3:55

Lovewell Mtn. Rd. (part of Monadnock–Sunapee Greenway) climbs through logged areas (follow markings carefully) to a level area at 0.9 mi., where ledges run down to the road past the stone wall that parallels it. Here, the foot trail (sign, cairns) turns left to cross through the stone wall. It ascends through old pastures and at 1.8 mi. enters a level section. At the end of this section, the trail turns right, ascends a steep, rough portion, and then continues on a fairly steep, rough, and ledgy pathway through mostly dark, mature coniferous woods. At 2.1 mi. a side path leads left 100 yd. to a piped spring. In a short distance another side path leads right 60 yd. to a southeast outlook, where views have been improved in recent years.

The trail reaches the summit cairn at 2.3 mi.; a nearby overlook (sign) provides views to the north and northeast. The trail then descends north along a broad ridge and crosses a shallow sag and a minor hump. After swinging around to the west and descending into a ravine, the trail crosses a small brook at 3.6 mi. It climbs to the crest of a lesser ridge and passes Max Israel Shelter on the left. From there it descends, crossing through several stone walls and passing the remains of old farms—a number of old cellar holes and foundations and the remnants of an apple orchard. After crossing through several more stone walls, the trail reaches Halfmoon Pond Rd. at 4.6 mi. This is 1.9 mi. north of the junction with Lovewell Mtn. Rd., where the description of this trail began. Turn left to return to the trailhead.

PILLSBURY STATE PARK

This 5,500-acre park, in the towns of Washington and Goshen, contains nine ponds and surrounding mountain ridges, including several miles of Monadnock–Sunapee Greenway. Refer to the USGS Washington and Sunapee Lake South quadrangles as well as this book's *AMC Southern New Hampshire Trail Map: Mount Sunapee and Pillsbury State Parks* (Map 2). A network of trails, mostly on logging roads, provides access to the Greenway and makes possible an extended hike to the fine viewpoint known as Lucia's Lookout, where there are expansive views to the surrounding peaks, including Mt. Sunapee and Mt. Monadnock. About 40 primitive campsites are available around the ponds. A day-use fee is charged for admission to the park, which is open from early May through late October and gated at other times. Contact NHDP for current operating schedules and fees. The area is remote and hiking use is generally light. Due to the many wetlands, it is an excellent place for wildlife sightings.

The park entrance is on NH 31, 4.2 mi. north of the general store in Washington. Pay the admission fee at the office 0.2 mi. from the entrance;

a park trail map is also available here. Trailhead parking is in a designated area by a playground near the shore of Mill Pond, 1.1 mi. from the entrance.

FIVE SUMMERS TRAIL (NHDP; MAP 2: G3–H4)

Cumulative from parking area (1,650 ft.) to:	↕	↗	⏱
Bear Pond Trail (1,660 ft.)	0.5 mi.	50 ft. (rev. 50 ft.)	0:15
Viewpoint at North Pond (1,650 ft.)	1.1 mi.	50 ft.	0:35
Monadnock–Sunapee Greenway (2,280 ft.)	3.8 mi.	700 ft.	2:15
Lucia's Lookout (2,490 ft.) via Greenway	4.0 mi.	900 ft.	2:25

This blue-blazed trail provides the most direct access to Lucia's Lookout. For much of its length it follows logging roads used as snowmobile trails—pleasant in the lower section, but often muddy, rough, and overgrown in the upper mile, though a relocation completed in 2014 by MSGTC has improved the footing. Check with park management about the current condition of this trail. (Bear Pond Trail provides a longer but probably better access to Monadnock–Sunapee Greenway and Lucia's Lookout.)

A gravel road leads north from the main parking area and swings right past Campsite 35. At 0.1 mi., just before an orange gate, Balance Rock Trail diverges left. Five Summers Trail continues past the gate, descending gradually alongside Mill Pond and crossing a bridge over the inlet brook. At 0.5 mi. Bear Pond Trail leaves on the right; Five Summers Trail heads left and soon comes within sight of North Pond, passing a side path on the left that leads to a campsite. At 1.1 mi. there is a viewpoint on the left that looks over the pond. The trail continues at easy grades on the grassy road, passing a town boundary marker at 1.5 mi. It leaves the park at 1.9 mi., crosses a bridge, swings right in a logging yard, and at 2.2 mi. crosses another bridge and bears right at a fork (sign). After crossing another bridge, the wide trail ascends through regenerating forest and becomes muddy and rough at times.

At 3.0 mi. the trail swings right, with a large beaver pond visible on the left. In another 0.1 mi. it bears left off the main road onto a footpath. Five Summers Trail then ascends gradually, with some wet footing, and meets the main road at 3.5 mi. It follows the road to the left for 20 yd., turns right off it (sign) onto a footpath with improved footing, and then ascends moderately to Monadnock–Sunapee Greenway at 3.8 mi. For Lucia's Lookout, turn left (north) and climb steeply for 0.2 mi. to a ledge with a view south. A side path descends 40 yd. right to a fine eastern outlook. For a view to the west, continue 90 yd. north on the main trail and take a short spur path to the left.

BEAR POND TRAIL (NHDP; MAP 2: G3–H3)

From Five Summers Trail (1,660 ft.) to:	⬇⬆	↗	↺
Monadnock–Sunapee Greenway (2,040 ft.)	1.2 mi.	400 ft.	0:50
From parking area (1,650 ft.) to:			
Lucia's Lookout (2,490 ft.) via Five Summers Trail, Bear Pond Trail, and Monadnock–Sunapee Greenway	4.8 mi.	1,150 ft. (rev. 300 ft.)	3:00

This blue-blazed trail follows a logging road/snowmobile trail from Five Summers Trail up to Monadnock–Sunapee Greenway, making possible a fairly long and remote hike to Lucia's Lookout. (*Note*: Some portions of the trail have wet footing.) Bear Pond Trail diverges right (sign) from Five Summers Trail 0.5 mi. from the parking area. At 0.1 mi. it passes close by a beaver swamp on the left. After crossing a bridge, it ascends to a point near the shore of Bear Pond at 0.5 mi., with a good view of the pond 20 yd. to the right. The trail ascends moderately, crosses two bridges, and then rises more steeply on an eroded section of road. At 0.9 mi. the grade eases, and in another 0.1 mi. the trail swings right at a fork and continues across a level area with muddy footing to meet Monadnock–Sunapee Greenway in a saddle. For Lucia's Lookout, turn left (north) on the Greenway, which winds around two humps on the south ridge of Mt. Sunapee, passes a side path on the left that leads to Steve Galpin Shelter at Moose Lookout at 1.7 mi. from the junction with Bear Pond Trail, and then reaches the junction where Five Summers Trail joins from the left at 2.9 mi. The Greenway climbs another 0.2 mi. to Lucia's Lookout.

BALANCE ROCK TRAIL (NHDP; MAP 2: G3)

From Five Summers Trail (1,700 ft.) to:	⬇⬆	↗	↺
Balance Rock (2,150 ft.)	1.0 mi.	500 ft. (rev. 50 ft.)	0:45

This orange-blazed trail leads from Five Summers Trail, 0.1 mi. from the parking area, to a restricted viewpoint over North Pond and a large boulder perched on a ledge. Balance Rock Trail diverges left (sign) from Five Summers Trail just before an orange gate. The trail follows a woods road for 70 yd. and then bears left onto another woods road (sign). At 0.2 mi. it bears right off the road (sign) and follows a well-worn footpath. It ascends a southern shoulder of Bryant Mtn., dips to a col at 0.5 mi., and then climbs steadily by switchbacks. The trail angles up across the east slope of the mountain and at 1.0 mi. reaches a ledge with a restricted but beautiful view of North Pond and the ridge to the east; Lovewell Mtn. is visible to the southeast. The trail continues another 50 yd. and ends at Balance Rock.

MAD ROAD TRAIL (NHDP; MAP 2: G2)

From Pillsbury State Park access road
(1,640 ft.) to:

NH 31 (1,670 ft.)	2.7 mi.	200 ft. (rev. 200 ft.)	1:25

This trail leaves the south side of the park access road just before the cul-de-sac at the road's end. It crosses a footbridge and runs at easy grades for 0.9 mi. to a junction with Ridge Link on the left, near the shore of swampy Bacon Pond. Mad Road Trail then swings right (southwest), climbs over a col on a ridge north of Jones Hill, and at 2.7 mi. descends to NH 31, 1.8 mi. south of the park entrance.

RIDGE LINK (NHDP; MAP 2: H2)

From Mad Road Trail
(1,670 ft.) to:

Monadnock–Sunapee Greenway (1,870 ft.)	0.5 mi.	200 ft.	0:20

This short connecting trail diverges to the east from Mad Road Trail near Bacon Pond and climbs for 0.5 mi. to Monadnock–Sunapee Greenway, 0.5 mi. south of Kittredge Hill and 1.8 mi. south of the junction with Bear Pond Trail.

MT. SUNAPEE (2,732 FT.)

Mt. Sunapee, the northern terminus of Monadnock–Sunapee Greenway, is an irregular, massive, heavily wooded mountain in the town of Newbury at the south end of Sunapee Lake. Lake Solitude, near its summit, is notable for its high elevation, remoteness, and beautiful setting. Nearby cliffs rise 300 ft. to White Ledges, where there is a fine view southeast over the wild country of the Merrimack–Connecticut watershed. The area is covered by this book's *AMC Southern New Hampshire Trail Map: Mount Sunapee and Pillsbury State Parks* (Map 2). Also, refer to the USGS Sunapee Lake South quadrangle. Mt. Sunapee State Park (2,893 acres) is on NH 103, 7.0 mi. east of Newport. Facilities include a small campground with tent platforms and lean-tos. A state-owned but now privately managed ski area lies on the north slope of the mountain. In addition to the trails described below, the mountain is easily climbed via the ski slopes (direct routes are about 1.5 mi. long; ski trails are closed to hiking during ski area operation).

SOLITUDE TRAIL (NHDP; MAP 2: G5–H5)

From Mt. Sunapee summit
(2,732 ft.) to:

Lake Solitude (2,510 ft.)	1.0 mi.	250 ft. (rev. 450 ft.)	0:40

This very popular trail connects the summit of Mt. Sunapee with beautiful Lake Solitude and the ledges that overlook it—ledges that are only slightly lower than the summit itself. The trail is also the northern end of Monadnock–Sunapee Greenway and a segment of Trail 1 of Sunapee–Ragged–Kearsarge Greenway (trail numbers indicate section of the SRKG as a whole). It is blazed in white and orange. From the summit of Mt. Sunapee, the trail descends on a gravel service road along the right edge of the ski slopes, with excellent views to the north, swinging right and passing under a chairlift. At 0.2 mi. the trail leaves the service road and ski trails and enters the woods on the right; just 30 yd. before this point, Goshen Trail, here a woods road, enters on the right. Solitude Trail follows a bumpy ridge through beautiful woods, and at 0.8 mi. a side path on the right leads 60 yd. across White Ledges to a fine viewpoint down to the lake and out to the east. The main trail descends sharply to Jack and June Junction at 0.9 mi. Here, Newbury Trail continues ahead, and the red-blazed trail (may be obscure) from the eastern side of the ski area diverges left at a junction. Solitude Trail bears right and descends to its junction with Andrew Brook Trail at the north end of Lake Solitude.

ANDREW BROOK TRAIL (CHVTC; MAP 2: H5)

Cumulative from Mountain Rd. (1,330 ft.) to:	↕	↗	○
Lake Solitude at the Solitude Trail jct. (2,510 ft.)	2.0 mi.	1,200 ft.	1:35
Mt. Sunapee summit (2,732 ft.) via Solitude Trail	3.0 mi.	1,650 ft. (rev. 250 ft.)	2:20

This trail ascends to beautiful Lake Solitude from the east and offers access to the summit of Mt. Sunapee via Solitude Trail. Leave NH 103 0.8 mi. east of its junction with NH 103A in Newbury, and follow Mountain Rd. 1.2 mi. to a woods road on the right just before Mountain Rd. crosses a bridge. Limited roadside parking is available here; do not block the woods road.

The blue-blazed trail follows the woods road, crossing Andrew Brook at 0.1 mi. and a tributary on a small bridge at 0.3 mi. At 0.5 mi. the trail bears right across Andrew Brook and follows it upstream. It climbs moderately, recrossing the brook at 1.0 mi. and 1.4 mi., finally reaching Lake Solitude at a point near some (illegal) campsites. The route follows the north shore of the pond and meets Monadnock–Sunapee Greenway, which enters on the left (south) and follows Solitude Trail uphill toward the summit of Mt. Sunapee. Even if you do not intend to visit the summit, you should not miss the views from White Ledge. To reach the outlook, follow Solitude Trail uphill for 0.2 mi. and then turn left across the ledges on an unmarked spur path.

For an alternate route, at the Greenway junction turn left and follow the Greenway south past Lake Solitude and along Sunapee Ridge, with occasional views. After crossing three humps on the ridge, at 1.5 mi. from Andrew Brook Trail the Greenway reaches a red-blazed spur leading 0.1 mi. left (east) to an open ledge with excellent views. Ascent along the ridge to this point is 250 ft. (rev. 250 ft.).

NEWBURY TRAIL (CHVTC; MAP 2: H5)

Cumulative from Lake View Ave. (1,150 ft.) to:	⤴⤵	↗	↻
Solitude Trail (2,580 ft.)	2.6 mi.	1,450 ft.	2:00
Mt. Sunapee summit (2,732 ft.) via Solitude Trail	3.5 mi.	1,850 ft. (rev. 250 ft.)	2:40

This orange-blazed trail ascends from the village of Newbury at the southern tip of Sunapee Lake to Solitude Trail at a point just above Lake Solitude. It is a segment of Trail 1 of Sunapee–Ragged–Kearsarge Greenway. Parking is very limited on the road just below the trailhead, so it is probably best to park in Newbury. (Possible parking locations include the town offices and post office; or check with the police department for a recommended location: 603-763-4104.) Follow the road that leaves NH 103 directly opposite the information booth (sign: "Newbury Hts."), and in less than 0.1 mi. take the second right, which is Lake View Ave. This leads in a short distance to the path, which is marked by a sign on the right side of the road. Mileages are given from the point where the trail leaves Lake View Ave.; distances from parking in Newbury are about 0.2 mi. longer each way.

Newbury Trail climbs steadily and at 0.4 mi. passes a red-blazed side path that leads to the right, crosses an attractive, ledgy brook in 80 yd. and and continues 0.2 mi. to Eagle's Nest, a ledgy outlook with a fine view across Sunapee Lake. Newbury Trail continues to climb at a moderate grade and then more steeply, turning right onto a relocated trail section at 0.8 mi. It angles up across the slope, crosses a ledge with a restricted view, and descends slightly to a junction at 1.1 mi. with Rim Trail.

At the junction, Newbury Trail turns sharply left and ascends steeply for 0.2 mi. to an outlook with a spectacular view north over Sunapee Lake. It turns right, climbs over several knolls, and turns right again onto the original route of the trail at 1.6 mi. The trail then follows a ridge, passing to the right of the south peak of Mt. Sunapee (2,620 ft.), and continues along a bumpy ridge crest with little change of elevation. At 2.6 mi. it meets Solitude Trail at Jack and June Junction, a short distance above the lake.

RIM TRAIL (SRKGC; MAP 2: H5–G5)

From cul-de-sac at end of paved road
(1,640 ft.) to: ⮏⮑ ⬈ ◷

Newbury Trail (2,090 ft.)	0.5 mi.	450 ft.	0:30

This yellow-blazed trail ascends from a cul-de-sac at the end of a 1.4-mi. paved road that leaves the east side of the main ski area access road 0.3 mi. from NH 103. The side road is sometimes gated, and hikers may have to walk all or part of it to reach the trail. Rim Trail enters the woods at a sign, immediately crosses Johnson Brook, and ascends steadily for 0.5 mi. on somewhat rough footing, at times in a streambed.

SUMMIT TRAIL (SRKGC; MAP 2: G5)

From ski area parking lot
(1,270 ft.) to: ⮏⮑ ⬈ ◷

Mt. Sunapee summit (2,732 ft.)	2.5 mi.	1,450 ft.	2:00

This trail provides an attractive, moderately graded route to the summit of Mt. Sunapee from the ski area parking lot. The upper part is a segment of Trail 1 of Sunapee–Ragged–Kearsarge Greenway. (*Note*: Future ski trail development may force relocations.) Reach the ski area by Sunapee Park Rd., which leads 0.8 mi. south from a traffic circle on NH 103 on the southwest side of Sunapee Lake. Walk to the far right (west) side of the parking lot, and follow a service road to the right of the Sunapee base lodge, between the New England Handicapped Sports building and the South Peak Learning Center. The road bears left in front of a chairlift, and in 200 yd. the red-blazed trail enters the woods on the right at the base of Lower Ridge ski trail (sign: "Hiking Trail to Summit").

Summit Trail crosses a footbridge over a small brook and parallels the ski trail for 125 yd. Then Summit Trail bears left and crosses the ski trail, reentering the woods higher up the slope. It climbs moderately through hardwoods to a T junction at 0.6 mi. Here, Summit Trail turns left, and a link in Sunapee–Ragged–Kearsarge Greenway (blazed in white) joins from the right.

(This link provides alternate access to Summit Trail. From the intersection of NH 103 and NH 103B in Newbury, drive 1.1 mi. west on NH 103, turn left onto Brook Rd., and in another 1.2 mi. turn left onto Old Province Rd. The trailhead [sign: "Province Trail"] is 0.5 mi. up on the right, with parking for several cars. The trail ascends an old woods road for 80 yd. and then turns right and runs nearly level, following a stone wall and the blue-blazed state park boundary, to the junction in 0.4 mi.)

From the junction, Summit Trail descends slightly for 0.1 mi. and then turns right onto an old woods road (bear left here on the descent). It ascends moderately, traverses a plateau through a beautiful spruce grove, crosses a small brook, and resumes the ascent. After crossing several more small brooks, the trail turns sharply left at 1.6 mi. and ascends the west slope of the mountain by switchbacks through birch and hardwood forest, then conifers. It passes an outlook west at 2.3 mi., and in another 0.1 mi. it bears right where a side path leads 40 yd. left to another outlook. After a fairly steep climb, the trail emerges on a grassy shelf on the south side of the summit lodge.

Descending, walk 50 yd. south across the lawn from the front of the summit lodge to the sign "Hiking Trail" at the edge of the woods.

GOSHEN TRAIL (NHDP; MAP 2: G5)

From Brook Rd. (1,350 ft.) to:	↕	↗	⟳
Mt. Sunapee summit (2,732 ft.)	2.6 mi.	1,400 ft.	2:00

Goshen Trail follows an old woods road once used to transport the materials to construct the summit lodge and provides an easy, if unexciting, route to the summit of Mt. Sunapee from the west. It begins in the town of Goshen, which is notable as the birthplace of John Gunnison, an early explorer of the West. (A town, a river, and a national forest in Colorado are named after him.) Follow NH 103 1.1 mi. west from the complicated traffic circle at the ski area entrance, and then take Brook Rd. (sign) south for 2.5 mi. to the point where the road makes a 90-degree turn to the right (west). At this corner, turn left onto a gravel road, where there is limited and rough roadside parking.

Walk up the gravel road across a bridge. Just after the road starts to climb, the blue-blazed trail turns left onto a gated gravel road with signs forbidding the use of motorized vehicles. At 0.7 mi. the trail enters a logged clearing and bears left, soon crossing a bridge over a brook and beginning to climb more seriously. At 1.4 mi. it passes to the right of a small gravel pit, and the path becomes much rougher, climbing to reach the ski trail used by Solitude Trail at 2.4 mi., just after passing a large boulder. For the summit, turn left and follow the left edge of the ski trail for 0.2 mi.; for Lake Solitude, turn right and enter the woods in 30 yd.

On the descent, the entrance to Goshen Trail is somewhat camouflaged, but once the trail is identified—it passes a light-blue-blazed beech tree and a large boulder after 40 yd.—it is unmistakable.

SECTION 2

CARDIGAN AND KEARSARGE REGION

SEC 2

INTRODUCTION

In the northern part of the hill country of western New Hampshire are a jumble of medium-size peaks south of the White Mtns. that generally do not group naturally into ranges. This area includes the highest and most impressive of these mountains, Mt. Cardigan (3,149 ft.), which with its subsidiary peaks supports the most extensive and interesting trail system in the region. Also included in this section of the guide is Mt. Kearsarge (2,935 ft.), only about 200 ft. lower than Cardigan and almost equally impressive due to its comparative isolation from other mountains and its relatively great rise from base to summit. Ragged Mtn. (2,287 ft.) and Bog Mtn. (1,785 ft.), two interesting smaller mountains in the neighborhood of Kearsarge, are crossed by Sunapee–Ragged–Kearsarge Greenway. The ledgy summits of Bald Knob (2,040 ft.) and Mt. Crosby (2,238 ft.) and other interesting features are reached by trails in Cockermouth Forest in Groton. Plymouth Mtn. (2,200 ft.), Cardigan's neighbor on the northeast side of Newfound Lake, has fine trails that are described here. Briefly described are trails in the Walter/Newton Natural Area in Plymouth, trails at New Hampshire Audubon's Paradise Point Wildlife Sanctuary on Newfound Lake, and trails to the open summit of Little Roundtop (1,006 ft.) in Slim Baker Conservation Area in Bristol. In New London are Morgan Hill (1,755 ft.), the town high point, and Clark Lookout (1,325 ft.), a short hike with a rewarding view over Lake Sunapee.

OVERNIGHT OPTIONS

AMC's Cardigan Lodge is open year-round and offers full service from late May through mid-October and on weekends January through March; self-service at other times. Also available are 20 primitive campsites located at the eastern base of the mountain, available for individuals, families, and groups, with tent platforms, a water source, and outhouses within walking distance; as well as Clark Brook backcountry group campsite (1.1 mi. from the lodge, capacity 24) and rustic and secluded High Cabin (2.2 mi. from the lodge, about 0.5 mi. below the summit, self-service, capacity 12 with bunk beds, roof, woodstove, propane cooktop, and composting toilet). As of 2019, Cardigan offers additional amenities for guests with autism. Advance reservations are required; for more information, visit outdoors.org/lodging, or call 603-466-2727. Crag Shelter is an open shelter (first come, first served, capacity 6) on Mowglis Trail, 1.1 mi. north of Mt. Cardigan's summit; it has no reliable water source.

Slim Baker Conservation Area offers the Slim Baker Lodge (near the trailhead parking area for Little Roundtop) and an Adirondack shelter (on the eastern side of Little Roundtop, 0.1 mi. below the summit) for overnight use (both for a fee, by reservation only). To inquire about staying at the shelter or lodge, email reservations@slimbaker.org or call 603-744-8094.

As with all sections in this book, unless otherwise noted, camping outside of these designated areas is not permitted.

SEC 2

SUGGESTED HIKES

■ Easy Hikes
LITTLE ROUNDTOP

LP via Worthen Trail and Stephens Trail	0.9 mi.	300 ft.	0:35

This small peak in Bristol offers excellent views from an outlook known as Inspiration Point near the summit. To begin, see Little Roundtop, p. 159.

WELTON FALLS

RT via Manning Trail from AMC's Cardigan Lodge	2.4 mi.	300 ft.	1:20

This scenic waterfall and gorge is easy to reach from the lodge, although there is a potentially difficult crossing of Fowler River along the route. To begin, see Manning Trail, p. 144.

MT. KEARSARGE

RT via Rollins Trail	1.2 mi.	350 ft.	0:45

This southern approach from the top of the Rollins State Park auto road follows a short but somewhat rough section of old carriage road to the bald summit, which features expansive views in all directions. To begin, see Rollins Trail, p. 179.

BOG MTN.

		🔁	🗠	⏱
RT via Bog Mtn. Trail		2.0 mi.	600 ft.	1:20

This route follows a segment of Sunapee–Ragged–Kearsarge Greenway to the summit of a small peak with several excellent ledge viewpoints. To begin, see Bog Mtn. Trail, p. 173.

BUTTERFIELD POND

		🔁	🗠	⏱
LP via orange-blazed trail		2.0 mi.	600 ft.	1:20

This small pond offers a backcountry feel away from civilization, with several viewpoints along the shore. To begin, see Orange Trail, p. 174.

■ Moderate Hikes
MT. KEARSARGE

		🔁	🗠	⏱
LP via Winslow Trail and Barlow Trail		2.7 mi.	1,100 ft.	1:55

This direct approach from Winslow State Park climbs steep and rough terrain to Kearsarge's open summit and excellent views, followed by a more gradual descent. To begin, see Winslow Trail, p. 176.

GOOSE POND AND LITTLE SUGARLOAF

		🔁	🗠	⏱
LP via Elwell Trail, Goose Pond Trail, and Pond Loop Trail	2.8 mi.	600 ft.	1:40

This trip starts with an easy and scenic loop around Goose Pond and then ascends to views over Newfound Lake from Little Sugarloaf. To begin, see Elwell Trail, p. 151.

PIKE'S PEAK

		🔁	🗠	⏱
RT via Sutherland Trail and Pike's Peak Spur	3.6 mi.	1,300 ft.	2:25

A moderate ascent leads to this open ledge outlook on the east side of Plymouth Mtn., with an excellent view northeast toward the White Mtns. To begin, see Sutherland Trail, p. 159.

ORANGE MTN.

RT via Holt Trail, Holt–Clark Cutoff, Vistamont Trail, and Skyland Trail	5.6 mi.	1,600 ft.	3:35

SEC 2

This southern spur of Mt. Cardigan offers both spectacular and serene views back to the primary peak and the surrounding countryside from various open ledges near the summit. To begin, see Holt Trail, p. 145.

RAGGED MTN., WEST TOP, OLD TOP, AND BALANCED ROCK

RT via Ragged Mtn. Trail	6.8 mi.	1,750 ft.	4:15

Part of Sunapee–Ragged–Kearsarge Greenway, a western approach reaches four viewpoints on this surprisingly rugged mountain. It also offers a round-trip hike to West Top and side trips to Old Top and the ledges just beyond Balanced Rock. To begin, see Ragged Mtn. Trail, p. 170.

MT. CARDIGAN

RT via West Ridge Trail	3.0 mi.	1,250 ft.	2:10

Many possible routes are available to climb central New Hampshire's finest peak and enjoy panoramic views from the bald summit. This approach is the shortest and most gradual, starting at Cardigan Mtn. State Park. To begin, see West Ridge Trail, p. 137.

LP via West Ridge Trail, Clark Trail, and South Ridge Trail	3.5 mi.	1,300 ft.	2:25

This variation on the route above includes a visit to the open ledge known as Rimrock, which offers spectacular views to the west toward Vermont. To begin, see West Ridge Trail, p. 137.

LP via Holt Trail, Holt–Clark Cutoff, Clark Trail, Mowglis Trail, and Manning Trail	5.7 mi.	1,900 ft.	3:50

This attractive loop over Mt. Cardigan and its northern subpeak, called Firescrew, offers abundant open ridge walking with extensive views in all directions. To begin, see Holt Trail, p. 145.

LP via Holt Trail, Holt-Clark Cutoff, Vistamont Trail, Skyland Trail, South Ridge Trail, Clark Trail, Mowglis Trail, and Manning Trail	7.8 mi.	2,300 ft.	5:05

This route extends the loop described above by including Orange Mtn. and Mt. Cardigan's bare South Peak, both of which provide excellent views. To begin, see Holt Trail, p. 145.

■ Strenuous Hikes
MT. CARDIGAN

OW via Elwell Trail, Mowglis Trail, Clark Trail, Holt–Clark Cutoff, and Holt Trail	15.2 mi.	4,760 ft.	10:00

This long trip requires a "car spot" (leaving a second car) and is suitable for experienced hikers only. It begins at Wellington State Park and ends at AMC's Cardigan Lodge. The remote backcountry trek follows quiet, lesser used trails north of Mt. Cardigan, with several viewpoints en route and excellent vistas on the ridge. To begin, see Elwell Trail, p. 151.

TRAIL DESCRIPTIONS

MT. CARDIGAN (3,149 FT.) AND VICINITY

The most outstanding mountain of west-central New Hampshire, Mt. Cardigan straddles two towns: Orange (near Canaan) and Alexandria (near Bristol). Excellent views are available from the steep-sided rock dome of Mt. Cardigan itself, as well as from South Peak (2,862 ft.) and from Firescrew (3,063 ft.), the north peak, named for a spiral of fire and smoke that rose from it during an 1855 blaze that denuded the upper slopes of the mountain. Though relatively low in elevation, Mt. Cardigan provides a great variety of terrain, from hardwood forests to the windswept summit. Its trails vary, going from gentle woods walks to easy West Ridge Trail (the easiest route up the mountain, and a traditional first "big mountain climb" for children) to tough Holt Trail, with upper ledges that constitute one of the more difficult scrambles among the regular hiking trails in New England. From the east, you can make a fine circuit by ascending Mt. Cardigan via Holt Trail, Holt–Clark Cutoff, and Clark Trail (or by taking the much more challenging Holt Trail all the way) and returning over Firescrew via Mowglis and Manning trails. From the west, you can make an excellent loop via West Ridge, Clark, and South Ridge trails.

The upper slopes of Mt. Cardigan and, to a lesser extent, Firescrew consist of bare ledges that are completely exposed to the weather. Some of them are quite steep. Use caution if the ledges are wet; they can be dangerous when snow or ice is present. If stormy weather is forecast, avoid the exposed areas. The summit of Mt. Cardigan, in particular, is no place to be caught during a thunderstorm.

In addition to the vistas from Mt. Cardigan, there are excellent views from several of the smaller mountains on the two long ridges that run east toward Newfound Lake. On the northeast ridge, Little Sugarloaf (997 ft.), Big Sugarloaf (1,374 ft.), and Bear Mtn. (1,844 ft.) are easy to reach and offer good views of the lake. Farther west along this ridge, there are viewpoints on spur ridges of Oregon Mtn. (2,246 ft.) and Mowglis Mtn. (2,370 ft.). (Although some sections are lightly used and obscure, Elwell Trail travels this ridge all the way from the edge of Newfound Lake to the north shoulder of Mt. Cardigan.) On the southeast ridge—traversed by Skyland Trail—Grafton Knob (2,201 ft.), Crane Mtn. (2,436 ft.), and especially Orange Mtn. (also known as Gilman Mtn., 2,684 ft.) offer interesting outlooks from various open ledges.

SEC 2

Most of the mountain is contained in the 5,000-acre Cardigan Mtn. State Forest. AMC's adjacent Cardigan Reservation occupies much of Shem Valley and portions of the east slopes of the mountain. The 1,200-acre reservation includes 50 mi. of hiking and backcountry ski trails.

AMC's Cardigan Lodge is the major eastern trailhead for Mt. Cardigan, with ample parking and a variety of possible loop hikes. Nearby Newfound Lake, with a major public beach at Wellington State Park, offers swimming, boating, and fishing. Two road approaches from Bristol are easily accessible from I-93 at Exit 23. Turn left (west) from NH 3A onto West Shore Rd. at the stone church at the foot of Newfound Lake. Continue straight on Cardigan Mtn. Rd. at 1.9 mi., bear right onto Fowler River Rd. at 3.1 mi., and turn left onto Brook Rd. at 6.3 mi. At 7.4 mi. from the church, turn right onto gravel Shem Valley Rd.; bear right at 7.5 mi. and continue to the lodge at 8.9 mi. An alternate route marked by small "AMC" arrow signs at intersections is slightly longer. To follow this route, bear left onto North Rd. at 3.1 mi. from the stone church, turn right onto Washburn Rd. at 4.0 mi., then right again onto Mt. Cardigan Rd. at 4.2 mi., reaching the junction of Brook Rd. (right, paved) and Shem Valley Rd. (straight ahead, gravel) at 7.9 mi. (the 7.4 mi. point on the other route), and the lodge at 9.4 mi. Shem Valley Rd. is plowed in winter but must be driven with great care.

Since 1987, maintainers have used a uniform system of blazing the Mt. Cardigan trails. Trails on the eastern slopes are blazed in yellow, those on the western slopes in orange, and those along the ridge crest in white. This can be helpful when choosing a trail for descent off the ridge. Note that on a few trails (such as Clark Trail, South Ridge Trail, and Skyland Trail), different blaze colors are used for different sections of the trail.

While many of the trails on Mt. Cardigan are heavily used and well beaten, others (noted in the individual descriptions) are lightly used, sparsely marked, and infrequently maintained. Such trails may be difficult to follow if not recently maintained in the early part of the season when a footway is not clearly established, or in the fall when covered by leaves. Although these trails are not recommended for the inexperienced, seasoned hikers can use them fairly readily. (*Note*: Carry a map and compass, keep track of your location on the map, and carefully follow any markings that do exist.) The main trails on Mt. Cardigan are covered by this book's *AMC Southern New Hampshire Trail Map* (Map 3: Mt. Cardigan) as well as the in-text Goose Pond–Sugarloaf map on p. 152; the mountain itself and some of the trails are shown on the USGS Mt. Cardigan quadrangle, with lesser amounts of outlying areas on the Newfound Lake, Grafton, and Danbury quadrangles.

Volunteer maintenance efforts at Mt. Cardigan include those by the Cardigan Highlanders Volunteer Trail Crew (cardiganhighlanders.com). AMC's Cardigan Volunteer Trail Crew also sponsors several work weekends each year. On some trails, the footway may be obscured by fast-growing vegetation during the summer months, particularly later in the season, when shrubs and berry bushes reach their maximum growth. Be alert and be prepared to return to your starting point if a trail is obscure or impassable. It would be wise to check with newenglandtrailconditions.com and Cardigan Lodge before attempting the less popular trails.

Mt. Cardigan forms the northern end of the Quabbin to Cardigan Initiative (Q2C), a major, long-term conservation project that involves more than 20 public and private partners, including AMC. Launched in 2003, the Q2C is a collaborative, landscape-scale effort to conserve a 100-mile span of highland in north-central Massachusetts and western New Hampshire. This 2 million-acre region stretches from the Quabbin Reservoir northward to Mt. Cardigan and the White Mountain National Forest and is bounded by the Connecticut River valley on the west and the Merrimack River valley on the east. It is one of the largest unfragmented and ecologically significant areas of forest in central New England.

WEST RIDGE TRAIL (CHVTC; MAP 3: D2–C4)

From Cardigan Mtn. State Park parking area (1,930 ft.) to:	⇅	↗	↺
Mt. Cardigan summit (3,149 ft.)	1.5 mi.	1,250 ft.	1:20

This is the main trail to Mt. Cardigan from the west, as well as the shortest and easiest route to the summit. From NH 118, 0.5 mi. north of Canaan, turn right (east) onto Orange Rd. at a large Cardigan Mtn. State Park sign. In 0.9 mi. stay left (straight) on Cardigan Mtn. Rd. Bear right 2.0 mi. from NH 118 and right again at 2.7 mi., shortly after crossing Orange Brook, staying on Cardigan Mtn. Rd. At 3.4 mi. turn left and continue to a parking area at 4.1 mi., where there are picnic tables and restrooms.

The well-beaten trail, blazed in orange, starts at a sign in the parking area. At 0.5 mi. South Ridge Trail diverges right with a sharp turn. West Ridge Trail climbs moderately, crosses a bridge over a small brook, and climbs some more to a junction with Skyland Trail on the right. It then crosses Cliff's Bridge at 1.1 mi. Shortly beyond that point, a branch path called Ranger Cabin Trail (marked by a cairn) leads to the right for 0.2 mi. to South Ridge Trail. West Ridge Trail—marked by cairns, paint on the rocks, and blaze boards—ascends the broad, open summit ledges and joins Clark Trail at a large cairn (signs) just below the summit.

Descending, follow white blazes southwest for 50 yd. to the junction with Clark Trail (sign) and bear right to stay on West Ridge Trail, following cairns and orange blazes.

SOUTH RIDGE TRAIL (CHVTC; MAP 3: D3–D4)

Cumulative from West Ridge Trail (2,250 ft.) to:	⮅	⬈	⟳
Skyland Trail at Rimrock (2,815 ft.)	0.7 mi.	590 ft.	0:40
Clark Trail (2,900 ft.)	1.3 mi.	700 ft. (rev. 50 ft.)	1:00
From Cardigan Mtn. State Park parking area (1,930 ft.) to:			
Starting point by complete loop over Mt. Cardigan summit via West Ridge, Clark, and South Ridge trails	3.5 mi.	1,300 ft.	2:25

This trail provides access to Mt. Cardigan, South Peak, and Rimrock and also makes possible a scenic loop in combination with West Ridge Trail. It is blazed in orange below Rimrock and white above. South Ridge Trail diverges right from West Ridge Trail 0.5 mi. from the state park parking area, crosses a brook, and climbs—steeply and roughly at times—to the open ledges of Rimrock, where there is a good view to the west. From there, it crosses Skyland Trail at 0.7 mi. (Descending, follow the left of two lines of cairns on the ledge below Rimrock.)

The trail, now blazed in white, continues across marked ledges, with good views of Mt. Cardigan ahead, and passes the open summit of South Peak on the right at 1.0 mi.; then it turns left and descends into the woods to the junction with Hurricane Gap Trail on the right. The trail dips to a col and then climbs to a T junction. Here, it turns sharply right (Ranger Cabin Trail leads left 0.2 mi. to West Ridge Trail) and continues across ledges to the warden's cabin and Clark Trail. To reach the summit of Mt. Cardigan, turn left onto Clark Trail and climb steeply over open ledges for 0.2 mi.

ORANGE COVE TRAIL (CHVTC; MAP 3: B3–A4, USGS MT. CARDIGAN QUAD)

From end of paved road (1,850 ft.) to:	⮅	⬈	⟳
Mowglis Trail (2,310 ft.)	1.6 mi.	450 ft.	1:00

This trail, a recently active gravel logging road (the old Groton–Orange highway) used as an access route, provides a relatively short approach from the west to Mowglis Trail, Crag Shelter, and the summit of Mt. Cardigan via the north ridge and Firescrew. Follow access directions above for West

Ridge Trail, but bear left onto New Colony Rd. 2.7 mi. from NH 118, immediately after crossing Orange Brook. Follow this road 1.3 mi. just past the end of the pavement and the state park boundary, and park on the right before the gate. (The last 0.2 mi. of this road was damaged by flooding in 2019 and as of this writing is not passable to the trailhead. The road is scheduled to be made passable by winter 2019 and will be repaired permanently in 2020.) The rough road has no sign but is easy to follow. It climbs gradually past a large beaver pond at 1.0 mi. to end at Mowglis Trail in a large clearing in the col between Firescrew and Cataloochee Mtn. Mowglis Trail continues straight ahead (northbound) on the old road to Groton and turns sharply right (southbound) onto a footpath to Firescrew and Mt. Cardigan.

SEC 2

MOWGLIS TRAIL
(CHVTC; MAP 3: A4–C4, USGS MT. CARDIGAN QUAD)

Cumulative from Sculptured Rocks Rd. (800 ft.) to:

	↕	↗	↻
Elwell Trail (2,450 ft.)	3.7 mi.	1,650 ft.	2:40
Firescrew summit (3,063 ft.)	5.1 mi.	2,300 ft. (rev. 50 ft.)	3:40
Mt. Cardigan summit (3,149 ft.)	5.7 mi.	2,550 ft. (rev. 150 ft.)	4:15

This trail provides access to Mt. Cardigan and Firescrew from the north. The northern 3.5 mi. follows logging roads with minimal markings through areas that may be actively logged; the southern 2.2 mi. is blazed and maintained. From the village of Hebron on the north end of Newfound Lake, drive west on Groton Rd. and then Sculptured Rocks Rd., following signs to Sculptured Rocks Natural Area. This geologic site on the Cockermouth River is an interesting glacial gorge with potholes and is a popular picnic spot with a good swimming hole. Continue 1.0 mi. farther on Sculptured Rocks Rd. (which becomes Province Rd.) to a point just beyond a green bridge over Atwell Brook.

Mowglis Trail (no sign, very limited parking) follows an old, rough dirt road from Groton to Orange (sign: "Orange Rd."), which leaves Sculptured Rocks Rd. on the left and follows Atwell Brook. The route ascends at a moderate grade for 1.4 mi. to a fork, where a newer logging road diverges left to a landing; the trail continues straight on the older road, which can be very muddy at times. The trail ascends through logged areas, bears right at a fork (blue blazes and Camp Mowglis wolf silhouette trail marker, the first trail markings along the route), and passes the state park boundary at 2.4 mi. It continues to a junction with Orange Cove Trail at 3.5 mi. in a large clearing in the col between Cilley's Cave and Cataloochee Mtn. Orange Cove Trail continues ahead on the road.

Mowglis Trail, from here on blazed in white, turns left (south) into the woods on a footpath (look for a white blaze on a tree beside an opening in the brush on the southeast side of the clearing) and climbs to a junction on the left with Elwell Trail at 3.7 mi. Just beyond, a spur trail (now abandoned) formerly led left 80 yd. to Cilley's Cave (a potentially dangerous spot). At 4.1 mi. a side path leads 0.1 mi. left to a fine view east at Hanging Rocks.

Mowglis Trail then ascends more steeply, and at 4.6 mi. passes Crag Shelter (an open shelter with no reliable water source; accommodates 6). It passes to the right of the shelter and climbs steeply to a ledgy area and a north outlook. Here, the trail turns sharply right and climbs to the summit of Firescrew at 5.1 mi., where it meets Manning Trail ascending from the left (east). Mowglis Trail then descends south across wide ledges deeply marked by glacial action and passes an unofficial and unblazed side trail on the left that descends 0.2 mi. and 200 ft. to Grotto Cave and a smaller boulder cave. The main trail continues south, ascending steeply over open ledges to the summit of Mt. Cardigan.

WELTON FALLS TRAIL (MAP 3: CARDIGAN AREA INSET MAP, USGS NEWFOUND LAKE QUAD)

From northern trailhead on Valley View Rd. (1,150 ft.) to:	⇅	↗	↻
Elwell Trail (1,630 ft.)	0.7 mi.	500 ft.	0:35

This trail (which actually does not go near Welton Falls) runs from a trailhead off Valley View Rd. in Hebron to Elwell Trail on the ridge crest. Parking is available at a log landing up a short driveway just east of the original, prelogged trailhead on Valley View Rd. For access to Welton Falls Trail, head southwest from the landing on a logging cut for about 20 yd.; look for a yellow-blazed tree and old corridor on the right. (Logging operations from 2015 to 2018 obliterated the former route of this trail south of Elwell Trail. Due to light use and the enormous amount of work required to build and maintain a sustainable route, that section of Welton Falls Trail should be considered abandoned.)

To reach the trailhead, take West Shore Rd. south from the village of Hebron and immediately turn right onto Hobart Hill Rd. At 0.7 mi. bear left on Valley View Rd. and follow it to the trail (sign) on the left at 1.6 mi., on a downhill curve to the right. Parking is available on a grassy shoulder on the right, across from the sign.

From the trailhead on Valley View Rd., yellow-blazed Welton Falls Trail climbs steeply up an embankment for 0.1 mi., offering a good view north at the top. It enters the woods, turns right in 35 yd., and descends gradually across an old woods road, two small brooks, and another woods road. It crosses another brook, ascends steeply, and at 0.3 mi. turns left onto another woods road and begins to climb steadily. At 0.5 mi., just after crossing another old road, the trail climbs across a power-line clearing; follow cairns carefully across this wide, brushy opening, which may be overgrown. The trail reenters the woods and ascends gradually to meet Elwell Trail (signs) in a brushy logged area at 0.7 mi. The junction with the abandoned southern section of Welton Falls Trail is an additional 0.6 mi. west on Elwell Trail.

OREGON MTN. TRAIL
(MAP 3: A6–A5, CARDIGAN AREA INSET MAP)

From eastern jct. with Elwell Trail (2,160 ft.) to:	⇅	↗	↻
Mowglis Mtn. summit and western jct. with Elwell Trail (2,370 ft.)	1.8 mi.	520 ft. (rev. 300 ft.)	1:10

This lightly used trail, obscure in places (though fairly well marked with yellow blazes), provides a ridge crest route between Elwell Trail near the south summit of Oregon Mtn. and Elwell Trail at the summit of Mowglis Mtn. It is not recommended for inexperienced hikers.

From its eastern junction with Elwell Trail (sign), Oregon Mtn. Trail descends over ledges and enters the woods, then climbs slightly across viewless ledges, passing just left of the north (true) summit of Oregon Mtn. It descends steeply to a col, where the footway is obscure, climbs over a viewless knob, and descends to a junction with Carter Gibbs Trail (sign) at 0.5 mi. Oregon Mtn. Trail now meanders along a shoulder, crosses a small brook, and climbs steeply. It crosses a ledge with a restricted view north and then eases, reaching the northeast knob of Mowglis Mtn. at 0.9 mi. The trail descends gradually through conifers, crosses a flat saddle, and ascends southwest at mostly easy grades to its western junction with Elwell Trail, a few yards east of the summit of Mowglis Mtn.

CARTER GIBBS TRAIL; MAP 3: A6, CARDIGAN AREA INSET MAP, USGS NEWFOUND LAKE QUAD)

Cumulative from Hardy Country Rd. (990 ft.) to:	⇅	↗	↻
Oregon Mtn. Trail (2,130 ft.)	2.1 mi.	1,150 ft.	1:35
Elwell Trail (1,930 ft.)	2.4 mi.	1,150 ft. (rev. 200 ft.)	1:45

This trail provides a northern approach to Elwell Trail between Oregon Mtn. and Mowglis Mtn. from a recently relocated trailhead. In its middle and upper sections it passes through several logged areas, where it must be followed with care. It is lightly used and not recommended for inexperienced hikers. To reach the trailhead, turn south onto Hardy Country Rd. from Sculptured Rocks Rd., 1.0 mi. west of its junction with Groton Rd. and North Groton Rd. in Groton. Drive 0.5 mi. up Hardy Country Rd. to a point where the road turns sharply left and becomes Spruce Ridge Rd. Carter Gibbs Trail (sign) starts on the right at this turn; there is parking space for several vehicles on the left, across the road from the trailhead. Additional parking is available in a small pull-off on the right, 20 yd. north of the trailhead.

The yellow-blazed trail runs briefly along the east side of Dane Brook and then crosses to the west side and ascends moderately well above the brook, crossing a tributary at 0.8 mi. At 1.0 mi. it leaves the woods to cross the edge of a recently logged area. Marked with small cairns, the path veers to the left and then reenters the woods; follow with care. The trail comes back near Dane Brook, crosses a logging road at 1.4 mi., and soon reaches the first of a series of cascades. At 1.7 mi. it swings left, crosses another logging road, then turns sharply right and climbs steadily to a four-way junction with Oregon Mtn. Trail at 2.1 mi. It then descends sharply, with a rope providing assistance over a steep, slippery ledge, to meet Elwell Trail, 0.2 mi. north of that trail's junction with the upper end of Old Dicey Rd.

OLD DICEY RD. (MAP 3: C7–A6, CARDIGAN AREA INSET MAP)

Cumulative from Welton Falls Rd. (1,000 ft.) to:	⭥	↗	○
Jct. with Back 80 Loop (1,400 ft.)	1.2 mi.	400 ft.	0:50
Jct. with Elwell Trail (1,860 ft.)	2.0 mi.	850 ft.	1:25

This trail follows a rough, eroded gravel road for much of its length. It can be a hot climb in summer and is not especially attractive, but it does make loop hikes possible with various connecting trails. To reach Old Dicey Rd.'s southern terminus at Welton Falls Rd., take the first route described above for Cardigan Lodge but bear right 6.3 mi. from the stone church and follow Welton Falls Rd. for another 1.2 mi. Where Cream Hill Rd. turns sharply right uphill, stop at that intersection and park on the left shoulder at the trailhead.

Follow minimally maintained Old Dicey Rd. straight ahead, crossing a bridge over a brook. At 0.3 mi. Manning Trail (no sign) diverges left on a cart track, while Old Dicey Rd. continues at easy to moderate grades to a clearing at 1.2 mi. Here, Back 80 Loop (sign) diverges left as Old Dicey Rd. swings right. Old Dicey Rd. climbs moderately up the gravel logging road, passing a spur that diverges right to a former wolf sanctuary, to a large clearing. At the upper end of the clearing, Old Dicey Rd. meets Elwell Trail at a T junction (sign); turn left (west) for Mowglis Mtn. and right (east) for Oregon Mtn.

SEC 2

BACK 80 LOOP (AMC; MAP 3: C5–B6)

From Old Dicey Rd. (1,400 ft.) to:	⇅	↗	○
Back 80 Trail (1,750 ft.)	0.8 mi.	350 ft.	0:35

This short yellow-blazed trail connects Old Dicey Rd. with Back 80 Trail and makes possible a circuit to Welton Falls from Cardigan Lodge. Where Old Dicey Rd. bears right 1.2 mi. from Welton Falls Rd., Back 80 Loop diverges left (sign) onto a woods road at a brushy clearing. It descends gradually for 0.1 mi. and then turns left onto another woods road and crosses an old bridge over a brook. After a short relocated section, it crosses Davis Brook above an attractive cascade and pool. The route climbs at easy to moderate grades, crosses another brook at 0.6 mi., crosses 93Z Ski Trail, and meets Back 80 Trail at a cellar hole.

BACK 80 TRAIL (AMC; MAP 3: C6–B4)

From Holt Trail (1,400 ft.) to:	⇅	↗	○
Elwell Trail (2,000 ft.)	2.4 mi.	600 ft.	1:30

This yellow-blazed trail diverges right from Holt Trail about 100 yd. west of Cardigan Lodge and follows an old logging road. At 0.3 mi. Short Circuit Ski Trail diverges right, and at 0.4 mi. Whitney Way Ski Trail diverges left. At 0.8 mi., where Allieway Ski Trail diverges left, Back 80 Trail turns sharply right and reaches a cellar hole and trail junction.

Back 80 Loop turns right here to Old Dicey Rd. Back 80 Trail bears left and follows a relocated section. It crosses 93Z Ski Trail at 1.0 mi. and then crosses two small brooks and a larger brook. The trail turns sharply left onto the old route at 1.4 mi. and runs along the yellow-blazed northern boundary of the Back 80 lot at the edge of a logged area. The trail soon skirts to the right of several beaver ponds and meadows; in this area it may be subject to periodic flooding and short relocations. At 1.8 mi., just after passing a junction with Duke's Link Ski Trail on the left, Back 80 Trail turns sharply right, crosses a brook, turns left, and skirts more beaver ponds and meadows, one of which offers a view of Firescrew. The trail then traverses a wooded slope with several minor ups and downs, enters Cardigan Mtn. State Forest, crosses a brook, and ends at Elwell Trail just south of the col between Mowglis Mtn. and Cilley's Cave.

A good viewpoint on Elwell Trail appears 0.4 mi. to the right (east) of this junction. To reach the summit of Mt. Cardigan, turn left onto Elwell Trail and ascend to the junction with Mowglis Trail.

MANNING TRAIL (AMC; MAP 3: C7–C4)

Cumulative from Old Dicey Rd. (1,050 ft.) to:	⬆⬇	↗	⟳
Cardigan Lodge (1,392 ft.)	1.5 mi.	400 ft. (rev. 50 ft.)	0:55
First open ledges (2,600 ft.)	3.2 mi.	1,600 ft.	2:25
Mowglis Trail near Firescrew summit (3,063 ft.)	4.0 mi.	2,050 ft.	3:15
From Cardigan Lodge (1,392 ft.) to:			
Mt. Cardigan summit (3,149 ft.) via Manning Trail and Mowglis Trail	3.1 mi.	1,900 ft. (rev. 150 ft.)	2:30

This trail was constructed by AMC as a memorial to the three Manning brothers—Robert, Charles, and Francis—who were killed by a train during a blizzard in 1924 while hiking on a section of railroad near Glencliff that was once frequently used as a shortcut between Dartmouth Outing Club trails. The lower part of the trail is easy and provides access to beautiful Welton Falls. The upper part of the trail is fairly steep and rough in places and crosses many open ledges on Firescrew, with fine views.

The trail (yellow blazes, no sign) leaves Old Dicey Rd. on the left (south) 0.3 mi. from Welton Falls Rd.; it is the second of two old roads, 90 yd. apart, that diverge left after crossing a bridge over a brook. It follows a cart path down to the Fowler River, crosses on stones, and enters Welton Falls Reservation (NHDP). Here, it continues to a deep, mossy ravine and the main falls. Many attractive falls and rapids, as well as spectacular potholes, lie above and below the main falls, which are at 0.3 mi. From Welton Falls, Manning Trail climbs and descends two small ridges. At 0.5 mi. it turns right, crosses the river on rocks (no bridge; difficult at high water), and climbs along a bank above the stream. It swings right at 1.1 mi., ascends to a plateau, where it crosses 93Z Ski Trail, and passes through a grove of spruces. The trail then descends through a picnic area to Cardigan Lodge at 1.5 mi. (To reach Manning Trail to Welton Falls from the lodge, ascend through the picnic area to the old road at the right of the outdoor fireplace.)

Manning Trail continues along the wide gravel road that leads west from the lodge parking area, coinciding with Holt Trail for 0.3 mi. and passing junctions with Back 80 Trail and a spur to a camping area, both on the right. Manning Trail then diverges right onto an older woods road (Holt Trail continues left on another woods road), soon passing a group camping area on the right. At 2.1 mi. it bears right off the woods road and begins a moderate ascent, crossing Allieway Ski Trail at 2.4 mi. After an easier section, the trail turns right and climbs, fairly steeply at times and with rough footing, crossing a ledge with a glimpse of Mt. Cardigan. It crosses a small brook, runs briefly in the brookbed, and at 3.2 mi. emerges on open ledges with fine views. From here, the trail climbs a steep and rough pitch through the woods (use caution in wet or icy conditions) and then continues steeply up more open ledges. At the top of the pitch, it swings right and follows cairns and paint markings across broad ledges, climbing at moderate and then easy grades to Mowglis Trail, just below the summit of Firescrew. A left turn onto Mowglis Trail leads to the summit of Mt. Cardigan.

HOLT TRAIL (AMC; MAP 3: C6–C4)

Cumulative from Cardigan Lodge (1,392 ft.) to:	⬇️⬆️	↗️	🕐
Grand Junction (1,750 ft.)	1.1 mi.	350 ft.	0:45
Mt. Cardigan summit (3,149 ft.)	2.2 mi.	1,750 ft.	2:00

This is the shortest but most difficult route from Cardigan Lodge to the summit of Mt. Cardigan. (*Caution*: The upper ledges are very steep, and the scramble up these ledges is much more difficult than on any other trail in this section and one of the most difficult in New England; it may be dangerous in wet or icy conditions.) Allow extra time for this challenging and strenuous climb, which is for experienced hikers only. It is not recommended for descent. The trail is named for Elizabeth Ford Holt, the founder of Camp Mowglis.

From Cardigan Lodge, yellow-blazed Holt Trail (coinciding here with Manning Trail) follows the wide gravel road that leads west from the parking area, passing junctions with Back 80 Trail and a camping area, both on the right, and then Nature Trail on the left. Manning Trail diverges right at 0.3 mi., while Holt Trail forks left onto a woods road. Nature Trail rejoins on the left at 0.4 mi., and Holt Trail continues on the woods road. It crosses the Croo Bridge over Bailey Brook at 0.8 mi. below a scenic

SEC 2

cascade and continues on a fairly rough and rocky footway past a restricted view of Elizabeth Holt Falls to Grand Junction. Here, yellow-blazed Holt–Clark Cutoff (Cathedral Forest Trail) diverges left, providing an easier ascent of Mt. Cardigan via Holt–Clark Cutoff and Clark Trail. Alexandria Ski Trail also diverges left here, and shortly beyond, Allieway Ski Trail diverges right. Holt Trail continues along Bailey Brook to a point directly under the summit and climbs steeply on a rocky path through woods. It emerges on open ledges and makes a rapid, very steep ascent, with several challenging scrambles, over marked ledges to the summit.

NATURE TRAIL (AMC; MAP 3: C6–C5)

From Manning Trail (1,400 ft.) to:	⇅	↗	⟳
Holt Trail (1,450 ft.)	0.4 mi.	50 ft.	0:15

This short yellow-blazed trail connects Manning and Holt Trails and offers pleasant walking beside Bailey Brook. It is an autism-aware trail that includes sensory-friendly activity stations and additional markers alerting hikers to what's coming up next on the route. Starting 0.1 mi. west of Cardigan Lodge, Nature Trail turns left off Manning Trail (sign) and passes through an area of campsites. It veers left at Site 10, crosses Bailey Brook on a footbridge, then turns right. The trail passes a junction at 0.1 mi. where Kimball Ski Trail (blue blazes) diverges left, then continues an easy ramble alongside the brook, climbing slightly. At 0.3 mi. it bears right at a fork where Bailey Brook Ski Trail (blue blazes) departs on the left, crosses the brook again on a footbridge, and ends at junction with Holt Trail at 0.4 mi.

HOLT–CLARK CUTOFF, AKA CATHEDRAL FOREST TRAIL (AMC; MAP 3: D5–D4)

From Holt Trail at Grand Junction (1,750 ft.) to:	⇅	↗	⟳
Clark Trail (2,250 ft.)	0.6 mi.	500 ft.	0:35
From Cardigan Lodge (1,392 ft.) to:			
Mt. Cardigan summit (3,149 ft.) via Holt Trail, Holt–Clark Cutoff, and Clark Trail	2.6 mi.	1,750 ft.	2:10

This yellow-blazed trail diverges left from Holt Trail at Grand Junction and ascends to Clark Trail in the Cathedral Forest, providing the easiest route to the summit of Mt. Cardigan from the east. About 100 yd. above the junction, Vistamont Trail branches left to Orange Mtn. Holt–Clark

Cutoff crosses a small brook, climbs past some large sugar maples, and then ascends moderately by switchbacks to Clark Trail.

CLARK TRAIL (AMC; MAP 3: D5–C4)

Cumulative from Woodland Trail (1,600 ft.) to:	↕	↗	⏱
Holt–Clark Cutoff (2,250 ft.)	1.1 mi.	650 ft.	0:50
Mt. Cardigan summit (3,149 ft.)	2.0 mi.	1,550 ft.	1:45

This yellow-blazed trail, which provides the upper part of the easiest route to Mt. Cardigan from the east, begins on Woodland Trail 1.2 mi. from Cardigan Lodge. Clark Trail continues straight ahead on a footpath at a point where Woodland Trail turns sharply left on the grassy road it has been following. Clark Trail passes an old cellar hole, enters the state reservation at a level grade in a beautiful forest, and then climbs steeply to cross Vistamont Trail at 0.8 mi.

The grade becomes easier, and Clark Trail reaches the Cathedral Forest, where Holt–Clark Cutoff (Cathedral Forest Trail) enters from the right at 1.1 mi. As Clark Trail continues a moderate ascent, Alexandria Ski Trail enters from the right near P.J. Ledge (views north and east) at 1.5 mi., and 30 yd. farther Hurricane Gap Trail leaves to the left. Clark Trail continues across a small brook and passes a side path on the left that leads to a spring and to AMC's High Cabin. It then climbs on ledges and through scrub and meets South Ridge Trail at 1.8 mi., at the warden's cabin. Up to this point Clark Trail is blazed in yellow; above here it is blazed in white. Turning right and now completely in the open, Clark Trail climbs steeply up marked ledges and joins West Ridge Trail at a large cairn with signs just below the summit.

Descending, follow the white blazes southwest for 50 yd. to the signed junction with West Ridge Trail, and bear left (south) toward a white-blazed wooden post.

HURRICANE GAP TRAIL (AMC; MAP 3: D4)

From Clark Trail (2,600 ft.) to:	↕	↗	⏱
South Ridge Trail (2,800 ft.)	0.4 mi.	200 ft.	0:20

This yellow-blazed trail leaves Clark Trail just above P.J. Ledge, passes an unsigned spur right to a spring, and then reaches AMC's High Cabin, where another spur leads right 60 yd. to the spring and 40 yd. farther to Clark Trail. Hurricane Gap Trail then climbs to South Ridge Trail at the height-of-land at 0.4 mi.

SEC 2

VISTAMONT TRAIL (AMC; MAP 3: D5–E4)

From Holt–Clark Cutoff (1,790 ft.) to:	⇅	↗	↻
Skyland Trail (2,650 ft.)	1.6 mi.	1,000 ft. (rev. 150 ft.)	1:20

This attractive trail connects Holt Trail with Skyland Trail at Orange Mtn. (also known as Gilman Mtn.) via Holt–Clark Cutoff. Blazed in yellow, it leaves Holt–Clark Cutoff (Cathedral Forest Trail) left about 100 yd. above Grand Junction. Vistamont Trail rises southeast, then southwest over a broad, low ridge, where it crosses Clark Trail at 0.6 mi. It drops to cross a branch of Clark Brook and then ascends steadily by switchbacks up the east spur of Orange Mtn. The grade eases at 1.4 mi., and the trail soon swings right (west) onto open ledges, where it is marked by cairns. It passes a good south outlook, dips slightly, and then climbs moderately on ledges and through scrub, with occasional views of Mt. Cardigan, to Skyland Trail 80 yd. southeast of the rocky summit, where there are fine views.

WOODLAND TRAIL (AMC; MAP 3: C6–E5, USGS GRAFTON QUAD)

Cumulative from Cardigan Lodge (1,392 ft.) to:	⇅	↗	↻
Beaver ponds (1,690 ft.)	2.1 mi.	350 ft. (rev. 50 ft.)	1:15
Skyland Trail (2,250 ft.)	3.3 mi.	900 ft.	2:05

This trail runs from Cardigan Lodge to Skyland Trail just northwest of the summit of Church Mtn., giving direct access from Cardigan Lodge to the interesting outlooks from the ledges along Skyland Trail. It is lightly used, and the upper section above the beaver ponds may be obscure and is not recommended for inexperienced hikers. The footing may be quite wet in the area around the beaver ponds. The route also crosses red-blazed and blue-blazed property lines several times; the trail itself is blazed in yellow.

Woodland Trail leaves the Cardigan Lodge parking lot at a sign. It passes to the left of the small pond on the lodge grounds, crosses a bridge over the outlet brook, and then passes two junctions with Nature Loop (0.5-mi. loop) on the left; between these junctions, Kimball Ski Trail diverges on the right. Woodland Trail continues through woods, with minor ups and downs, past the Brock Farm cellar hole, and turns right on a grassy logging road at 0.7 mi. (To the left, this road, formerly the lower part of Clark Trail, leads 0.5 mi. to Shem Valley Rd.) A new designated backcountry group tentsite with five platforms (available by reservation through AMC) is on the left at 1.0 mi. At 1.2 mi., where Clark Trail continues straight ahead on a footpath, Woodland Trail follows the grassy road as it swings left and descends to cross a brook and then a field with an abandoned trailer.

The trail climbs moderately and runs nearly level, with wet footing, to a large beaver pond complex on the left at 2.1 mi. From here, the trail, though generally well blazed in yellow, is harder to follow, and great care must be used. It swings right (west) along the edge of the ponds and then left to cross the inlet brook. The trail now doubles back to the east along the hillside above the ponds, swings to the south, and then meanders gradually up the slope, with several turns that must be carefully followed. It ascends to the left of a small brook for a time before crossing a blue-blazed boundary into the Mt. Cardigan State Forest. Woodland Trail then climbs steadily to end at Skyland Trail on the northwest shoulder of Church Mtn.

SEC 2

SKYLAND TRAIL (CHVTC; MAP 3: E4–D3, USGS GRAFTON QUAD)

Cumulative from Alexandria Four Corners (1,800 ft.) to:	⇅	↗	○
Woodland Trail (2,250 ft.)	1.3 mi.	600 ft. (rev. 150 ft.)	0:55
Orange Mtn. (2,684 ft.)	3.3 mi.	1,400 ft. (rev. 350 ft.)	2:20
South Ridge Trail at Rimrock (2,815 ft.)	4.4 mi.	1,790 ft. (rev. 250 ft.)	3:05
West Ridge Trail (2,650 ft.)	4.6 mi.	1,800 ft. (rev. 200 ft.)	3:10
Mt. Cardigan summit (3,149 ft.) via South Ridge Trail and Clark Trail	5.2 mi.	2,150 ft. (rev. 50 ft.)	3:40
From Cardigan Lodge (1,392 ft.) to:			
Mt. Cardigan summit (3,149 ft.) via Woodland Trail, Skyland Trail, South Ridge Trail, and Clark Trail	7.2 mi.	2,450 ft. (rev. 700 ft.)	4:50

This trail runs from Alexandria Four Corners to West Ridge Trail just below Cliff's Bridge. It follows the western and southern boundaries of Shem Valley, and over 4.5 mi. crosses five of the six peaks that extend south and southeast from Mt. Cardigan's summit. Blazed in white except for the last 0.2 mi. (blazed in orange), Skyland Trail is lightly used, particularly south of Orange Mtn., where it must be followed with great care. It is, however, a very scenic route, with several fine outlooks.

The trail starts at the crossroads known as Alexandria Four Corners. To reach the crossroads, begin at the junction of West Shore Rd. and Cardigan Mtn. Rd. on the southwest side of Newfound Lake, and drive west for 1.3 mi. on Cardigan Mtn. Rd. Then turn left onto North Rd. At 2.3 mi. turn right onto Washburn Rd. and follow it through the village of Alexandria, bearing left at a fork at 2.5 mi. and turning right at 3.2 mi., where the main road (Cass Mill Rd.) turns sharply left for Danbury. Follow Washburn Rd., which soon becomes gravel, for another 4.0 mi. to the crossroads. The best parking is here; do not block roads above.

The trail follows Knowles Hill Rd., which runs right (north) from the crossroads, and in 0.1 mi. bears left onto Church Hill Rd. (*Note*: These roads are marked with green street signs.) At 0.3 mi. the trail turns sharply left (arrow-shaped Skyland Trail sign on the right) on a short grassy road to a clearing; in 35 yd. there is another sign for Skyland Trail. The trail ascends moderately through woods to the edge of an open field. It climbs through woods again to a limited outlook near the wooded summit of Brown Mtn. (2,257 ft.) and then turns left and crosses a col to the east knob of Church Mtn. at 1.1 mi., where there is a ledge with a limited view. Skyland Trail continues over the flat, wooded summit of Church Mtn., passing a junction (right) at 1.3 mi. with Woodland Trail coming up from Cardigan Lodge.

The trail descends to a col and then climbs through two brushy clear-cuts with abundant berry growth (follow blazes and blaze posts with care) over Grafton Knob, with a view south from ledges. It dips to another col before making a steep climb up the south shoulder of Crane Mtn., circling around to the right of a large rock face. The route continues at easier grades over the summit of Crane Mtn. at 2.1 mi., crossing ledges with limited views near the top, and then descends across a ledge with a good outlook to Orange Mtn. and Mt. Cardigan. The trail drops rather steeply to a broad col, runs at easy grades across it, and then ascends the south shoulder of Orange Mtn. Along the shoulder, it crosses two large open ledges with excellent views: the first looks south and west, and the second looks southeast. Skyland Trail then ascends steadily to Orange Mtn. at 3.3 mi., where Vistamont Trail enters on the right just before an open ledge with fine views north and east, particularly of Mt. Cardigan and Firescrew.

From the ledge Skyland Trail swings left up to the summit (with an excellent outlook southwest from a ledge a short distance to the left) and then bears right across ledges with additional viewpoints. It descends steadily, with rather rough footing, to a broad col, runs nearly level for 0.2 mi., and then climbs fairly steeply to the open ledges of Rimrock (good view west) at 4.3 mi., where it crosses South Ridge Trail. Here, the blazing for Skyland Trail changes from white to orange. The trail descends along a ledge (follow the right of two lines of cairns), drops rather steeply, and soon enters West Ridge Trail just below Cliff's Bridge.

SKI TRAILS AT CARDIGAN LODGE

AMC maintains a number of ski trails in the woods around Cardigan Lodge, in addition to the hiking trails. A map available at the lodge shows most of these ski trails and their ratings, which range from novice cross-country to expert alpine terrain (on the ledges of Mt. Cardigan and Firescrew). Some of these trails were cut as alpine trails in the days before modern tows became common. (*Note*: Ski trails are not maintained for summer use, and hikers are requested not to use them at any time of the year.) For more on these ski trails, see *Best Backcountry Skiing in the Northeast*, by David Goodman (AMC Books).

SEC 2

SUGARLOAF RIDGE–GOOSE POND AND VICINITY

The summits of Little Sugarloaf (997 ft.) and Big Sugarloaf (1,374 ft.), which offer views of Newfound Lake as well as nearby Goose Pond, are now within the 418-acre Sugarloaf Ridge–Goose Pond Conservation Area, owned by Lakes Region Conservation Trust. A small network of trails makes possible a number of short loop hikes in this area; a map of these is available at lrct.org. The descriptions of these trails in this guide use the names on the LRCT map. The long-distance Elwell Trail, which runs from Newfound Lake to near Mt. Cardigan, begins within the LRCT property. Adjacent to this area is Bear Mtn. (1,847 ft.), reached by steep approaches via Elwell or Bear Mtn. trails.

ELWELL TRAIL (LRCT/CAMP PASQUANEY/AMC/CHVTC; CARDIGAN AREA MAP, AMC SUGARLOAF RIDGE–GOOSE POND MAP, MAP 3: A7–B4, LRCT MAP, USGS NEWFOUND LAKE AND MT. CARDIGAN QUADS)

Cumulative from parking area off West Shore Rd. (620 ft.) to:	⬇⬆	↗	⟳
Little Sugarloaf summit (997 ft.)	0.7 mi.	400 ft.	0:35
Sugarloaf summit (1,374 ft.)	1.7 mi.	950 ft. (rev. 200 ft.)	1:20
Bear Mtn. summit (1,844 ft.)	3.3 mi.	1,750 ft. (rev. 300 ft.)	2:30
Welton Falls Trail (1,630 ft.)	4.6 mi.	2,000 ft. (rev. 450 ft.)	3:20
Oregon Mtn. Trail, eastern jct. (2,150 ft.)	7.0 mi.	2,900 ft. (rev. 300 ft.)	4:55
Old Dicey Rd. (1,860 ft.)	7.5 mi.	2,900 ft. (rev. 300 ft.)	5:10
Mowglis Mtn. summit and Oregon Mtn. Trail, western jct. (2,370 ft.)	8.8 mi.	3,450 ft. (rev. 50 ft.)	6:10
Back 80 Trail (2,000 ft.)	9.8 mi.	3,500 ft. (rev. 370 ft.)	6:40
Mowglis Trail (2,450 ft.)	10.4 mi.	3,950 ft. (rev. 350 ft.)	7:10

Elwell Trail extends more than 10 mi. from Newfound Lake to Mowglis Trail at a junction 2.0 mi. north of Mt. Cardigan. It is named in honor of

SEC
2

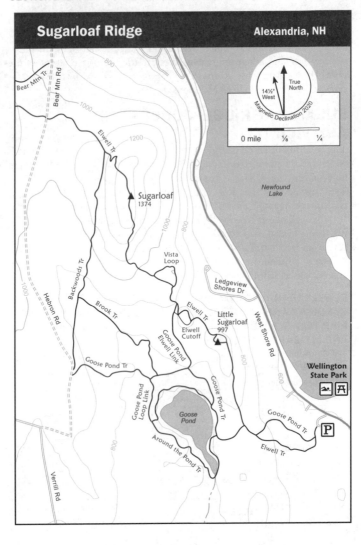

Sugarloaf Ridge

Alexandria, NH

True North

14½° West

Magnetic Declination 2020

0 mile   ⅛   ¼

Bear Mtn Tr

Bear Mtn Rd

Elwell Tr

800

1000

1200

1000

800

▲ Sugarloaf
1374

Newfound
Lake

Vista
Loop

Ledgeview
Shores Dr

Hebron Rd

Backwoods Tr

Brook Tr

Elwell Tr

Little
Sugarloaf
997

West Shore Rd

Elwell
Cutoff ▲

Goose Pond
Elwell Link

Goose Pond Tr

Goose Pond Tr

Wellington
State Park

Goose Pond
Loop Link

Goose
Pond

Goose Pond Tr

Around the Pond Tr

Elwell Tr

P

Verrill Rd

800

1000

Col. Alcott Farrar Elwell, who directed Camp Mowglis for 50 years and helped develop many of the trails in this region. It is marked with yellow blazes and Camp Mowglis signs, which are also often painted yellow. The lower (eastern) part of the trail, within Wellington State Park and the LRCT's Sugarloaf Ridge–Goose Pond Conservation Area, is fairly heavily used and provides easy access to scenic Goose Pond and fine views from Little Sugarloaf and Sugarloaf (also called Big Sugarloaf). For some time, the middle section of the trail (Bear Mtn. to the ridge east of Oregon Mtn.) received no regular maintenance and was badly overgrown and very difficult to follow. A few years ago, this section was recleared and reblazed by volunteers and crews from Camp Pasquaney. However, a major logging operation in 2016 heavily affected this section, making it once again difficult to follow through the brushy logged areas. This and some other sections of the trail are very lightly used, must be followed with great care, and are not recommended for inexperienced hikers. Additional logging operations could further disrupt parts of the middle section in the future; hikers intending to travel through this section should check with Cardigan Lodge for current conditions and should be prepared to navigate with map and compass.

Yellow-blazed Elwell Trail begins at a parking area (sign) off the west side of West Shore Rd., about 100 yd. north of the entrance to Wellington State Park; this is 2.9 mi. north of the junction of West Shore Rd. and NH 3A and 4.1 mi. south of the village of Hebron. Elwell Trail enters the woods at a kiosk, and in 60 yd. orange-blazed Goose Pond Trail diverges right at a sign listing trail mileages. Goose Pond Trail ascends to rejoin Elwell Trail in 0.3 mi. About 40 yd. past this junction, Elwell Trail turns right at a sign for Goose Pond and the Sugarloaves, crosses bog bridges over a muddy area, and climbs moderately. At 0.3 mi. from the trailhead along Elwell Trail, Goose Pond Trail rejoins from the right, and at 0.4 mi. it diverges left (sign: "Goose Pond"). Elwell Trail continues ahead and climbs easily through woods and then over semi-open ledges, where an alternate snowshoe route (sign) runs parallel to the main trail on the left. At 0.7 mi., as Elwell Trail swings left up a ledge to the flat, wooded summit of Little Sugarloaf, a side path to the right leads 20 yd. down to a ledge with an excellent view over Newfound Lake and a distant vista of the Franconia and Twin ranges. From the ledge a red-blazed bypass continues 75 yd., down and across the slope, and rejoins Elwell Trail on the north side of Little Sugarloaf.

At the 7.0 mi. point above, Elwell Trail runs across Little Sugarloaf's summit, descends past a glimpse of Sugarloaf ahead, and drops steeply to a col, turning sharply left where the red-blazed bypass rejoins on the right.

SEC 2

Elwell Trail then climbs and turns sharply right through a narrow rock crevice, where a lightly used, red-blazed alternate path continues ahead. Elwell Trail crosses the top of a minor knob and dips to another col. Just above the col, the red-blazed path (which skirts the west side of the knob) rejoins from the left. In a few steps a yellow-blazed connector on the left descends 30 yd. to an orange-blazed connector (named Goose Pond–Elwell Link by LRCT). The orange-blazed path descends 0.2 mi. left to Goose Pond Trail, making possible a loop that visits the pond. Elwell Trail descends another 75 yd. to the east end of the col at 1.1 mi., where it comes to a junction on the left with the upper end of Goose Pond–Elwell Link. From the col, Elwell Trail ascends 150 yd. to a junction with a red-blazed trail on the right (sign: "Rest Area Loop"; Vista Loop on LRCT map). This 0.2-mi. loop runs out to a spacious ledge with limited views and then swings left and returns to Elwell Trail. In another 150 yd. Elwell Trail passes the upper junction with Vista Loop and crosses a small brook and a minor shoulder.

The trail then climbs steeply up the south slope of Sugarloaf, passing a clifftop ledge 15 yd. to the right. (Use caution if descending to this viewpoint.) The grade soon eases, and at 1.6 mi. Elwell Trail passes a former junction with a white-blazed trail on the left; this trail has been closed due to severe erosion. Elwell Trail reaches the flat, ledgy summit of Sugarloaf, with a good view of Newfound Lake, at 1.7 mi. Beyond here, the path is less used but well blazed. After continuing at easy grades for about 100 yd., the trail descends moderately by switchbacks through a beautiful forest of hemlock and red pine. Then it drops steeply to a junction on the left with blue-blazed Backwoods Trail (sign for Goose Pond) at 1.9 mi. Here, Elwell Trail bears right and descends. At 2.2 mi. (sign: "Green Loop") it runs fairly level across Bear Mtn. Rd., a section of the old Alexandria–Hebron turnpike. (This rough, sometimes wet woods road may be followed 0.9 mi. left [south] to a junction with Backwoods Trail and Goose Pond Trail at an LRCT kiosk.) After passing through some sections that were relocated around wet areas and recent logging, Elwell Trail climbs by steep switchbacks, with rough footing, and passes a junction on the right with Bear Mtn. Trail at 2.8 mi., where the grade moderates. Soon the trail passes a good outlook over Newfound Lake and keeps climbing, steeply at times, to the summit of Bear Mtn. at 3.3 mi., where there is a restricted view. Elwell Trail continues along the ridge through logged areas (follow with care), swinging to the west and crossing several humps; then it descends and enters a wide power-line clearing at 4.4 mi. Here, the obscure and often overgrown footway is marked by cairns and blazed posts. The route runs 50 yd. through brush and then turns right onto a service road and follows it for 50 yd. It turns left off the service road and continues for another 70 yd. before it reenters the woods and proceeds through brushy logged areas, where it may be very difficult to follow. In another 0.1 mi. it reaches a signed junction on the right with the northern part of Welton Falls Trail (may be difficult to follow due to logging). Elwell Trail descends and then continues over the next two humps on the ridge. At 5.2 mi., in a spruce grove near the top of the second hump, the abandoned southern part of Welton Falls Trail (obliterated by logging) descends to the left.

SEC 2

Elwell Trail soon turns left, descends a steep pitch, and passes a junction where a snowmobile trail joins from the left. (In the reverse direction, bear left at this fork.) At 5.3 mi. Elwell Trail turns right off the snowmobile trail and continues along the ridge with several ups and downs, passing two partial views south at 5.6 mi. and crossing a skid road between two logging cuts at 6.0 mi. At 6.2 mi., at the top of a sharp ascent (with a short, steep scramble at the top), the trail emerges on a ledge on an eastern spur of Oregon Mtn. with a view east. It passes an outlook to the south in another 100 yd. At 6.7 mi. the trail climbs steeply out of a col to an extensive area of open ledge with views south, east, and north—the best outlook on upper Elwell Trail. (Coverage of Elwell Trail on Map 3 begins just east of this outlook.) The trail continues gradually up the ridge with occasional views until it reaches a fork with Oregon Mtn. Trail at 7.0 mi., which leads 0.2 mi. to the right to the south summit of Oregon Mtn. and rejoins Elwell Trail in another 1.6 mi.

From the fork, go left to remain on Elwell Trail, which descends gradually over ledges and then drops steeply to meet the upper end of Old Dicey Rd. at 7.5 mi., at the top of a large gravel log landing. In 50 yd. Elwell Trail swings left and descends briefly. In another 50 yd. it turns right onto a woods road and climbs gradually to a junction at 7.7 mi., where the south end of Carter Gibbs Trail continues straight ahead. Here, Elwell Trail enters a short relocated section and climbs gradually past logged areas with limited views to the summit of Mowglis Mtn. at 8.8 mi. Just before the summit, there is a boulder on the right with a tablet that honors Camp Mowglis. On the opposite side of the boulder is the junction with the western end of Oregon Mtn. Trail (sign).

Elwell Trail descends past more logged areas and then climbs to a knoll with a good view south at 9.4 mi. It swings right and descends again to a col at 9.8 mi., where Back 80 Trail diverges left for Cardigan Lodge. Elwell Trail then climbs fairly steeply by switchbacks to an abandoned spur trail leading left 130 yd. to Cilley's Cave (a potentially dangerous spot) and descends slightly to end at Mowglis Trail.

GOOSE POND TRAIL (LRCT; AMC SUGARLOAF RIDGE–GOOSE POND MAP, USGS NEWFOUND LAKE QUAD)

From lower jct. with Elwell Trail (750 ft.) to:	↓↑	↗	↺
Goose Pond (692 ft.)	0.2 mi.	0 ft. (rev. 50 ft.)	0:05
Upper jct. with Elwell Trail (890 ft.)	0.7 mi.	200 ft.	0:25

This orange-blazed loop trail from lower Elwell Trail provides easy access to scenic Goose Pond. It diverges left from Elwell Trail 0.4 mi. from the parking area off West Shore Rd. and follows a wide path down to Goose Pond, passing the south end of red-blazed Around the Pond Trail on the left at 0.1 mi. At 0.2 mi. a side path descends 15 yd. left to the shore. Goose Pond Trail soon passes the north end of Around the Pond Trail on the left, climbs along the slope above the pond, crosses a small brook, and ascends to a T junction at 0.4 mi. Here, it turns right onto a woods road (sign: "Sugarloaves") and runs at easy grades to the col south of Sugarloaf. As Goose Pond Trail enters the col, a yellow-blazed connecting path diverges right and climbs 30 yd. to Elwell Trail; turn right here for Little Sugarloaf. Goose Pond Trail continues 65 yd. ahead to meet Elwell Trail at the east end of the col; turn left here for Sugarloaf.

AROUND THE POND TRAIL (LRCT; AMC SUGARLOAF RIDGE– GOOSE POND MAP, USGS NEWFOUND LAKE QUAD)

From southern jct. with Goose Pond Trail (720 ft.) to:	↓↑	↗	↺
Northern jct. with Goose Pond Trail (720 ft.)	0.9 mi.	100 ft. (rev. 100 ft.)	0:30

This red-blazed trail loops around scenic Goose Pond, starting and ending on Goose Pond Trail. The south end of the loop leaves Goose Pond Trail 0.1 mi. west of that trail's southern junction with Elwell Trail. It descends to a spot on the shore with a view of Sugarloaf and then runs up and down above the east shore of the pond's southern arm. At 0.2 mi. the trail dips to cross the pond's outlet brook; then it swings right (north) and meanders up and down along the west side of the pond. At 0.4 mi. it joins a wide woods road and follows it for 0.2 mi. (blazing is sparse in this section). At 0.6 mi., after a short ascent, the trail turns right onto a spur road and descends 35 yd. to a point near the shore; to the right, beyond a clearing, is a good view of the pond. Here, Around the Pond Trail turns left and follows a footpath around the north side of the pond, crossing two inlet brooks at 0.7 mi. and ascending to rejoin Goose Pond Trail, 0.1 mi. north of the south end of the loop.

BROOK TRAIL (LRCT; AMC SUGARLOAF RIDGE–GOOSE POND MAP, LRCT MAP, USGS NEWFOUND LAKE QUAD)

From Goose Pond Trail (740 ft.) to:	�	↗	↻
Backwoods Trail (840 ft.)	0.5 mi.	100 ft.	0:20

This white-diamond-blazed trail ascends the valley of a small brook from Goose Pond Trail, 0.9 mi. from the West Shore Rd. parking area, to Backwoods Trail, 0.3 mi. north of its junction with Goose Pond Trail and 0.5 mi. south of its junction with Elwell Trail. Brook Trail diverges north from Goose Pond Trail a few yards east of a bridge over the brook. It follows a meandering route on a recently opened footpath, making two turns to the left and another to the right. Then it turns right again onto an old woods road and ascends gently to meet Backwoods Trail in a brushy meadow.

BACKWOODS TRAIL (LRCT; AMC SUGARLOAF RIDGE–GOOSE POND MAP, LRCT MAP, USGS NEWFOUND LAKE QUAD)

Cumulative from Goose Pond Trail (960 ft.) to:	�	↗	↻
Brook Trail (840 ft.)	0.3 mi.	0 ft. (rev. 100 ft.)	0:10
Elwell Trail (1,130 ft.)	0.8 mi.	350 ft. (rev. 50 ft.)	0:35

This blue-diamond-blazed trail leads north from the west end of Goose Pond Trail, at the junction with Hebron Rd. (a section of the old Alexandria–Hebron turnpike), to Elwell Trail on the northwest slope of Sugarloaf. It follows an old woods road that is wet and eroded in places. Backwoods Trail diverges right (northeast) off the old turnpike, 40 yd. north of the LRCT kiosk at the west end of Goose Pond Trail. It descends gradually and crosses a small brook at 0.3 mi. On the far side, it enters a brushy meadow where Brook Trail (white diamond blazes) diverges right. Backwoods Trail soon reenters the woods and ascends moderately. It crosses a knoll in a rocky area on the flank of Sugarloaf and descends to meet Elwell Trail 0.2 mi. north of the summit of Sugarloaf.

BEAR MTN. TRAIL (CAMP MOWGLIS; MAP 3: CARDIGAN AREA INSET MAP, USGS NEWFOUND LAKE QUAD)

Cumulative from Bear Mtn. Rd. (old Alexandria–Hebron turnpike) (900 ft.) to:	�	↗	↻
Elwell Trail (1,600 ft.)	0.5 mi.	700 ft.	0:35
Bear Mtn. (1,844 ft.) via Bear Mtn. Trail and Elwell Trail	1.0 mi.	950 ft.	0:55

This steep, rough, lightly used trail provides an alternate route up the steep eastern side of Bear Mtn. from Bear Mtn. Rd. (a section of the old Alexandria–Hebron turnpike) to Elwell Trail 0.5 mi. south of the summit of Bear Mtn. The ledges are slippery when wet. (This trail should not be confused with New Hampshire Audubon's Bear Mtn. Trail [NH Audubon sign; does not lead to the summit], which leaves directly from West Shore Rd. 1.5 mi. north of Bear Mtn. Rd. and climbs about 1.1 mi. up the northeastern slope of Bear Mtn., with 600 ft. elevation gain, offering limited views of Newfound Lake.)

To reach the trailhead, follow Bear Mtn. Rd., which leaves West Shore Rd. 2.0 mi. south of Hebron and 2.5 mi. north of Wellington State Park. After 0.3 mi., follow the gravel road to the left as the paved road swings right toward a housing development. Depending on driving conditions, it may be advisable to park at the gravel road and walk the rest of the way; there is ample parking space on the right at the start of the road. Drivers with high-clearance vehicles may be able to continue on the rough gravel road (the old Alexandria–Hebron turnpike) 0.6 mi. uphill to the trail (sign), which is on the right, 0.2 mi. below the junction of the road with Elwell Trail in the saddle between Sugarloaf and Bear Mtn. (*Note*: The gravel road was slightly improved in 2018 for a logging operation but has become somewhat rough again.) Limited parking is available just above the trailhead at a fork; do not block the gated road on the left. Additional parking is available in a pull-off on the left, 0.3 mi. before the trailhead.

The yellow-blazed trail enters the woods and soon follows a relocation by a small brook around a logged area; then it swings left and attacks the steep, rocky eastern slope of Bear Mtn., climbing steeply by longer then shorter switchbacks. It reaches Elwell Trail 0.5 mi. above Elwell Trail's junction with the old Alexandria–Hebron turnpike and 0.5 mi. below the main summit of Bear Mtn. The best outlook on Bear Mtn. is on Elwell Trail 0.1 mi. to the right (north) of this junction.

LITTLE ROUNDTOP (1,006 FT.)

This small mountain just outside the town center of Bristol offers excellent views north from an open area known as Inspiration Point. A small network of trails in the Slim Baker Conservation Area provides several options for easy loop hikes that include Inspiration Point. A trail map and descriptions are available at slimbaker.org. To inquire about staying at the hiker shelter or lodge, email reservations@slimbaker.org or call 603-744-8094.

To reach the trailhead parking area, take NH 3A south from its junction with NH 104 in downtown Bristol. In 0.1 mi. turn right onto High St., and in another 0.2 mi. turn right onto New Chester Mtn. Rd. and follow it 0.6 mi. uphill to the trailhead parking area on the right.

LITTLE ROUNDTOP TRAILS (SBFOE; SBFOE MAP)

SEC 2

Cumulative from New Chester Mtn. Rd. (830 ft.) to:	↥↧	↗	⟳
Inspiration Point via Worthen Trail (1,000 ft.)	0.2 mi.	170 ft.	0:10
Starting point via Worthen Trail and Stephens Trail	0.9 mi.	300 ft. (rev. 300 ft.)	0:35

This short loop provides access to Inspiration Point. Starting across the road from the trailhead kiosk, unblazed Worthen Trail, a fairly steep multiuse woods road, leads to the viewpoint. Here, a branch of red-blazed Stephens Trail leaves sharply right for a shorter 0.4-mi. loop option back to the trailhead. Bear right onto the southern section of Stephens Trail and descend steeply south off the summit. At 0.3 mi. turn right where yellow-blazed Greenan Trail diverges left past the hiker shelter. Stephens Trail descends into a ravine, where orange-blazed Cabin Trail diverges left at 0.5 mi.; Stephens Trail then swings right (north) and ascends 100 ft. to Slim Baker Lodge at 0.9 mi. Continue 150 yd. ahead on the road to return to the parking area. Other loops are possible using Greenan Trail or Cabin Trail and New Chester Mtn. Rd.

PLYMOUTH MTN. (2,200 FT.)

Plymouth Mtn. is in the town of Plymouth, northeast of Newfound Lake. The true summit is wooded, but nearby open ledges afford good views. The AMC Plymouth Mtn. map shows all of the trails listed in this section. Well-maintained Sutherland Trail provides an attractive approach from the north. Plymouth Mtn. Trail, an older route on private land, ascends from the end of Pike Hill Rd. to the west.

SUTHERLAND TRAIL (PCC; USGS ASHLAND QUAD)

Cumulative from Old Hebron Rd. (790 ft.) to:	↥↧	↗	⟳
Side path to Pike's Peak (2,100 ft.)	1.8 mi.	1,300 ft.	1:35
Plymouth Mtn. summit (2,200 ft.)	2.2 mi.	1,400 ft.	1:50

This trail from Plymouth, maintained by the Plymouth Conservation Commission, provides access to a knob locally called Pike's Peak, a ledge

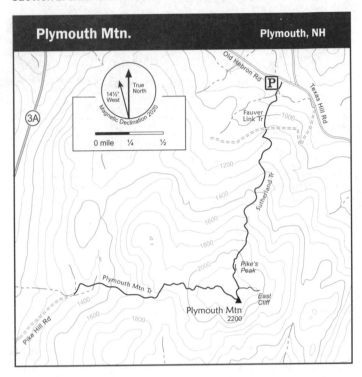

Plymouth Mtn.   **Plymouth, NH**

with an excellent view north and east. Between Pike's Peak and the Plymouth Mtn. summit, the trail is rough and somewhat obscure and requires care to follow, and the ledges in this section are very slippery when wet. From US 3/NH 25 at the south end of downtown Plymouth, take Warren St. for 0.2 mi. to a crossroads with four-way stop signs. Go through this intersection with a slight curve to the right onto Texas Hill Rd. At 2.5 mi. turn right onto Old Hebron Rd., where there is a boulder in the triangular island between the converging roads. The trailhead parking area is on the left at 2.6 mi.

The yellow-blazed trail leaves the south end of the parking area (sign: "Fauver Link Trail"), passes a kiosk, and in 100 yd. crosses a bridge over a small brook. It ascends moderately through Fauver Preserve (owned by the town of Plymouth), crossing a second brook (often dry) and bearing left before crossing an overgrown logging road at 0.4 mi.; look for a sign ("Sutherland Trail") and arrow on the far side of the road. In another 30 yd., Sutherland Trail joins its original route, which enters from the left. The land that the trail now passes through is protected by a conservation easement. The trail climbs moderately through hemlock woods, making a sharp turn to the left before it dips to cross an old logging road and continues upward. At 0.9 mi. it turns sharply right where a side path leads left 40 yd. to a rocky knob (no view). The trail climbs to a ridge crest, where in places it may be overgrown with brambles in summer, but it is well marked with blazes. It crosses a small brook at 1.4 mi. and then continues up the ridge, skirting to the right of a low rocky knob (please stay on the marked trail and off the revegetation area) to arrive at a trail junction (sign: "Pikes Peak" and double blaze) at 1.8 mi. The yellow-blazed side path to the left runs 100 yd. to an excellent outlook north to the White Mtns. and east to Squam Lake and the Ossipee Range.

Beyond this junction, Sutherland Trail is marked with new yellow plastic blazes, though it is still obscure in places. In 100 yd. it reaches the rough upper ledges of Plymouth Mtn., which are slippery when wet. The trail crosses numerous small rocky knobs; take great care to follow cairns and blazes as the route winds over and between ledges. At 2.0 mi., just after a scramble up a sharp-edged ledge, an unsigned and very obscure side path leads 0.2 mi. left to a good viewpoint from the East Cliff. (This path is suitable for experienced hikers only. Look for cairns just inside the start of the path.)

Sutherland Trail continues over more ledges, crossing one high rock knob and skirting to the right of another; both knobs provide views north and east. Near the second knob, the trail swings right and in another 50 yd. reaches the wooded summit ledge (benchmark and sign) at 2.2 mi. Descending, Sutherland Trail departs from the eastern side of the summit. (Avoid a path farther down that leads to the southwest and is posted against trespassing.)

PLYMOUTH MTN. TRAIL
(CAMP MOWGLIS; USGS HOLDERNESS QUAD)

From parking (1,290 ft.) to:	⇅	↗	↻
Plymouth Mtn. summit (2,193 ft.)	1.6 mi.	930 ft.	1:15

This lesser used western approach to Plymouth Mtn. was in a state of quasi-abandonment but has been receiving maintenance in recent years from trail crews from nearby Camp Mowglis. The trail still has some wet and muddy sections along its lower third but has been greatly improved overall. It leaves from the end of Pike Hill Rd. in Hebron, just west of the Plymouth town line. From I-93, take Exit 26 and follow NH 25 west for 3.9 mi. At the traffic circle, take the second exit onto NH 3A and drive 4.9 mi. Then turn left onto Pike Hill Rd. and continue 1.2 mi. to the junction with unsigned Wade Hill Rd. on the right, which is also a snowmobile trail junction. Parking is limited to only a couple of vehicles. Do not block the nearby private driveway or park in the pull-off across the street, which has been posted as no parking by the landowner. In winter, parking at this junction is not possible. The nearest parking spot is at a plowed pull-off 0.7 mi. from NH 3A, where Pike Hill Rd. officially becomes a Class VI (unmaintained) road. Parking here adds 0.5 mi. and 190 ft. elevation gain to the hike.

Plymouth Mtn. Trail provides a mostly easy ascent to the summit with a few short steeper sections. Footing is generally good, although rocky in places. The route is marked with Camp Mowglis' small wooden black-and-white signs featuring the image of a wolf. From parking, continue up Pike Hill Rd. for 0.1 mi. to where it continues ahead as a snowmobile trail and a private drive leaves left. (There is a sign here, "Plymouth Mtn. Trail," but it is high in a tree and hard to see.) The trail ascends easily along the muddy, eroded road and then bears right off it (signs) at 0.2 mi. onto a brushy old logging road. It dips slightly to cross George's Brook and then begins a steady climb, with rocky footing, at easy to moderate grades, crossing a small stream at 0.6 mi. At 0.8 mi. the trail reaches the height-of-land in a small saddle and swings left for an initially steep ascent that becomes easier. It soon enters a conifer forest, swings right, and meanders mostly level along a beautiful, wooded plateau (1,970 ft.). The trail then ascends at easy grades to reach the false summit at 1.4 mi. before descending over ledges to a low muddy spot. It then climbs gradually, with a short scramble up a rocky slot, and reaches the wooded but ledgy summit (sign) at 1.6 mi. Yellow-blazed Sutherland Trail continues straight ahead.

No signs are posted for the two major trails that leave the summit, and various beaten paths can cause some confusion. Plymouth Mtn. Trail leaves the west side of the summit and immediately bears right at a fork where an unmarked path diverges left.

WALTER/NEWTON NATURAL AREA

At the northeast base of Plymouth Mtn. is the town of Plymouth's 163-acre Walter/Newton Natural Area, with a trailhead on Cummings Hill Rd. 0.8 mi. from US 3. (Cummings Hill Rd. leaves the west side of US 3, 2.1 mi. south of the square in downtown Plymouth.) In addition to the

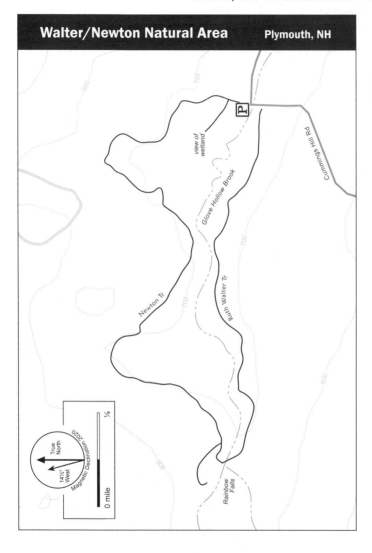

Walter/Newton Natural Area   Plymouth, NH

SEC
2

Cummings Hill Rd

view of wetland

Glove Hollow Brook

Newton Tr

Ruth Walter Tr

Rainbow Falls

True North

14½° West

Magnetic Declination 2020

⅛

0 mile

in-text map in this guide, refer to the USGS Ashland quadrangle. Hikers can make an easy 1.5-mi. loop to 30-ft. Rainbow Falls by following Ruth Walter Trail up the south side of Glove Hollow Brook and returning along Newton Trail on the north side of the brook. The trails pass scenic beaver wetlands, and a side path leads to the top of the falls.

PARADISE POINT WILDLIFE SANCTUARY

This scenic 43-acre property owned by New Hampshire Audubon is on a peninsula at the north end of Newfound Lake. Four trails are open from dawn to dusk year-round. A nature center is open in summer only, with varying hours. Reach the parking area via a short, steep driveway that leaves the south side of North Shore Rd. 1.0 mi. west of its junction with NH 3A. Make an attractive 1.3-mi. loop with 100-ft. elevation gain via Ridge, Lakeside, and Loop trails, with a short side path leading to the Point, a sloping ledge with a wide view of Newfound Lake and the mountains to the west. For more information, visit nhaudubon.org.

COCKERMOUTH FOREST

The 1,002-acre Cockermouth Forest, owned by SPNHF, is on the west slopes of Mt. Crosby in the town of Groton. A network of woods roads and trails provides access to several features, most notably the open summits of Mt. Crosby (2,238 ft.; within the small Mt. Crosby State Forest) and its southern spur, Bald Knob (2,040 ft.). Both summits offer fine views, though to the north and east those views now include a number of wind turbines on nearby Tenney Mtn. and Fletcher Mtn. Woods roads and trails on the western part of the property lead to Little Pond, surrounded by a 9-acre bog, and two ledgy outlooks (via Cliffs Loop).

The trails are marked and blazed in yellow and are signed at most junctions. Sections on old woods roads and recently used logging roads are easy to follow for most hikers. Other sections may show little evidence of a footway, but they are well marked and fairly easy to follow for experienced hikers. The trails are shown on the in-text map in this guide. Trail information and a trail map can also be found at forestsociety.org.

To reach the trailhead, follow North Shore Rd. west from NH 3A for 2.4 mi. to the village of Hebron at the north end of Newfound Lake. Continue straight ahead on Groton Rd. At 4.0 mi. bear right onto North Groton Rd. and follow it to a sign for Cockermouth Forest and John F. Woodhouse Trail on the right at 6.0 mi. Drive 0.1 mi. down the rough woods road in front of the sign and park on the left before a gate; do not block the gate.

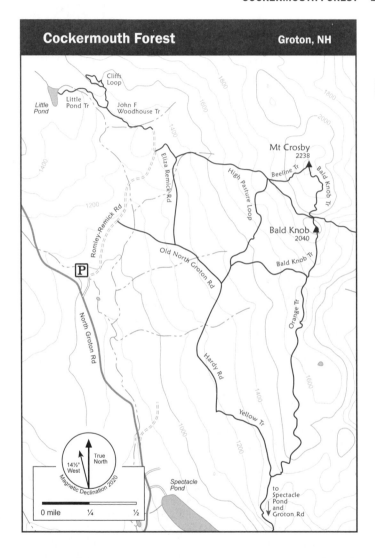

Cockermouth Forest

Groton, NH

SEC 2

Little Pond

Cliffs Loop

Little Pond Tr

John F Woodhouse Tr

Eliza Remick Rd

Romley-Remick Rd

P

North Groton Rd

Mt Crosby 2238

Beeline Tr

Bald Knob Tr

High Pasture Loop

Bald Knob 2040

Old North Groton Rd

Bald Knob Tr

Orange Tr

Hardy Rd

Yellow Tr

True North

14½° West

Magnetic Declination 2020

0 mile   ¼   ½

Spectacle Pond

to Spectacle Pond and Groton Rd

BALD KNOB AND MT. CROSBY TRAILS
(SPNHF; AMC COCKERMOUTH FOREST MAP, SPNHF MAP,
USGS NEWFOUND LAKE QUAD)

Cumulative from gate (970 ft.) via Romley-Remick Rd., Old North Groton Rd., High Pasture Loop, and Bald Knob Trail to:	⇵	↗	○
Bald Knob (2,040 ft.)	2.0 mi.	1,090 ft.	1:30
Mt. Crosby (2,238 ft.)	2.4 mi.	1,390 ft. (rev. 100 ft.)	1:55
Loop with descent via Beeline Trail, High Pasture Loop, Old North Groton Rd., and Romley-Remick Rd.	4.5 mi.	1,390 ft.	2:55

The principal route to Bald Knob and Mt. Crosby follows several newer and older woods roads as well as Bald Knob Trail. From the gate, follow Romley-Remick Rd., a wide gravel road, across a bridge over a brook. (Trail maps may be available at a kiosk beyond the bridge.) The road climbs easily to a junction at 0.4 mi., where the route to Bald Knob turns right onto grassy Old North Groton Rd. (sign). This road descends slightly to cross a footbridge over a brook at 0.5 mi., then ascends moderately, with logged areas on the left and stone walls lining both sides of the old road. At 0.8 mi. Eliza Remick Rd. (sign) diverges left, leading in 0.4 mi. to the old Remick homestead and a junction with the upper end of High Pasture Loop.

The route to Bald Knob continues to climb on Old North Groton Rd., crosses two small brooks, and then levels. At 1.1 mi. it turns left (sign) onto the lower end of High Pasture Loop, another woods road, at a point where Old North Groton Rd. begins to descend. At 1.2 mi. the route bears right off High Pasture Loop onto Bald Knob Trail (sign: "To Bald Knob") and climbs moderately on another woods road, with occasional wet footing, while swinging to the southeast. At 1.7 mi. Bald Knob Trail turns left off the road at a signed junction. Here, a new orange-blazed trail joins from the right, after ascending 3.2 mi. from Groton Rd. in Hebron through the Hebron Town Forest; its trailhead is on the north side of Groton Rd., 0.9 mi. west of the junction with West Shore Rd. and North Shore Rd. in Hebron. From the junction with the new trail, Bald Knob Trail climbs to the ridge crest on an obscure but well-blazed footway and then ascends steeply up the ridge to the north to the open ledges of Bald Knob at 2.0 mi. Various outlooks around the summit offer views of Newfound Lake, Mt. Cardigan, and the southern White Mtns.

From Bald Knob, the route to Mt. Crosby—marked with yellow blazes and old Camp Mowglis signs with the silhouette of a wolf—descends north over ledges and makes a short, steep drop to a col. Here, a yellow-blazed connecting trail diverges left and descends 0.3 mi. to High Pasture Loop, 0.6 mi. above that trail's junction with Old North Groton Rd. The main route to Mt. Crosby swings left for a short distance through the col and then turns right and climbs along the ridge, with occasional short descents. After crossing a ledge with a view east at 2.3 mi., the route reaches the summit at 2.4 mi., with views north and east, including many peaks in the White Mtns. Here, Beeline Trail (sign) diverges left and descends steeply for 0.3 mi. to High Pasture Loop, making several loop hikes possible.

SEC 2

LITTLE POND AND CLIFFS LOOP (SPNHF; AMC COCKERMOUTH FOREST MAP, SPNHF MAP, USGS NEWFOUND LAKE QUAD)

From gate (970 ft.) for round trip to:	⬇︎⬆︎	⬈	↻
Little Pond and ledge viewpoint via Romley-Remick Rd., John F. Woodhouse Trail, Little Pond spur, and Cliffs Loop	3.8 mi.	800 ft.	2:20

Trails on the western side of Cockermouth Forest provide access to a pond and bog and a ledgy viewpoint in the eco-reserve section of the property. From the trailhead, follow Romley-Remick Rd. as described in the Bald Knob and Mt. Crosby trip. At 0.4 mi., where Old North Groton Rd. diverges right, continue ahead on Romley-Remick Rd., which ascends moderately. At 0.6 mi. the road crosses a bridge over a brook with cascades on the left. After passing a log landing on the right, the road bears left at a fork at 0.9 mi. (yellow blazes and sign for Little Pond and Ledges Loop).

In another 0.1 mi., bear left on a grassy road at a sign for Little Pond, and 20 yd. after that, turn left onto John F. Woodhouse Trail, marked by a cairn. The trail soon crosses a brook and, just after crossing another brook, reaches a junction at 1.4 mi. Here, the spur trail to Little Pond diverges left and ascends along a small ridge to the right of the pond's ledgy outlet brook, passing small cascades. It crosses the brook near the outlet, climbs over a knoll, and ends at a ledge overlooking the pond and surrounding bog, 0.3 mi. from the junction. From the junction, Cliffs Loop (Ledges Loop on signs) bears right and climbs to the loop junction in 0.1 mi. Taking the right fork, Cliffs Loop, 0.3 mi. long, climbs steeply, with several twists and turns, and then swings left to a ledge with a view of Little Pond and Mt. Cardigan. The trail runs along the ledge, turns left where a side path leads 15 yd. ahead to another viewpoint, and descends past an overhanging ledge back to the loop junction.

HEBRON TOWN FOREST

This 458-acre parcel, owned by the town of Hebron and protected through a conservation easement held by the SPNHF, abuts the Cockermouth Forest to the north. From NH 3A in East Hebron, follow North Shore Rd. west for 2.4 mi. to Hebron. Continue straight onto Groton Rd. for 0.9 mi. to the trailhead and parking area on right. A map of the forest is available at hebronnh.org.

COCKERMOUTH LEDGE TRAIL (HCC; HEBRON TOWN FOREST MAP, USGS NEWFOUND LAKE QUAD)

Cumulative from parking area (600 ft.) to:	⇅	↗	○
Southern outlook (810 ft.)	0.7 mi.	210 ft.	0:25
Northern outlook (810 ft.)	1.1 mi.	240 ft.	0:40
Starting point via complete loop (600 ft.)	2.3 mi.	240 ft.	1:15

This loop trail (actually composed of two smaller loops) ascends to two open ledge outlooks with good views atop an 840-ft. knob. The yellow-blazed trail is also marked with maps at junctions. Watch markings carefully, as this trail makes something like a figure-eight loop and crosses itself a few times, which could be confusing for inexperienced hikers. Grades are easy to moderate, with a couple of steep sections, and the footing is generally good.

From the parking area, head north along a wide woods road to cross a bridge over Cockermouth River and arrive at the trailhead (sign) and a kiosk on the left at 0.1 mi. Trail maps and a guest register are available here. The trail turns sharply left off the road and descends slightly along the northern bank of the river to reach the first loop junction at 0.2 mi. Bear right at the junction (an arrow sign here points left in the direction of other end of loop) and begin a short but steep climb up an old woods road. Cockermouth Ledge Trail turns sharply right as grades ease and then becomes level to meet the first of two junctions with the second loop trail at 0.6 mi. Cockermouth Ledge Trail turns right at this first junction and immediately continues straight through the second junction just a few yards farther. It then climbs moderately up the side of a small ridge, turning left to meet the crest before continuing to the southern ledge outlook on the right at 0.7 mi., with views to Newfound Lake. Use caution here if the ledges are wet or icy as there is a significant dropoff.

The trail then swings northwest, ascends easily over the wooded high point of a bump, and then descends easily to bear right through two cairns at a fork. It emerges in an open, ledgy area. (Please stay on the trail in this area to avoid trampling fragile vegetation.) The trail ascends briefly over ledges to an open slab at 1.0 mi., where there is a restricted view. It turns sharply left here and then quickly turns left again down a sloping ledge at an easy-to-miss spot. Straight ahead, a spur path marked with small cairns descends 25 yd. to a northern ledge outlook with good views up the Cockermouth River valley. The main trail swings left (south) along a hairpin turn and descends back to the earlier fork marked by double cairns at 1.2 mi. It turns sharply right here, descends a steep pitch, continues moderately to a low spot, and then climbs easily back to a set of two junctions with the first loop trail. Cockermouth Ledge Trail turns right at the first junction and immediately continues straight through the second. The trail then curves left and makes a long, gradual descent, northwest at first and then turning southeast, to rejoin the river bank and first loop junction at 2.1 mi. Continue straight along the bank to the kiosk and then turn right to recross the river and return to the parking area at 2.3 mi.

SUNAPEE–RAGGED–KEARSARGE GREENWAY (SRKGC)

Sunapee–Ragged–Kearsarge Greenway (SRKG), a loop trail about 75 mi. long, connects these three major mountains in western Merrimack County. SRKG makes use of some previously existing trails as well as some newer ones on Mt. Kearsarge, Mt. Sunapee, and Ragged Mtn. Camping is not allowed anywhere along the Greenway. Most of the route is marked with white trapezoid blazes, both painted and plastic. Information about SRKG and about volunteer maintenance activities can be obtained from the Sunapee–Ragged–Kearsarge Greenway Coalition. The sections of the Greenway are divided by the SRKGC into 14 numbered segments running in a clockwise direction, starting and ending at the village of Newbury on NH 103 at the foot of Lake Sunapee. Space constraints prevent full and detailed coverage of SRKG in this guide; it is described in detail in the *SRKG Trail Guide*, 3rd edition (2015), available at srkg.com. The segments of the route on Ragged Mtn., Bog Mtn., and Mt. Kearsarge are described below; those on Mt. Sunapee are described in Section 1 of this guide.

RAGGED MTN. (2,287 FT.)

Ragged Mtn. is a sprawling ridge in the towns of Danbury and Andover with several summits of nearly equal elevation. A ledge on West Top, the west knob of East Peak, offers a sweeping vista to the south and west. Old Top (2,257 ft.), a spur of the eastern and highest summit, has a ledgy top with good views north. On the east side of East Peak is the Bulkhead

(1,850 ft.), an impressive cliff with wide views that is reachable by paths developed by Proctor Academy, an independent preparatory boarding school. On West Peak (2,225 ft.), Ragged Mtn. Ski Area offers views north. Trail 9 of the Sunapee–Ragged–Kearsarge Greenway traverses Ragged Mtn. from Andover on the southeast to Wilmot on the west.

RAGGED MTN. TRAIL (SRKGC; SRKG GUIDE, USGS ANDOVER QUAD)

Cumulative from parking lot at Proctor Academy (650 ft.) to:	⇅	⤴	↺
Balance Rock spur (2,050 ft.)	2.5 mi.	1,400 ft.	1:55
East Ridge Trail (2,170 ft.)	2.7 mi.	1,500 ft.	2:05
Ragged Mtn. Ski Area (2,225 ft.)	3.8 mi.	1,850 ft. (rev. 300 ft.)	2:50
New Canada Rd. (1,010 ft.)	6.5 mi.	1,900 ft. (rev. 1,250 ft.)	4:10

This route, well marked with white trapezoid blazes and in some places with white metal squares, uses a combination of logging and skid roads, previously existing hiking and cross-country ski trails, and newer segments of trail. The entire route is on private land. Signs at both trailheads designate it as Ragged Mtn. Trail, but signs along the ridge have the original name for that portion: Ridge Trail. Parts of this route pass through logged areas, where markings must be followed with care. Logging and ski trail construction may cause future disruption and even relocation of some trail sections; check srkg.com for updates. All in all, this trek is rougher and more strenuous than the distance and elevation figures indicate.

The southeast trailhead (from which an out-and-back trip is more appealing) uses the parking area for Farrell Field House of Proctor Academy on US 4 just west of the Andover town center. Turn north onto Field House Lane and bear left into the parking lot. The trail (sign) starts on a gravel driveway at the far left corner of the parking lot, below the tennis courts. Additional parking may be found near the playing fields on the south side of US 4. The west trailhead is on New Canada Rd., which leaves from the east side of US 4, 1.8 mi. north of its junction with NH 11 in Andover. Drive 0.9 mi. up New Canada Rd. and park on the left; the trail (sign) starts on the right at a gated logging road.

From the field house parking lot, the trail ascends 70 yd. up the gravel driveway and turns right onto an old road (a cross-country ski trail) at a yellow blaze. In another 125 yd. it bears right, and a path from the tennis courts joins from the left. At 0.3 mi. Ragged Mtn. Trail turns left off the road onto a white-blazed footpath just before the road descends to a wooden bridge. The trail climbs moderately, crosses a stone wall, and then eases. At 0.8 mi. it turns left onto a grassy road and rises at an easy grade, passing a private side path on the left at 1.1 mi. and crossing a bridge over a small brook at 1.5 mi. Another private path joins from the left, and the trail soon ascends to a stop sign that faces the opposite direction.

The trail then climbs an eroded section into a brushy logged area, going directly across a major logging road at 1.8 mi.; follow blazes carefully here. It continues up an old road, bearing left and then right on a relocated section at 1.9 mi. to bypass a badly eroded portion of the road. At 2.0 mi. the relocated trail turns left to rejoin the road. It soon swings left and climbs moderately, crosses a little col, and passes an obscure trail diverging left. It then ascends steadily to a junction at 2.5 mi., where a side path marked with metal disks diverges right (sign: "BAL RK"), leading 0.1 mi. to Balanced Rock, a boulder perched atop a hogback ledge. Here, the side path turns left (sign: "Bulkhead") and continues another 100 yd. across a ledge with restricted views, leading up to an open outcropping with a wide vista south and east.

From the junction with the Balanced Rock side path, Ragged Mtn. Trail/SRKG climbs to a junction at 2.7 mi. Here, a spur path, East Ridge Trail, diverges right, climbs over several ledgy knobs (including the mountain's highest summit, a wooded ledge a short distance to the right of the trail), and ends at open ledges on Old Top, where there are excellent views north. This lightly used spur is intermittently marked with cairns and metal squares; follow with care. Distance to Old Top: 0.4 mi., 100 ft. (rev. 50 ft.).

From the junction with East Ridge Trail, SRKG turns left (west) on a section signed as West Ridge Trail. It dips through a brushy col, runs over a knoll with new ski trail construction to the right, and at 2.8 mi. passes a side path that leads 30 yd. left to a ledge with a view south. In another 40 yd. a private trail (sign: "MT TR") comes in from the left. SRKG swings right and climbs to a ledge on the left at 2.9 mi. with an extensive vista south and west. In another 50 yd. it reaches its high point on West Top and then descends, negotiating two very steep pitches with poor footing, to a col at 3.3 mi. It then rises moderately, crossing a red-blazed boundary several times, and swings right to the cleared area at the top of Ragged Mtn. Ski Area at 3.8 mi. (In the reverse direction, SRKG enters the woods to the right of the ski patrol building, crossing under a power line.)

The trail now makes a horseshoe turn to the left behind a chairlift terminal and onto a grassy road that leads up toward a communications tower. (At this turn, descend a short distance right to the top of the ski trails for good views to the hills and mountains to the north.) The trail skirts the left side of the fenced tower enclosure and descends, crossing and recrossing a ski trail. It drops down a steep pitch to the base of a cliff, meanders over a

SEC
2

ledgy hump, and then swings left and descends to a ferny glade surrounded by high ledges at 4.4 mi. Here, the private Ash Trail continues down the ravine, while SRKG turns right to ascend a steep pitch to the crest of Buswell Ridge, a long southern spur.

The route descends along the ridge through spruce woods and over ledges, with occasional short ascents and limited views. At 4.8 mi. SRKG turns right at a ledge with a partial view. (For a better look at Mt. Kearsarge, descend the ledges 30 yd. to the left.) In another 0.2 mi. the trail drops steeply to a logged area and crosses a skid road twice. It continues down the ridge to a sign at 5.3 mi., where it turns right (west) to descend off the ridge. It enters another logged area and descends steadily on a potentially confusing network of logging roads, bearing left at 5.7 mi. Follow markings carefully through this area. SRKG continues down on logging roads, with two brook crossings, to a large logging yard at 6.3 mi. The trail crosses the yard to the far right corner, turns right onto a gravel road, and continues to New Canada Rd.

BULKHEAD TRAIL (SRKG GUIDE, USGS ANDOVER QUAD)

From Balanced Rock view ledge (2,050 ft.) to:	�	↗	⟳
The Bulkhead (1,850 ft.)	0.5 mi.	100 ft. (rev. 300 ft.)	0:20

From the view ledge beyond Balanced Rock, Bulkhead Trail, a rough and obscure path with little evident footway, suitable for experienced hikers only, leads down to the top of a cliff called the Bulkhead, where there are excellent views to the east. The trail is marked with yellow diamonds. It briefly continues across the ledges on a rough traverse, makes an obscure entry into the woods, and descends a steep, rugged pitch over broken rock. At 0.2 mi. from Balanced Rock, Bulkhead Trail turns left, ascends briefly, and then descends moderately to a small brook at 0.4 mi. It then climbs easily to a signed junction behind the Bulkhead. From here, a side path leads 35 yd. ahead to the clifftop.

THE BULKHEAD (1,850 FT.) AND MUD POND (USGS ANDOVER QUAD)

From Proctor Academy (650 ft.) to:	↕	↗	⟳
The Bulkhead, with side trip to Mud Pond (1,850 ft.)	2.4 mi.	1,300 ft. (rev. 100 ft.)	1:15

Hikers experienced in navigating obscure routes can follow this trip composed of Proctor Academy trails up to secluded Mud Pond and the scenic views from the Bulkhead. These trails are only occasionally marked and are lightly maintained.

From the Proctor Academy field house parking lot, follow SRKG/Ragged Mtn. Trail for 0.3 mi. and then turn right onto a wide, unmarked ski trail. At 0.6 mi. the main route turns left onto a wide woods road. It turns left again and leads 100 yd. to a junction at 1.2 mi. Here, an unmarked path descends 100 yd. left to the shore of Mud Pond.

From the junction, SKRG turns right onto an unmarked footpath and in 100 yd. turns left onto an overgrown but obvious road. The trail turns left at 1.5 mi. and continues ahead to a marked junction at 1.6 mi. where a side path turns right for a private cabin. The route now ascends easily, using or crossing several old skid roads, and swings left at 1.9 mi. It crosses two small brooks, climbs steadily, and then turns left at a junction at 2.3 mi. (sign in the reverse direction: "M. Pond"). From here, the trail ascends steeply to the Bulkhead viewpoint at 2.4 mi.

BOG MTN. (1,785 FT.)

This small mountain in the town of Wilmot, traversed by SRKG, provides excellent views from several ledges. Bog Mtn. Trail and Kimpton Brook Trail (which runs west from Stearns Rd. to NH 4A) form Trail 7 of SRKG. Refer to the USGS New London quadrangle.

BOG MTN. TRAIL
(SRKGC; SRKG GUIDE, USGS NEW LONDON QUAD)

Cumulative from Stearns Rd. (1,200 ft.) to:	⇅	↗	↻
Bog Mtn. summit (1,785 ft.)	1.0 mi.	600 ft.	0:50
Wilmot Public Library (900 ft.)	3.2 mi.	750 ft. (rev. 1,050 ft.)	2:00

The ascent from the west is considerably shorter, but the eastern approach has better parking. The east trailhead and parking is at the Wilmot Public Library in the village of Wilmot, on North Wilmot Rd. just off NH 4A. For the west trailhead, take NH 4A west from NH 11 for 4.8 mi. Turn right onto gravel Stearns Rd. and follow it for 0.7 mi. to where Bog Mtn. Trail begins on the right (sign). Parking for two cars is available on the west (left) side of the road just north of the trailhead. (Kimpton Brook Trail leaves the west side of the road at a sign 25 yd. north of the parking pull-off.)

From Stearns Rd., Bog Mtn. Trail climbs moderately through attractive woods, swinging left onto the ridge crest at 0.4 mi. and reaching an outlook ledge to the south at 0.6 mi. It continues to climb, winding on or near the ridge crest, until it scrambles up a broad, open ledge at 1.0 mi. with excellent views southwest. On the west side is a granite memorial bench. On the east side is a spur path (sign: "Overlook") that leads 70 yd. to a southeast outlook, including Mt. Kearsarge. Heading north from behind the ledge, a short side path leads over the true summit of Bog Mtn., marked by a cairn, and descends slightly to a cleared outlook with a view to Mt. Cardigan.

From the north end of the summit ledge, SRKG angles to the right into the woods and soon descends steeply, with several turns, through a grassy, ledgy oak forest. In this area the footway is indistinct in places (though well blazed with the white trapezoids of SRKG) and must be followed with care. At 1.4 mi. the trail turns right at a ledge with a view of Ragged Mtn. and Mt. Kearsarge and descends a very rocky section. At 1.6 mi. it turns left onto an old logging road, and the grade eases. The trail bears right at a fork at 1.9 mi., ascends easily for 250 yd., and then turns left off the road, passing through a stone wall. It descends for 0.1 mi. through a hemlock grove and then turns right and follows the contour of the slope, crossing a skid road at 2.4 mi. In another 0.1 mi. the trail turns right again and climbs alongside a stone wall; then it swings left and meanders through more stone walls and a wet area to the east trailhead (sign: "No Parking") on gravel Pinnacle Rd. at 2.8 mi. (On the lower section of the trail, follow markings carefully through recent logging.) Turn left and follow the road, bearing left at a fork. At 3.1 mi., turn right on paved North Wilmot Rd. and follow it 0.1 mi. to the parking area at the Wilmot Public Library on the right.

BUTTERFIELD POND

This small pond in Wilmot is also within the 6,675-acre Gile State Forest and offers a quiet backcountry feel. Access is via Gardner Memorial Wayside Park along NH 4A, 7.0 mi. north of its junction with US 4 in Andover. A loop trail around the pond offers several viewpoints and passes through areas of glacial boulders and small cliffs. Footing is generally good, but there are some rougher sections. Grades are mostly easy, with numerous ups and downs. Refer to the USGS New London quadrangle.

ORANGE TRAIL (NHDP/NHFG; USGS NEW LONDON QUAD)

Cumulative from Gardner Memorial Wayside Park (1,290 ft.) to:	⇅	↗	↻
Loop jct. (1,360 ft.)	0.5 mi.	90 ft.	0:15
Starting point via complete loop	1.8 mi.	180 ft. (rev. 180 ft.)	1:00

From Gardner Memorial Wayside Park, the unsigned but orange-blazed Orange Trail crosses a bridge over Kimpton Brook and ascends easily along an old woods road. At 0.1 mi. it turns right off the road onto a footpath and climbs easily over a minor ridge, passing a precariously placed glacial boulder on the left. The trail then descends to a loop junction at the shore of a pond at 0.5 mi. From this point the loop can be done in either direction, but it is described clockwise here.

Bearing left at the junction, Orange Trail runs at easy grades, with many minor ascents and descents, along the west side of the pond, reaching a small peninsula with a view on the right at 0.6 mi. It swings left at 0.7 mi. where an unmarked path continues ahead. Then it swings right along the base of some rock outcroppings and boulders. At 1.0 mi. the trail crosses the pond's inlet brook and swings to the south. It crosses the outlet brook at 1.2 mi., passes a view of the pond on the right, and then returns to the loop junction at 1.3 mi. Turn left for an easy 0.5-mi. walk back to the trailhead.

NEW LONDON CONSERVATION COMMISSION TRAILS

	⟳↕	⟋↗	◯
Clark Lookout Trail	0.4 mi.	100 ft.	0:15
Morgan Hill	0.8 mi.	170 ft. (rev. 170 ft.)	0:30

The New London Conservation Commission maintains a 26-mi. trail network offering hikes of varying length and difficulty, some of which connect to the Sunapee–Ragged–Kearsarge Greenway. Two of the hikes are briefly described below. Camping is not allowed along any of these trails without prior permission from the town, and fires are not permitted at any time. Dogs are welcome but must be under control at all times, per a town ordinance. The NLCC also offers a patch to hikers who complete all of the trails. Maps, trail descriptions, and more information are available at nl-nhcc.com. A large printed map of all the trails is also available for purchase at the New London town offices and the Tracy Memorial Library.

Clark Lookout Trail (NLCC). This route leads to the excellent Clark Lookout viewpoint (1,325 ft.) on a shoulder of Davis Hill that overlooks Lake Sunapee. The nearest public parking is at the Park & Ride lot on NH 103A, reached by Exit 12 off I-89. From the lot, cross NH 103A to the gate where the trail starts (signs), and ascend easily along a series of well-graded woods roads to the viewpoint. Return via the same route.

SEC 2

SEC 2

Morgan Hill (NLCC). Morgan Hill (1,755 ft.) is the highest point in New London. A combination of Kidder Trail, Morgan Hill Loop, and Morgan Hill Trail allow for a loop hike over the wooded summit. From downtown New London, take NH 114 north for 1.1 mi. Then turn right onto Morgan Hill Rd. and proceed 1.6 mi. to a small parking area for Kidder Trail on the left (this road becomes private at 1.4 mi., but hikers are welcome).

MT. KEARSARGE (2,935 FT.)

Mt. Kearsarge is a high, very prominent isolated mountain in Warner, Wilmot, Andover, and Salisbury. Its bare summit, topped by a fire tower (refurbished in 2019) and communications towers, offers magnificent vistas in all directions. On one seventeenth-century map the name appears as "Carasarga," but since the 1816 Carrigain map of New Hampshire "Kearsarge" has remained the accepted spelling. Winslow, Barlow, and Rollins trails and the upper part of Lincoln Trail are covered by the Mt. Kearsarge map included in this guide. The remainder of Lincoln Trail is covered by the *SRKG Trail Guide*. Refer to the USGS Andover quadrangle for the summit and most of the upper part of the mountain, and to the Warner, Bradford, and New London quadrangles for the lower slopes.

WINSLOW TRAIL (NHDP; AMC MT. KEARSARGE MAP)

From parking area, Winslow State Park (1,820 ft.) to:	⮃	⬈	↻
Mt. Kearsarge summit (2,935 ft.)	1.1 mi.	1,100 ft.	1:05

This trail, sometimes called Wilmot or Northside Trail, provides a direct route, steep and rough, from the north. Major improvements were made on this trail in 2013. From NH 11 between Wilmot Flat and Elkins, take Kearsarge Valley Rd. south for 1.5 mi. Turn left onto Kearsarge Mtn. Rd. at a sign for Winslow State Park, and follow the road uphill through several turns, passing a gate at 3.8 mi. Stop at the old Winslow House (caretaker's cabin, picnic area, water, and parking), 4.1 mi. from NH 11. Visitors pay an admission fee in season. (In winter, Kearsarge Mtn. Rd. is gated 0.7 mi. below the trailhead. Limited plowed parking is available outside the gate. Parking is not allowed along the south side of Kearsarge Mtn. Rd. or adjacent Twist Hill Rd., per posted signs; violators will be ticketed. Skiers and snowmobilers often use the access road; hikers should keep to the side.)

Winslow Trail starts from the upper end of the parking area to the left of a service garage, at the same point as Barlow Trail (kiosk). It is well beaten and marked with red paint. Winslow Trail crosses under power

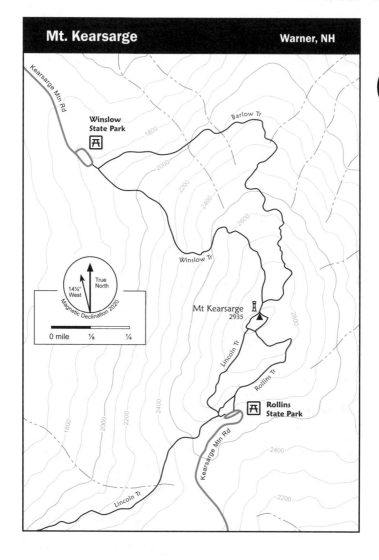

Mt. Kearsarge

Warner, NH

Kearsarge Mtn Rd

Winslow
State Park

Barlow Tr

1800

2000

2200

2400

2600

Winslow Tr

True North

14½°
West

Magnetic Declination 2020

0 mile   ⅛   ¼

Mt Kearsarge
2935

2800

Lincoln Tr

Rollins Tr

2400

Rollins
State Park

Kearsarge Mtn Rd

2400

2000

2200

1800

2200

Lincoln Tr

SEC
2

lines and climbs moderately to the foot of Halfway Rock, where it climbs more steeply. It then angles to the left, climbing moderately again past an outlook to the north, before turning south and ascending over increasingly bare ledges, marked with orange paint. Barlow Trail joins from the left about 100 yd. below the summit, and the two trails coincide as they ascend over ledges to the top.

BARLOW TRAIL (SRKGC/NHDP; AMC MT. KEARSARGE MAP)
From Winslow State Park parking area
(1,820 ft.) to:

	⇅	↗	↺
Mt. Kearsarge summit (2,935 ft.)	1.6 mi.	1,100 ft.	1:20

This yellow-blazed trail is a segment of Trail 11 of Sunapee–Ragged–Kearsarge Greenway. It provides a very scenic and gentler alternative to the steeper and rockier Winslow Trail, which leaves from the same parking area. Visitors pay an admission fee in season. Barlow Trail is particularly enjoyable for the descent of the mountain. (In winter, Kearsarge Mtn. Rd. is gated 0.7 mi. below the trailhead. Limited plowed parking is available outside the gate. Parking is not allowed along the south side of Kearsarge Mtn. Rd. or adjacent Twist Hill Rd., per posted signs; violators will be ticketed. Skiers and snowmobilers often use the access road; hikers should keep to the side.)

The trail leaves on the left at a kiosk just above the parking area, at the same place where Winslow Trail continues ahead. It crosses under the power line and runs nearly level for the first 0.1 mi. Then it angles up and across to the east, climbing at easy to moderate grades. It swings right (south) at 0.7 mi., entering a fine spruce forest, and continues up at a moderate grade over some viewless ledges. At 1.2 mi. a side path leads right 25 yd. to a northern outlook. Barlow Trail then turns sharply right onto a dramatic open ledge with a wide northern view and climbs to the top, reaching the end of the mountain's northeast shoulder at 1.4 mi. (For the descending hiker approaching this point, it appears for a short distance that one is about to step off the edge of the mountain—an exciting prospect.) The trail passes a small pond in a swampy area on the right; then it dips down on the south side of the ridge to pass a sharp, canyon-like formation on the ridge crest before wandering back to the north side of the ridge to join Winslow Trail (trail signs) on the open ledges 100 yd. below the summit. Barlow and Winslow trails coincide as they ascend open ledges to the top.

Descending, Barlow Trail diverges right 100 yd. below the summit at a sign and proceeds 40 yd. through scrub to another sign, where it emerges on ledges on the northeast shoulder.

ROLLINS TRAIL (NHDP; AMC MT. KEARSARGE MAP)

From Rollins State Park parking area (2,600 ft.) to:	⇅	⌁	○
Mt. Kearsarge summit (2,935 ft.)	0.6 mi.	350 ft.	0:30

This trail, sometimes called Warner or Southside Trail, provides the shortest route to the summit of Mt. Kearsarge. From NH 103 in Warner turn north onto Kearsarge Mtn. Rd. and follow signs 4.9 mi. to the tollgate at Rollins State Park. Visitors pay an admission fee in season (mid-May to mid-October; the gate is open from 9 A.M. to 4 P.M.). A picnic area includes tables, fireplaces, and water. From here, Kearsarge Mtn. Rd. mainly follows the route of an old carriage road along the crest of Mission Ridge and ends at a parking area 3.7 mi. above the tollgate. Toilets, picnic tables, and fireplaces are available here, but there is no water.

Rollins Trail (not blazed) follows the badly eroded old carriage road to a ledge with a fine view. The trail then swings left and rises to the foot of the summit ledges. Lincoln Trail (sign) enters from the left. Rollins Trail turns right and, now bearing Lincoln Trail's white blazes, climbs ledges to the south knob, continuing to the true summit and the fire tower. Descending, follow white arrows across the ledges of the south knob and down to the junction with Lincoln Trail at its base; here, Rollins Trail turns left and enters the woods (sign) to descend to the parking area.

LINCOLN TRAIL
(SRKGC/NHDP; AMC MT. KEARSARGE MAP, SRKG GUIDE)

Cumulative from Kearsarge Valley Rd. (850 ft.) to:	⇅	⌁	○
Top of wooded knob (1,650 ft.)	2.0 mi.	800 ft.	1:25
Connector to Rollins State Park parking area (2,600 ft.)	4.2 mi.	1,850 ft. (rev. 100 ft.)	3:00
Mt. Kearsarge summit (2,935 ft.)	4.6 mi.	2,200 ft.	3:25

This interesting and varied trail runs from Kearsarge Valley Rd. along a meandering route up the western ridge of Black Mtn. to the summit of Mt. Kearsarge, passing near the parking area at Rollins State Park. It is much less used than the other shorter, more popular trails from Winslow and Rollins state parks and provides a wilder, rougher experience than those heavily trodden routes. It may also be periodically affected by logging operations. It is a segment of Trail 11 of Sunapee–Ragged–Kearsarge Greenway and is well marked with white SRKG blazes. Lincoln Trail begins on Kearsarge Valley Rd. at a large turnout 0.4 mi. south of the golf course entrance and 0.4 mi. north of North Rd. It is signed initially as "Link Trail" because the original route of Lincoln Trail started at Kearsarge Regional High School off North Rd.—what was once a link to the main trail has become the official trail. Link Trail was heavily affected by a logging operation in 2018; follow newly placed white SRKG blazes carefully.

Lincoln Trail leaves the parking area, enters a large logged clearing, and ascends gradually on a winding route through an area of boulders and logging slash. At 0.4 mi. it turns right onto a snowmobile trail and then quickly left off it (arrows). At 0.5 mi. Lincoln Trail turns left uphill onto a gravel logging road and again coincides with a snowmobile trail (joining from the right at this junction is an alternate approach from the end of Mastin Rd., where there is limited parking). Lincoln Trail follows the logging road straight through a large clearing and at 1.5 mi. turns left onto an older woods road (trail sign), traveling uphill in company with the snowmobile route. At 2.0 mi. it reaches the top of a wooded knob and turns right where an obscure snowmobile spur (sign: "Baker's Ledge") leaves to the left. About 30 yd. after the right turn, Lincoln Trail enters a brushy clear-cut. The trail descends through the clear-cut, following white-blazed stakes, reenters the woods, crosses a saddle, and ascends easily. It then turns right and ascends steeply to a grassy knoll, where there is a glimpse of Mt. Cardigan to the north.

Here, the trail turns left and continues on a long section through fine hardwood forest. It crosses a small brook and climbs by alternately easy and moderate grades across the western shoulder of Black Mtn., a subsidiary peak on the southern flank of Mt. Kearsarge. The trail ascends moderately through an attractive birch grove, skirts a wet area on a boardwalk, and at 4.2 mi. reaches a short connector leading right to the western end of the upper parking area in Rollins State Park. (From the parking area, the heavily used and more gradual Rollins Trail provides an easier route to the summit.) Lincoln Trail soon turns left uphill and climbs steeply, emerging on a massive open ledge with wide views south. (*Caution:* This is a very steep, rough climb through talus and over ledges; use caution in wet or icy conditions.)

From here, the trail climbs at easy to moderate grades up a ledgy southwestern shoulder, with occasional views. At 4.6 mi. it reaches a junction at the foot of the south summit knob of Mt. Kearsarge, where Rollins Trail joins from the right. The trails coincide up the ledges of the south knob and across to the true summit and the fire tower. Descending, follow white arrows across the ledges of the south knob and down to the junction at its base. Here, Rollins Trail diverges left as Lincoln Trail (sign) continues ahead.

SECTION 3
THE MERRIMACK VALLEY

INTRODUCTION

The Merrimack River divides the southern part of New Hampshire nearly in half. For more than two centuries, this central artery has provided a route for transportation and travel and a supply of water power that helped establish the state's three largest cities: Manchester, Nashua, and Concord. The Merrimack was once said to "turn more spindles than any other river in the world"—a reference to the massive textile industry that spawned the mills in Manchester and Nashua, as well as in the Massachusetts cities of Haverhill, Lawrence, and Lowell. The extent of the river-powered industry is most noticeable to the casual visitor in the line of old brick mill buildings—now preserved as a historical landmark—that borders the Merrimack across from the Everett Turnpike in Manchester, below Amoskeag Falls. The falls themselves (now the site of a fishway educational center), along with the rapids below them, remain an impressive sight despite having been dammed for more than a century.

Although there are no high mountains in the Merrimack Valley, there are a number of hills and other features worth seeing, as well as myriad historical sites along the Merrimack River itself.

The largest hiking area covered in this section is 9,300-acre Bear Brook State Park, several miles east of the river, roughly midway between Concord and Manchester, and boasting more than 40 mi. of trails (not all described in this guide). Although views from the few low hills in the park are limited, the trail system offers many opportunities for short or extended woods walks that visit interesting wetlands and other natural features. Trails are also described on the Uncanoonuc Mtns. in Goffstown, Hooksett Pinnacle in Hooksett, Great Hill in Bow, Neville Peak in Epsom, and Oak Hill in Loudon and Concord. Also in Concord are Jerry Hill and Broken Ground, both part of the city's extensive 81-mi. trail network. Several of the many conservation areas managed by towns and nonprofit organizations are also briefly described here; these have trail systems—some of them quite extensive—and offer a variety of easier hikes and walks.

In addition, short walks with an emphasis on ecology and conservation are available at the state headquarters of New Hampshire Audubon (nhaudubon.org) and the Society for the Protection of New Hampshire Forests (Forest Society; forestsociety.org) and their respective trail systems, both in Concord. NHA headquarters, called the Susan N. McLane Audubon Center, is easily reached by following signs from I-89 at Exit 2. Turn left off the exit ramp onto Clinton St. and then turn right at the first blinking light onto Silk Farm Rd. The McLane Center is on the left. The principal trail is a 1.2-mi. loop that descends to the shore of Great Turkey Pond. SPNHF headquarters is on Portsmouth St., reached from I-93 at the east side of Exit 16 either by following East Side Dr. uphill to the right and then turning right onto Portsmouth St. (sign: "Conservation Center"), or by turning right onto Eastman St. and then sharply left onto Portsmouth St. at a small park. The main building, which incorporates a number of advanced energy conservation measures, is on top of a bluff overlooking the Merrimack River; the trails lie on the floodplain at the foot of the bluff. Loop hikes of 1.5 mi. or longer are possible.

SEC 3

OVERNIGHT OPTIONS

Bear Brook State Park, the largest of New Hampshire's developed state parks, features a 101-site campground (fee; reservations only), open late May through late October. For campground information, call 603-485-9869. For reservations, contact ReserveAmerica at reserveamerica.com or 877-647-2757.

As with all sections in this book, unless otherwise noted, camping outside of these designated areas is not permitted.

SUGGESTED HIKES

■ Easy Hikes
GREAT HILL

LP via Hamilton's Path, Great Hill Loop, and Walter's Way	1.2 mi.	140 ft.	0:40

An easy and gradual loop over Great Hill gives way to expansive northern views to the Lakes Region and the southern White Mtns. from the partly open summit. To begin, see Great Hill, p. 196.

NORTH UNCANOONUC MTN.

RT via White Dot Trail	1.4 mi.	750 ft.	1:05

A steady climb leads to this attractive, semi-open summit with several viewpoints. See White Dot Trail, p. 190.

JERRY HILL

	↻↑	↗	○
LP via Blue Loop, Yellow Trail, and Orange Trail	1.7 mi.	310 ft.	0:55

An easy loop over this summit, which once bore an observation tower, offers two vistas: one looking north over Penacook Lake to the Belknap Range and the other looking southwest toward Crotched Mtn. and Mt. Monadnock. To begin, see Blue Loop, p. 208.

HAYES MARSH

	↻↑	↗	○
LP via Lane Trail, Carr Ridge Trail, and Hayes Farm Trail	1.6 mi.	50 ft.	0:50

A pleasant loop within Bear Brook State Park follows a nearly level walk to scenic Hayes Marsh and through two fields. To begin, see Bear Brook State Park, p. 197.

CATAMOUNT HILL (SHORT LOOP)

	↻↑	↗	○
LP via One Mile Trail, Catamount Hill, and Shortcut Trail	2.0 mi.	350 ft.	1:10

An easy loop hike passes two scenic vistas on Catamount Hill within Bear Brook State Park. To begin, see Bear Brook State Park, p. 197.

BROKEN GROUND

	↻↑	↗	○
LP via Howard C. Nowell Trail	2.6 mi.	220 ft.	1:25

The longest loop through Broken Ground follows a mix of footpaths and old woods roads through beautiful forest that has remained undeveloped since the nineteenth century and past a large, scenic beaver pond. To begin, see Howard C. Nowell Trail, p. 211.

■ Moderate Hikes
SOUTH UNCANOONUC MTN.

	↻↑	↗	○
LP via Incline Trail, Walker Trail, and Summit Trail	2.2 mi.	750 ft.	1:30

A partial loop visits several open ledges with good views; add a short side trip for a western outlook. To begin, see South Ucanoonuc Mtn. Trails, p. 186.

PULPIT ROCK

LP via Kennard Trail, Tufts Trail, and Ravine Trail	2.7 mi.	300 ft.	1:30

Follow a rocky, cascading stream through a gorge to Pulpit Rock, an interesting formation. To begin, see Pulpit Rock Conservation Area, p. 191.

OAK HILL

RT via Tower Trail	4.0 mi.	530 ft.	2:30

This popular hike to a fire tower with good views climbs at easy to moderate grades. Make various interesting loop hikes with more views by using the extensive network of trails on the western slopes. To begin, see Tower Trail, p. 206.

NEVILLE PEAK

LP via Neville Ridge Scout Foot Trail and Neville Ridge Trail	3.1 mi.	580 ft.	1:50

This subpeak of Nottingham Mtn. features excellent views north to the White Mtns. from its ledgy summit. To begin, see Neville Ridge Scout Foot Trail, p. 203.

CATAMOUNT HILL (LONG LOOP)

LP via One Mile Trail, Catamount Trail, Cascade Trail, Carr Ridge Trail, Hayes Farm Trail, and Lane Trail	5.8 mi.	700 ft.	3:15

This loop visits some of the best scenery in Bear Brook State Park, including two ledges with views, a brook with cascades in a hemlock ravine, and scenic Hayes Marsh. To begin, see Bear Brook State Park, p. 197.

SEC 3

TRAIL DESCRIPTIONS

SOUTH UNCANOONUC MTN. (1,321 FT.) AND NORTH UNCANOONUC MTN. (1,328 FT.)

These two nearly symmetrical rounded hills in Goffstown are visible from many points in the Merrimack Valley. Over the years the Goffstown Conservation Commission has greatly expanded the trail system and opened new viewpoints, making the Uncanoonucs a more attractive destination. The trails are shown on the in-text map in this guide, and a trail map can be downloaded at goffstowntrails.com/pdf/Uncanoonuc-Trails-2017.pdf. Also, refer to the USGS Pinardville quadrangle. Most of the trails are on town conservation land and water precinct land. South Uncanoonuc Mtn., also known as South Mtn., supports what is probably the finest forest of communications towers in New Hampshire (the former fire tower has been removed), giving it a distinctively bristly appearance even from a considerable distance. A paved road leads to the heavily developed summit, and the actual high point is within a fenced-off area. However, trails on the slopes just below the summit area offer good views in many directions, and several loop hikes are possible. North Uncanoonuc Mtn., also known as North Mtn., is wooded and undeveloped; the summit area offers partial views. A connecting trail makes it possible to climb both mountains in a single hike.

South Uncanoonuc Mtn. Trails

To reach the primary trailhead for the trails on South Mtn., start from NH 114 0.6 mi. east of its junction with NH 13, and take Wallace Rd. south, immediately passing Goffstown High School. Turn right onto Mountain Base Rd. at 1.5 mi. from NH 114, and follow it 1.0 mi. to its end at the small town beach on Uncanoonuc Lake. A parking area and kiosk with trail map are behind the beach.

INCLINE TRAIL (GCC; GCC MAP)

From Mountain Base Rd. (660 ft.) to:	⇅	↗	↻
Gravel road near South Mtn. summit (1,260 ft.)	0.5 mi.	600 ft.	0:35

Incline Trail starts to the left of the trailhead kiosk and follows the grade of the former incline railway, which once carried fashionable tourists to the summit. It climbs steeply, with loose, rocky footing, following a small power line. At 0.4 mi. yellow-blazed Walker Trail diverges right, and Incline Trail ascends to its terminus at a private gravel road just below the

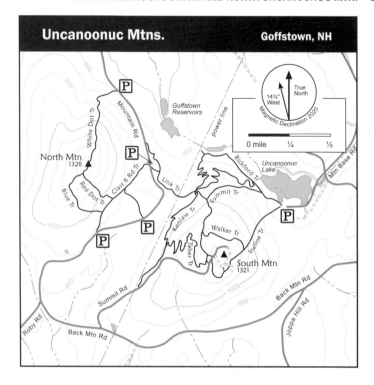

summit at 0.5 mi. Continue ahead (south) on the gravel road to reach the upper end of Summit Trail in 40 yd. (no sign), at a point where the gravel road turns sharply left and leads downhill to residences. The paved road that ascends to the right from the terminus of Incline Trail climbs 50 yd. to Perimeter Rd., which makes a 0.3-mi. loop around the summit area and its many communications towers.

WALKER TRAIL (GCC; GCC MAP)

From Incline Trail (1,140 ft.) to:	⇅	↗	◷
Summit Trail (1,180 ft.)	0.3 mi.	100 ft. (rev. 100 ft.)	0:10

Yellow-blazed Walker Trail diverges right from Incline Trail 0.4 mi. from the trailhead. It crosses two ledges with views toward Manchester, enters the woods and first ascends, then descends, passing a restricted view north to end at Summit Trail in 0.3 mi.

SUMMIT TRAIL (GCC; GCC MAP)

From Mountain Base Rd. (660 ft.) to:	⇅	↗	○
Dirt road near South Mtn. summit (1,310 ft.)	1.2 mi.	650 ft.	0:55

From the kiosk, red-blazed Summit Trail follows the road to the right for 0.1 mi. along Uncanoonuc Lake and then turns left into the woods at a sign for Summit and Bickford trails. At 0.2 mi. Bickford Trail diverges right; Summit Trail turns left and climbs moderately to the west to a junction at 0.6 mi., where Link Trail (sign) diverges right. At this junction, Summit Trail swings left (south) and climbs fairly steeply. It bears right at a fork at 0.8 mi., where Walker Trail diverges left. Summit Trail swings around the west side of the mountain, and at 0.9 mi. a spur (sign: "The View") diverges left and leads 100 yd. to a large opening with a good view west; from here, a lightly used path continues another 0.1 mi. to the northern outlook on Walker Trail. About 100 yd. past the junction with the view spur, Summit Trail crosses the paved summit access road. (To the left, it is 35 yd. up this road to Perimeter Rd., which makes a loop around the summit.) Summit Trail then travels through hardwoods around the south side of the mountain, reaching an opening with a view south, where the Boston skyline is visible on a clear day, at 1.1 mi. Just above the viewpoint, Summit Trail turns right onto an old gravel road and ends at a sharp turn on a private dirt road at 1.2 mi. To descend via Incline Trail, walk 40 yd. ahead on this dirt road and continue straight on the trail (no sign) where a paved road ascends left to Perimeter Rd.

BICKFORD TRAIL (GCC; GCC MAP)

From Mountain Base Rd. (660 ft.) to:	⇅	↗	○
Power-line clearing (640 ft.)	0.7 mi.	0 ft.	0:20

This blue-blazed trail diverges right from Summit Trail 0.2 mi. from the kiosk (sign). Bickford Trail ascends at easy grades to a junction with orange-blazed Scout Trail on the right at 0.3 mi. (Scout Trail, a short 0.3-mi. loop, descends steeply to a causeway at the northwest corner of Uncanoonuc Lake. It turns sharply left here [sign] and runs at easy grades along the edge of a beaver pond to rejoin Bickford Trail.) From the junction, Bickford Trail runs level and then descends easily to a second junction with Scout Trail on the right at 0.5 mi. Bickford Trail swings left here, climbs a moderate pitch, and then descends and ascends easily to a junction with unblazed Kenlaw Trail on the left at 0.6 mi. Bickford Trail swings right, descends, and ends at a power-line clearing at 0.7 mi.

LINK TRAIL (GCC; GCC MAP)
From Summit Trail
(970 ft.) to:

	↧↥	↗	↻
Mountain Rd. (720 ft.)	0.5 mi.	250 ft. (rev. 250 ft.)	0:15

This white-blazed trail provides a connection between the trails on South Mtn. and those on North Mtn. Departing from Summit Trail on South Mtn., it descends steadily, crosses under a power line, and continues down through a series of well-marked turns on and off various snowmobile trails. Link Trail ends in 0.5 mi. at a pull-off on Mountain Rd. across from the start of Class 6 Rd. Trail on North Mtn.

KENLAW TRAIL (GCC; GCC MAP)
From Bickford Trail
(670 ft.) to:

	↧↥	↗	↻
Summit Rd. (950 ft.)	1.5 mi.	380 ft. (rev. 100 ft.)	0:55

This unblazed trail, which traverses the quieter northwest side of South Mtn., connects Bickford Trail and Summit Rd., allowing for various loop hike options. Kenlaw Trail begins at the western end of Bickford Trail, 0.6 mi. from Mountain Base Rd. parking area. Kenlaw Trail switchbacks southwest at generally easy grades and passes through a four-way junction with Link Trail at 0.6 mi. It then bears right at a fork at 1.2 mi., where Taber Trail leaves left, before descending easily to meet Summit Rd. at 1.5 mi., where there is very limited roadside parking.

TABER TRAIL (GCC; GCC MAP)
From Kenlaw Trail
(1,050 ft.) to:

	↧↥	↗	↻
Summit Trail (1,270 ft.)	0.9 mi.	220 ft.	0:35

Taber Trail, formerly known as Mountain Trail, connects Kenlaw Trail and Summit Trail on the west side of the mountain. Taber Trail, which is unblazed, begins at a junction along Kenlaw Trail 0.3 mi. northeast from that trail's southern terminus at Summit Rd. From the junction, Taber Trail climbs moderately eastward by short switchbacks and then swings south and climbs more easily. At another series of short switchbacks, the trail again turns east, passing a junction with a spur path on the right at 0.7 mi. The spur path leads 100 yd. to Summit Rd. Taber Trail turns left and ascends gradually to end at a junction with Summit Trail at 0.9 mi.

North Uncanoonuc Mtn. Trails

Hikers can ascend North Mtn. from two trailheads on Mountain Rd., which runs through the col between North and South Mtns. To reach White Dot Trail, the traditional route to the summit, start from NH 114 in Goffstown, just east of the junction with NH 13, and follow Mountain Rd. south, bearing left at 0.9 mi. The trailhead is on the right at 1.4 mi., nearly opposite a small parking area.

The second main trailhead for North Mtn. is 0.5 mi. south of the White Dot Trail trailhead on Mountain Rd. Parking is available on the east side of the road, where Link Trail comes down from South Mtn.

WHITE DOT TRAIL (GCC; GCC MAP)

From Mountain Rd. (590 ft.) to:	⇅	↗	○
North Mtn. summit (1,328 ft.)	0.7 mi.	750 ft.	0:45

This trail leads directly to the summit of North Mtn. It is marked with white circles and white-painted can tops. White Dot Trail begins on private property; please stay on the marked trail and obey all posted signs. The trail climbs the bank above Mountain Rd. and soon passes through a stone wall and in front of a small cave. It climbs steeply through a fine hemlock forest, with some rough and rocky footing, and then moderates. It passes a very limited northern outlook at 0.5 mi. and approaches the summit through an oak forest, passing a side path that leads 25 yd. left and down to a partial view east. In another 75 yd., at 0.7 mi., the trail reaches the broad, grassy, and ledgy summit of North Mtn., where there is a view of South Mtn.

NORTH MTN., SHORT ROUTE (GCC; GCC MAP)

From Mountain Rd. (720 ft.) to:	⇅	↗	○
North Mtn. summit via Class 6 Rd. Trail and Red Dot Trail (1,328 ft.)	0.7 mi.	600 ft.	0:40

The shortest route to North Mtn. starts from the west side of Mountain Rd. on Class 6 Rd. Trail (sign), opposite the second parking area described above. Follow Class 6 Rd. Trail as it ascends along an old woods road, quickly bears left, and then takes the right branch at a fork at 0.2 mi. At a junction with Red Dot Trail at 0.3 mi., turn right onto Red Dot Trail, marked with red circles. This trail climbs rather steeply, bears left at a fork 0.6 mi. from Mountain Rd., and soon turns right onto a wide footway.

Follow the footway across a grassy plateau to the summit of North Mtn. at 0.7 mi.

NORTH MTN., LONG ROUTE (GCC; GCC MAP)

From Mountain Rd. (720 ft.) to:	⇅	↗	⟳
North Mtn. summit via Class 6 Rd. Trail, snowmobile trail, Blue Trail, and Red Dot Trail (1,328 ft.)	1.0 mi.	600 ft.	0:50

A longer route to the summit of North Mtn. starts from the same trailhead as above and follows Class 6 Rd. Trail for 0.1 mi. beyond its junction with Red Dot Trail. Here, the route turns right onto a snowmobile trail (sign: "North Mtn."), climbs an eroded pitch, bears right at a fork (from here on, it is shown as Blue Trail on the GCC trail map), and turns right at a four-way intersection, marked by three cairns, at 0.8 mi. Class 6 Rd. Trail then merges with Red Dot Trail, which joins from the right, and continues to the North Mtn. summit at 1.0 mi. from Mountain Rd. (600 ft. ascent). Descending, Red Dot and Blue trails coincide and lead south from the summit, and White Dot Trail leaves to the north.

PULPIT ROCK CONSERVATION AREA

The primary feature of this 338-acre reservation owned by the town of Bedford and managed by Bedford Land Trust (BLT) is the interesting rock formation known as Pulpit Rock (or the Pulpit), a gorge and large pothole that were carved by the swirling action of glacial meltwater at the end of the last ice age. A small network of trails provides walks in the range of 1.5 to 3.0 mi. A trail map can be downloaded at bedfordnh.org. Also, refer to the in-text AMC Pulpit Rock Conservation Area map or the USGS Pinardville quadrangle.

The trailhead is at a parking area on New Boston Rd. a few yards east of the Bedford–New Boston town line. A trail map is posted at the trailhead. From I-293 in Manchester, take NH 101 west to the traffic lights at its junction with NH 114, where NH 101 turns sharply left. Follow NH 114 straight ahead for 0.7 mi. Turn left onto New Boston Rd. at the next set of traffic lights. The trailhead is on the left in another 5.7 mi. From NH 101 in Amherst, at the Horace Greeley Birthplace historical marker, follow Horace Greeley Rd. for 1.2 mi. and then bear left onto Chestnut Hill Rd. At 4.2 mi. the road passes the New Boston Air Force Station and makes a sweeping turn to the right. The trailhead is on the right at 5.1 mi.

SEC 3

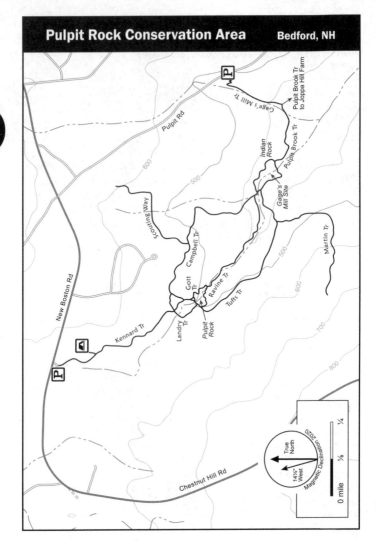

Pulpit Rock Conservation Area   Bedford, NH

PULPIT ROCK, SHORT WALK (TBCC/BLT; TBCC MAP)

From New Boston Rd.
(570 ft.) to:

	⇅	↗	○
Starting point by loop via Kennard Trail, Granite Trail, and Ravine Trail	1.5 mi.	200 ft. (rev. 200 ft.)	0:50

This short loop hike with three small brook crossings begins on white-blazed Kennard Trail, which follows a boardwalk through a swamp and travels through woods with minor ups and downs. At 0.4 mi. a spur leads 50 yd. right to a ledge overlooking a marsh. Kennard Trail soon passes a junction with Campbell Trail on the left and Blue (Landry) Trail on the right. After another junction, where a green-blazed woods road diverges sharply left, the path crosses a bridge over Pulpit Brook and reaches a kiosk at Pulpit Rock at 0.6 mi. Here, the route makes a short loop down through the gorge and pothole area, turning left onto yellow-blazed Granite (Gott) Trail and then right onto the upper part of rough, orange-blazed Ravine Trail, ascending to a junction with Tufts and Kennard trails; turn right to return to the parking area. (Because Granite Trail has generally better footing, it is recommended to descend Granite Trail and ascend Ravine Trail.)

PULPIT ROCK, LONG WALKS (TBCC/BLT; TBCC MAP)

From New Boston Rd.
(570 ft.) to:

	⇅	↗	○
Starting point by loop via Kennard Trail, Granite Trail, Tufts Trail, and Ravine Trail	2.7 mi.	300 ft. (rev. 300 ft.)	1:30
From New Boston Rd. (570 ft.) to:			
Starting point by loop via Kennard Trail, Granite Trail, Campbell Trail, and Ravine Trail	2.7 mi.	300 ft. (rev. 300 ft.)	1:30

The longer loops also start on Kennard Trail and then use either white-blazed Tufts Trail (on the west side of the brook) or red-blazed Campbell Trail (on the east side of the brook) to approach the south end of Ravine Trail. Ravine Trail leads back up the brook to Pulpit Rock. At the south end of the conservation area, the trails end at an old mill dam and pond. The distances indicated above include a trip from the parking area to the mill dam and back. Many old woods roads and beaten paths lie in the area, so carefully follow trail markings, which are mostly painted wooden squares or diamonds. (*Caution*: This is an excellent trip for small children, but supervise them closely in the vicinity of the potentially dangerous Pulpit Rock ledges.)

SEC
3

JOE ENGLISH RESERVATION

This 558-acre property owned by the town of Amherst has a color-coded trail network of more than 10 mi. that traverses varied, sometimes rough terrain. Most of the trails are reserved for foot travel only. Refer to the USGS Pinardville and New Boston quadrangles. The main access point is a parking area at the north end of Brook Rd. From NH 101, about 2.3 mi. north of the main exit for the Amherst town center, turn left (north) onto Horace Greeley Rd. In 0.4 mi. turn left onto Brook Rd. and follow it about 1.5 mi. to the trailhead. Alternate access to the reservation is from Chestnut Hill Rd. on the east. From the reservation, the town's Bicentennial Trail extends about 4 mi. south across conservation land and private land to its southern terminus on Dodge Rd. A trail map of Joe English Reservation is on the website for the Amherst Conservation Commission, amherstnh.gov. The Commission has also published maps and guides for over 25 mi. of trails on conservation land in the town.

BEAVER BROOK ASSOCIATION

Beaver Brook Association (BBA), an educational and land-stewardship nonprofit organization founded in 1964, now owns more than 2,000 acres of land in Hollis, Brookline, and Milford. Refer to the USGS Pepperell and Townsend quadrangles. More than 35 miles of trails—some designated as multiuse for hiking, mountain biking, and horseback riding, and others restricted to foot travel—are available for public use during daylight hours. No fee is charged for use of the trails, though donations are always welcome. The trails lead through generally easy forested terrain and pass numerous ponds and wetlands. Many loop hikes of various lengths are possible. Trail maps and other information about BBA lands are available at beaverbrook.org. Visitors to Hollis can stop at the BBA office (open Monday through Friday; 603-465-7787; info@beaverbrook.org) at Maple Hill Farm, 117 Ridge Rd., to obtain maps (small fee) and trail information. From Exit 6 off US 3 in Nashua, follow NH 130 about 6 mi. west (entering Hollis in 2.6 mi.), and then turn left (south) onto NH 122. In 1.0 mi. turn right onto Ridge Rd. At 1.0 mi. from NH 122, the office is on the right. Trailhead parking is available at the office and at several other locations around the property.

HOOKSETT PINNACLE (485 FT.)

This small but steep-sided prominent hill (also known as the Pinnacle) in the town of Hooksett rises abruptly from the west edge of the Merrimack River, just east of I-93. The summit monolith is composed of tough, erosion-resistant quartzite and offers interesting views of the river and nearby hills to the northeast. Henry David Thoreau, in *A Week on the Concord and Merrimack Rivers*, praises the view of the river from this little peak, commenting that the Pinnacle affords "a scene of rare beauty and completeness, which the traveler should take pains to behold." An imaginative modern visitor might be able to reconstruct the bucolic scene that Thoreau enjoyed from the Pinnacle's ledges. Refer to the USGS Manchester North quadrangle.

SEC 3

The former approach to the Pinnacle on private land from Ardon Dr. has been closed, and access is now via the town-owned Pinnacle Park. From I-93, Exit 11, follow Hackett Hill Rd. to NH 3A and turn left (north) onto NH 3A. In 0.7 mi. turn left (west) onto Pinnacle St. and follow it 0.1 mi. to a parking area (sign: "Pinnacle Park") on the right, just beyond the junction with Birch Hill Rd. on the left.

HOOKSETT PINNACLE TRAILS
(THCC; USGS MANCHESTER NORTH QUAD)

From parking area on Pinnacle St. (270 ft.) to:	↓↥	↗	↻
Hooksett Pinnacle summit (485 ft.) via main trail	0.5 mi.	215 ft.	0:20

Pinnacle Park contains many official and unofficial trails, with only one being signed and none being blazed. This can cause confusion because although many side paths connect official routes, others diverge toward surrounding private property. Follow the description below carefully to avoid wandering off-trail. A proposed new section of trail will allow for a longer loop hike option over the Pinnacle in the future.

The main route to the summit follows segments of an old carriage road and footpaths and starts near a sign displaying the park regulations. In 45 yd. it bears left and ascends easily, turning left again at 0.1 mi. at a junction marked by a summit sign. In 50 yd. the route continues ahead where Switchback Trail (a lightly used alternate route 125 yd. long) diverges right before looping back to rejoin the main trail. The main trail, meanwhile, climbs a short, steep pitch to the crest of a ridge and a four-way junction, where an alternate side path turns left (this path can be used for a loop descent) and ascends moderately up the ridge. Switchback Trail comes in on the right. The main trail continues straight and descends to a gate on the right (sign: "Summit") at 0.2 mi. It turns left here and ascends moderately up a section of the carriage road by two short switchbacks. At the second switchback, at 0.4 mi., the alternate side path comes in from the left. The main trail swings right and ascends easily, skirting the west side of the Pinnacle. Then it turns sharply left (here, a beaten path diverges right and descends slightly for 45 yd. to an open ledge with good views south) and reaches the rocky summit at 0.5 mi. Embedded in the summit ledges are iron remnants from an observation tower that stood at this spot from 1892 to 1923 and provided panoramic views.

GREAT HILL (875 FT.)

Great Hill, within Nottingcook Forest in Bow, offers wide views north toward the White Mtns. from its open, grassy summit, which has been cleared as a result of logging. On clear days, visitors can see the Sandwich Range, Franconia Ridge, and Mt. Washington. To reach the trailhead, take Exit 1 off I-89 and follow Logging Hill Rd. south. Logging Hill Rd. changes to Bow Center Rd. at 1.0 mi. and then to Woodhill Rd. at 2.8 mi. At 5.0 mi. turn left onto South Bow Rd. and continue 0.9 mi. to the trailhead on the left. Limited parking is available along both sides of the road. The organization Bow Open Spaces (BOS) provides a trail map at bowopenspaces.com.

GREAT HILL TRAILS (BOS; BOS MAP)

Cumulative from South Bow Rd. (735 ft.) to:	↧↥	↗	↻
Great Hill summit (875 ft.)	0.6 mi.	140 ft.	0:20
Starting point by loop via Hamilton's Path, Great Hill Loop, and Walter's Way	1.2 mi.	140 ft. (rev. 140 ft.)	0:40

The route to Great Hill, beginning on Hamilton's Path, starts on private property. Please stay on the trail and obey all posted signs. From the trailhead, yellow-blazed Hamilton's Path climbs easily northeast with two short moderate pitches to a junction with an old logging road, where it bends left and reaches an outlook ledge at 0.2 mi. with views southwest to Crotched Mtn. and Mt. Monadnock. Continuing ahead on the old road, the trail runs level, crosses a snowmobile trail, and passes junction on left with Walter's Way at 0.3 mi. At 0.4 mi. Hamilton's Path ends at a junction with Great Hill Loop (on left and straight ahead) and Nancy's Trail (on right; this trail descends to intersect with other trails within Nottingcook Forest that are not described in this guide).

The eastern branch of red-blazed Great Hill Loop continues ahead past a cleared outlook with wide views to the northeast. At the outlook, the trail bends left (northwest), descends a short rocky section into a small col, then climbs moderately to a three-way junction with Walter's Way (straight ahead) and the western branch of Great Hill Loop (left) at 0.6 mi. The open summit with bench and sign describing the view is several yards ahead on Walter's Way.

The route descends from the summit by following Walter's Way, blazed in orange, which swings left and descends easily along the western side of the summit plateau, where footing is rocky in places. It crosses an old logging road and continues a gentle descent to a junction with Hamilton's Path at 0.9 mi. Turn right here onto Hamilton's Path for 0.3 mi. return to the trailhead.

SEC 3

BEAR BROOK STATE PARK

This park of nearly 10,000 acres lies mostly in Allenstown, with smaller portions in Deerfield, Hooksett, and Candia. In this area of generally rolling terrain there are only a few significant hills—including Hall Mtn. (940 ft.), Bear Hill (827 ft.), and Catamount Hill (721 ft.)—but there are several interesting streams, ponds, and wetlands, as well as extensive and varied stands of fine forest. The park's wide-ranging system of multiuse trails, about 40 mi. in total, comprises mostly woods walks with few long-distance views. The New Hampshire State Parks trail map, covering all the trails in the park, is available at the park's tollbooth and information offices or online at nhstateparks.org. A trail guide with brief descriptions (including difficulty ratings) of all 26 trails in the park is also available both at the park and online. Bear Brook State Park is covered by four USGS quadrangles that meet almost in the center of the property, a short distance to the northwest of Bear Hill: Suncook (northwest), Gossville (northeast), Manchester North (southwest), and Candia (southeast).

The officially maintained trails in the park are generally clear, easy to follow, and reasonably well signed. Some are blazed in yellow, while others have small white plastic trail markers. Trails in the remote southwestern section of the park are less often maintained, requiring some care to follow, and are very wet in places. Sections of some trails are occasionally disrupted or even obliterated by logging operations. Bear Brook's trails are often used by mountain bikers (and snowmobilers in winter); hikers should be aware that they may encounter mountain bikers on any trail in the park. The New England Mountain Bike Association has been heavily involved in trail maintenance activities. In addition to the official park trails, there are numerous old woods roads, snowmobile trails, and unofficial paths (used primarily by mountain bikers) that are potentially confusing.

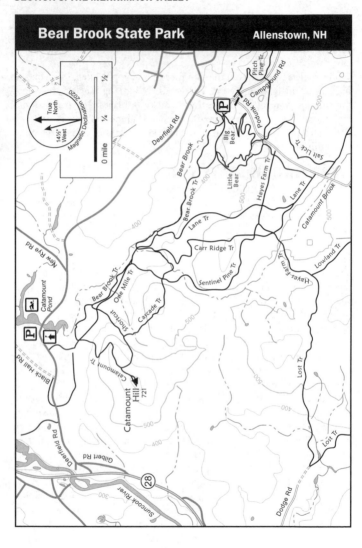

Bear Brook State Park   Allenstown, NH

The park offers a walk-in lean-to for camping at Smith Pond, with access via Broken Boulder Trail from a trailhead on Campground Rd. (advance reservation required; 877-647-2757). Two sizes of walk-in cabins are available for rent at Bear Hill Pond (603-485-9874). Otherwise, camping is allowed only at the park campground at Beaver Pond. (*Note:* Pets must be leashed at all times within the park.)

To reach the park's main entrance, take NH 28 north for 3.0 mi. from its intersection with US 3 in Suncook or south for 5.8 mi. from its intersection with US 4 at the Epsom traffic circle. Then take Deerfield Rd. (sign for park) east. The park's main tollbooth is on the right at 1.0 mi. from NH 28, just west of the developed recreation facilities near Catamount Pond. An admission fee is required during the operating season (May through October), which may be paid at this tollbooth or at a second tollbooth at the Podunk Rd. entrance. In 2019, the main tollbooth opened at 9 A.M. weekdays and 8 A.M. on weekends. The park gates close at 8 P.M. every day. (Check nhstateparks.org for current information on fees and operating hours, or call 603-485-9874; off-season 603-485-1031.) If you arrive before the park opens, deposit the fee in one of the "iron ranger" fee tubes at the tollbooths.

To reach the trails in the northwestern part of the park during operating hours (except in winter), park in the large beach parking lot across Deerfield Rd. from the tollbooth. If the gate to this lot is closed, there is room for several cars to park outside the gate; do not block the gate. With the exception of Black Hall Rd., all trails in this area of the park are reached via One Mile Trail, which leaves the south side of Deerfield Rd. just west of the tollbooth.

The other main access to the park's trails is Podunk Rd., which leaves Deerfield Rd. (signs for park) on the right (south) side, 2.2 mi. east of the main tollbooth. In 0.3 mi. Podunk Rd. reaches a fork, a second tollbooth, and the park's winter office. Just before this fork there is a large parking area for hikers and mountain bikers on the right (west) side, with a short path connecting to Little Bear and Bear Brook trails. At the fork, paved Campground Rd. diverges left and leads 2.9 mi. southeast past several trailheads (limited parking) to the entrance for the public campground at Beaver Pond; there is no hiker parking at the campground. (For campground reservations [fee; reservation only], contact ReserveAmerica at reserveamerica.com or 877-647-2757.) Podunk Rd. continues right from the fork, leading 2.4 mi. south past several trailheads, some with limited parking, to a point where gated Bear Hill Rd. (not open to public travel)

SEC 3

diverges right. A large parking area sits at Hayes Field, on the right (west) side of Podunk Rd. at 0.8 mi. from the fork with Campground Rd. At 1.8 mi. from the fork, Spruce Pond Rd. diverges left (southeast) and leads 2.0 mi. past several trailheads to the entrance of the campground at Beaver Pond, where it meets Campground Rd.

Many of the trails in Bear Brook State Park—in particular those between Podunk Rd. and Campground Rd.—are ideal for snowshoeing and cross-country skiing, though the major through routes are heavily used by snowmobilers. Skier parking is available at the Podunk Rd. parking area near the park's winter office. Winter access to trails in the northwest part of the park is from a snowmobiler parking area off Deerfield Rd. 0.1 mi. west of the main tollbooth; from here, a connector leads to One Mile Trail.

Space limitations in this guide preclude a complete description of the Bear Brook trail system. A few of the more attractive hike options are briefly described below.

Smith Pond, a beautiful pond and bog with a shelter above its shore, can be reached from the west side of Campground Rd. (limited parking), 1.0 mi. south of its junction with Podunk Rd., via an easy stroll through pine forest on Broken Boulder Trail and a side path. The round trip is 1.0 mi. with no elevation gain. A visit to Smith Pond can also be incorporated into various longer trips.

A pleasant, nearly level loop hike to scenic Hayes Marsh, passing through two fields, starts at the Hayes Field trailhead on Podunk Rd. (0.8 mi. south of its junction with Campground Rd.) and follows Lane, Carr Ridge, and Hayes Farm trails (with a short side trip to the Hayes Marsh viewpoint), returning on Lane Trail. (Hayes Marsh is a beautiful open wetland along Catamount Brook. The best view is from the north end of a causeway over Catamount Brook; follow Hayes Farm Trail 0.1 mi. southwest from its junction with Carr Ridge Trail.) The loop is 1.6 mi. with 50-ft. elevation gain.

An interesting loop in the central section of the park starts at the trailhead for Bear Hill Trail (limited parking) on the west side of Podunk Rd., 1.2 mi. south of its junction with Campground Rd. The loop—3.1 mi. with 400-ft. elevation gain—follows Bear Hill Trail over Bear Hill, Ferret Trail for a short distance, and Ledge Trail back to Bear Hill Trail. Highlights include the summit of Bear Hill, a former fire tower site with no views but an impressive collection of anthills; a beautiful view of Bear Hill Pond from a rocky promontory on the northwest shore, reached by a 150-yd. side path off Ferret Trail; and a series of rugged rock outcroppings and boulders along Ledge Trail.

A shorter loop and a longer loop can be made over Catamount Hill in the northwest part of the park, passing two vistas from semi-open ledges—one to the east and one to the northwest toward Mt. Kearsarge and Concord. Both loops start on One Mile Trail, which leaves Deerfield Rd. just west of the tollbooth and beach parking area at the park's main entrance. The shorter loop—2.0 mi. with 350-ft. elevation gain—follows One Mile Trail, Catamount Trail, and Shortcut Trail. The longer loop—5.8 mi. with 700-ft. elevation gain—includes some of the best scenery in Bear Brook State Park. Following One Mile, Catamount, Cascade, Carr Ridge, Hayes Farm, and Lane trails, this route visits the two semi-open ledges on Catamount Hill, a series of cascades along Catamount Brook in a beautiful hemlock ravine, and scenic Hayes Marsh.

SEC 3

NEVILLE PEAK (1,191 FT.)
AND EPSOM TOWN FOREST

Neville Peak, a lower subpeak of Nottingham Mtn., features excellent views north to Mt. Cardigan, Mt. Moosilauke, Franconia Ridge, and the Sandwich and Belknap ranges from its ledgy summit clearing, which also offers abundant blueberries in season. The peak is within the Epsom Town Forest, which contains a network of old roads, cellar holes, stone walls, and other relics from the area's agricultural past, all managed by the Epsom Conservation Commission. A hand-drawn map is available at epsomnh.org. Printed maps are sometimes available from a mailbox at the parking area.

To reach the trailhead from the Epsom traffic circle, take US 4/US 202/ NH 9 east for 1.6 mi., turn right on Center Hill Rd. and drive 1.3 mi., and then turn right onto Mountain Rd. and drive 0.5 mi. At the fork, bear left onto Tarlton Rd. and continue 0.25 mi. to the parking area at the left of the gate (beyond the gate, Tarlton Rd. forms the backbone of the forest from which other trails branch off). High clearance is recommended for this road, but regular cars can pass if careful. It is not maintained all the way to the trailhead in winter. Roadside/winter parking is available at the junction of Mountain Rd. and Tarlton Rd. Parking is prohibited at the end of the maintained portion of Tarlton Rd.; do not block the private driveways here.

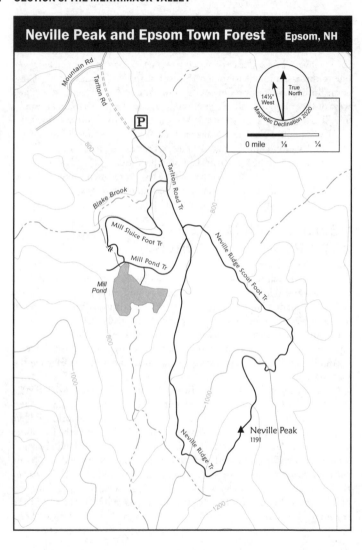

Neville Peak and Epsom Town Forest   Epsom, NH

Mountain Rd

Tarlton Rd

P

14½° West   True North   Magnetic Declination 2020

0 mile   ⅛   ¼

Blake Brook

Tarlton Road Tr

Mill Sluice Foot Tr

Mill Pond Tr

Mill Pond

800

Neville Ridge Scout Foot Tr

1000

Neville Ridge Tr

Neville Peak
1191

1200

NEVILLE RIDGE SCOUT FOOT TRAIL (ECC; ECC MAP, AMC NEVILLE PEAK AND EPSOM TOWN FOREST MAP)

Cumulative from gate on Tarlton Rd. (710 ft.) to:

	⇅	↗	↻
Start of Neville Ridge Scout Foot Trail (770 ft.)	0.4 mi.	110 ft.	0:15
Neville Peak (1,191 ft.)	1.6 mi.	530 ft.	1:05
Starting point via complete loop using Neville Ridge Trail	3.1 mi.	580 ft. (rev. 580 ft.)	1:50

SEC 3

This red-blazed trail ascends to the summit of Neville Peak and its excellent views. After falling into a state of disuse, the trail was restored and improved by Eagle Scout Davis Marston in 2015. Grades are easy to moderate, and footing is generally good.

From the gate, descend along the unmaintained portion of Tarlton Rd. to cross Blake Brook (this area is sometimes prone to flooding due to beaver activity). Pass the junction on the right with orange-blazed Mill Sluice Foot Trail, and then climb moderately to the junction at 0.4 mi. where Neville Ridge Scout Foot Trail begins on the left. An interesting cellar hole from the Tarlton Homestead is on the right.

(*Note*: Despite the similar name, Neville Ridge Scout Foot Trail is a different route than Neville Ridge Trail, which begins 0.1 mi. ahead and also ascends to the summit.)

Neville Ridge Scout Foot Trail follows an eroded, sometimes muddy snowmobile trail for 0.1 mi. and then bears right onto a wide path and ascends easily, with excellent footing, passing a wall-like ledge outcropping on the left at 0.7 mi. At 0.9 mi. the trail swings left through a more open area and descends gradually through a section of outcroppings. Then it swings right to cross a footbridge over a small stream. Footing becomes rougher as the trail ascends easily, bearing right at 1.0 mi. and climbing up a short, steep pitch, after which it becomes a narrow footpath lined by low plants. The footpath descends slightly and then swings left twice to begin a winding climb up the steep northern shoulder of Neville Peak. The trail swings right and descends to a restricted viewpoint on the right; then it curves left, ascends over the height-of-land, and descends gently to a ledge at 1.3 mi., with a restricted view of nearby McCoy Mtn. It traverses a ledgy area and then reenters the woods for an easy, level ramble. The trail then resumes a moderate climb, breaking out into the open for an easy walk up the ridge to the open, ledgy summit clearing at 1.6 mi. For wider views, carefully descend northwest a short distance to the lower ledges (walk on rock and do not trample fragile vegetation). Return via the same route or by a loop using Neville Ridge Trail.

NEVILLE RIDGE TRAIL (ECC; ECC MAP, AMC NEVILLE PEAK AND EPSOM TOWN FOREST MAP)

From Tarlton Rd. (720 ft.) to:	⬇⬆	↗	◔
Neville Peak (1,191 ft.)	1.2 mi.	470 ft.	0:50

This trail provides an alternate ascent route to the summit and can also be used as part of a loop hike with Neville Ridge Scout Foot Trail. It begins on Tarlton Rd., 0.5 mi. from the gate and parking area and 0.1 mi. south of Neville Ridge Scout Foot Trail. The route is unmarked and is only signed at the bottom.

At a fork where Mill Pond Trail diverges right, Neville Ridge Trail continues ahead (sign: "Neville Ridge Trail"), coinciding with Tarleton Rd. It ascends gradually, with good footing, and turns sharply left (sign: "Neville Peak") at 0.8 mi. onto a jeep road, where footing changes to rough and eroded. The trail ascends steeply and then easily to the summit of Neville Peak at 1.2 mi. Here, Neville Ridge Scout Foot Trail continues ahead.

MILL SLUICE FOOT TRAIL (ECC; ECC MAP, AMC NEVILLE PEAK AND EPSOM TOWN FOREST MAP)

Cumulative from Tarlton Rd. (685 ft.) to:	⬇⬆	↗	◔
Mill Pond Trail (770 ft.)	0.7 mi.	60 ft.	0:20
Starting point by loop via Mill Sluice Foot Trail, Mill Pond Trail, and Tarlton Rd.	1.3 mi.	90 ft. (rev. 120 ft.)	0:40

This trail, blazed in orange, begins on Tarlton Rd. (sign), 0.2 mi. south of the gate, and in conjunction with Mill Pond Trail, can be used to form a loop hike. The trail diverges right off the road (sign) and descends easily to cross small brook on a bridge. At 0.2 mi. it swings right, crosses another bridge, then makes a long level traverse along a north-facing slope. It swings left and stays level, then swings left again at 0.6 mi. alongside Mill Sluice, an area of ledgy cascades sliding down Blake Brook on right. The trail rises gently and briefly follows the brook, then bears left away from it and ascends easily to a junction with Mill Pond Trail at 0.7 mi.

MILL POND TRAIL (ECC; ECC MAP, AMC NEVILLE PEAK AND EPSOM TOWN FOREST MAP)

Cumulative from Tarlton Rd. (775 ft.) to:	⬇⬆	↗	◔
Mill Sluice Foot Trail (770 ft.)	0.3 mi.	30 ft.	0:10
End of trail (775 ft.)	0.4 mi.	40 ft.	0:10

This unmarked trail begins on Tarlton Rd. 0.5 mi. south of the gate at a fork where Neville Ridge Trail continues ahead, and in conjunction with Mill Sluice Trail can be used to form a loop hike. At the fork, Mill Pond bears right (sign) and descends slightly on a wide woods road, passing a junction on the left with an unmarked side path at 0.2 mi. that gently descends 0.1 mi. to a bench at the shore of Mill Pond, a lovely sitting spot. The main trail climbs gradually then descends again to reach Mill Pond and an old dam on the left and a junction with Mill Sluice Foot Trail on the right at 0.3 mi., then continues ahead on the road and ends at the town forest boundary at 0.4 mi.

SEC 3

OAK HILL (IN LOUDON; 941 FT.)

Oak Hill is a long ridge running east and west in Loudon and Concord. A fire tower on the wooded summit was refurbished in 2019 and offers pleasant views of the surrounding countryside and hills. Other outlooks lie lower on the mountain.

OAK HILL SUMMIT RD.
(NHDFL; USGS PENACOOK AND LOUDON QUADS)

From Oak Hill Rd. (570 ft.) to:	⇅	⟋	↻
Oak Hill summit (941 ft.)	1.3 mi.	370 ft.	0:50

The easiest route to the top of Oak Hill is via the access road from the east that ascends to the summit and fire tower. From I-93, Exit 16 (eastern off-ramp), go around the traffic circle and take the second exit onto Shawmut St. Bear left at 0.7 mi. as Shawmut St. becomes Oak Hill Rd. at the junction with Appleton St. Pass Turtletown Pond and continue up Oak Hill Rd.; the summit road (gated; sign for fire tower) is on the left, 4.0 mi. from Exit 16, just before the height-of-land on Oak Hill Rd. Parking is very limited; park carefully along the roadside across from the entrance to the summit road, avoiding areas with No Parking signs posted. From the gate next to a recently logged area, unmarked Oak Hill Summit Rd. ascends at mostly easy grades, bearing left at a fork with a large cellar hole on the right, and reaches the flat summit clearing and fire tower at 1.3 mi.

City of Concord's Conservation Commission Trails

The city of Concord's Conservation Commission maintains an extensive network of well-blazed and signed trails on the western slopes of Oak Hill. These trails pass two outlooks and are connected to the summit by Tower Trail. Rewarding loops of up to 7.0 mi. are possible. Two trailheads are on Shaker Rd. From I-93, Exit 16 (eastern off-ramp), turn left onto Mountain

Rd. and then bear right onto Shaker Rd. in 0.3 mi. The southern trailhead (390 ft.), a pull-off with room for several cars, is 2.3 mi. from the off-ramp; Vista Way starts here. The northern trailhead (410 ft.; sign: "Oak Hill City Forest") is 0.5 mi. beyond. This is the main trailhead and has the best parking; Tower Trail starts here. A third trailhead (390 ft.), with limited parking, is on Oak Hill Rd., 2.0 mi. from I-93, Exit 16 (see directions above for Oak Hill Summit Rd.). It is on the left (sign for Luti Loop) at the top of the first hill beyond Turtletown Pond. Download an excellent trail map at concordnh.gov. Also refer to the USGS Penacook and Loudon quadrangles.

TOWER TRAIL (CCCC; CCCC MAP)

From Shaker Rd. (410 ft.) to:	⬍	⬈	⟳
Oak Hill summit (941 ft.)	2.0 mi.	530 ft.	1:15

This yellow-blazed trail is the most direct route to the summit and fire tower from the main Shaker Rd. trailhead and also serves as a trunkline trail where several other trails branch off, making various loop hikes possible. Grades are generally easy the whole way and footing is mostly good aside from a few rocky sections. The immediate area around the summit has been impacted by logging but the trail itself is only slightly affected.

Tower Trail leaves the parking area at a kiosk and branch of Concord's Little Free Public Library and ascends easily along a wide path to a junction at 0.2 mi. where blue-blazed Lower Trail diverges right for the Vista Way trailhead. Tower Trail bears left, immediately passes the closed former section of Ledges Trail on the right, then in 25 yd. passes a junction on the right with the current route of that red-blazed trail. At 0.5 mi. Tower Trail passes a junction on the right with red-blazed Upper Trail, which leads to the scenic vista and Oak Hill Rd. trailhead. It ascends easily, levels as it passes north of Potter Ridge, then descends to a four-way junction at 0.9 mi. where red-blazed Dancing Bear Trail leaves left (turn left onto this trail to reach the Swope Slope Vista) and blue-blazed Potter Ridge Trail leaves right.

Tower Trail continues straight ahead and footing becomes rockier. At 1.2 mi. it passes through a lower four-way junction with blue-blazed Krupa Loop, climbs easily over an unnamed 775 ft. bump, then descends to an upper four-way junction with Krupa Loop at 1.3 mi. Tower Trail continues an easy ascent, with a few minor ups and downs, and reaches an old stone wall at 1.7 mi. which, along with an engraved granite post on left, marks the boundary between Concord and Loudon. Here, red-blazed Ron's Way departs right.

Tower Trail passes through the wall, turns sharply left and follows a power-line corridor at easy to moderate grades. At 1.9 mi. the fire tower comes into view as the trail makes the final ascent to the summit. The trail crosses two newer skid roads, jogging left then right at the second one, and emerges onto the broad summit clearing at 2.0 mi. When leaving the summit, Tower Trail diverges right at a fork (sign: "Tower Trail") where Oak Hill Summit Rd. bears left by the communications tower.

VISTA WAY LOOP (CCCC; CCCC MAP)
Cumulative from Shaker Rd.

(410 ft.) to:	🔄	📈	🕐
Oak Hill outlook (560 ft.)	0.6 mi.	150 ft.	0:20
Starting point via complete loop	1.2 mi.	250 ft. (rev. 250 ft.)	0:45

This short loop starts at the northern trailhead on Shaker Rd. and makes an easy ascent up Oak Hill to a cleared outlook on Vista Way that provides fine views west and northwest to Mt. Kearsarge, Ragged Mtn., and Mt. Cardigan. From the northern trailhead at the main parking area on Shaker Rd., follow yellow-blazed Tower Trail, red-blazed Ledges Pass, and red-blazed Vista Way.

OAK HILL SUMMIT LOOP (CCCC; CCCC MAP)
Cumulative from Shaker Rd.

(410 ft.) to:	🔄	📈	🕐
Oak Hill summit (941 ft.)	2.0 mi.	530 ft.	1:15
Starting point via complete loop	4.0 mi.	530 ft. (rev. 530 ft.)	2:15

To begin this meandering multitrail trek from the northern trailhead, follow yellow-blazed Tower Trail at easy grades, and then bear left at a junction at 0.2 mi. where Lower Trail diverges right. Immediately turn right onto red-blazed Ledges Pass. At 0.4 mi. turn right onto red-blazed Upper Trail and continue to a junction with Tower Trail at 0.8 mi. Bear right here to rejoin Tower Trail. At 1.1 mi. turn left onto red-blazed Dancing Bear Trail. This trail continues to the Swope Slope Vista at 1.5 mi., where there are good views to Mt. Kearsarge, Ragged Mtn., and Mt. Cardigan. From the Vista, continue ahead on blue-blazed Krupa Loop, and then bear left at 1.7 mi. to once again rejoin Tower Trail. Ascend easily on Tower Trail to the Concord–Loudon town line, indicated by an engraved granite boundary marker beside the trail at a break in a stone wall. Tower Trail turns sharply left here and makes the final easy climb to the summit and fire tower at 2.0 mi. For a more direct and quicker descent route, follow Tower Trail all the way back to the trailhead at 4.0 mi.

JERRY HILL (737 FT.) AND SWOPE PARK

Jerry Hill is a small but interesting hill in Concord, within 77-acre Marjory Swope Park, offering easy hiking within 15 min. of downtown. The formerly open summit once featured an observation tower, the footings of which remain. Cleared outlooks along Blue Loop and Orange Trail offer nice views. Footing is generally good on all trails, aside from a few rocky stretches. The trails are blazed in colors according to their names. Marjory Swope Park is owned by the city of Concord, with a conservation easement held by Five Rivers Conservation Trust. To reach the trailhead, take Long Pond Rd. north from NH 202/NH 9 for 0.7 mi. to the parking area and kiosk (sign: "Swope Park") on the left. An AMC map is on p. 209, and one from the city of Concord's Conservation Commission is available at concordnh.gov.

BLUE LOOP (CCCC/FRCT; CCCC MAP)

From Long Pond Rd. (460 ft.) to:	⇅	↗	↻
Starting point via complete loop	1.7 mi.	300 ft. (rev. 300 ft.)	1:00
Jerry Hill summit by loop via Yellow Trail with side trip to Mountain Vista (737 ft.)	1.7 mi.	310 ft. (rev. 310 ft.)	1:00

This blue-blazed trail circumnavigates Jerry Hill and is described here in the counterclockwise direction. From the parking area and kiosk, turn left where red-blazed Swope Winant Connector turns right. Pass a branch of Concord's Little Free Public Library and ascend easily 30 yd. to the loop junction. Bearing right, Blue Loop angles up the eastern slope of Jerry Hill, alternating between easy and moderate grades, with occasional dips. At 0.5 mi. it reaches a cleared outlook and bench with a view northeast to Penacook Lake and the Belknap Range. From this outlook, Blue Loop swings left and descends moderately to the northern junction with Yellow Trail on the left at 0.6 mi. Continuing straight ahead, Blue Loop curves south and descends easily before ascending to meet a blue-and-orange-blazed connecting trail on the right at 0.8 mi. Then at 0.9 mi. it climbs moderately to the junction with Orange Trail. (Turn left here to ascend 0.2 mi. and 100 ft. to Mountain Vista, a cleared outlook with views southwest to Mt. Monadnock, Crotched Mtn., Mt. Wallingford, and Craney Hill.) Blue Loop descends southeast over rolling terrain at easy grades to the southern junction with Yellow Trail at 1.4 mi.; then it curves northeast, arriving back at the loop junction and trailhead at 1.7 mi.

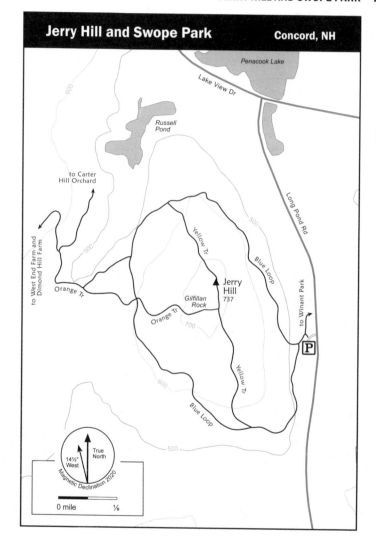

Jerry Hill and Swope Park — Concord, NH

Penacook Lake

Lake View Dr

SEC 3

Russell Pond

to Carter Hill Orchard

600

500

to West End Farm and Dimond Hill Farm

Orange Tr

Yellow Tr

Blue Loop

500

Long Pond Rd

Jerry Hill 737

Gilfillan Rock

Orange Tr

700

to Winant Park

Yellow Tr

Blue Loop

600

Blue Loop

P

500

True North

14½" West

Magnetic Declination 2020

0 mile   ⅛

YELLOW TRAIL (CCCC/FRCT; CCCC MAP)

Cumulative from northern jct. with Blue Loop (570 ft.) to:	⮏⮑	⬈	↻
Southern jct. with Blue Loop with side trip to Mountain Vista (550 ft.)	0.8 mi.	170 ft. (rev. 190 ft.)	0:30
Jerry Hill summit by loop via Blue Loop with side trip to Mountain Vista (737 ft.)	1.7 mi.	310 ft. (rev. 310 ft.)	1:00

This trail, combined with Blue Loop, allows for a loop hike over the summit of Jerry Hill; the route is described here in the steeper north–south direction. From the northern junction with Blue Loop, 0.6 mi. north of the trailhead, Yellow Trail begins climbing moderately south along a wide old road. (At 0.2 mi., near a boulder on the right, look back for a framed view northwest to Mt. Kearsarge.) The grade eases as the trail reaches the wooded summit of Jerry Hill and the former observation tower footings at 0.3 mi. Yellow Trail then descends gently 120 yd. to the junction on the right with Orange Trail. (Turn right here for a level 0.1-mi. side trip to Mountain Vista and Gilfillan Rock, an interesting inscribed and uplifted ledge.) Yellow Trail continues at easy grades along the wooded ridge crest to its southern junction with Blue Loop, 0.3 mi. south of the trailhead.

BROKEN GROUND

This multiuse trail system in Concord was completed in 2016 on land that, aside from farming use in the nineteenth century, has remained undeveloped since the city was first settled in 1725. Three major loop trails can be used on their own or combined to form longer options. Grades are easy, and footing is good on all trails. Follow blazes and signs carefully because the three trails overlap in areas. A map is available at concordnh.gov. Dogs are permitted on Howard C. Nowell Trail and Pond Loop, but they must be leashed in the vicinity of the beaver pond to protect wildlife.

To reach the northern trailhead (380 ft.), take Exit 2 off I-393. Follow East Side Dr./NH 132 north for 0.3 mi., and then turn right onto South Curtisville Rd., which becomes Curtisville Rd. Continue straight on Curtisville Rd. to the parking area on the left at 1.3 mi. To reach the southern trailhead (355 ft.), take Exit 2 off I-393 and follow East Side Dr./NH 132 north for 0.2 mi. Turn right onto Broken Ground Dr. and drive 0.2 mi. Then turn right onto Portsmouth St. and continue to a gravel pull-off on the left at 0.6 mi.

HOWARD C. NOWELL TRAIL (CCCC; CCCC MAP)
From Curtisville Rd.
(300 ft.) to:

	⇵	⤢	↻
Starting point via complete loop	2.4 mi.	150 ft. (rev. 150 ft.)	1:15

This is the longest of the three loop trails. It leaves from the northern trailhead, is blazed in blue, and is indicated as Nowell Trail on some signage. From the parking area, cross Curtisville Rd. and enter woods to descend easily along the east side of a beaver pond. At 0.3 mi. an unmarked spur path on the right leads 25 yd. to the shore. The trail passes through a stand of tall pines, climbs a short, moderate pitch, and then levels out again to reach a junction at 0.7 mi. with Pond Loop and Marsh Loop. Howard C. Nowell Trail turns left onto an old town road to meet a junction at 0.9 mi. where Marsh Loop leaves right. Howard C. Nowell Trail continues straight and climbs easily before leveling out. It curves left and then bears left off the old road at a fork at 1.2 mi.—where Ry's Way Mountain Bike Trail diverges right—and continues straight to join another woods road that comes in from the left. Howard C. Nowell Trail quickly bears left off that road onto a footpath and begins a gradual descent over rolling terrain to a junction with a snowmobile trail at 2.0 mi. Here, the route bends left and descends easily to a junction at 2.2 mi. where the snowmobile trail and red-blazed Curtis Trail diverge right (Curtis Trail makes a 0.4-mi. alternate loop back to the parking area). Howard C. Nowell Trail continues straight along a woods road, bears right onto a footpath just before a gate, and then descends easily past a cellar hole from an old homestead to the parking area at 2.4 mi.

POND LOOP (CCCC; CCCC MAP)
From Curtisville Rd.
(300 ft.) to:

	⇵	⤢	↻
Starting point via complete loop	1.5 mi.	30 ft.	0:45

This yellow-blazed trail makes a loop around a large beaver pond and adjacent wetlands, where the residents can sometimes be seen at work. Pond Loop starts from the northern trailhead in the parking area and crosses Curtisville Rd. to enter the woods. The first section of this trail coincides with Howard C. Nowell Trail; see that description for details. From the junction at 0.7 mi. where Howard C. Nowell Trail and Marsh Loop turn left, Pond Loop turns right, ascending past a beaver swamp on the left. When it reaches a junction at 0.8 mi. where Marsh Loop turns left, Pond Loop turns sharply right, descends gradually, and levels out (with minor ups and downs) through an area of tall pines. The trail crosses a small brook, swings right to pass between the foundations of an old homestead and barn, and then descends slightly to Curtisville Rd. at 1.3 mi. Turn right for an easy 0.2-mi. walk back to the parking area.

MARSH LOOP (CCCC; CCCC MAP)
From Portsmouth St.
(355 ft.) to:

	⇅	↗	↻
Starting point via complete loop	1.6 mi.	90 ft. (rev. 90 ft.)	0:50

This orange-blazed trail departs from the southern trailhead and makes a loop around a beaver pond and wetland. From the parking area, walk northeast along a paved road for 0.2 mi. to where the trail enters the woods on the left, just before a gate. (Purple-blazed Ry's Way Mountain Bike Trail continues straight here.) Marsh Loop ascends easily northeast, slowly curves left to pass an attractive beaver pond on the left, and then continues, mainly level, to a junction with an old woods road at 0.6 mi. Here, Marsh Loop bears right and climbs easily to a junction with Howard C. Nowell Trail at 0.8 mi. Marsh Loop turns left, overlaps Howard C. Nowell Trail, and descends gradually to a junction at 1.1 mi., where Howard C. Nowell Trail leaves right. At 1.2 mi. Marsh Loop turns left, ascends briefly, and then continues level to cross a wide power-line cut. The trail angles across the open cut (marked by orange-blazed posts) and joins an overgrown access road on the southwest side; it follows the road back to the parking area at 1.6 mi.

SECTION 4
THE LAKES REGION

INTRODUCTION

South of the White Mtns. and east of the natural dividing line formed by the Merrimack River and its northern extension, the Pemigewasset River, a multitude of medium and small mountains and hills, many with interesting views, ripple New Hampshire's terrain. But the dominant feature of this region is the fine collection of lakes and ponds generously scattered among the hills, including New Hampshire's largest lake, Lake Winnipesaukee, and numerous smaller lakes, of which Squam Lake is the most prominent.

For the purposes of this book, coverage of the Lakes Region is restricted to the area east of the Pemigewasset River and south and east of Squam Lake. (The mountains in the Squam Lake area—the Squam Range, the Rattlesnakes, and Red Hill—are covered in AMC's *White Mountain Guide*, 30th edition.) The unifying theme of the hills and mountains in this section is that views often include a significant lake, most often Lake Winnipesaukee. The mountains with trails described here include Green Mtn. in Effingham, south of Ossipee Lake; the Ossipee Range, east of Lake Winnipesaukee; the Belknap Range and Mt. Major, west of Lake Winnipesaukee; and Copple Crown Mtn. in Brookfield and the Moose Mtns. in Middleton, south of Lake Winnipesaukee. Other locations covered in this section are Whiteface Mtn. in Wolfeboro, Fogg Hill Conservation Area in Center Harbor, and Whitten Woods Conservation Area in Ashland.

Lakes Region Conservation Trust's Explorer Patch Program offers a patch for hikers who visit twenty of LRCT's conservation areas throughout the Lakes Region; more information is available at lrct.org.

OVERNIGHT OPTIONS

Camping is generally not permitted in the Belknap Mtns., but Belknap County's Gunstock Mtn. Resort (603-293-4341; gunstock.com) offers camping on 270 sites in summer (Memorial Day through Columbus Day) and winter (early December through late April).

As with all sections in this book, unless otherwise noted, camping outside of these designated areas is not permitted.

SUGGESTED HIKES

■ Easy Hikes

BALD LEDGE

RT via Bald Ledge Trail	1.6 mi.	100 ft.	0:25

Ascend easily to this open ledge, high above Winona Lake with excellent views toward the White Mtns. See Bald Ledge Trail, p. 240.

WHITTEN WOODS CONSERVATION AREA (SOUTH PEAK)

RT via Main Junction and South Peak Trail	1.8 mi.	400 ft.	0:40

This small, partly open peak provides good views of Squam Lake, Little Squam Lake, and surrounding mountains. To begin, see Main Junction, p. 242.

PIPER MTN.

RT via Piper Mtn. Trail	2.6 mi.	1,000 ft.	1:50

A short but fairly steep climb leads to the open, ledgy north summit of Piper Mtn., which offers views toward the eastern Belknap Range, Manning Lake, and Sunset Lake. To begin, see Piper Mtn. Trail, p. 251.

BELKNAP MTN.

LP via Red Trail and Blue Trail	2.0 mi.	700 ft.	1:20

Of the several routes to this peak, one of the nicest ascends from the upper Carriage Rd. parking area. A fire tower on the summit offers panoramic views in all directions over the Lakes Region. To begin, see Red Trail, p. 248.

■ Moderate Hikes

WHITEFACE MTN. (WOLFEBORO)

RT via White Trail	2.2 mi.	600 ft.	0:55

A large open ledge just past the summit provides excellent views toward the White Mtns. as a reward for the short but somewhat challenging climb. To begin, see White Trail, p. 248.

BAYLE MTN.

RT via snowmobile trail and unofficial Bayle Mtn. Trail			2.8 mi.	950 ft.	1:10

This summit is uniquely situated within the center of the Ossipee Range and offers excellent views in all directions from its open ledges. To begin, see Bayle Mtn., p. 238.

SEC 4

MT. MAJOR

LP via Mt. Major Trail, Belknap Range Trail, and Brook Trail			3.9 mi.	1,150 ft.	2:30

A large area of open rock with wide views over Lake Winnipesaukee makes this one of the most popular and scenic hikes in southern New Hampshire. To begin, see Mt. Major Trail, p. 263.

BALD KNOB

RT via Shannon Brook Trail, Bald Knob Cutoff, and Bald Knob Trail			4.0 mi.	1,140 ft.	2:35

This open rock knob on the south side of the Ossipee Range features a sweeping, unobstructed vista over Lake Winnipesaukee. To begin, see Shannon Brook Trail, p. 224.

MOOSE MTNS. RESERVATION

LP via Burrows Farm Trail, North Trail, Beauty Ledge Trail, Beauty Knob Trail, Phoebes Nable Loop, and Phoebes Nable Mtn. Trail			4.3 mi.	1,050 ft.	2:40

An attractive loop visits two open southerly viewpoints and a nineteenth-century farmstead. To begin, see Moose Mtns. Reservation, p. 274.

GUNSTOCK MTN., BELKNAP MTN., AND PIPER MTN.

LP via Gunstock Mtn. Trail, Brook Trail, Saddle Trail, Blue Trail, White Trail, Old Piper Trail, and Piper Mtn. Trail	4.7 mi.	1,850 ft.	3:15

A three-peak loop from the lower Carriage Rd. parking area affords numerous vistas of the Lakes Region from the ski area on Gunstock Mtn., the fire tower on Belknap Mtn., and the open north summit of Piper Mtn. To begin, see Gunstock Mtn. Trail, p. 252.

MT. ROBERTS

SEC 4

RT via Mt. Roberts Trail	5.4 mi.	1,400 ft.	3:25

A mostly moderate route ascends over a series of open ledges along the south ridge of Mt. Roberts, which provide vistas over Lake Winnipesaukee; at the summit is a view north to the White Mtns. See Mt. Roberts Trail, p. 234.

■ Strenuous Hikes
MT. SHAW

RT via Bridle Path, Oak Ridge Cutoff, and High Ridge Trail	8.6 mi.	2,050 ft.	5:20

Visit the highest peak in the Ossipee Range, where there are sweeping views north and east, starting from the Ossipee Park Rd. trailhead on the grounds of Castle in the Clouds. The hike can be lengthened with any of several loop options for the return trip. To begin, see Bridle Path, p. 230.

BELKNAP RANGE TRAVERSE

OW via Belknap Range Trail	12.5 mi.	3,850 ft.	8:10

This challenging trek requires a "car spot" (leaving a second car) and traverses the entire Belknap Range from west to east, starting at the Gunstock Resort parking area and ending at the Mt. Major trailhead. The route follows the long-distance Belknap Range Trail—which encompasses other trails, in whole or in part—and showcases the finest scenery and summits in the range, all in one hike. See Belknap Range Trail, p. 266.

TRAIL DESCRIPTIONS

WHITEFACE MTN. (IN WOLFEBORO; 1,349 FT.)

Not to be confused with Whiteface Mtn. in the Belknap Range or Mt. Whiteface in the Sandwich Range, this small peak in Wolfeboro offers a 180-degree view toward the White Mtns. and western Maine from open ledges atop a sheer 250-ft. white cliff (from which the mountain gets its name) on its east side. In 2016, the Student Conservation Association constructed a new white-blazed trail from Browns Ridge Rd. to the summit and ledges. In 2018, the Land Bank of Wolfeboro-Tuftonboro and the Wolfeboro Conservation Commission purchased a 120-acre parcel on the east side of the mountain, including the summit, which was placed into protection under an easement held by Lakes Region Conservation Trust. As of this writing, there was no formal trail map available; refer to the USGS Wolfeboro quadrangle.

To reach the trailhead from NH 28 in Ossipee, take NH 171 south for 0.2 mi. Then bear right onto Browns Ridge Rd. and continue 2.1 mi. to a small, unmarked parking area (easy to miss) on the right, through a break in a stone wall, located under power lines.

WHITE TRAIL (WCC/LBWT/LRCT; USGS WOLFEBORO QUAD)

From Browns Ridge Rd.
(740 ft.) to:

	⇅	↗	↺
Whiteface Mtn. summit (1,349 ft.)	1.1 mi.	610 ft.	0:50

The trail ascends the steeper eastern side of the mountain, angling up below the cliff (not visible from the trail when the trees are in full leaf) and swinging around to the summit and view ledges. The footbed is not evident in some spots, but the route is clearly blazed with white plastic diamonds. Footing is generally good. Despite the short distance, this is a fairly stiff climb, but short switchbacks help ease the grades.

White Trail leaves the left side of the parking area and quickly turns right, where blazing begins. It ascends easily past a huge glacial boulder and along a stone wall, dipping slightly to cross a small brook on step stones. At 0.2 mi. it bears right onto a woods road and then immediately bears right again onto a footpath (watch blazes carefully in both directions at this turn). The footpath ascends easily through young birch and beech woods. More moderate to steep climbing begins as the trail bears right onto an old logging road at 0.4 mi. (in the reverse direction, bear left here), following it along an angling route across the steep slope. At 0.6 mi. the old road diverges left and descends, while the trail continues straight onto another footpath. It turns right at 0.8 mi. and ascends by short switchbacks to the ridge.

At 1.0 mi. White Trail turns right at a junction where an unofficial trail comes in on the left. This route is also blazed in white, so in the reverse direction, turn left at this junction to stay on the correct trail (sign: "Browns Rdg Rd"). Grades become much easier as the trail meanders up the ridge crest with one minor descent, passes the high point of the mountain on the right, and then descends slightly 30 yd. to the open ledges and a guest register.

GREEN MTN. (1,911 FT.)

Green Mtn. is an isolated small mountain in the town of Effingham. The state owns 15 acres on the summit, where there is a 61-ft. fire tower. The views from the tower are good, though those to the north toward the White Mtns. are restricted by tree growth; there are no significant views from the ground.

In addition to the fire warden's trail on the north side of the mountain, called High Watch Trail, there are two trails on the south side, Dearborn Trail and Libby Rd. Trail, that make a loop hike possible. Much of the north side of the mountain, as well as the corridor of Dearborn Trail, is in the SPNHF's 2,171-acre High Watch Preserve. The trails are covered by the in-text map in this guide. A trail map and additional information can be found at forestsociety.org. Also, refer to the USGS Freedom quadrangle.

HIGH WATCH TRAIL
(SPNHF; AMC GREEN MTN. MAP, USGS FREEDOM QUAD)

From crossroads on High Watch Rd. (740 ft.) to:	⤵⤴	↗	↻
Green Mtn. summit (1,911 ft.)	1.4 mi.	1,180 ft.	1:15

From the western junction of NH 25 and NH 153 (northbound) near Effingham Falls, go south on Green Mtn. Rd. for 1.3 mi., and then turn left onto Winter Rd. (sign: "Green Mt. Fire Tower"). Follow Winter Rd. for 0.1 mi. to a T intersection with High Watch Rd. Turn left here and follow High Watch Rd. In another 1.1 mi., just past the Lakeview Neurorehabilitation Center, the paved road becomes rough gravel and continues another 0.1 mi. to a crossroads in the woods (sign: "Green Mt. Fire Tower"). Park here. (High Watch Trail is shown accurately on the USGS Freedom quadrangle.)

The orange-blazed trail follows the road to the right (south), passing a High Watch Preserve sign. This old woods road is moderately steep and

SEC
4

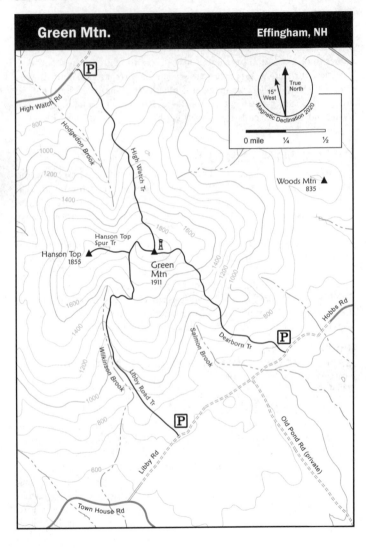

Green Mtn.

Effingham, NH

True North

15°
West

Magnetic Declination 2020

0 mile   ¼   ½

High Watch Rd

Hodgedon Brook

High Watch Tr

800

1000

1200

1400

Woods Mtn
835

1800   1600

Hanson Top
Spur Tr

Hanson Top
1855

Green
Mtn
1911

1600

1400

1200   1000

800

Hobbs Rd

1600

Wilkinson Brook

Libby Road Tr

Salmon Brook

Dearborn Tr

1200

1000

800

Libby Rd

600

Old Pond Rd (private)

Town House Rd

severely eroded in places, so watch your footing. It runs toward the fence of the Lakeview Center's parking area and then climbs across a service road that leads to a fenced-in building on the left at 0.4 mi. Soon it bears left at a fork, where the road to the right is becoming overgrown, and ascends moderately through an attractive softwood forest. At 0.9 mi. the grade becomes easy for a while, but then the trail grows steeper and rougher until it swings to the left. After that it becomes progressively less steep until it reaches the summit and fire tower at 1.4 mi.

DEARBORN TRAIL (SPNHF; AMC GREEN MTN. MAP)

Cumulative from Hobbs Rd. (550 ft.) to:	⇅	↗	↻
Green Mtn. summit (1,911 ft.)	1.4 mi.	1,380 ft.	1:25
Starting point by complete loop via Libby Rd. Trail, Libby Rd., and Hobbs Rd.	4.2 mi.	1,450 ft.	2:50

This yellow-blazed trail ascends Green Mtn. from the southeast and is part of the SPNHF's High Watch Preserve. It is probably the most attractive trail on Green Mtn. because of the relatively light use it has received and the ledgy, wooded terrain it passes through. The trailhead for Dearborn Trail is on Hobbs Rd. From NH 153 on the north edge of Center Effingham, at a junction where there is a historical marker for the First Normal School in New Hampshire, follow Hobbs Rd. for 1.3 mi. (the last 0.2 mi. is rough). The trailhead is at a parking lot (not plowed in winter) on the right at the height-of-land opposite a house. An SPNHF kiosk sits at the back edge of the lot. To reach the trailhead for Libby Rd. Trail on foot from this trailhead, follow Hobbs Rd. (not passable for most cars) west to the junction with Old Pound Rd. (passable for cars) at 0.3 mi., and then bear right onto Libby Rd. (no sign; not passable for most cars) to a woods road with a green gate on the right at 1.0 mi.

From the trailhead, Dearborn Trail climbs moderately, entering a section of large pines at about 0.7 mi., which permits glimpses across the valley. At 0.9 mi. there is a split boulder to the right of the trail that looks as if it had been sliced into three pieces with a knife. At 1.1 mi. the trail runs level on a shoulder for a short distance. Then it swings right, climbs moderately past a yellow-blazed property boundary, and continues to ascend below a rocky ridge crest to the left of the trail. It becomes less steep and winds through woods with ledges, crosses the blue-blazed state land boundary, and reaches the Green Mtn. summit.

LIBBY RD. TRAIL
(NHDFL; AMC GREEN MTN. MAP, USGS FREEDOM QUAD)
From Libby Rd.
(720 ft.) to:

⮌↥   ⬈   ⟳

Green Mtn. summit (1,911 ft.)	1.8 mi.	1,180 ft.	1:30

The fire warden uses this white-blazed woods road to ascend the mountain in an ATV. The route has much loose rock footing and is not particularly attractive, but it is easy to follow and makes possible a loop hike in combination with Dearborn Trail. Some of the forest along this trail was damaged by a tornado in 2008. From NH 153 in Center Effingham, opposite the Baptist church, take Town House Rd. west for 1.8 mi. Then turn right onto Libby Rd. (sign: "Green Mt. Fire Tower") and follow it for 0.5 mi. to a woods road with a green gate on the left (sign: "Green Mt. Fire Tower"). Libby Rd. is rough but passable to this point for most cars; limited parking is available. To reach the trailhead for Dearborn Trail on foot from here, follow Libby Rd. (not passable for most cars at this point) east to the junction with Old Pound Rd. (passable for cars) at 0.7 mi. Then bear left onto Hobbs Rd. (no sign; not passable for most cars) to a parking lot on the left at 1.0 mi. (sign: "Roland Libby Trail"). (Libby Rd. Trail is accurately shown on the USGS Freedom quadrangle.)

Libby Rd. Trail follows the woods road past the gate, passing a private cabin on the left at 0.2 mi. and reaching a small brook at 0.7 mi. At 0.9 mi. the trail swings to the right, away from the brook, and climbs moderately through the tornado-damaged area to a junction with Hanson Top Spur Trail on the left at 1.6 mi. Blue-blazed Hanson Top Spur Trail passes through a saddle, ascends briefly, and then runs at easy grades to an outlook south beyond the summit of Hanson Top (1,855 ft.), 0.4 mi. from Libby Rd. Trail.

Just after this junction, Libby Rd. Trail makes a hairpin turn to the right. (Avoid an eroded woods road that diverges left here; it rejoins the main path higher up.) The trail climbs past the fire warden's cabin to the summit and tower. To find Libby Rd. Trail from the summit, descend to the front of the fire warden's cabin; the woods road can be seen clearly from there.

OSSIPEE MTNS.

These mountains, just northeast of Lake Winnipesaukee, occupy a nearly circular tract about 9 mi. in diameter. They are the result of an unusual geologic formation called a ring dike, in which magma wells up into a circular fracture in the earth's crust. The range shelters beautiful Dan Hole

Pond on its southeast edge and harbors areas of old-growth forest and a great diversity of vegetation, including several rare species.

Mt. Shaw (2,990 ft.), the highest of the Ossipees, affords outstanding views north toward the White Mtns. and other mountains to the east from its partly cleared summit; it may be ascended by a combination of trails in the Castle in the Clouds Conservation Area. A southern shoulder called Black Snout (2,803 ft.) offers excellent vistas to the south and west, particularly of Lake Winnipesaukee. (This is not the Black Snout shown on USGS maps, which is at the north end of the range and is not reachable by any trails.) The rocky promontory Bald Knob (1,800 ft.) also provides fine views of Lake Winnipesaukee. Other outlooks are on the south slope of Faraway Mtn. (2,782 ft.), at the summit and on the south ridge of Mt. Roberts (2,584 ft.), on Turtleback Mtn. (2,205 ft.), and on Oak Ridge.

SEC 4

The 5,381-acre Castle in the Clouds Conservation Area, owned and managed by Lakes Region Conservation Trust, encompasses most of the south slopes of the range, including all the summits listed above. (No admission is charged to enter the estate grounds, but there is a fee for a guided tour of the mansion on the site, called Castle in the Clouds.) LRCT has created more than 30 mi. of trails, marked with paint blazes and diamond markers. Many of these routes were originally carriage roads and bridle paths built in the late 1800s and early 1900s when the area was a private estate, owned first by Benjamin Shaw (for whom Mt. Shaw is named) and later by the eccentric millionaire Thomas Plant. These routes are now available as public hiking trails. LRCT has published a topographic trail map (created by AMC cartographer Larry Garland) showing these trails; it may be purchased from LRCT. Sections of the LRCT trail system are shown on the Ossipee Mtns. maps in this guide. Several other blazed trails lead off the LRCT property onto adjacent private land, some of which may be posted against trespassing; these trails are not maintained by LRCT and are not described in this guide or shown on the LRCT trail map. Use them only if you have obtained permission from the landowner.

Two hiker parking areas provide trailhead access. The large Shannon Brook trailhead parking area, with a kiosk and well marked by signs, is on LRCT land on the south side of NH 171 in Moultonborough, 0.2 mi. east of the main entrance to Castle in the Clouds and just east of the junction with Severance Rd. The second parking area, on Ossipee Park Rd., is just outside the gate to the estate grounds and is convenient to several trails; Ossipee Park Rd. leaves NH 171 0.5 mi. southeast of its junction with NH 109 and rises steeply for 1.3 mi. to the signed parking area on the right.

Drivers should be alert for tractor-trailers going to and from the spring-water bottling plant near the gate. (If this fairly small upper parking area is full, hikers must use the lower lot on NH 171.) To reach the major trail junction on the estate grounds near a kiosk at Shannon Pond, walk up the paved road past the gate. In 0.1 mi. turn right at a T intersection, and then soon turn left onto a gravel road that crosses a dike at the south end of the pond, reaching the kiosk at 0.2 mi. from the parking area. (Another 125 yd. ahead on the paved road, beyond the left turn, is the upper end of Brook Walk.) LRCT requests that hikers not park on the estate grounds inside the gate, as the access road gates are locked from late afternoon through midmorning during summer and fall, and at all times in winter and spring. No camping, overnight use, fires, or wheeled vehicles are permitted on LRCT land. A few of the trails receive heavy snowmobile use in winter. These trails may be indicated by orange arrow signs at turns.

The carriage road trails are generally wide with easy grades; the amount of vegetation on a trail may vary. Several connecting paths make possible a variety of rewarding loop hikes. LRCT offers a Hiker Achievement Patch for those who have climbed five summits on the property (Bald Knob, Black Snout, Mt. Shaw, Mt. Roberts, and Turtleback Mtn.) and have hiked all nineteen designated trails, totaling 30 mi., that lie within the property. For more information, visit lrct.org.

SHANNON BROOK TRAIL
(LRCT; AMC MT. SHAW MAP, LRCT TRAIL MAP)

Cumulative from trailhead on NH 171 (730 ft.) to:	⮑⮏	↗	⟳
Bald Knob Cutoff (1,080 ft.)	0.7 mi.	350 ft.	0:30
Connector Trail (1,170 ft.)	1.1 mi.	440 ft.	0:45
Shannon Pond via Connector and Turtleback Mtn. trails (1,230 ft.)	1.4 mi.	520 ft.	0:55

This red-blazed trail is the access route from the LRCT trailhead on NH 171 to the various trails that lead from the Castle in the Clouds grounds to the higher summits of the Ossipees. In 2019, the upper 0.4 mi. of the trail was closed permanently due to erosion caused by repeated flooding from Shannon Pond Dam. Shannon Brook Trail begins as a gated woods road on the north side of NH 171, 0.2 mi. east of the main entrance to the Castle in the Clouds and across from the designated hiker parking area. It follows the woods road, soon swinging left past one of the estate buildings and approaching Shannon Brook at 0.3 mi. The route climbs moderately, keeping well above the brook, and passes the junction with Bald Knob Cutoff on the right at 0.7 mi. Then it swings left and descends to cross a bridge over a branch of the brook at 0.8 mi. It passes a junction with Brook Walk on the left at 0.9 mi., and at 1.0 mi. the trail ends at a gate and junction with red-and-yellow-blazed Connector Trail on the right. To continue to Shannon Pond, follow Connector Trail for 0.1 mi. and then turn left onto Turtleback Mtn. Trail for 0.3 mi.

BALD KNOB CUTOFF
(LRCT; AMC MT. SHAW MAP, LRCT TRAIL MAP)

From Shannon Brook Trail (1,080 ft.) to:	⬆⬇	↗	⟳
Bald Knob Trail (1,690 ft.)	1.0 mi.	650 ft. (rev. 50 ft.)	0:50
From Shannon Brook Trail parking area on NH 171 (730 ft.) to:			
Bald Knob (1,800 ft.) via Shannon Brook Trail, Bald Knob Cutoff, and Bald Knob Trail	2.0 mi.	1,100 ft. (rev. 50 ft.)	1:35

This trail links Shannon Brook Trail with the upper part of Bald Knob Trail, providing the best route to Bald Knob and its excellent views. It is blazed in yellow and blue. Bald Knob Cutoff leaves Shannon Brook Trail on the right (east), 0.7 mi. from the trailhead on NH 171, and climbs by switchbacks to a ledge with a view southwest at 0.4 mi. Here, the trail turns left twice and then quickly right; it begins to climb northeast, passing to the left of a rocky knob and crossing the height-of-land at 0.6 mi. It then descends to an old woods road, turns right, and traverses a flat area, where a short alternate route to the right bypasses a wet spot. At 0.9 mi. a spur (sign) leads 25 yd. left to some interesting rocks that are a fine example of columnar jointing. Bald Knob Cutoff then climbs moderately to meet Bald Knob Trail; turn right to reach the ledges in 0.3 mi.

BALD KNOB TRAIL
(LRCT; AMC MT. SHAW MAP, LRCT TRAIL MAP)

Cumulative from Turtleback Mtn. Trail (1,700 ft.) to:	⬆⬇	↗	⟳
Bald Knob Cutoff (1,690 ft.)	0.4 mi.	0 ft.	0:10
Bald Knob (1,800 ft.)	0.7 mi.	100 ft.	0:25
From kiosk at Shannon Pond (1,230 ft.) to:			
Bald Knob via Turtleback Mtn. Trail and Bald Knob Trail	2.7 mi.	550 ft.	1:40

The portion of this trail that ascends to Bald Knob from NH 171 near the Moultonborough–Tuftonboro town line crosses private land and is not included in this guide or on the LRCT map. Ascend to Bald Knob from either the LRCT trailhead on NH 171 (via Shannon Brook Trail and Bald Knob Cutoff) or the trailhead on Ossipee Park Rd. on the Castle in the Clouds grounds (via Turtleback Mtn. Trail). The maintained portion of Bald Knob Trail now begins on Turtleback Mtn. Trail, 2.0 mi. from the kiosk at Shannon Pond on the estate grounds. The white-blazed trail follows an old carriage road south at a nearly level grade along the side of Turtleback Mtn. At 0.4 mi. Bald Knob Cutoff enters on the right. Bald Knob Trail now ascends gradually, breaking into the open at 0.6 mi. and ending at the old carriage road turnaround at 0.7 mi., just behind the open ledges of Bald Knob with their fine views of Lake Winnipesaukee. An unofficial trail leading north from Bald Knob toward Turtleback Mtn. has been closed by LRCT due to erosion and to protect sensitive vegetation. Signage indicating the closure has been posted, and hikers should not use this trail.

BROOK WALK
(LRCT; AMC MT. SHAW MAP, LRCT TRAIL MAP)

Cumulative from paved road on Castle in the Clouds grounds (1,230 ft.) to:	⮃	↗	⟳
Bridge below Falls of Song (930 ft.)	0.6 mi.	0 ft. (rev. 300 ft.)	0:20
Shannon Brook Trail (1,130 ft.)	0.8 mi.	200 ft.	0:30

This white-blazed trail follows the route of a historical path used by guests visiting Ossipee Park in the late 1800s and early 1900s. It is exceptionally scenic, passing seven named waterfalls on Shannon Brook, accompanied by interpretive signs. (*Note*: Parts of the route are rough along the steep brook bank.) Reach Brook Walk from the hiker parking area on NH 171 (via Shannon Brook Trail) or at the upper end of Ossipee Park Rd. In 2019, the short segment of a snowmobile trail that connected Brook Walk to Shannon Pond Trail was closed permanently due to erosion caused by repeated flooding from Shannon Pond Dam.

The upper end of the longer and more scenic western section of Brook Walk begins at a kiosk near a paved road on the Castle in the Clouds grounds, 125 yd. south of Shannon Pond. Here, the trail descends gradually on a grassy road for 0.1 mi., turns left onto a snowmobile trail for 10 yd., and then turns right into the woods, descending along the west side of Shannon Brook past Roaring Falls, Twin Falls, and Whittier Falls. At 0.3

mi. it turns left onto an old road, follows it for 100 yd. past Harriet's Cascades, and then turns left off the road and descends along the brook, with rough footing in places, passing Emerald Pool Falls. The route continues down to a beautiful view of Bridal Veil Falls at 0.5 mi., swings away from the brook briefly, and then descends to a flat area on the left near the top of the 60-ft. Falls of Song. (*Caution*: Use great care in this area. Do not venture near the edge of the falls.) The trail descends steeply over rock steps, turning left at the bottom at 0.6 mi. It then crosses a short bridge to a boardwalk that leads left 50 yd. to a viewing platform at the base of the Falls of Song. An extension of the trail continues ahead (southwest) for 0.1 mi. to a parking area at a hairpin turn on Castle in the Clouds' entrance road, 0.4 mi. above the gate on NH 171. Brook Walk crosses a bridge over Shannon Brook, then swings left (northeast) and climbs steeply to the east of and away from the brook, meeting Shannon Brook Trail 0.9 mi. above NH 171 and 0.5 mi. below Shannon Pond.

TURTLEBACK MTN. TRAIL
(LRCT; AMC MT. SHAW MAP, LRCT TRAIL MAP)

Cumulative from Shannon Brook Trail (1,230 ft.) to:	⤒⤓	↗	◯
Bald Knob Trail (1,700 ft.)	2.0 mi.	450 ft.	1:15
Turtleback Summit Trail (2,070 ft.)	3.0 mi.	850 ft.	1:55
High Ridge Trail (2,410 ft.)	5.2 mi.	1,200 ft.	3:10

This yellow-blazed trail follows old carriage roads across the south slopes of the Ossipees, connecting the Shannon Pond area with trails leading to Bald Knob, Turtleback Mtn., Black Snout, and Mt. Shaw. It leaves sharply right (east) from Shannon Brook Trail near the kiosk by the shore of Shannon Pond and runs at easy grades. At 0.4 mi. it passes a connector on the right that descends 0.1 mi. to Shannon Brook Trail. In another 85 yd. it passes a branch of Oak Ridge Trail on the left, and at 0.5 mi. it passes another branch of that same trail. At 1.1 mi., after a short, moderate ascent, Turtleback Mtn. Trail passes two entrances to Faraway Mtn. Trail, also on the left. It swings around a brook ravine, crosses the brook on a culvert at 1.3 mi., and then climbs by easy switchbacks. At 2.0 mi. it meets white-blazed Bald Knob Trail, which continues ahead 0.7 mi. to Bald Knob. Turtleback Mtn. Trail, meanwhile, turns sharply left and climbs by short, then longer, switchbacks to the height-of-land between Turtleback Mtn. and Middle Mtn. at 3.0 mi. Here, Turtleback Summit Trail leaves on the right, while Turtleback Mtn. Trail soon turns left (north) and then swings

SEC 4

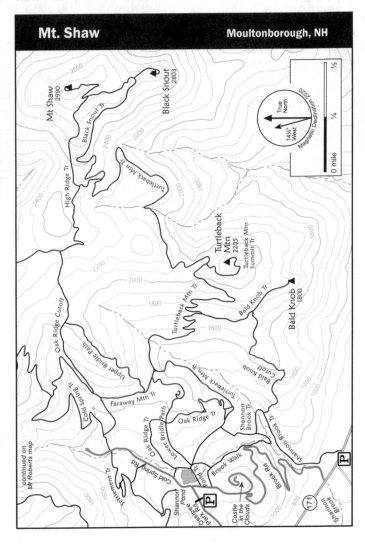

Mt. Shaw

Moultonborough, NH

Mt Shaw 2990

Black Snout Tr

Black Snout 2803

High Ridge Tr

Turtleback Mtn Tr

Turtleback Mtn 2205

Turtleback Mtn Summit Tr

Bald Knob Tr

Bald Knob 1800

Oak Ridge Cutoff

Upper Bridle Path

Turtleback Mtn Tr

Faraway Mtn Tr

Bald Knob Cutoff

Copps Spring Tr

Oak Ridge Tr

Lower Bridle Path

Shannon Brook Tr

Shannon Brook

Settlement Tr

Cold Spring Rd

Pond Tr

Brook Walk

Brook Rd

continued on Mt Roberts map

Shannon Pond

Ossipee Park Rd

Castle in the Clouds

Shannon Brook

171

True North

Magnetic Declination 2020

14½° West

0 mile   ¼   ½

right (east) again, crossing a bridge over a brook at 3.7 mi. It follows the brook for a short distance before swinging right around a minor ridge. At 4.4 mi. the trail turns sharply left and climbs to the junction with Black Snout Trail on the right at 5.0 mi. Here, Turtleback Mtn. Trail turns sharply left and then ascends gently to meet High Ridge Trail near a stagnant pool.

TURTLEBACK SUMMIT TRAIL
(LRCT; AMC MT. SHAW MAP, LRCT TRAIL MAP)

From Turtleback Mtn. Trail (2,070 ft.) to:	�??↕	↗	○
Turtleback Mtn. summit (2,205 ft.)	0.5 mi.	150 ft.	0:20

This orange-blazed spur trail follows an old carriage road from Turtleback Mtn. Trail—at the height-of-land 3.0 mi. from the Shannon Pond trailhead—to open ledges at the summit of Turtleback Mtn. The trail curves left and right and then follows the contour of the west slope of Turtleback Mtn. It then swings left at 0.3 mi. and ascends easily by switchbacks to the ledges, where there is a fine close-up view of Mt. Shaw and the main ridge of the Ossipees.

OAK RIDGE TRAIL
(LRCT; AMC MT. SHAW MAP, LRCT TRAIL MAP)

Cumulative from Turtleback Mtn. Trail (1,290 ft.) to:	↕	↗	○
Oak Ridge Lookout (1,490 ft.)	0.4 mi.	200 ft.	0:20
Kiosk at Shannon Pond (1,230 ft.)	1.3 mi.	200 ft. (rev. 250 ft.)	0:45

This blue-blazed trail makes possible an easy loop over the southern end of a low ridge, passing a good viewpoint above Lake Winnipesaukee. An interpretive guide, keyed to eighteen stations along the route, can be purchased from LRCT. Oak Ridge Trail begins on either of two short branches (each about 100 yd. long) that leave Turtleback Mtn. Trail, 0.4 mi. and 0.5 mi., respectively, from Shannon Brook Trail. From the point where the two branches join, Oak Ridge Trail follows a carriage road through several turns before reaching a short loop that leads to Oak Ridge Lookout on the left at 0.4 mi. Oak Ridge Trail crosses the flat crest of the ridge and descends gradually, crossing Bridle Path at 0.7 mi. From here, it descends moderately on a woods road, making a long curve around to the left (south). At 1.2 mi. it meets orange-blazed Pond Trail; here, it turns left, and the two trails coincide until they reach the junction with Shannon Brook Trail near the kiosk by the east shore of Shannon Pond.

BRIDLE PATH (LRCT; AMC MT. SHAW MAP, AMC MT. ROBERTS MAP, LRCT TRAIL MAP)

Cumulative from kiosk at Shannon Pond (1,230 ft.) to:	⇅	↗	↻
Faraway Mtn. Trail, lower jct. (1,580 ft.)	0.9 mi.	400 ft. (rev. 50 ft.)	0:40
Oak Ridge Cutoff (2,030 ft.)	1.9 mi.	900 ft. (rev. 50 ft.)	1:25
Mt. Shaw (2,990 ft.) via Oak Ridge Cutoff and High Ridge Trail	4.1 mi.	1,900 ft. (rev. 50 ft.)	3:00

This green-blazed trail, consisting of lower and upper sections, ascends along Oak Ridge, passing two outlooks. Lower Bridle Path begins behind the kiosk by the east shore of Shannon Pond and ascends easily on an old and sometimes muddy road, with one short bypass to the right. It crosses Oak Ridge Trail at 0.3 mi., and at 0.5 mi. it turns right. Here, a spur path diverges left and climbs 0.1 mi. by switchbacks to a ledge with a view of Lake Winnipesaukee. The main trail descends gradually north to a low spot and then ascends slightly to Faraway Mtn. Trail at 0.9 mi. The route turns left here and follows Faraway Mtn. Trail for 0.1 mi., where Upper Bridle Path diverges right 30 yd. beyond a 90-degree right turn. Becoming rougher, Upper Bridle Path ascends moderately up the ridge, passing an outlook on the right at 1.4 mi. At 1.6 mi. it gains the crest of the ridge and crosses several minor humps before ending at Oak Ridge Cutoff, 0.5 mi. above that trail's junction with Faraway Mtn. Trail.

OAK RIDGE CUTOFF
(LRCT; AMC MT. ROBERTS MAP, LRCT TRAIL MAP)

Cumulative from Faraway Mtn. Trail (1,610 ft.) to:	⇅	↗	↻
Bridle Path (2,030 ft.)	0.5 mi.	400 ft.	0:25
High Ridge Trail (2,350 ft.)	1.0 mi.	750 ft.	0:55

This white-blazed trail connects Faraway Mtn. Trail, 0.5 mi. north of Turtleback Mtn. Trail, with High Ridge Trail, 1.7 mi. west of Mt. Shaw. Oak Ridge Cutoff forms part of the shortest route from the Shannon Pond area to Mt. Shaw and Black Snout. From Faraway Mtn. Trail, Oak Ridge Cutoff climbs moderately northeast along the west side of Oak Ridge on an old woods road; then it swings right (east) and at 0.5 mi. passes a junction with Upper Bridle Path on the right. It continues climbing moderately and meets High Ridge Trail via either of two short branches.

COLD SPRING TRAIL
(LRCT; AMC MT. ROBERTS MAP, LRCT TRAIL MAP)

Cumulative from kiosk at Shannon Pond (1,230 ft.) to:	↧↥	↗	↻
Right turn off Cold Spring Rd. via Pond Trail (1,370 ft.)	0.6 mi.	150 ft.	0:20
Faraway Mtn. Trail (1,840 ft.)	1.9 mi.	600 ft.	1:15

This red-blazed trail follows a paved road and an old bridle path from Shannon Pond to the middle section of Faraway Mtn. Trail. From the kiosk by Shannon Pond, the most scenic route follows orange-blazed Pond Trail to the right (north) into the woods, passing the junction with Oak Ridge Trail on the right, bearing left across a bridge over Shannon Brook, and reaching paved Cold Spring Rd. at 0.2 mi.; Cold Spring Trail turns right here. (Pond Trail makes a 0.5-mi. loop around the pond, using roads part of the way.)

Pond Trail's junction with Cold Spring Rd. can also be reached in 0.2 mi. from the parking area near the gate on Ossipee Park Rd. Walk up the paved road past the gate for 0.1 mi. and turn left at a T intersection. In another 80 yd. bear right to continue on the paved road, avoiding a gravel road ahead that leads to Mt. Roberts Trail, and walk past a sign for Cold Spring Trail and a gate to the junction with Pond Trail. Mileages given below include the 0.2-mi. approach by either route.

Cold Spring Trail follows the road uphill at easy grades. At 0.4 mi., by the Copp cellar hole, blue-blazed Whitten Trail diverges left. It climbs past the Whitten family gravesite and cellar hole and ascends 100 ft. to meet Settlement Trail in 0.2 mi. At 0.6 mi., opposite the northern terminus of Settlement Trail, Cold Spring Trail turns right into the woods onto an old bridle path; travel is prohibited on the road beyond this point, as it leads to an inholding (i.e., privately owned land located within a parcel of public land). The trail soon passes to the right of the Roberts cellar hole, and at 0.7 mi. Faraway Mtn. Connector (marked with red and orange diamonds) diverges right, ascending 0.3 mi. and 200 ft. to Faraway Mtn. Trail. Cold Spring Trail climbs moderately through several turns, with occasional wet footing. At 1.0 mi. it bears right at a fork and ascends by long, grassy switchbacks to Faraway Mtn. Trail, which can be followed left for 1.7 mi. to High Ridge Trail.

FARAWAY MTN. TRAIL (LRCT; AMC MT. SHAW MAP, AMC MT. ROBERTS MAP, LRCT TRAIL MAP)

Cumulative from Turtleback Mtn. Trail (1,550 ft.) to:	⇅	↗	↺
Cold Spring Trail (1,840 ft.)	1.2 mi.	300 ft.	0:45
High Ridge Trail (2,450 ft.)	2.9 mi.	900 ft.	1:55

This orange-blazed trail follows an old carriage road and connects Turtleback Mtn. Trail, 1.1 mi. from the kiosk at Shannon Pond, with High Ridge Trail, 0.9 mi. east of Faraway Mtn. Lookout. Leaving Turtleback Mtn. Trail by either of two forks, Faraway Mtn. Trail ascends gently past junctions with Bridle Path on the left at 0.1 mi. and, after a sharp right turn, on the right at 0.2 mi. At 0.5 mi. Faraway Mtn. Connector enters on the left, having ascended 0.3 mi. from Cold Spring Trail, and in another 90 yd. Oak Ridge Cutoff diverges right. At 0.8 mi. Faraway Mtn. Trail turns sharply left across a bridge over a branch of Shannon Brook. It turns right where Cold Spring Trail enters on the left at 1.2 mi. Faraway Mtn. Trail then makes a long traverse to the left and climbs by several switchbacks to end at High Ridge Trail.

■ MT. SHAW (2,990 FT.)

Mt. Shaw is the highest peak in the Ossipee Range and the entire Lakes Region. Its partly open summit offers a panoramic vista of the White Mtns. and western Maine. The route described below uses a combination of trails that follow woods roads and old carriage roads. It leaves from the hiker parking area at the top of Ossipee Park Rd. Grades are easy to moderate, and footing is generally smooth along the old roads.

MT. SHAW TRAILS (LRCT; LRCT MAP)

Cumulative from Ossipee Park Rd. (1,250 ft.) to:	⇅	↗	↺
Cold Spring Trail (1,370 ft.)	0.8 mi.	120 ft.	0:25
High Ridge Trail (2,360 ft.)	2.3 mi.	1,110 ft.	1:40
Mt. Shaw summit (2,990 ft.)	4.0 mi.	1,740 ft.	2:50

From the parking area, follow paved Ossipee Park Rd., turn left at the first junction at 0.1 mi., and then quickly bear right onto red-blazed Cold Spring Rd. (part gravel and part paved). The gentle ascent includes two junctions: one with orange-blazed Pond Trail on the right at 0.2 mi. and the other with blue-blazed Whitten Trail on the left at 0.5 mi. At a four-way junction at 0.8 mi., turn right onto red-blazed Cold Spring Trail, which follows an old woods road past the Roberts cellar hole (Mt. Roberts was named for this family). At 0.9 mi. bear right onto Faraway Mtn.

Connector, blazed in both red and orange. The connector trail climbs moderately to a junction with orange-blazed Faraway Mtn. Trail at 1.2 mi. Turn left here. At 1.3 mi. bear right at the fork onto white-blazed Oak Ridge Cutoff. Following an old woods road, this trail climbs at easy to moderate grades, with rocky footing in places, and passes a junction on the right with green-blazed Upper Bridle Path at 1.8 mi. before coming to a branched junction with blue-blazed High Ridge Trail at 2.3 mi.

Turn right onto High Ridge Trail, a former carriage road, for an easy ramble along the highest ridge in the Ossipee Range (the trail doesn't dip below 2,300 ft.). At 3.0 mi. turn left at a junction where yellow-blazed Turtleback Mtn. Trail diverges right. High Ridge Trail ascends easily at first, then moderately. Bear right at a fork at 3.5 mi. where a snowmobile trail comes in on the left (in the reverse direction, bear left here). At 3.6 mi., after a junction on the right with white-blazed Black Snout trail, High Ridge Trail makes the final easy ascent to the summit at 4.0 mi. and loops around it. The outlook is on the northern side of this loop; the high point is on the southern side.

SEC 4

MT. SHAW TRAIL

The portion of the unofficial red-blazed trail to Mt. Shaw that ascends from NH 171 near its junction with Sodom Rd. crosses private land. It is not described in this guide or shown on the LRCT map.

HIGH RIDGE TRAIL
(LRCT; LRCT TRAIL MAP, AMC MT. ROBERTS MAP)

Cumulative from Mt. Shaw summit (2,990 ft.) to:	↥↧	↗	↻
Jct. with Turtleback Mtn. Trail (2,410 ft.)	1.1 mi.	0 ft. (rev. 600 ft.)	0:35
Oak Ridge Cutoff (2,350 ft.)	1.7 mi.	50 ft. (rev. 100 ft.)	0:55
Faraway Mtn. Trail (2,450 ft.)	2.9 mi.	200 ft. (rev. 50 ft.)	1:35
Mt. Roberts summit loop (2,570 ft.)	5.2 mi.	500 ft. (rev. 200 ft.)	2:50

This blue-blazed trail follows carriage roads along the crest of the range between Mt. Shaw on the southeast and Faraway Mtn. and Mt. Roberts on the northwest. The amount of vegetation on the trail may vary, depending on how recently the trail was cleared and how much foot traffic it has received. Grades are mostly easy. At its southeast end, High Ridge Trail makes a short loop around the summit of Mt. Shaw; the viewpoint is on the north end of the loop. At the southeast side of the loop, yellow-and-red-blazed Gorilla Trail diverges. This rough, rocky path is not maintained by LRCT and is not shown on the LRCT or AMC trail maps; in 1.2 mi.

it leads onto private land and then rises to the ledgy summit of Mt. Flagg (2,390 ft.), with excellent views, at 1.4 mi.

From the loop at the summit of Mt. Shaw, High Ridge Trail descends south by two switchbacks to its junction with Black Snout Trail at 0.4 mi. Here, High Ridge Trail turns sharply right as Black Snout Trail continues ahead. At 0.6 mi. High Ridge Trail turns left where a snowmobile trail continues ahead. It descends to a junction with Turtleback Mtn. Trail on the left by a stagnant pool at 1.1 mi. Here, High Ridge Trail turns right and meanders along the ridge. At 1.5 mi. the trail turns sharply right (north) and follows the contour of the west side of a knob, passing a junction with Oak Ridge Cutoff on the left at 1.7 mi. After crossing a saddle, High Ridge Trail swings left (west) around the north side of a knob, descends to another saddle, and ascends easily to a junction with Faraway Mtn. Trail on the left at 2.9 mi. It angles upward along the east side of Faraway Mtn.'s south ridge and then makes a hairpin turn left (south) and curves back to the right, reaching Faraway Mtn. Lookout at 3.8 mi., where there is a good view south over Lake Winnipesaukee.

High Ridge Trail swings north through boreal forest, passes an old road diverging right, and curves around the ravine at the head of Shannon Brook. At 4.3 mi. it swings right and crosses a bridge over Shannon Brook. It descends to a saddle and then climbs by switchbacks to a 0.2-mi. loop around the summit of Mt. Roberts at 5.2 mi. The left branch of the loop leads 60 yd. to a good view north to the Sandwich Range and Mt. Washington, visible beyond Black Snout. The right branch of the loop reaches the upper terminus of Mt. Roberts Trail in 110 yd.

■ MT. ROBERTS (2,584 FT.)

Mt. Roberts is one of the most popular hikes in the Lakes Region, offering spectacular vistas over Lake Winnipesaukee from its open south ridge, which Mt. Roberts Trail traverses. A side path on the ascent leads to a good viewpoint west, and an outlook near the summit provides views north to the White Mtns.

MT. ROBERTS TRAIL
(LRCT; AMC MT. ROBERTS MAP, LRCT TRAIL MAP)

Cumulative from parking area on Ossipee Park Rd. (1,250 ft.) to:	�	↗	↻
Spur path to first outlook (1,650 ft.)	1.2 mi.	400 ft.	0:50
High Ridge Trail and Mt. Roberts summit loop (2,570 ft.)	2.7 mi.	1,350 ft. (rev. 50 ft.)	2:00

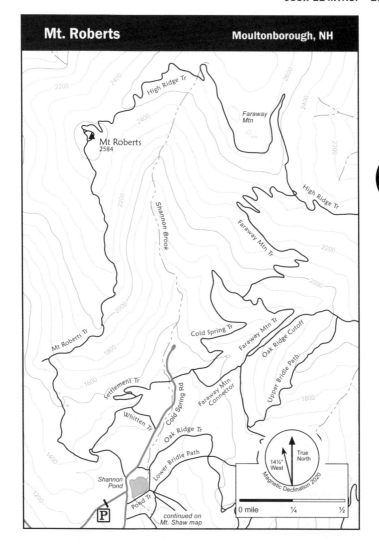

Mt. Roberts

Moultonborough, NH

SEC
4

continued on
Mt. Shaw map

Starting on the Castle in the Clouds grounds, this orange-blazed trail ascends Mt. Roberts via its ledgy south ridge. The route offers several excellent outlooks and passes through an unusual and extensive forest of scrub oak. Grades are moderate. From the trailhead parking area at the top of Ossipee Park Rd., walk around the gate and proceed up the road until you reach a T intersection at 0.1 mi. Bear left here. In another 85 yd. continue straight up a gravel driveway where the paved road (the start of Cold Spring Trail) swings right. Follow the driveway for 100 yd. When the driveway bears left to the stables, continue ahead across a field for 75 yd. to where Mt. Roberts Trail (blazes and sign) enters the woods.

The trail follows an old bridle path, bearing left at a fork at 0.4 mi. from the parking area, where Settlement Trail diverges right. Mt. Roberts Trail ascends for a short distance and then swings right across the top of a field (view) and onto a short relocated section. In another 50 yd. the trail turns right, going back into the woods. It ascends moderately, levels out, and descends slightly. At 0.8 mi. it turns right onto an older route of the trail. The grade is easy across a shoulder, and then the steadier ascent begins. At 1.2 mi. a spur path leads 70 yd. left to a fine view west. Here, Mt. Roberts Trail swings right (northeast) and climbs steadily, reaching the next outlook at 1.6 mi. It continues up the ridge, alternating between scrub oak forest and open ledges with fine views south over Lake Winnipesaukee and east to Mt. Shaw. (*Note:* Follow the blazes and cairns carefully across the ledgy areas, as it is important to avoid ecologically sensitive areas.) Mt. Roberts Trail reaches the highest open ledge at 2.3 mi. Here, it enters conifer woods, descends briefly, and then climbs moderately to the west end of blue-blazed High Ridge Trail, which makes a 0.2-mi. loop around the summit of Mt. Roberts. (Follow the loop 100 yd. to the right to reach a fine outlook north to the White Mtns.)

SETTLEMENT TRAIL (LRCT; AMC MT. ROBERTS MAP, LRCT MAP)

From Mt. Roberts Trail (1,300 ft.) to:	⇵	↗	↻
Cold Spring Rd. (1,360 ft.) via left fork of Settlement Loop	1.1 mi.	150 ft. (rev. 100 ft.)	0:40

This white-blazed trail, with a loop in its middle section, follows old roads at easy grades through an area of settlements from the early 1800s. It diverges right (northeast) from Mt. Roberts Trail 0.4 mi. from the parking area on Ossipee Park Rd. and ascends gradually, crossing two spots that were paved with cobblestones 200 years ago. At 0.3 mi. blue-blazed Whitten Trail diverges right and descends 0.2 mi. to Cold Spring Rd., passing the Whitten family gravesite and cellar hole and the Copp cellar hole. Settlement Trail swings left and reaches the lower junction with Settlement Loop at 0.5 mi. The right branch of the loop ascends 50 yd. to the upper loop junction. The left branch (the main route) continues ahead for 0.1 mi. and then turns right and leads to the upper loop junction at 0.7 mi. Here, Settlement Trail turns left, then swings right and descends gradually, crossing a brookbed just before reaching Cold Spring Rd. across from the start of the footpath section of Cold Spring Trail.

BLACK SNOUT TRAIL (LRCT; LRCT TRAIL MAP)

Cumulative from jct. with Turtleback Mtn. Trail (2,390 ft.) to:	⬇⬆	↗	⟳
Spur path to Black Snout (2,730 ft.)	1.2 mi.	350 ft.	0:45
Jct. with High Ridge Trail (2,820 ft.)	1.5 mi.	450 ft.	1:00

This white-blazed trail follows carriage roads along the southwest side of Mt. Shaw, connecting with several other trails and providing access (via a spur path) to fine views from Black Snout. Its west end diverges to the east from Turtleback Mtn. Trail, 0.2 mi. south of High Ridge Trail. Black Snout Trail climbs by switchbacks and then turns right and traverses southeast across the slope, passing the junction with red-blazed Mt. Shaw Trail on the right at 1.0 mi. (This trail, not maintained by LRCT and not shown on the LRCT or AMC trail maps, leads down to private land and should not be used without landowner permission.) At 1.2 mi. Black Snout Trail swings to the left; here, a spur path on the right follows an old carriage road 0.3 mi. at easy grades to a short loop at the summit of Black Snout, where there are fine views west and south. At 0.2 mi. from the main trail, the spur passes blue-blazed Ball Mtns. Trail on the left. (This trail, also known as Banana Trail, is not maintained by LRCT and not shown on the LRCT or AMC trail maps. It descends onto private land and should not be used without landowner permission.) A few yards beyond the junction with the spur, Black Snout Trail passes the start of obscure, yellow-blazed Thunderbird Trail (which also descends onto private land, is not maintained by LRCT, is not shown on the LRCT or AMC trail maps, and should not be used without landowner permission) on the right. It then ascends northwest to its junction with High Ridge Trail at 1.5 mi.; from here, it continues straight and reaches the summit of Mt. Shaw in 0.4 mi.

SEC 4

■ BAYLE MTN. (1,845 FT.)

This small, ledgy peak, which is almost in the center of the Ossipee Mtns. ring dike complex, offers excellent views in all directions from its bare summit, including an unusual and unique perspective on the higher summits of the range. In May 2015, a forest fire burned 275 acres on the mountain over a five-day period, but as of mid-2019 the upper slopes and summit had recovered beautifully, with only a few signs of the blaze remaining. The route to Bayle Mtn. consists of an approach on a snowmobile trail and a steep and rugged climb up the unofficial red-blazed Bayle Mtn. Trail.

From NH 16, 2.4 mi. south of its junction with NH 25 in West Ossipee, follow Pine Hill Rd., a good gravel road, west for 3.3 mi., and then turn right onto Conner Pond Rd. In another 0.6 mi. turn right onto Marble Rd., narrow but sound, and drive 0.6 mi. to a signed, designated parking pull-off on the right, just before a bridge over Lovell River and directly opposite a cabin. Do not park in front of any gates or in any spot that obstructs the road.

This route described below is entirely on private land and has been the subject of a dispute regarding access in the past. The landowner has graciously given permission for the description to appear in this guide. Please stay on the marked trail and respect the land; unauthorized trail maintenance is prohibited.

UNOFFICIAL BAYLE MTN. TRAILS
(USGS TAMWORTH AND OSSIPEE LAKE QUADS)

Cumulative from parking area on Marble Rd. (1,010 ft.) to:	↥↧	↗	⟳
Unofficial Bayle Mtn. Trail (1,110 ft.)	0.7 mi.	200 ft. (rev. 100 ft.)	0:25
Bayle Mtn. summit (1,853 ft.)	1.4 mi.	940 ft.	1:10

From the parking pull-off, continue up Marble Rd. a very short distance and turn sharply right onto an unsigned snowmobile trail with an orange gate, just before the bridge over Lovell River. The wide trail, with good footing, leads northeast, then north, with minor ups and downs; old woods roads join from the left at 0.1 mi. and from the right at 0.4 mi. Bear right at a prominent fork (arrow) at 0.5 mi. At 0.7 mi., at a high spot, Bayle Mtn. Trail leaves left at a new location, 0.1 mi. south of its former trailhead (now closed); the entrance to the trail is marked by a cairn and small sign.

This section of the route, on a footpath, is very lightly maintained and requires care to follow, especially in its middle portion and when leaving the summit. Pay close attention to the blazes, small cairns, and occasional flagging.

Bayle Mtn. Trail ascends moderately northwest across the slope for 0.2 mi.; then it turns left at the base of a boulder field where the former route comes in on the right (in reverse, turn right here). Now marked with faded red blazes, the trail ascends steeply with rough footing, winding through an area of large glacial boulders. At 1.1 mi. it climbs a very steep, slippery ledge beside a large slab; an overgrown bypass route is on left. The main trail continues up through the woods and across semi-open ledges, marked by small cairns. It reaches a high rock wall, scrambles up the right side, and then makes a short traverse along the edge of the wall (use caution). Above the wall, the trail levels briefly and then climbs moderately, breaking out into the open and ascending easily up broad ledges (not marked) to the bare summit at 1.4 mi.

The stretch between entering onto the ledges and the summit is not marked, so hikers should make note of where they emerge from the woods onto an open ledge ramp. The trail leaves the summit by descending along the prominent ramp on the south side and then bearing right at a turn; a small cairn sits beside a dead tree stub several yards ahead.

HAMLIN-EAMES-SMYTH RECREATION AND CONSERVATION AREA

This 500-acre tract on Wicwas (also spelled Wickwas) Lake in Meredith has an extensive trail system developed by the Meredith Conservation Commission. Attractions include several beaver ponds, old-growth forest, Crockett's Ledge (view of Belknap Range), White Mtns. Ledge (view of Sandwich Range), and an undeveloped section of shoreline on the lake. Various loop hikes of up to 5 mi. or more are possible. A trail map is available at the Meredith town offices and town library; also, refer to the USGS Winnisquam Lake quadrangle. To reach the trailhead, turn south onto Meredith Center Rd. from NH 104, 5.0 mi. east of I-93. In 0.9 mi. turn right onto Chemung Rd. Bear right at 2.5 mi. and follow Chemung Rd. to trailhead parking on the right at 2.9 mi. from NH 104. Trail maps are sometimes available at the kiosk.

BALD LEDGE (1,100 FT.)

Bald Ledge is a fine and easy-to-reach outlook on a bluff along the southwest side of Winona Lake in New Hampton. Bald Ledge Trail, on old woods roads and a short section of footpath, is mostly within Sky Pond State Forest; the outlook itself is on town conservation land. Though unblazed, it is easily followed. From US 3 in Ashland, follow NH 132 south and turn left onto Winona Rd. in 0.2 mi. At 1.0 mi. from US 3 turn right on Dana Hill Rd. At 1.7 mi. turn left on Lower Oxbow Rd. Turn left again on gravel Sky Pond Rd. at 2.9 mi. Follow it to the end of the maintained section at 3.8 mi., where there is limited parking on the right (do not block access) and signs for Sky Pond State Forest and Bald Ledge Trail on the left. Additional parking is available at the Sky Pond boat launch, which is off a spur road on the right just before the trailhead.

BALD LEDGE TRAIL (NHDFL; USGS HOLDERNESS QUAD)
From Sky Pond Rd.
(1,100 ft.) to:

	⇅	◢	◷
Bald Ledge (1,100 ft.)	0.8 mi.	100 ft. (rev. 100 ft.)	0:25

From the end of the maintained road, proceed on foot up the rough extension of Sky Pond Rd. At 0.2 mi. turn left onto a gated woods road, which descends through a grassy, brushy area before it levels, crosses a small brook, and swings left (northeast). At 0.6 mi. turn right onto a footpath (sign for Bald Ledge Trail) that ascends slightly and leaves Sky Pond State Forest. It immediately passes a yellow-blazed path on the left that descends 0.2 mi. to a small outlook. The footpath itself descends a short distance to the main outlook on Bald Ledge. The view includes the Squam, Sandwich, and Ossipee ranges, Red Hill, the Belknap Range, and parts of several lakes.

FOGG HILL (986 FT.)
This peak is within the 235-acre Fogg Hill Conservation Area in Center Harbor, which also features a large wetland area containing a rare kettle hole bog, a small beaver pond, and the larger Bear Pond. To the southwest of the summit are several scattered white oaks estimated to be more than 300 years old. From NH 104 in Meredith, take Winona Rd. northwest for 1.6 mi. Turn right onto Waukewan Rd. and follow it for 2.0 mi. Turn left onto Piper Hill Rd. and continue 1.5 mi. to trailhead and parking area on the left. A map is available at lrct.org.

FOGG HILL TRAIL (LRCT; LRCT MAP)
Cumulative from parking area
(620 ft.) to:

	⇅	◢	◷
Bear Pond Trail (620 ft.)	0.1 mi.	0 ft.	0:05
Bog Trail (860 ft.)	0.9 mi.	240 ft.	0:35
Fogg Hill summit (986 ft.)	1.0 mi.	370 ft.	0:40

This yellow-blazed trail offers a direct route to the summit of Fogg Hill. Grades are easy to moderate, with good footing. From the parking area, head southwest across a grassy field, bearing right through a gate (where blazes begin) onto a short section of woods road. Fogg Hill Trail quickly turns left off the road and onto a footpath; it passes a junction with Bear Pond Trail on the left at 0.1 mi. (this short trail leads 0.1 mi. to the southwest shore of the pond).

Fogg Hill Trail crosses a small stream at 0.2 mi. and then meanders at easy grades with a few zigzags to pass a picturesque beaver pond on the right at 0.4 mi. Just past the pond, the trail swings sharply left at a hairpin turn and begins a winding, moderate ascent, briefly joining an old logging road just before the junction with Bog Trail on the right at 0.9 mi. (Orange-blazed Bog Trail follows an old woods road and descends moderately 0.6 mi. to the turnaround at the end of Fogg Hill Rd.; parking is prohibited here.)

Climbing continues moderately as the trail winds its way up to the wooded summit of Fogg Hill at 1.0 mi., where a large split boulder is perched. This spot offers limited views south to the Belknap Range, though they are better in winter when the trees are bare.

SEC 4

WHITTEN WOODS CONSERVATION AREA

This 495-acre conservation area near downtown Ashland offers pleasant hiking along old woods roads through an area known as the Squam Uplands, a section of the watershed for Squam Lake and Little Squam Lake that sits above 900 ft. in elevation. The trails are mostly easy, with good footing, and provide access to excellent views over Squam Lake and Little Squam Lake to the surrounding mountains. The woods are named after Reuben Whitten, a local resident and farmer who successfully grew wheat and potatoes on the sunny south slopes of Indian Hill following the 1815 eruption of Indonesia's Mt. Tambora, which resulted in severe global crop failures. The property is managed through a partnership between the Squam Lakes Association, the Squam Lakes Conservation Society, New England Forestry Foundation, the town of Ashland, and the New Hampshire Land and Community Heritage Investment Program.

To reach the trailhead, take Exit 24 off I-93 and follow US 3 South/NH 25 East for 0.7 mi. Just past downtown Ashland, turn sharply left onto Highland St. and follow it 1.0 mi. to the trailhead and parking on the left. Refer to the Whitten Woods Conservation Area in-text map on p. 242.

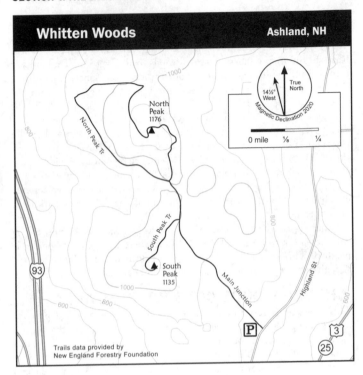

Whitten Woods   Ashland, NH

MAIN JUNCTION (SLA/SLCS/NEFF/ACC/LCHIP; SLA MAP)

From parking area (740 ft.) to:	↕	↗	↻
Jct. with North Peak Loop and South Peak Trail (1,000 ft.)	0.6 mi.	260 ft.	0:25

This red-blazed trail leaves the parking area and connects to South Peak Trail and North Peak Loop. Main Junction passes through the gate and ascends easily northwest along a wide woods road among tall pine trees, curving left through a large clearing. Above this clearing, the road narrows and climbs gradually to meet South Peak Trail (left) and North Peak Loop (straight ahead and right) at 0.6 mi.

NORTH PEAK LOOP (SLA/SLCS/NEFF/ACC/LCHIP; SLA MAP)

Cumulative from jct. with Main Junction and South Peak Trail (1,000 ft.) to:	⇅	⬈	◷
North Peak (1,173 ft.)	0.5 mi.	175 ft.	0:20
Starting point via complete loop	1.9 mi.	330 ft.	1:25

This blue-blazed trail allows for a loop hike over North Peak, with one good outlook on the way. The route is described here in the steeper counterclockwise direction and starts at the junction of Main Junction and South Peak Trail 0.6 mi. from the parking area and gate. Proceed northwest easily along an old woods road to the loop junction at 0.2 mi. Main Junction turns right (north) and ascends moderately to a cleared outlook on the right at 0.3 mi., with a view over Squam Lake and Little Squam Lake to Red Hill and the Ossipee Range. The trail enters the woods on a newer footpath section and climbs moderately by switchbacks, passing a framed view on the right to Jennings Peak and Sandwich Dome at 0.4 mi.; then it curves left to the wooded summit of North Peak at 0.5 mi.

From the summit, Main Junction bends right and descends easily, soon joining an old woods road. At 0.9 mi., the trail turns sharply left onto a very short footpath (avoid the old road that continues straight), immediately turns left again onto another road, and descends easily to a junction at 1.2 mi. Here, it turns left (avoid the road to the right) and climbs easily along the grassy woods road, continuing straight where an older road comes in on the right. (*Note:* This section was somewhat overgrown in 2018.) Main Junction reaches the loop junction at 1.7 mi. and descends easily to end at the junction with South Peak Trail at 1.9 mi.

SOUTH PEAK TRAIL (SLA/SLCS/NEFF/ACC/LCHIP; SLA MAP)

From jct. with Main Junction and North Peak Loop (1,000 ft.) to:	⇅	⬈	◷
South Peak (1,136 ft.)	0.3 mi.	140 ft.	0:15

This short, green-blazed side trail climbs to South Peak, which offers excellent views east and northeast. It begins at the junction of Main Junction and North Peak Loop 0.6 mi. from the parking area and gate. South Peak Trail ascends southwest along an old woods road at easy grades, passing a logged clearing with a view back to Jennings Peak and Sandwich Dome on the right at 0.2 mi. Past the clearing, the trail descends briefly, climbs a short, steep section, and curves left to reach the ledgy, semi-open summit of South Peak at 0.3 mi. A cleared outlook offers a nearly

SEC 4

180-degree vista to Mt. Prospect, the Squam, Ossipee and Sandwich ranges, Squam Lake, Little Squam Lake, and Red Hill.

THE BELKNAP RANGE AND MT. MAJOR (1,787 FT.)

The Belknap Mtns. are a prominent range west of Lake Winnipesaukee in the towns of Gilford, Gilmanton, and Alton. The range and the county in which it rises were named for Jeremy Belknap (1744–1796), author of the first comprehensive history of New Hampshire and a member of one of the early (1784) scientific expeditions to Mt. Washington, though Belknap himself did not reach the summit. The principal peaks on the main ridge, from north to south, are Mt. Rowe (1,676 ft.), Gunstock Mtn. (2,247 ft.), Belknap Mtn. (2,384 ft.), and Piper Mtn. (2,041 ft.). A fire tower on Belknap Mtn. and the cleared summit of Gunstock Mtn., as well as numerous scattered ledges on all the peaks, provide fine views of Lake Winnipesaukee, the Ossipee and Sandwich ranges, and Mt. Washington.

Principal trailheads are at the Gunstock Mtn. Resort (east side) and on Carriage Rd. (west side). East Gilford Trail also ascends from the east, beginning at a parking area on private land off Wood Rd. Paths along the ridge connect all four summits. Mt. Major (1,787 ft.), which has excellent views over Lake Winnipesaukee, is in Alton, east of the main Belknap Mtns. A long, lumpy ridge runs east from Belknap Mtn. to Mt. Major, consisting of Straightback Mtn. (1,909 ft.) and several other humps that are officially nameless but have been given local names by the Boy Scouts of the Griswold Scout Reservation: Mt. Klem (2,000 ft.), Mt. Mack (1,943 ft.), and Mt. Anna (1,676 ft.). A parallel ridge to the north is sometimes called the Quarry Mtns. The jewel of this range is Round Pond, a beautiful and secluded mountain pond lying at the foot of Mt. Klem, just south of the main ridge crest, at an elevation of 1,652 ft. The USGS West Alton and Laconia quadrangles cover the Belknap Range.

The area's trail systems have been greatly expanded and improved in recent years, with better blazing and signage, though some trails described below may still require considerable care to follow. All the trails described here are shown on this book's *AMC Southern New Hampshire Trail Map* (Map 4). In addition to the map in this guide, a detailed map of the Belknap Range is available at belknaprangetrails.org; printed color copies are usually available for purchase for a nominal fee at local libraries, including those in Gilford, Laconia, Gilmanton, Alton, Meredith, Barnstead, Sanbornton, and Tuftonboro. This map shows all the trails described here, plus others that may be extremely obscure and rough or require the permission of the landowner for hiking use. It also labels several minor knobs with names that are not recognized by any authority. An unofficial "Belknap Range Hiker" patch is available from the Belknap County Sportsmen's Association for climbing twelve peaks in the Belknap Range: Rowe, Gunstock, Belknap, Piper, Whiteface, Mack, Klem, Rand, Anna, West Quarry, Straightback, and Major. For information, see belknapcountysportsmens.org. In addition, a separate red-lining patch is available to hikers who complete the approximately 65 mi. of trails in the range. See belknaprangetrailtenders.org for details. In 2018, Lakes Region Conservation Trust published a full-color map of the range, available for purchase at lrct.org.

Public and quasi-public organizations own most of the peaks and slopes of the Belknap Mtns. Public ownership includes Belknap County (Gunstock Mtn. Resort), the state of New Hampshire (Belknap Mtn. State Forest), and the town of Gilford. The Griswold Scout Reservation, owned by the Daniel Webster Council Boy Scouts of America, encompasses much of the land to the south of the eastern ridge and a considerable portion of the ridge itself, including most of Round Pond (the western shore is part of Belknap Mtn. State Forest) and Mts. Klem, Mack, and Anna. A volunteer organization, the Belknap Range Trail Tenders, has assumed primary responsibility for the maintenance of many trails in the Belknap Range.

In general, camping and fires are prohibited in this area; Gunstock Mtn. Resort (603-293-4341; gunstock.com) offers camping in summer (Memorial Day through Columbus Day) and winter (early December through late April).

A major network of trails is maintained in Griswold Scout Reservation, southwest of Belknap Mtn. State Forest; the trails on and near the ridge crest, described below, are open to public use. The trails leading from the main camp areas northward up to the ridge trails are not described here, though they are shown on the trail maps referred to above. These trails are open to public use from September through May without advance permission, with parking available at Camp Bell (on Manning Lake Rd. in Gilmanton) and at Camp Hidden Valley (off Places Mill Rd., also in Gilmanton). Hikers should leave a basic trip plan in their vehicle's window. During the camp season, June through August, hikers are asked to check in and log out at the administration building at each camp. For driving directions, see nhscouting.org.

The trails in the Mt. Major, Straightback Mtn., and Quarry Mtns. areas are on private land, with the exception of a small state forest at the top of

SEC
4

Mt. Major. In 2014, the Society for the Protection of New Hampshire Forests (Forest Society) and the LRCT completed a campaign to conserve four parcels of land, totaling 950 acres, around Mt. Major, Piper Mtn., Belknap Mtn., North Straightback Mtn., and the Quarry Mtns.

Gunstock Mtn. Resort (gunstock.com), operated by Belknap County, is a four-season recreation area off NH 11A, 2.8 mi. east of its junction with NH 11B. An access road leads to a large parking area in 0.7 mi.; several trails begin here. The resort includes a major downhill ski area on Mt. Rowe and Gunstock Mtn. and a large campground. The chairlift on Gunstock Mtn. operates at times in summer and fall; call 603-293-4341 for information. The ski trails can be used during the nonwinter months to ascend Gunstock Mtn. and Mt. Rowe, and there is also an extensive network of cross-country ski trails (fee charged in winter), many of which are available as multiuse trails during the nonwinter months. A trail map is available at the resort's information center. Ellacoya State Park on Lake Winnipesaukee is nearby.

Carriage Rd. provides access to all trails on the west side of the Belknap Range; reach it by leaving NH 11A at the village of Gilford and following Belknap Mtn. Rd. south, bearing left at 0.8 mi. and right at 1.4 mi. At 2.4 mi. Carriage Rd. forks left and leads in 0.2 mi. to a gate, which is locked from 6 P.M. to 9 A.M. in summer and fall. (In winter the road is plowed to the gate, where limited parking may be available; do not block the gate. The gate may be open for snowmobile traffic if there is sufficient snow cover, but the road is not plowed beyond the gate, and automobile travel is forbidden.) A small parking area sits on the left just before the gate. Gunstock Mtn. and Piper Mtn. Trails begin a short distance above the gate. From the gate, proceed carefully up Carriage Rd., which has steep grades and sharp turns and is rough in places. Another parking area is located 1.3 mi. above the gate. Various relatively easy loop hikes may be made from this trailhead. For Warden's (Green), Red, and Blue trails, walk up Carriage Rd. toward the fire warden's garage (signs on wall). White Trail begins 0.2 mi. back down the road on the left. Overnight parking and camping are not allowed anywhere in this area.

A separate small trail network (consisting of Lakeview Trail and Quarry Trail), not described in detail here, provides a 1.8-mi. loop (450-ft. ascent) with two viewpoints on Lockes Hill (1,057 ft.), a low northern spur of the Belknap Range. Access is from a trailhead parking area for Gilford's 280-acre Kimball Wildlife Forest on the south and west sides of NH 11 about 2 mi. east of its junction with NH 11B; refer to the USGS Laconia and West Alton quadrangles.

Additional hiking trails are available on the south side of the Belknap Range at the Forest Society's 431-acre Morse Preserve in Alton. From a parking area on Avery Hill Rd., yellow-blazed Arlene Frances Morse Trail and Dana & Arthur Morse Loop Trail make a 1.7-mi. loop with a 300-ft. ascent through woods, brushy areas, and blueberry barrens to an open shoulder of Pine Mtn. (1,410 ft.), with excellent views north. From NH 11 in Alton Bay, turn left onto Rand Hill Rd. Turn left onto Alton Mtn. Rd. at 0.7 mi. from NH 11. Turn left onto Avery Hill Rd. at 2.6 mi., and reach a parking area in Mike Burke Town Forest on the right at 2.8 mi. From the parking area, cross Avery Hill Rd. and walk 70 yd. right to the sign for Morse Preserve. Information and a trail map are available at forestsociety .org. Also, refer to the USGS Gilmanton Ironworks quadrangle.

SEC 4

BLUE TRAIL (BRATTS; MAP 4: G2)

Cumulative from upper Carriage Rd. parking area (1,670 ft.) to:	↥↧	↗	↻
Belknap–Gunstock col (2,000 ft.)	0.6 mi.	350 ft.	0:30
Belknap Mtn. summit (2,384 ft.)	1.1 mi.	700 ft.	0:55

This blue-blazed trail runs from the upper parking lot on Carriage Rd. to the summit of Belknap Mtn. It follows the extension of the carriage road past the warden's garage and the junctions with Warden's (Green) and Red trails on the right, descends slightly to cross a brook, and then diverges right and climbs to the Belknap-Gunstock col at 0.6 mi. Here, orange-blazed Overlook Trail continues straight while white-blazed Saddle Trail diverges left for Gunstock Mtn. Blue Trail, now coinciding with Belknap Range Trail, turns right and climbs, crossing a meadow with a limited outlook to Gunstock Mtn. at 0.7 mi. It passes a cleared outlook north on the left at 1.0 mi. and continues at easier grades up through coniferous woods to the summit. Descending, Blue Trail starts near the northeast side of the summit's fire tower.

WARDEN'S TRAIL, AKA GREEN TRAIL (BRATTS; MAP 4: G2)

From upper Carriage Rd. parking area (1,670 ft.) to:	↥↧	↗	↻
Belknap Mtn. summit (2,384 ft.)	0.8 mi.	700 ft.	0:45

Warden's Trail (Green Trail), which starts at the upper parking area on Carriage Rd., is the shortest route to Belknap Mtn. but is rather steep, with ledges that are slippery when wet, particularly on descent. The green-blazed trail leaves the Carriage Rd. extension behind the warden's garage and ascends on a service road, crossing under a telephone line. It continues to climb, passes a well on the right (not dependable), and reaches the fire tower at the summit. Descending, Warden's Trail begins on the southwest side of the fire tower.

RED TRAIL (BRATTS; MAP 4: G2)

From upper Carriage Rd. parking area (1,670 ft.) to:	↕	↗	◔
Belknap Mtn. summit (2,384 ft.)	0.9 mi.	700 ft.	0:50

This red-blazed trail, less steep and more scenic than Warden's Trail, but rough in parts, climbs from the upper parking area on the Carriage Rd. extension to the summit of Belknap Mtn. It leaves just beyond the Warden's Trail junction, climbs past a good outlook to the west at 0.5 mi., and continues to the summit, bearing to the right of a communications building and leveling out near the top. Descending, Red Trail begins near the north side of the fire tower.

WHITE TRAIL (BRATTS; MAP 4: G2)

Cumulative from upper Carriage Rd. parking area (1,670 ft.) to:	↕	↗	◔
Old Piper Trail (1,800 ft.)	0.4 mi.	200 ft. (rev. 50 ft.)	0:15
Belknap Mtn. summit (2,384 ft.)	1.3 mi.	750 ft	1:00

This white-blazed trail ascends to the summit of Belknap Mtn. via the Belknap-Piper col. It begins on Carriage Rd. about 0.2 mi. below the upper parking area, just below the highest bridge; there is no parking here. White Trail ascends 0.2 mi. to a point about 50 yd. below the pass between Belknap Mtn. and Piper Mtn. and turns left where orange-blazed Old Piper Trail continues straight to the pass and then turns right to Piper Mtn. White Trail winds up a relocated section to an outlook to the south and west on the right at 0.6 mi. from the upper parking area. Here, the trail turns sharply left and reaches an excellent outlook to the southeast, where it turns left again. White Trail soon swings right and climbs steadily, passing through some beautiful, shady coniferous woods, to the junction with East Gilford Trail, which enters from the right on the ledges at 1.1 mi. The two trails, which also coincide with Belknap Range Trail in this segment, ascend together (now blazed in both white and yellow) at an easy grade, leading north. They soon swing right onto a relocated section around a communications tower and then rejoin the original route and follow it under a power line to the summit and fire tower.

Descending, White Trail and East Gilford Trail begin at the summit ledge on the south side of the fire tower; they follow a power line for 70 yd. and then diverge left onto the relocation.

OLD PIPER TRAIL (BRATTS; MAP 4: G2–H2)

From White Trail (1,800 ft.) to:	Distance	Elevation gain	Time
Piper Mtn. north summit (2,030 ft.)	0.5 mi.	250 ft.	0:20

This orange-blazed trail ascends Piper Mtn. from White Trail 0.4 mi. from the upper parking area on Carriage Rd. and 50 yd. below the Belknap-Piper col. It turns right upon reaching the col, and in 30 yd. it passes a junction on the left with green-blazed Round Pond–Piper Link, which joins Belknap Range Trail at the bottom of Boulder Trail and continues on to Round Pond. Old Piper Trail ascends at easy grades for 0.2 mi. and then climbs moderately through woods and over ledges, passing an excellent outlook east over the Moulton Brook valley at 0.3 mi. It emerges on open ledges by an east-facing rock throne at the north summit of Piper Mtn., where it meets Piper Mtn. Trail and Piper–Whiteface Link.

SEC 4

WHITEFACE MTN. TRAIL (BRATTS; MAP 4: H1–H2)

Cumulative from end of Belknap Mtn. Rd. (1,050 ft.) to:	Distance	Elevation gain	Time
Piper–Whiteface Link (1,510 ft.)	0.7 mi.	450 ft.	0:35
Whiteface Mtn. summit (1,671 ft.)	1.6 mi.	700 ft. (rev. 100 ft.)	1:10

This trail leads from the end of Belknap Mtn. Rd. to the open summit of Whiteface Mtn. and also provides access to Piper Mtn. via Piper–Whiteface Link. Its lower part is on land owned by Lakes Region Conservation Trust, while the upper part follows a jeep road that has been heavily affected by ATV use. To reach the trailhead, follow Belknap Mtn. Rd. past the junction with Carriage Rd. 2.4 mi. from NH 11A. Turn left at 3.4 mi. and park on the right at the end of the paved road at 3.8 mi. Public parking is prohibited beyond this point. Walk up the gravel continuation of the road, passing two houses on the left, and in 110 yd., just before a third house, turn left into the woods at a sign ("Hiking Trail").

The blue-blazed trail ascends moderately on an eroded old roadbed, passing an LRCT kiosk. At 0.4 mi. it swings right, crosses a small brook, and then climbs to the ridge crest, meeting Piper–Whiteface Link at 0.7 mi. Here, Whiteface Mtn. Trail bears right through a gap in a stone wall and descends slightly, passing an unmarked path that descends left, to an open meadow with a view of the summit ahead. The trail swings right across the meadow and then turns left to join a rocky jeep road badly eroded by ATV use. Whiteface Mtn. Trail follows the road along the ridge, crossing an intermediate hump with partial views. It makes a short, steep ascent to open ledges on the north side of the summit, with excellent views north and west, and then continues to a large clearing at the true summit, where there are views to the south.

PIPER–WHITEFACE LINK (BRATTS; MAP 4: H2)

Cumulative from Whiteface Mtn. Trail (1,510 ft.) to:	⇅	↗	⟳
Vista Trail (2,010 ft.)	0.6 mi.	500 ft.	0:35
Piper Mtn. north summit (2,030 ft.)	0.8 mi.	500 ft.	0:40

This trail, blazed in green, connects Whiteface Mtn. Trail with Piper Mtn. Piper–Whiteface Link leaves Whiteface Mtn. Trail on the ridge crest 0.7 mi. from the trailhead on Belknap Mtn. Rd., and soon begins a steady ascent to the northeast through oak woods. Higher up, it crosses semi-open ledges with some views to the south. Follow the footway with care across the ledges, where it is marked by cairns and green blazes. At 0.5 mi., at the top of a large sloping ledge, there is an excellent outlook south and west. The trail climbs a short distance farther and then bears right into conifers. At 0.6 mi., shortly before reaching the open south end of the Piper Mtn. summit ridge, it arrives at a posted junction where Vista Trail diverges sharply right. Piper–Whiteface Link bears left, then right, across a ledgy area with views of Belknap Mtn. and out to the east. The trail winds across ledges and through scrub along the nearly level ridge. Follow cairns carefully; blueberry pickers have created many paths. At 0.8 mi. the trail emerges in a large, open, ledgy area and crosses it to reach two rock thrones on the north summit of Piper Mtn. Here, orange-blazed Old Piper Trail leaves north, and red-blazed Piper Mtn. Trail descends northwest.

VISTA TRAIL (BRATTS; MAP 4: H2)

Cumulative from Piper–Whiteface Link (2,010 ft.) to:	⇅	↗	⟳
Ledges on southeast ridge of Piper Mtn. (1,870 ft.)	0.4 mi.	0 ft. (rev. 150 ft.)	0:15
Swett Mtn. viewpoint (1,535 ft.)	1.3 mi.	85 ft. (rev. 590 ft.)	0:40

This yellow-blazed trail provides access to open ledges on the southeast ridge of Piper Mtn., ending at a viewpoint just beyond the summit of

Swett Mtn. Vista Trail diverges to the east from Piper–Whiteface Link near the south end of the Piper Mtn. summit ridge (sign: "S. Piper, Swett"). It soon swings right and descends moderately over ledges and through patches of woods, with some views to the southwest. At 0.3 mi. it levels in a spruce grove and then emerges on an expanse of open ledges with wide views south and east at 0.4 mi. Continuing southeast, Vista Trail descends the ledges, marked by paint blazes and cairns, with one steep section, to reenter the woods. The trail bears right and descends very steeply down a rough rockfall (use caution, especially in wet or icy conditions); then it turns left to gain the ridgeline, passing a large glacial boulder on the right. Walking is easy along this beautiful wooded ridge. At 1.1 mi. the trail passes through a stone wall and briefly enters private property before ascending easily to the wooded summit of Swett Mtn. at 1.3 mi. A good viewpoint northeast to Mt. Mack and Mt. Anna is 70 yd. to the east. Just beyond the summit, Vista Trail swings around to the southwest and ends at a partly open ledge with a good view south.

SEC 4

PIPER MTN. TRAIL (BRATTS; MAP 4: G2–H2)

From Carriage Rd. (1,030 ft.) to:	↕	↗	○
Piper Mtn. north summit (2,030 ft.)	1.3 mi.	1,000 ft.	1:10

This red-blazed trail provides direct access to Piper Mtn. from the lower end of Carriage Rd. Grades are mostly moderate. The trailhead on the right (south) side of Carriage Rd. is 0.4 mi. from Belknap Mtn. Rd., just beyond a bridge over Gunstock Brook. Parking is available 0.1 mi. below the trailhead (on the left, just before the gate) or 0.1 mi. above it (a pull-off on the right); parking is not permitted at the trailhead itself.

Leaving Carriage Rd., Piper Mtn. Trail soon swings left and crosses a footbridge over a brook; then it ascends rather steeply along the blue-blazed boundary of Belknap Mtn. State Forest. At 0.2 mi. the grade eases as the trail enters private land that has been selectively logged. At 0.6 mi. the trail crosses a muddy logging road (go straight across, following signs and blazes), leaves the logged area, and ascends through mixed forest. At 0.8 mi. Piper Mtn. Trail swings left and climbs through a ledgy area, passing a restricted outlook northwest. It continues climbing over ledges and through patches of oak woods, with several turns; follow blazes and cairns carefully. Passing a good view southwest to Mt. Kearsarge at 1.1 mi., the trail continues up through spruce forest and emerges on open ledges at the north summit of Piper Mtn. A stone chair here offers a view west. The trail continues another 25 yd. across open ledges to a second rock throne, with an excellent view east. Orange-blazed Old Piper Trail joins from the left (north) and green-blazed Piper–Whiteface Link joins from the right (south). Descending, Piper Mtn. Trail drops northwest into the woods from the west-facing rock throne; look for a fingerlike cairn with a red blaze.

GUNSTOCK MTN. TRAIL (BRATTS; MAP 4: G2)

Cumulative from Carriage Rd. (1,030 ft.) to:	⇅	↗	↻
Winter Short Cut (1,800 ft.)	0.7 mi.	750 ft.	0:45
Spur path to outlook (1,880 ft.)	0.8 mi.	850 ft.	0:50
Gunstock Mtn. summit (2,247 ft.)	1.1 mi.	1,200 ft.	1:10

This orange-blazed trail leads from the lower end of Carriage Rd. to the summit of Gunstock Mtn. and makes possible a loop hike including Gunstock, Belknap, and Piper mtns. with descent via Piper Mtn. Trail. Grades are steady and occasionally steep. Gunstock Mtn. Trail departs Carriage Rd. at a sign on the left (north) side, 0.3 mi. from Belknap Mtn. Rd. and 60 yd. beyond the gate; parking is available on the left just before the gate.

Leaving the road, the trail climbs steadily northeast and then north up a minor southwestern ridge of Gunstock Mtn., passing through a stone wall at 0.3 mi. It rises into ledgy oak woods, bearing right (northeast) at 0.6 mi. At 0.7 mi. it bears right again where green-blazed Winter Short Cut diverges left. (This alternate route, less ledgy than the main trail, ascends steeply for 0.3 mi. to Ridge Trail, 35 yd. below that trail's junction with Gunstock Mtn. Trail.) At 0.8 mi. Gunstock Mtn. Trail turns left (north) in a ledgy area, where side paths lead to a large sloping ledge on the right with excellent views south and west. The main trail continues its steep ascent through ledgy spruce forest, scrambling up through a jumble of rocks at 1.0 mi. Just above, an obscure path leads 20 yd. right to a ledge with an improved view south, and then white-blazed Ridge Trail joins from the left (sign). Blazed in both white and orange, the combined trails pass an outlook to the east and climb steadily to a junction with Brook Trail on the right and turn left; in another 40 yd. the three combined trails, now marked in orange, white and yellow, emerge at the summit beside the Safety Services building of Gunstock Mtn. Resort's ski area. The top of the ski slopes a short distance ahead offers fine views. To the right, a ski trail leads 30 yd. down to the upper terminus of Brook Trail.

Combined Gunstock Mtn. Trail and Ridge Trail, and Brook Trail begin the descent behind the left side of the Safety Services building and adjacent restroom (signs; orange, white, and yellow blazes).

RIDGE TRAIL (BRATTS; MAP 4: F2–G2)

Cumulative from Gunstock Mtn. Resort parking lot (930 ft.) to:	⬇⬆	↗	⟳
Mt. Rowe summit (1,676 ft.)	0.9 mi.	730 ft.	0:50
Gunstock Mtn. summit (2,247 ft.)	2.8 mi.	1,500 ft. (rev. 200 ft.)	2:10

This white-blazed trail, a segment of Belknap Range Trail, runs from the main parking lot at Gunstock Mtn. Resort to the summit of Mt. Rowe and then continues along the ridge to the summit of Gunstock Mtn. A major relocation in 2013 moved the upper part of the trail off the Gunstock resort's ski slopes and into the woods. From the main parking lot, follow the walkway down to the front of the main base lodge; then take the paved road to the right of the lodge, between the building and a pond. In 100 yd. follow the road left around the building; turn right onto Alpine Ridge Rd. and then left onto Single Chair Path (a gravel service road for the communications tower on Mt. Rowe). The trail (sign, white blazes) starts to the right of the main Mountain Coaster amusement ride building.

Ridge Trail climbs easily alongside the Mountain Coaster, bears left at a fork, and at 0.3 mi. passes a junction on the left with a signed ("Road Bypass"), white- and green-blazed footpath to the summit. (This alternate bypass route provides a 0.8-mi. alternative to walking on the road and rejoins the main route of Ridge Trail at the true summit of Mt. Rowe, just south of the communications tower. 0.6 mi. up this path, a spur trail [sign: "View"] leaves on the right and leads 100 yd. to an excellent view east and northeast over Lake Winnipesaukee to the Ossipee Range from the site of a former ski area warming hut.) Ridge Trail now ascends fairly steeply along the service road, bearing left at a fork at 0.4 mi. It continues climbing to the communications tower near the flat summit of Mt. Rowe at 0.9 mi. from the parking area. The trail continues to the left on a woods road along the nearly level ridge, passing over the wooded true summit at the upper end of the road bypass trail (sign), soon coming into the open with excellent views of Gunstock Mtn. and Lake Winnipesaukee and passing to the left of a USGS monitoring station. (Take care to stay on the blazed route, avoiding side roads and paths. A network of blazed paths originating at Gilford Elementary School ascends the ridge from the west; these intersect Ridge Trail in two places but are not described in this guide.) At some smooth ledges at 1.3 mi., Ridge Trail (cairn and white-blazed post) bears left where blue-blazed Mt. Rowe Trail from Gilford Elementary School enters on the right. Ridge Trail descends into a small ravine and then climbs up into blueberry patches with more views. It comes within sight of

SEC
4

a ski trail and turns right, staying to the right of (above) the ski trail as it climbs through patches of woods and ledges.

At 1.7 mi., where Ridge Trail formerly joined a ski trail, it continues ahead on the 2013 relocation; here, purple-blazed Benjamin Weeks Trail from Gilford Elementary School leaves on the right. Ridge Trail climbs at easy to moderate grades, by many short switchbacks, through woods to the west of the ski trail. Passing through conifer woods, it largely follows the west side of Gunstock Mtn., passes a short view spur (sign: "View") on the left, and reaches an outlook north at 2.6 mi. At 2.7 mi. Ridge Trail turns sharply left and uphill, where green-blazed Winter Short Cut, an alternate route for a steep section of Gunstock Mtn. Trail, joins from the right. Ridge Trail climbs 35 yd. to a junction where orange-blazed Gunstock Mtn. Trail joins from the right, and both trails coincide, now blazed in both white and orange. Ridge Trail passes a cleared outlook and picnic table on the right with an excellent view east, then turns left at a junction with yellow-blazed Brook Trail on the right. From this point, Ridge Trail, Gunstock Mtn. Trail and Brook Trail all run together, blazed in white, orange, and yellow, to the summit of Gunstock Mtn. at 2.8 mi., where fine views are available from the ski slopes a short distance ahead, near the top of a chairlift.

Leaving the summit, the combined Ridge Trail, Gunstock Mtn. Trail, and Brook Trail begin to the left of the Gunstock ski area's Safety Services building and adjacent restroom (signs; white, orange, and yellow blazes).

BROOK TRAIL (BRATTS; MAP 4: F2–G2)

From Gunstock Mtn. Resort parking lot (930 ft.) to:	⇅	↗	⟳
Gunstock Mtn. summit (2,247 ft.)	1.7 mi.	1,300 ft.	1:30

This yellow-blazed trail is the most direct hiking route from Gunstock Mtn. Resort to the summit of Gunstock Mtn. It is rather steep and rough in places. Start from the south side of the parking area, following a gravel service road to the left of the resort's prominent Panorama chairlift. In 100 yd.—to the right of a kiosk with a yellow blaze and a stone fireplace, both on the left—head up a grassy ski trail. Follow the ski trail for 90 yd. and then bear left off it into the woods (sign; yellow blazes). The trail immediately crosses a brook, follows its bank, and crosses another ski trail. After reentering the woods, Brook Trail crosses and quickly recrosses another brook, and soon begins to climb away from the brook as it ascends in the valley. At 0.5 mi. it crosses another ski trail and climbs, steeply at times, passing through a ski glade until it meets a stone wall. Brook Trail turns left along the wall, crosses another ski trail at 1.2 mi., and ascends along the left edge to the junction with yet another ski trail. Brook Trail then climbs to a junction with Saddle Trail on the left at 1.5 mi. and turns right, where it becomes a segment of Belknap Range Trail. The trail climbs up a relocated section around a steep and wet area to a junction with the combined Ridge Trail and Gunstock Mtn. Trail on the left (white and orange blazes) and continues ahead as all three trails now coincide and ascend to the summit of Gunstock Mtn.

Leaving the summit, the combined Brook Trail Trail, Gunstock Mtn. Trail and Ridge Trail begin to the left of the Gunstock ski area's Safety Services building and adjacent restroom (signs; yellow, orange and white blazes).

SADDLE TRAIL (BRATTS; MAP 4: G2)

From Belknap-Gunstock col (2,000 ft.) to:	⇅	↗	◯
Brook Trail jct. (2,050 ft.)	0.1 mi.	50 ft.	0:05

This very short, white-blazed trail, also a segment in Belknap Range Trail, connects the col between Belknap Mtn. and Gunstock Mtn. with Brook Trail. Leaving the junction with Overlook Trail and Blue Trail in the col, it crosses the flat sag and climbs moderately to the junction where Brook Trail enters on the right.

ROUND POND TRAIL (BRATTS; MAP 4: F2–G3)

Cumulative from Gunstock Mtn. Resort parking lot (930 ft.) to:	⇅	↗	◯
Jct. with Short Oak Trail and divergence of Overlook Trail (1,140 ft.)	0.9 mi.	200 ft.	0:35
Lower jct. with East Gilford Trail (1,230 ft.)	1.8 mi.	400 ft. (rev. 100 ft.)	1:05
Round Pond–Piper Link (1,710 ft.)	3.0 mi.	1,000 ft. (rev. 100 ft.)	2:00
Northwest shore of Round Pond (1,652 ft.)	3.1 mi.	1,000 ft. (rev. 50 ft.)	2:05

This multiuse trail in the Gunstock Mtn. Resort trail system runs from the main ski area parking lot to Round Pond. In addition to providing access to the pond from the recreation area, it connects with Overlook Trail, East Gilford Trail, and Round Pond–Piper Link, making possible a great variety of loop hikes from several trailheads. For the first 0.9 mi. it coincides with Overlook Trail and is blazed in both red and orange; thereafter it is blazed in red.

From the ski area parking lot, follow the access road back past the last of the maintenance buildings and then turn right onto a gravel road leading across a small stone bridge. Note the signs for Round Pond and Overlook trails; this road is also called Cobble Mtn. X-C Trail. In 35 yd. the gravel road crosses another road that leads to the maintenance buildings on the right. Continue straight here, and in another 30 yd. turn right onto Maple Trail, a wide woods road. After 0.3 mi. the woods road bears right where Short Cut Trail joins from the left, and in another 40 yd. it swings left where an alternate access route (Connector Trail) from Cobble Mtn. Stables joins from the right. Round Pond Trail, still a wide road, climbs to the top of a rise, where it passes through a stone wall, bears right uphill at a fork, and passes through another stone wall. The road then levels and descends slightly, and at 0.9 mi. orange-blazed Overlook Trail, also the route of Short Oak Trail, diverges right.

Continue ahead on the main road (sign for Round Pond Trail; now blazed in red). In 40 yd. a woods road comes in from the right at a sharp angle. In another 10 yd. Round Pond Trail (arrow), still coinciding with Maple Trail, diverges right off the main woods road onto an older woods road and descends. In 100 yd. a side path connecting with Birch Path diverges left; Round Pond Trail continues straight and descends into a meadow. It crosses along the right edge of the meadow and in 50 yd. turns right onto the southern end of Oak Trail. (Birch Path is to the left here.) Round Pond Trail follows Oak Trail into the woods and across a bridge over a small brook. (Beyond the bridge, avoid a well-worn private footpath that diverges left and leads to a private residence.) Follow red blazes as Round Pond Trail soon bears left and uphill (sign) while Oak Trail continues to the right on a woods road. After two switchbacks Round Pond Trail passes through a stone wall; it then crosses a small brook, a larger brook at 1.4 mi., and another small brook. After a short rise, an old woods road enters from the left; Round Pond Trail bears right (sign) along the woods road, runs level and then uphill across a skid road, and turns left off the end of the woods road just as the road reaches the edge of a swamp. Round Pond Trail climbs rather steeply for a short distance before it levels off and reaches East Gilford Trail at 1.8 mi.

Round Pond Trail turns right and coincides with yellow-blazed East Gilford Trail for 0.3 mi.; the section where the trails coincide is blazed in both red and yellow. Round Pond Trail then leaves on the left (sign) and runs with minor ups and downs to a woods road at 2.3 mi. It follows this woods road to the left across a bridge over a brook, and 20 yd. past the brook it turns sharply right at a junction with East Gilford Fire Rd. (left) onto another woods road and climbs moderately through a fine hardwood forest. At 3.0 mi., just before Round Pond Trail reaches the height-of-land, green-blazed Round Pond–Piper Link (Belknap Range Trail) enters on the right. The combined trails, blazed in both red and green, continue ahead and descend moderately to a beautiful secluded spot on the northwest shore of Round Pond, where Round Pond Trail ends. Round Pond–Piper Link swings left and runs northeast along the shore, continuing around the pond to reach Red Trail (Mt. Klem–Mt. Mack Loop section) in 0.4 mi.

OVERLOOK TRAIL (BRATTS; MAP 4: G3–G2)

Cumulative from Gunstock Mtn. Resort parking lot (930 ft.) to:	⇅	↗	↻
Short Oak Trail jct. (1,140 ft.)	0.9 mi.	200 ft.	0:35
Divergence from Oak Trail (1,150 ft.)	1.2 mi.	250 ft. (rev. 50 ft.)	0:45
Overlook (1,500 ft.)	1.7 mi.	600 ft.	1:10
Belknap–Gunstock col (2,000 ft.)	2.9 mi.	1,150 ft. (rev. 50 ft.)	2:00
Belknap Mtn. summit (2,384 ft.) via Blue Trail	3.4 mi.	1,550 ft.	2:30
From Gunstock Mtn. Resort parking lot (930 ft.) to:			
Gunstock Mtn. summit (2,247 ft.) via Saddle Trail and Brook Trail	3.2 mi.	1,400 ft.	2:20

This orange-blazed trail connects the main parking lot at Gunstock Mtn. Resort with the col between Belknap Mtn. and Gunstock Mtn., providing a convenient route to either peak and offering a fine viewpoint along the way. The trail, carefully placed to avoid steep areas that are vulnerable to damage by erosion, opened in November 1998.

Overlook Trail leaves the main parking area by following Round Pond Trail (see trail description), with which it coincides, to the junction with Short Oak Trail at 0.9 mi.; this section is blazed in both red and orange. Here, Overlook Trail turns right onto and follows Short Oak Trail. The combined trails descend to a junction with a gravel road at 1.1 mi. Overlook Trail turns right onto the road, follows it for 0.1 mi., and then turns left onto Oak Trail, a woods road. Overlook Trail descends with Oak Trail for 50 yd. and then turns sharply right off the road (sign for Overlook Trail). It immediately descends across a branch of Poorfarm Brook and then begins to climb.

Constantly winding about to avoid steep grades, Overlook Trail ascends to the upper edge of a steep slope and, at 1.7 mi. from the parking area, reaches open ledges covered with low juniper bushes, where there is a fine outlook to the east across the valley. The trail swings right and reenters the woods, descends through a dip, and resumes its climb. At 2.1 mi. it crosses a small brook that falls in tiny needles of water over a 5-ft. vertical ledge to the left. After crossing more small brooks, the grade becomes easier, but then gets steeper again as Overlook Trail enters the main ravine below the ridge crest. At 2.9 mi. it reaches the Belknap-Gunstock col. For Gunstock Mtn., turn right onto white-blazed Saddle Trail and follow it to yellow-blazed Brook Trail. For Belknap Mtn., turn left onto blue-blazed Blue Trail. Straight ahead is Blue Trail descending to the upper end of Carriage Rd.

EAST GILFORD TRAIL (BRATTS; MAP 4: G3–G2)

Cumulative from parking area off Wood Rd.
(1,110 ft.) to:

	⇅	↗	⟳
Jct. with Boulder Trail (2,100 ft.)	1.4 mi.	1,000 ft.	1:10
Belknap Mtn. summit (2,384 ft.)	1.9 mi.	1,250 ft.	1:35

This attractive, yellow-blazed trail is sometimes referred to as Yellow Trail. The trailhead and lower part of the trail are on private land protected by a conservation easement; dogs must be leashed in this area. From NH 11A, 1.7 mi. south of Gunstock Mtn. Resort Rd., or 2.7 mi. west of NH 11, turn west onto Bickford Rd. At 0.2 mi. turn left onto Wood Rd. In another 0.1 mi., just before reaching a house, bear left on a narrow, rough gravel road and follow it for 0.1 mi. to a parking area in an old gravel pit. A strict five-car limit exists at this parking area, which is sometimes used for logging operations and is closed to vehicles after dusk. There is no overflow area, and parking is prohibited along Wood Rd. and Bickford Rd. by the town of Gilford.

Continue along the road on foot past a gate, descending slightly. At 0.1 mi. East Gilford Trail (sign: "trail") bears right at a fork where East Gilford Fire Rd. diverges left across a bridge over a brook. East Gilford Trail runs briefly along the brook and then turns right, away from it. At 0.3 mi. the trail crosses a skid road between two clear-cuts. Soon multiuse, red-blazed Round Pond Trail from Gunstock Mtn. Resort to Round Pond enters on the right, and at 0.6 mi. it diverges on the left; the section where the trails coincide is blazed in both yellow and red. East Gilford Trail enters Belknap Mtn. State Forest (blue boundary blazes), climbs moderately, and crosses a drainage. It swings right, then sharply left, and climbs more steeply. At 0.9 mi., on a very steep pitch, it passes to the left of an interesting rock formation, where frost action has carved almost perfectly rectangular blocks of rock from a ledge. The trail winds back and forth, angling up the ledgy face of the mountain. Restricted views begin to appear, and the trail climbs steeply over two sections of ledge, which are slippery when wet.

At 1.4 mi., just above an outlook over Lake Winnipesaukee, blue-blazed Boulder Trail (Belknap Range Trail) enters on the left (sign). Now coinciding with Belknap Range Trail, East Gilford Trail swings right (northwest) and continues across ledges and through patches of woods at a moderate grade. It passes a ledge with excellent views north and east, and in another 70 yd. joins White Trail, which enters from the left on a ledge at 1.7 mi. The trails coincide (blazed in both yellow and white from this point) and ascend at an easy grade, soon swinging right onto a section relocated around a communications tower. Then they rejoin the original route and follow it under a power line to the summit and fire tower.

Descending, the combined East Gilford and White trails begin at the summit ledge on the south side of the fire tower and follow under a power line for 70 yd.; then they diverge left onto the relocated section.

ROUND POND–PIPER LINK (BRATTS; MAP 4: G2–G3)

Cumulative from Belknap–Piper col (1,800 ft.) to:	⇅	↗	⟳
Boulder Trail jct. (1,550 ft.)	1.0 mi.	100 ft. (rev. 350 ft.)	0:35
Northwest shore of Round Pond (1,652 ft.)	1.9 mi.	400 ft. (rev. 200 ft.)	1:10
Red Trail (Mt. Klem–Mt. Mack Loop section) (1,652 ft.)	2.3 mi.	400 ft.	1:20

This green-blazed trail links the col between Belknap Mtn. and Piper Mtn. with the lower end of Boulder Trail, where it joins Belknap Range Trail. Round Pond–Piper Link then continues east to meet Red Trail (Mt. Klem–Mt. Mack Loop section) on the northeast shore of Round Pond. It gives convenient access to the fine ledges on the east side of Belknap Mtn. and to Round Pond from Carriage Rd.

Round Pond–Piper Link leaves Old Piper Trail 30 yd. south of its junction with White Trail. The route descends to cross a small brook and then descends on a relocated section that formerly dropped down a steep, rocky slope. At 0.4 mi. it reaches the bottom of the descent and swings left uphill; at 0.5 mi. it passes a ledge with a good view up to Piper Mtn. After crossing a minor ridge, the trail descends easily, with occasional small ascents, to a well-signed junction on the left at 1.0 mi. with Boulder Trail. (Turn left uphill to ascend Belknap Mtn.)

SEC 4

Now coinciding with Belknap Range Trail, Round Pond–Piper Link makes several turns across a col and then continues east along the northern slope of Suncook Mtn., with one significant climb and several minor ups and downs. It crosses a small brook at 1.7 mi., and at 1.8 mi. it meets red-blazed Round Pond Trail coming up from the left (north). Round Pond–Piper Link turns right here, and the two trails coincide (blazed in both green and red), descending moderately 0.1 mi. to a beautiful secluded spot on the northwest shore of Round Pond, where Round Pond Trail ends. Round Pond–Piper Link turns left onto a relocated section of trail and runs northeast, hugging the northwest shore. It turns right at 2.1 mi. and right again onto a woods road at 2.2 mi. (This woods road can no longer be reached from its former trailhead on Grant Rd.) The trail continues south along the shore, and in another 0.1 mi. it reaches a junction with Red Trail, which goes left (the Mt. Klem–Mt. Mack Loop section) and ahead (the Round Pond–Mt. Mack Trail section).

BOULDER TRAIL (BRATTS; MAP 4: G2)

Cumulative from Round Pond–Piper Link jct. (1,550 ft.) to:

	⇅	↗	⟳
East Gilford Trail jct. (2,100 ft.)	0.4 mi.	550 ft.	0:30
Belknap Mtn. summit (2,384 ft.) via East Gilford Trail	0.9 mi.	850 ft.	0:50

This route, a segment of Belknap Range Trail, ascends the east ledges of Belknap Mtn. It is steep and rough and better suited for ascent than descent; use extra caution in wet or icy conditions. Boulder Trail is well marked with blue blazes and blue-topped cairns. It diverges northwest from Round Pond–Piper Link at the foot of the east ledges, 1.0 mi. east of Old Piper Trail. It climbs over a slope of loose talus blocks and then up a series of ledges with ever-improving views, swinging right near the top to meet East Gilford Trail (sign) just above an outlook ledge on that trail. Turn left onto East Gilford Trail to get to the summit of Belknap Mtn.

ROUND POND WOODS RD.

This trail from Grant Rd. to Round Pond has been closed by development, and hiking access from this trailhead is prohibited. A short segment at the south end of this route is still used as part of Round Pond–Piper Link and Belknap Range Trail.

EAST GILFORD FIRE RD. (MAP 4: G3)

Cumulative from parking area off Wood Rd. (1,110 ft.) to:	⬇⬆	↗	⟳
Round Pond Trail (1,330 ft.)	0.7 mi.	200 ft.	0:25
Round Pond–Piper Link via Round Pond Trail (1,710 ft.)	1.4 mi.	600 ft.	1:00
Red Trail (Mt. Klem–Mt. Mack Loop section) (1,652 ft.) via Round Pond–Piper Link	1.8 mi.	600 ft. (rev. 50 ft.)	1:15

Although Round Pond Woods Rd. and Grant Rd. access to Round Pond is closed, an alternate and slightly longer route to Round Pond and access to the central section of the Belknap Range is available from the trailhead parking area for East Gilford Trail. The trailhead and lower part of the trail are on private land protected by a conservation easement. Dogs must be leashed in this area.

From NH 11A, 1.7 mi. south of Gunstock Mtn. Resort Rd., or 2.7 mi. west of NH 11, turn west onto Bickford Rd.; at 0.2 mi. turn left onto Wood Rd. In another 0.1 mi., just before reaching a house, bear left on a narrow, rough gravel road and follow it for 0.1 mi. to a parking area in an old gravel pit. A strict five-car limit exists at this parking area, which is sometimes used for logging operations and is closed to vehicles after dusk. There is no overflow area, and parking is prohibited along Wood Rd. and Bickford Rd. by the town of Gilford.

Continue along the road on foot past a gate, descending slightly. At 0.1 mi. from the parking area, cross a bridge on the left over Poorfarm Brook as East Gilford Trail (sign) diverges right. East Gilford Fire Rd. ascends moderately and reaches another fork at 0.2 mi. The route continues to climb, and the grade eases. At 0.7 mi., just after crossing the Belknap Mtn. State Forest boundary (and just before the road crosses a brook), East Gilford Fire Rd. meets red-blazed Round Pond Trail.

Round Pond Trail turns left here and leads 0.7 mi. to Round Pond–Piper Link (Belknap Range Trail). From that junction, the combined trails descend to the northwest shore of Round Pond in 0.1 mi. Round Pond–Piper Link then leads around the north end of the pond to the junction with Red Trail (Mt. Klem–Mt. Mack Loop section) on the east shore in another 0.4 mi.

SEC
4

RED TRAIL, MT. KLEM–MT. MACK LOOP SECTION
(GSR/BRATTS; MAP 4: G3–H3)
From jct. on northeast shore of Round Pond
(1,652 ft.) to:

Jct. near Mt. Mack summit (1,943 ft.)	1.6 mi.	550 ft. (rev. 250 ft.)	1:05

This route, a segment of Belknap Range Trail and Griswold Scout Reservation's Red Trail, runs from Round Pond over Mt. Klem to a point just east of the summit of Mt. Mack. Marked with red wooden diamonds nailed to trees and some red blazes, it is fairly easy to follow, although some care is needed, particularly in the open areas.

This loop section of Red Trail begins on the northeast shore of Round Pond at a junction with Round Pond–Piper Link and Red Trail's Round Pond–Mt. Mack section. At this junction the loop section is marked by two red wooden diamonds and a sign pointing the way to Mt. Klem. Leaving the shore of Round Pond, Red Trail climbs steadily northeast through a dense coniferous forest before leveling out and passing through a small sag. It then climbs more easily, passing a view of Belknap Mtn. at 0.3 mi., and crosses a stone wall. After ascending to a ledgy area, the trail swings left, descending slightly, and then ascends across another ledgy outcropping. It dips through a shallow sag and then curls around the north end of Mt. Klem at 0.6 mi. At 0.8 mi. it passes a beautiful outlook to the north and swings right. Then the trail runs almost level for some distance, passing a junction with white-blazed Dave Roberts' Quarry Trail (sign: "Rand") on the left at 0.9 mi. Here, a white-blazed spur leads 140 yd. right to the wooded summit of Mt. Klem (sign).

Red Trail descends and crosses an open area with views southeast at 1.0 mi. It descends across another ledgy spot with a view into a sag at 1.2 mi. and then climbs up to a rocky knob, crosses a small dip, and climbs to a junction near the summit of Mt. Mack at 1.6 mi. Here, Belknap Range Trail, of which Red Trail is a segment, diverges left and continues east toward Mt. Anna; Red Trail's Round Pond–Mt. Mack section, blazed in both red and orange, leads to the right over the summit of Mt. Mack and back down to Round Pond.

RED TRAIL, ROUND POND–MT. MACK SECTION
(GSR/BRATTS; MAP 4: H3)

From upper jct. with Red Trail (Mt. Klem–Mt. Mack Loop section) on Mt. Mack (1,943 ft.) to:	↓↥	↗	↺
Lower jct. with Red Trail (Mt. Klem–Mt. Mack Loop section) at Round Pond (1,652 ft.)	0.7 mi.	0 ft. (rev. 300 ft.)	0:20

This section of Griswold Scout Reservation's Red Trail leads from a junction with the upper end of Red Trail's Mt. Klem–Mt. Mack Loop section near the summit of Mt. Mack down to Round Pond and the lower end of the loop, completing the circuit over those two peaks.

From the upper junction, the trail section, blazed in both red and orange, leads west, crossing the summit of Mt. Mack in 50 yd. and passing to the right of two communications towers before it starts to descend. At 0.1 mi. a side path leads 15 yd. left to a ledge with a wide view south and west. Red Trail continues down an eroded and recently widened road, turns right at a cleared outlook west, and crosses orange-blazed Mack Ridge Trail at 0.3 mi., at a point where the road splits and quickly comes back together. (To the left, Mack Ridge Trail descends to Griswold Scout Reservation; to the right, it rejoins Red Trail in 0.3 mi.) Red Trail descends across a skid road; at 0.5 mi. it turns left onto a wide gravel logging road, follows it for 40 yd., and then turns right at a sign into the woods. (Red Trail also continues to the left, descending with the logging road to Griswold Scout Reservation.) The trail crosses a brook and in another 100 yd. enters a small clearing among the pines (a campsite of the Griswold Scout Reservation), where Mack Ridge Trail enters on the right. Now blazed solely in red, Red Trail descends to the edge of Round Pond and follows the shore for 0.1 mi. to its lower junction with the Mt. Klem–Mt. Mack Loop section of Red Trail.

SEC 4

MT. MAJOR TRAIL (SPNHF; MAP 4: G5)

Cumulative from parking area on NH 11 (650 ft.) to:	↓↥	↗	↺
Brook Trail jct. (930 ft.)	0.7 mi.	300 ft.	0:30
Mt. Major summit (1,787 ft.) via Mt. Major Trail	1.5 mi.	1,150 ft.	1:20
Mt. Major summit (1,787 ft.) via Mt. Major Trail and Brook Trail	2.4 mi.	1,150 ft.	1:45
Starting point via complete loop	3.9 mi.	1,150 ft.	2:30

Mt. Major offers views that are among the best in southern New Hampshire for the effort required, but the steep upper ledges are dangerous in wet or icy conditions. These treacherous ledges and the easy-to-reach nature of the mountain have combined to produce a number of serious injuries, particularly in late fall and winter when ice is present. In such conditions Brook Trail is probably safer, and it may also be a better choice for the descent at other times—as well as providing good views from the open west ridge that are not duplicated by the main trail.

Mt. Major Trail, part of Belknap Range Trail and well blazed in blue, begins at a parking area on the west side of NH 11, 4.2 mi. north of Alton Bay and 2.4 mi. south of the junction of NH 11 with NH 11A. The trail leaves the right side of the parking area and follows a lumber road west, ascending a steep, severely eroded section where several alternate roads diverge and rejoin; the road farthest to the right (ascending) offers slightly better footing than the others. At 0.4 mi., at the top of this steep section, the road becomes nearly level and smooth. An unmarked path diverges left at 0.6 mi., and at 0.7 mi. Mt. Major Trail diverges sharply left on a path as Brook Trail continues ahead on the lumber road.

Mt. Major Trail climbs steeply through second-growth forest and over ledges, with some steep scrambles near the top. At 1.3 mi. there are two alternate routes, both signed and blazed in blue: the "Main Trail via ledges" route forks to the right and climbs steep ledges (potentially dangerous when wet or icy), while the "Main Trail—ledge detour" diverges left, avoiding the steepest scrambles. The routes rejoin at 1.4 mi. (Revegetation efforts have closed other unofficial routes in this area.) The summit, with the ruins of a stone hut (Mr. Phippen's Hut), is at 1.5 mi.

To descend on Mt. Major Trail, follow the blue blazes northeast directly down the ledges (starting to the west of the ruins) toward the southern part of Lake Winnipesaukee. To descend on the alternate route (Brook Trail), walk southwest down the ledges toward Straightback Mtn., following the blue and yellow blazes. At 0.5 mi. from the summit, turn right onto yellow-blazed Brook Trail (sign).

BROOK TRAIL (SPNHF; MAP 4: G5–G4)

From jct. with Mt. Major Trail (930 ft.) to:	⇅	↗	⟳
Mt. Major summit (1,787 ft.)	1.7 mi.	850 ft.	1:15

At its junction with blue-blazed Mt. Major Trail 0.7 mi. from the parking area on NH 11, yellow-blazed Brook Trail continues ahead nearly level on a lumber road. (Mt. Major Trail [Belknap Range Trail] leaves on the left.)

At 0.2 mi. from this junction, after a slight descent, Brook Trail bears left and uphill as an unmarked path diverges right. At 0.5 mi. the lumber road appears to end, but a lesser woods road bears right toward a small brook, crosses it, and continues to climb. It recrosses the brook at 0.7 mi. and ascends alongside it, with loose footing on some severely eroded sections (some of which have been bypassed). At 0.9 mi. Brook Trail swings left away from the edge of the valley, where green-blazed North Straightback Link continues ahead. Brook Trail climbs to the saddle between Mt. Major and Straightback Mtn. at 1.2 mi., where it meets blue-blazed Belknap Range Trail at a signed intersection. The coinciding Brook and Belknap Range trails, blazed in both yellow and blue, bear left (east) from the intersection, passing a junction on the right with red-blazed Jesus Valley–Beaver Pond Trail (not described in this guide) at 1.4 mi., and climbing mostly over open ledges with good views to the summit at 1.7 mi.

SEC 4

BOULDER LOOP TRAIL (SPNHF; MAP 4: G5–H5)

From parking area on NH 11 (650 ft.) to:	⇅	◢	○
Mt. Major summit (1,787 ft.)	1.6 mi.	1,150 ft.	1:25

This orange-blazed trail provides an attractive route up the south side of Mt. Major from the trailhead parking area on NH 11. The upper section of Boulder Loop Trail has a steep and rough segment. The lower section follows a snowmobile trail that leaves the left side of the parking area, crosses two plank bridges, and in 30 yd. turns right up a bank past a boulder, where a woods road continues straight. The route climbs moderately up a woods road also used as a snowmobile trail to a T junction at 0.4 mi., where red-blazed Jesus Valley–Beaver Pond Trail (not described in this guide) diverges left and descends south toward Jesus Valley Rd. Here, Boulder Loop Trail turns right; in 40 yd. it bears left at a fork and ascends south along the woods road. At 0.7 mi., where the road becomes wet and curves to the left, the trail continues ahead into the woods on a footpath.

Boulder Loop Trail ascends steadily through an area strewn with boulders, swings right (west) at 1.0 mi., squeezes between and under boulders at 1.2 mi., and then climbs a steep, gravelly pitch with poor footing. At the top of the pitch it turns right, then left, and runs north at easy grades through pine and oak woods before ascending gradually to the summit over open ledges, with increasing views east and south. To descend by this trail, walk south across the ledges from the ruins of a stone hut and look for cairns and orange-blazed posts. On the descent, take care to distinguish the main trail from several unmaintained paths that diverge along the upper section.

BELKNAP RANGE TRAIL (BRATTS/GSR; MAP 4: F2–G5)

Cumulative from Gunstock Mtn. Resort parking lot (930 ft.) to:	↕	↗	⟳
Gunstock Mtn. summit (2,247 ft.)	2.8 mi.	1,500 ft. (rev. 200 ft.)	2:10
Belknap Mtn. summit (2,384 ft.)	3.6 mi.	1,900 ft. (rev. 250 ft.)	2:45
Northwest shore of Round Pond (1,652 ft.)	5.4 mi.	2,200 ft. (rev. 1,050 ft.)	3:50
Mt. Mack summit (1,943 ft.)	7.4 mi.	2,750 ft. (rev. 250 ft.)	5:05
Mt. Anna summit (1,676 ft.)	8.8 mi.	3,250 ft. (rev. 750 ft.)	6:00
South Peak of Straightback Mtn. (1,888 ft.)	10.0 mi.	3,650 ft. (rev. 200 ft.)	6:50
Mt. Major summit (1,787 ft.)	11.1 mi.	3,850 ft. (rev. 300 ft.)	7:30
Trailhead parking area on NH 11 (650 ft.)	12.5 mi.	3,850 ft. (rev. 1,150 ft.)	8:15

This trail extends along the length of the Belknap Range from Gunstock Mtn. Resort to the summit of Mt. Major and down to the trailhead on NH 11, using all or part of several other trails along the way. Much of the route is easy to follow, and the rest requires only reasonable care.

Leaving the Gunstock Mtn. Resort main parking lot, Belknap Range Trail follows white-blazed Ridge Trail over Mt. Rowe to the summit of Gunstock Mtn. (coinciding with orange-blazed Gunstock Mtn. Trail in the upper part) at 2.8 mi. It then descends on yellow-blazed Brook Trail and white-blazed Saddle Trail to the Belknap-Gunstock col at 3.1 mi.; from here, it follows blue-blazed Blue Trail to the summit of Belknap Mtn. at 3.6 mi. It descends on yellow-blazed East Gilford Trail (coinciding with white-blazed White Trail for 0.2 mi.) and then blue-blazed Boulder Trail, becoming quite steep until it reaches a sag at 4.5 mi. and turns left onto green-blazed Round Pond–Piper Link.

Belknap Range Trail follows Round Pond–Piper Link to reach the northwest shore of Round Pond at 5.4 mi., coinciding with red-blazed Round Pond Trail for the last 0.1 mi. to the shore. It continues on green-blazed Round Pond–Piper Link around to the east shore, where it turns left onto Griswold Scout Reservation's Red Trail (Mt. Klem–Mt. Mack Loop section; red blazes) at 5.8 mi. It follows Red Trail over Mt. Klem and up to a point just east of the summit of Mt. Mack at 7.4 mi., where a different section of Red Trail (the red-and-orange-blazed Round Pond–Mt. Mack section, formerly part of Belknap Range Trail) joins from the right. (For the next 3.2 mi., Belknap Range Trail does not coincide with other trails.)

At this junction, Belknap Range Trail, still blazed in red, turns left, then left again, and descends at easy to moderate grades. In all, it descends more than 500 ft.—the last part with several minor ups and downs—until it reaches its low point at a mossy brook at 8.1 mi. From here, the trail begins to climb a bit. After passing through a stone wall on the Gilford–Gilmanton town line, it climbs more seriously (descending briefly at one point to cross a brook), reaching a trail junction on the flat, viewless summit of Mt. Anna at 8.8 mi. A blue-blazed trail to the right (southwest) and a red-blazed trail straight ahead (southeast) descend toward Griswold Scout Reservation. (An easy 0.2-mi. descent on the blue-blazed trail leads to a fine southern outlook.) At this junction, Belknap Range Trail turns left (northeast) and its blazing changes to blue.

The trail runs across the flat top of Mt. Anna, descends over a ledge, and drops down a short, steep, rocky pitch into a sharp col at 9.0 mi. It runs briefly left through the col and then climbs to a signed junction on the right with purple-blazed Precipice Trail (not described in this guide) at 9.1 mi. From this point, Belknap Range Trail makes numerous small ascents and descents, sometimes through slightly obscure places. At 9.2 mi. it passes a junction with Marsh Crossing Trail on the left, and at 9.5 mi. it runs through another col and climbs steeply to the left of an overhanging rock face. It then climbs moderately and reaches an open ledgy area at 9.8 mi. with views ahead to part of Straightback Mtn. (and, higher up, back to Belknap Mtn.). The general route across this area is obvious, but it is poorly marked; this poses little problem in clear weather, but in fog it could be difficult to cross the area correctly without following a compass course. At 9.9 mi. Belknap Range Trail climbs past junctions with purple-blazed Precipice Trail on the right and then white-blazed Dave Roberts' Quarry Trail on the left; it reaches a junction with Straightback Mtn. Trail just north of the south summit of Straightback Mtn. at 10.0 mi. The various ledges and open areas of this summit merit exploration.

At this junction, the somewhat obscure Straightback Mtn. Trail continues ahead (east) across the ledges, reaching an especially fine open area in 0.2 mi. It eventually descends the southeast side of the mountain. Belknap Range Trail turns sharply left (north) at the junction and soon descends, mostly in the woods, often angling to the left. It passes a junction with orange-blazed Quarry Spur, a branch of Dave Roberts' Quarry Trail, on the left at 10.3 mi. At 10.4 mi. it crosses a ledge with a glimpse of Lake Winnipesaukee; then it turns right and descends to the col between Straightback Mtn. and Mt. Major, reaching a trail junction on the Mt. Major side of the col at 10.6 mi. The path on the left here is yellow-blazed Brook Trail, which descends to the parking area on NH 11 in 1.9 mi. Belknap Range Trail, now coinciding with Brook Trail and blazed

SEC 4

in both blue and yellow, ascends the ridge, soon coming into the open. It passes a junction on the right with red-blazed Jesus Valley–Beaver Pond Trail (not described in this guide) at 10.8 mi. and then follows a somewhat poorly marked but fairly obvious route up to the summit of Mt. Major at 11.1 mi., where there are magnificent views and the remains of a stone hut. From here, Belknap Range Trail follows blue-blazed Mt. Major Trail, descending ledges to the northeast and north (starting to the west of the stone hut), continuing down through the woods to the trailhead parking area on NH 11.

NORTH STRAIGHTBACK LINK (SPNHF; MAP 4: G4)

From Brook Trail (1,300 ft.) to:	↥	↗	◷
Dave Roberts' Quarry Trail (1,909 ft.)	0.5 mi.	600 ft.	0:35

This lightly used, green-blazed trail leads from Brook Trail to Dave Roberts' Quarry Trail at the north summit of Straightback Mtn., making various loop hikes possible. It continues ahead where Brook Trail turns left, 0.9 mi. from Mt. Major Trail and 1.6 mi. from the Mt. Major trailhead on NH 11. North Straightback Link dips to cross a small brook and then ascends steadily through hardwood forest. The trail crosses two old skid roads at 0.4 mi. and climbs steeply through a ledgy spruce forest to meet Dave Roberts' Quarry Trail on the flat north summit of Straightback Mtn. (sign) at 0.5 mi.

DAVE ROBERTS' QUARRY TRAIL (BRATTS; MAP 4: H4–G3)

Cumulative from Belknap Range Trail near Straightback Mtn. south summit (1,830 ft.) to:	↥	↗	◷
East Quarry Mtn. summit (1,894 ft.)	1.1 mi.	250 ft. (rev. 200 ft.)	0:40
West Quarry Mtn. summit (1,890 ft.)	1.7 mi.	350 ft. (rev. 100 ft.)	1:00
Rand Mtn. summit (1,880 ft.)	2.7 mi.	650 ft. (rev. 300 ft.)	1:40
Red Trail (Mt. Klem–Mt. Mack Loop section) (1,970 ft.)	3.3 mi.	950 ft. (rev. 200 ft.)	2:10

This white-blazed trail traverses an interesting ridge from the south peak of Straightback Mtn. to Mt. Klem, passing several viewpoints and crossing over or near the summit of the north peak of Straightback Mtn. (1,909 ft.) and the unofficially named summits of East Quarry Mtn., West Quarry Mtn., and Rand Mtn. The route is named in honor of Dave Roberts, who blazed, mapped, and maintained many of the trails in the Belknap Range. It makes possible various loop hikes over the east-central section of the range. Dave Roberts' Quarry Trail is well blazed, but several short, steep, and rough stretches and other sections may require care to follow. Active logging has taken place along parts of the route, especially along Quarry Spur; around the north summit of Straightback Mtn.; east of East Quarry Mtn.; and between East Quarry Mtn. and West Quarry Mtn. Take particular care to follow markings in these areas; problem spots are often marked with yellow tape.

At its east end, Dave Roberts' Quarry Trail diverges north from Belknap Range Trail at an open ledgy area 0.1 mi. west of the south summit of Straightback Mtn. It descends into the woods and then ascends easily through the woods and across open areas, where it must be followed with care, passing a view northeast to Mt. Major. At 0.4 mi., atop a large sloping ledge, orange-blazed Quarry Spur (sign), a 0.3-mi. branch path, diverges right. (This path descends 200 ft. and then climbs 50 ft. to Belknap Range Trail at a point 0.3 mi. west of the Straightback–Major col.) In another 100 yd., Dave Roberts' Quarry Trail reaches the wooded north summit of Straightback Mtn. (sign). Just beyond, green-blazed North Straightback Link diverges right, and Dave Roberts' Quarry Trail turns left and descends steeply to a saddle. It then ascends the south slope of the long, low ridge northwest of Straightback Mtn., and at 0.9 mi. it turns sharply left at a ledge with a view northeast. The trail passes a steep, rough side path on the right that descends to boulder caves in a rockfall (use caution if taking this side path), and a short spur, also on the right, that descends to a ledge with a fine view east and a steep dropoff below.

The trail climbs through spruces, with one short scramble, to the partly wooded summit of East Quarry Mtn. (sign) at 1.1 mi. and then descends a short, steep pitch to a ferny sag, where blue-blazed Reed Road Trail joins from the right. Dave Roberts' Quarry Trail ascends across a knob through several open brushy areas—follow the blazes carefully. The trail then descends slightly and swings left (south) across a plateau, where the footing may be wet. At 1.6 mi. it swings left to a ledge overlooking a beaver pond at the base of Straightback Mtn. The trail climbs over the wooded summit of West Quarry Mtn. (sign) at 1.7 mi., passing a junction with yellow-blazed Marsh Crossing Trail on the left; it then descends and bears right (northwest) past an outlook on the left toward Mt. Mack and Mt. Klem.

Dave Roberts' Quarry Trail continues down through old-growth spruces to an informational sign and a left turn at 2.0 mi. Here, a bypass path, also marked with white blazes, continues ahead. The main trail descends a very steep pitch, soon swinging right across exposed sloping ledges with a view west (this area is potentially dangerous if wet). It descends another steep pitch over mossy ledges, and the bypass path joins from the right at 2.1 mi.

SEC 4

The trail swings left and descends to an old quarry site on the left before continuing down to a saddle at 2.3 mi. It then ascends and crosses a logging road; at 2.7 mi. it crosses the wooded summit of Rand Mtn. (sign) before turning sharply left and winding down to a right turn and a fine outlook south at 2.8 mi. The trail descends and ascends briefly and then drops very steeply to a notch, where there is a small, stagnant brook. From here, the trail climbs steadily up the east slope of Mt. Klem. After crossing a stone wall, it eases and runs through an open area to meet Red Trail (Mt. Klem–Mt. Mack Loop section) just east of the summit. Turn left for Mt. Mack or right for the most direct descent to Round Pond, passing a beautiful north outlook in 0.1 mi. A white-blazed spur at this junction continues 140 yd. ahead (west) to the wooded true summit of Mt. Klem.

REED ROAD TRAIL (SPNHF; MAP 4: G4)

Cumulative from parking area (990 ft.) to:	↧↥	↗	↻
Right turn off logging road (1,300 ft.)	0.6 mi.	310 ft.	0:25
Dave Roberts' Quarry Trail (1,820 ft.)	1.3 mi.	830 ft.	1:05

This trail, opened in 2016, provides access to the central part of the Belknap Range from the north. It is within the Forest Society's Quarry Mtn. Forest and ascends to Dave Roberts' Quarry Trail 0.1 mi. west of East Quarry Mtn. Grades are easy to moderate, with good footing.

From NH 11 in Alton, follow NH 11A for 1.3 mi. Turn left onto Reed Rd. at the Alton–Gilford town line, and then bear right at the fork at 0.1 mi. Pavement ends at 0.4 mi., and the road becomes narrower and rougher, continuing to a parking area on the left (sign: "Quarry Mountain Forest") at 0.6 mi. In winter, Reed Rd. is plowed (though often icy), but the parking area may not be. Parking is prohibited along the road itself.

From the parking area, walk up Reed Rd., continuing straight at the junction where a private driveway turns left (parking is prohibited here) and the maintained road ends. Pass through a gate at 0.2 mi. and continue up a rocky, eroded logging road. Pass a logged clearing on the left at 0.4 mi. with a good view north to the Sandwich Range, and reach stone steps on the right at 0.6 mi. Reed Road Trail bears right off the road here, and blue blazes begin. This junction features an expansive vista, stretching from Belknap Mtn., Gunstock Mtn., and Mt. Rowe over to the Sandwich and Ossipee ranges.

Reed Road Trail enters the woods and begins a moderate climb southeast, at first by numerous short switchbacks, reaching a spot with a good view back to Belknap Mtn. and Gunstock Mtn. at 1.0 mi. The trail briefly joins a brushy skid road, wet and muddy at times, and then bears right off the road. It then merges with an old woods road and ascends easily to the ridge and the junction with Dave Roberts' Quarry Trail at 1.3 mi.

MARSH CROSSING TRAIL (MAP 4: H4)

From Belknap Range Trail (1,660 ft.) to:	↕↑	↗	↺
Dave Roberts' Quarry Trail (1,890 ft.)	0.4 mi.	230 ft.	0:20

This yellow-blazed trail, located mostly on private land, connects the Belknap Range Trail between Mt. Anna and the south peak of Straightback Mtn. with Dave Roberts' Quarry Trail near the summit of West Quarry Mtn., making possible several loop hikes over this part of the range. It is lightly maintained, and portions of it are steep.

From Belknap Range Trail, 0.4 mi. east of the summit of Mt. Anna, Marsh Crossing Trail leaves north near an obvious stand of dead trees on the left; the junction is unsigned. The route, which runs level and is often wet, passes a sign ("Marsh Crossing Trail") and the first yellow blaze in 30 yd. After crossing a stream that feeds a small marsh, the trail climbs steeply, passing through a boulder field with a few easy scrambles. At the top of the boulder field, grades ease as Marsh Crossing Trail arrives at a junction with Dave Roberts' Quarry Trail at 0.4 mi. near the summit of West Quarry Mtn.

When descending, Marsh Crossing Trail leaves Dave Roberts' Quarry Trail to the left of a tree bearing a sign for West Quarry Mtn. The trail sign and a yellow blaze are 15 yd. down the trail.

COPPLE CROWN MTN. (1,875 FT.)

This mountain rises south of Lake Winnipesaukee in the towns of Brookfield and New Durham. The summit area is within a large tract of land owned by Lakes Region Conservation Trust. The ledgy summit offers restricted views over low brush to Lake Winnipesaukee and the Belknap, Squam, and Sandwich ranges beyond. A beautiful cliff-top outlook on the slightly lower east knob provides views of the gentler, more pastoral region to the south. A trail map is available at lrct.org. Also, refer to the AMC Copple Crown Mtn. map on p. 272 or the USGS Wolfeboro quadrangle.

To reach the trailhead, follow NH 109 west 1.2 mi. from its junction with NH 16, and then turn left onto Governors Rd. Follow this road for 0.4 mi.; then turn right onto Moose Mtn. Rd. and follow it for about 1.5 mi. to the end of the pavement. Bear left at a fork (sign for Copple Crown) and continue 0.4 mi. to the parking area for Ellis R. Hatch Wildlife

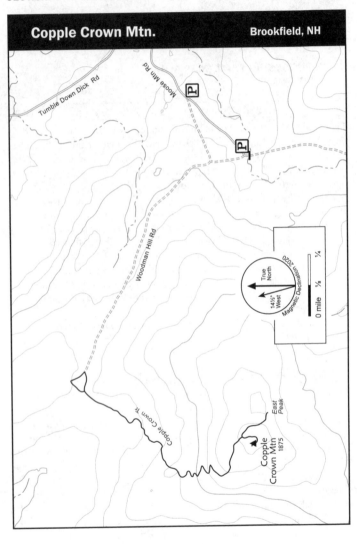

Copple Crown Mtn.   Brookfield, NH

SEC
4

Management Area, past which the road is gated. An LRCT kiosk is at the parking area. (*Note*: The road to the left of the fork is rough and may not be passable for all vehicles, in which case it may be best to park along the road at the fork and proceed on foot.)

COPPLE CROWN TRAIL
(LRCT; LRCT MAP, USGS WOLFEBORO QUAD)

Cumulative from Ellis R. Hatch Wildlife Management Area parking area (860 ft.) to:	⬇⬆	↗	⟳
LRCT kiosk (1,100 ft.)	1.3 mi.	260 ft.	0:45
Copple Crown Mtn. summit (1,875 ft.), including side trip to east knob outlook	3.0 mi.	1,110 ft.	2:05

SEC 4

From the parking area kiosk, Copple Crown Trail follows a gravel road (unblazed in this section) to the right for 0.2 mi. to a junction where it joins another gravel road that comes in from the right—this is the road that bears right at the fork 0.4 mi. before the parking area. The trail continues ahead on the main gravel road from this junction, ascending gradually. In 2019, a logging operation affected the woods on the south side of this road but did not affect the trail or the road. At 1.3 mi. the trail passes a woods road (left) and shortly reaches a second LRCT kiosk on the left.

Now blazed in blue, the trail turns left (southwest) off the gravel road at the kiosk, runs through the woods for a short distance, and joins the woods road that it passed at 1.3 mi. (If this junction is missed on the descent there is no problem, since the woods road leads to the gravel road at virtually the same point as the trail.) At 1.6 mi. the trail turns left onto another woods road (arrow and sign for Copple Crown) and soon becomes a footpath. The path climbs gradually, then more steeply—with some poor footing on the steepest eroded sections—through dense second-growth hardwoods in a logged area. At 1.9 mi. it emerges from the logged area into fine conifer woods, where it climbs the steep, rocky slope by switchbacks at easy grades. At 2.3 mi. a side trail enters on the right a few steps before a sharp left turn; be careful not to follow this trail on the descent—it leads to the private Copple Crown Community and is not open to the public. Copple Crown Trail now ascends easily, with mostly excellent footing, through beautiful woods to a junction at 2.5 mi. Here, a side path diverges left (sign: "East Peak"), descends through a small col, and then climbs easily to an excellent cliff-top outlook on the east knob at 0.2 mi. Copple Crown Trail bears right here and soon bears right again, continuing a short distance to the summit and the ledgy viewpoint a few steps beyond.

MOOSE MTNS. RESERVATION

This series of peaks (highest summit, 1,749 ft.) runs along a ridge southeast of Copple Crown Mtn. The 2,332-acre Moose Mtns. Reservation, on the south slopes of the range in Brookfield and Middleton, is owned by the Society for the Protection of New Hampshire Forests (Forest Society) and is managed for forestry, wildlife habitat, water quality, and recreation. More than 3,800 acres of protected and public land surround the peaks of the Moose Mtns. ridge, including the Middleton Town Forest on Piper Mtn. and the 1,493-acre Ellis R. Hatch Wildlife Management Area (owned by the New Hampshire Fish and Game Department). Moose Mtns. Reservation includes several miles of old logging roads, snowmobile trails, and hiking paths. The hiking paths, maintained by SPNHF volunteers, lead to a historical farm site, two ledgy viewpoints, and an unusual ridge-top pitch-pine forest. A trail map is available at forestsociety.org. Also, refer to the in-text map on p. 275 or the USGS Sanbornville quadrangle.

The SPNHF maintains a small parking area (may not be maintained in winter) and information kiosk on New Portsmouth Rd. in Middleton. From the junction of NH 16 and NH 153 in Wakefield, drive 0.3 mi. south on the combined NH 153 and NH 125, and then turn right onto NH 153. In 0.6 mi. turn right onto Ridge Rd. After 1.2 mi. turn right onto New Portsmouth Rd. Follow this road for 1.2 mi. (the last 0.5 mi. is gravel) to the parking area.

BEAUTY LEDGE TRAILS
(SPNHF; SPNHF MAP, USGS SANBORNVILLE QUAD)

From trailhead on New Portsmouth Rd. (630 ft.) to:	⇅	↗	↻
Beauty Ledge (1,180 ft.) via Burrows Farm Trail, North Trail, and Beauty Ledge Trail	1.2 mi.	600 ft. (rev. 50 ft.)	0:55

This open ledge on an eastern spur of the Moose Mtns. offers a fine view south. From the parking area, continue past the gate on a yellow-blazed gravel road called Burrows Farm Trail. In 0.3 mi., as Burrows Farm Trail bears left, bear right onto unblazed North Trail (an old logging road). North Trail ascends and bears left (sign) in a clearing at 0.5 mi., where another road diverges right toward Bowser Pond and Piper Mtn. At 0.7 mi. turn left onto blue-blazed Beauty Ledge Trail (sign) and ascend, steeply at first, on a winding route past Snapping Turtle Rock. The trail follows the base of the ledge and ascends via switchbacks to the junction with Beauty Knob Trail at 1.1 mi. from the parking area. Bear left as Beauty Knob Trail

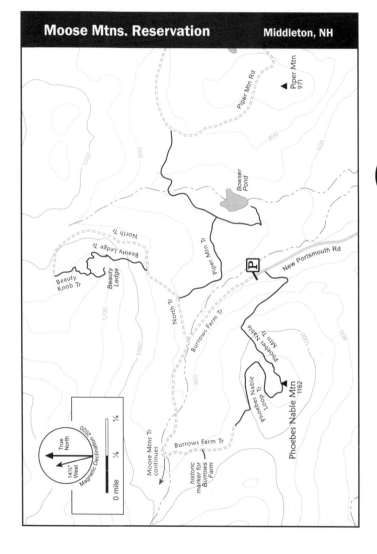

Moose Mtns. Reservation

Middleton, NH

SEC
4

Piper Mtn Rd

Piper Mtn
971

800

600

1000

800

Bowser
Pond

North Tr

Beauty Ledge Tr

Beauty
Knob Tr

Beauty
Ledge

North Tr

Piper Mtn Tr

New Portsmouth Rd

1200

Burrows Farm Tr

Phoebes Nable
Mtn Tr

1000

800

Phoebes Nable
Loop Tr

Phoebes Nable Mtn
1182

900

1000

Moose Mtns Tr
continues

Burrows Farm Tr

historic
marker for
Burrows
Farm

True North

14½°
West

Magnetic Declination 2020

⅛

¼

0 mile   ⅛   ¼

diverges right, cross over Beauty Knob, and then descend slightly to the view ledge at 1.2 mi.

On the return trip, for a loop with an easier descent, bear left onto Beauty Knob Trail and descend 0.2 mi. to North Trail in a clearing. Turn right onto North Trail (this junction is marked by two cairns), which descends to the lower Beauty Ledge Trail junction in 0.6 mi. (This is 0.4 mi. longer than the direct descent via Beauty Ledge Trail.)

PHOEBES NABLE MTN. TRAILS
(SPNHF; SPNHF MAP, USGS SANBORNVILLE QUAD)

Cumulative from trailhead on New Portsmouth Rd. (630 ft.) to:	⬆⬇	↗	⟳
Phoebes Nable Mtn. summit (1,182 ft.) via Burrows Farm Trail, Phoebes Nable Loop Trail, and Phoebes Nable Mtn. Trail	1.6 mi.	550 ft.	1:05
Return to trailhead (630 ft.)	2.2 mi.	550 ft. (rev. 550 ft.)	1:20

An outlook at the summit of Phoebes Nable Mtn. offers a good view south. Make a loop hike over this mountain using Burrows Farm Trail, Phoebes Nable Loop Trail, and Phoebes Nable Mtn. Trail.

From the parking area, follow yellow-blazed Burrows Farm Trail straight past the gate, and bear left at 0.3 mi. where North Trail diverges right. At 0.8 mi. Burrows Farm Trail turns left as Moose Mtns. Trail continues ahead. (Moose Mtns. Trail ascends on an old road, steeply at first, then moderately, for 700 ft., reaching a beautiful area of ledges and pitch pines on the privately owned crest of the Moose Mtns. ridge in 0.8 mi.) At 0.9 mi. Burrows Farm Trail enters a large, open field marking the former site of Burrows Farm, an isolated hill farm that dated to the early 1800s. The trail passes two nineteenth-century cemeteries on the left; a spur reaches the farm site to the right. A boulder and plaque mark the spot where the house once stood.

In 0.1 mi. there are views back to Bald Mtn. (named for the sheep pasture that once spread across the ridge-top) and ahead to Phoebes Nable Mtn. The trail swings left (sign) off the road in the middle of the clearing and soon enters the woods. At 1.1 mi. the route turns left onto Phoebes Nable Loop Trail; beyond this point Burrows Farm Trail is no longer maintained. Phoebes Nable Loop Trail, blazed in yellow, ascends east across the north slope of the mountain past boulders and ledges, swings around to the west at 1.4 mi., and then climbs south, ascending a volunteer-built rock staircase. It bears left onto a woods road (the original route of Phoebes Nable Trail) shortly before reaching the summit of

Phoebes Nable Mtn. at 1.6 mi. Here, a spur continues ahead 25 yd. to the outlook. To complete the loop, yellow-blazed Phoebes Nable Mtn. Trail leaves the summit to the left of the outlook spur and descends steadily to the northeast. It turns right at 1.9 mi., turns left at 2.1 mi., and continues at easy grades. In 100 yd. the trail turns right again and leads 70 yd. to the parking area on New Portsmouth Rd.

KNIGHT'S POND CONSERVATION AREA

Portions of this 307-acre property in Alton are owned by Lakes Region Conservation Trust, and other parcels are protected by conservation easements held by LRCT or by the state of New Hampshire. The conservation area's centerpiece is 31-acre Knight's Pond. From the blinking light at the sharp corner on NH 28 in South Wolfeboro, drive 1.6 mi. south on NH 28 and turn left (east) onto Rines Rd. (This turn is 7.5 mi. north of the traffic circle and junction with NH 11 in Alton.) At 1.1 mi. from NH 28 bear left at a fork. In 0.5 mi. turn left at a sign for Knight's Pond Conservation Area and drive 0.4 mi. down a dirt road (may be rough) to trailhead parking. A trail map is available at lrct.org.

SEC 5

KNIGHT'S POND TRAILS (LRCT; LRCT MAP)

From parking area (680 ft.) to:	⤵	⤢	↻
Starting point via Main Trail and Peninsula Trail	2.8 mi.	0 ft. (rev. 50 ft.)	1:25

From the parking area, descend along a continuation of the access road for 0.4 mi. to the beginning of blue-blazed Main Trail. This trail makes a 1.7-mi. loop around Knight's Pond through boulder fields and past beaver dams. An additional 0.3-mi. loop is possible via white-blazed Peninsula Trail.

BIRCH RIDGE COMMUNITY FOREST

This 2,000-acre conservation area in New Durham was permanently protected in 2019 through a cooperative effort between Southeast Land Trust of New Hampshire, Merrymeeting Lake Association, and Moose Mtns. Regional Greenways. The forest rises over Merrymeeting Lake, with views of Mt. Molly and Mt. Bet, and includes an informal network of 13 mi. of multiuse trails. Management and stewardship plans and a formal trail system are still being developed. See seltnh.org for updates.

SECTION 5
SOUTHEASTERN NEW HAMPSHIRE

SEC 5

INTRODUCTION

The southeastern portion of New Hampshire extends northwest from the seacoast to the first significant ranges of hills: the Pawtuckaway Mtns., which are just shy of 1,000 ft. in elevation, in Nottingham and Deerfield, about 25 mi. from the Atlantic Ocean; and the Blue Hills, which reach an elevation of 1,400 ft. in Strafford and Farmington, about 30 miles inland.

New Hampshire's coastline totals only 18 mi.—the fewest of any state that has a coastline—but those miles provide a great variety of scenery and terrain, from rocky headlands and salt marshes to the fine harbor at the mouth of the Piscataqua River, shared by Portsmouth, New Hampshire, and Kittery, Maine. The two most significant features of this area are not on the coastline itself, however. About 10 mi. out to sea, the rocky and picturesque Isles of Shoals (access available through Isles of Shoals Steamship Company in Portsmouth; 603-431-5500, islesofshoals.com) rise several dozen feet above the weather-driven surf, while just a few miles inland lies the 4,500-acre tidal estuary called Great Bay—perhaps the crown jewel of the area.

**SEC
5**

Beyond the coast, the region's low, rolling hills consist largely of piles of gravel left behind by retreating glaciers. Many of the more prominent hills are drumlins. These heaps of gravel, usually about a mile long and a quarter-mile wide, are oriented parallel to the track of the glacier in a northwest–southeast direction, and they rise 100 to 150 ft. above the surrounding countryside. Perhaps the most prominent of these hills, with easy access, is Stratham Hill in the town of Stratham, south of Great Bay. Farther inland, hills become higher. Some of them are formed from bedrock, with occasional rocky outcroppings. Eventually the first real ranges appear: the Pawtuckaways and the Blue Hills.

Included in this section are the trail network in 5,535-acre Pawtuckaway State Park and a number of scattered hills and other natural features that offer interesting walks, including Piscassic Greenway, Howard Swain Memorial Forest, Odiorne Point State Park, the Great Bay area, Stratham Hill, Stonehouse Pond, and Blue Job Mtn. and Parker Mtn. in the Blue Hills Range.

OVERNIGHT OPTIONS

Pawtuckaway State Park Campground offers campsites and cabins near or on Pawtuckaway Lake. In-season (Memorial Day to Columbus Day), make reservations through ReserveAmerica at reserveamerica.com or 877-647-2757. In the off-season (early spring and late fall), camping is allowed on a first-come, first-served basis, weather permitting; use the onsite "iron ranger" pay station to deposit the fee.

As with all sections in this book, camping outside of these designated areas is not permitted unless otherwise noted.

SUGGESTED HIKES

■ Easy Hikes
STRATHAM HILL

LP via Tuck Trail, Lincoln Trail, Kitty Rock Trail, and Old Tote Rd.	1.3 mi.	150 ft.	0:45

Stratham Hill offers extensive views from its observation tower, accessible by a pleasant and easy loop hike. To begin, see Stratham Hill, p. 291.

LITTLE BLUE JOB MTN.

RT via Fire Tower Loop and Little Blue Job Trail	1.8 mi.	280 ft.	1:00

Little Blue Job Mtn., while small in stature, affords panoramic views in all directions from its bare, ledgy summit, making it one of the finest viewpoints in this region. To begin, see Fire Tower Loop, p. 314.

PISCASSIC GREENWAY, MRAZ TRAIL

LP via Mraz Trail	1.3 mi.	90 ft	0:40

This loop hike offers a pleasant trek through attractive forests and along stone walls through the western section of the Greenway. To begin, see Mraz Trail, p. 288.

STONEHOUSE POND

| LP via Locke Trail, Overlook Trail, and Ledges Loop | 1.5 mi. | 160 ft. | 0:50 |

This beautiful small pond features an interesting rock formation that can be ascended for excellent views. To begin, see Locke Trail, p. 308.

HOWARD SWAIN MEMORIAL FOREST

| LP via Howard's Path and Quarry Trail | 1.8 mi. | 180 ft. | 1:00 |

An attractive loop that visits a secluded pond with views of cliffs on the Pawtuckaway Mtns. To begin, see Howard Swain Memorial Forest, p. 306.

SOUTH PAWTUCKAWAY MTN., SHORT LOOP

| LP via Mountain Trail, Tower Trail Connector, South Ridge Trail, South Ridge Connector, and Tower Rd. | 2.3 mi. | 450 ft. | 1:20 |

A loop hike traverses small, ledgy South Pawtuckaway Mtn., which features interesting rock formations, boulders, and fine views from a fire tower. To begin, see Mountain Trail, p. 301.

FUNDY COVE

| RT via Fundy Trail | 3.4 mi. | 0 ft. | 1:40 |

This level, pleasant hike passes an interesting swamp, a scenic lake, and traces of an old farming village. See Fundy Trail, p. 304.

■ Moderate Hikes
PARKER MTN.

| LP via Spencer Smith Trail, Link Trail, and Mooers Loop Trail | 4.1 mi. | 850 ft. | 2:30 |

A scenic loop over Parker Mtn., with a side trip to the mountain's south view ledges, offers a wide vista over Bow Lake. To begin, see Spencer Smith Trail, p. 317.

SWEET TRAIL TO GREAT BAY

OW via Sweet Trail	4.6 mi.	100 ft.	2:20

This hike in Durham and Newmarket provides an extended woods walk, passing many interesting wetlands and ending at the edge of Great Bay. A one-way trip can be made with a relatively easy car spot. Shorter out-and-back trips can be made from three different trailheads. See Sweet Trail, p. 285.

NORTH PAWTUCKAWAY MTN., BOULDER FIELDS, AND DEVIL'S DEN

LP via North Mtn. Trail, Boulder Trail, Round Pond Rd., and North Mtn. Bypass	5.0 mi.	1,000 ft.	3:00

SEC 5

This trio of mountains offers fine views, many interesting rock formations, and an unusual assemblage of large glacial erratic boulders. The distance given is for the approach from the southwest (Reservation Rd.), which has easier vehicular access; the distance for the loop with an approach from the northeast (Round Pond Rd.) is 1.0 mi. (30 min.) less. To begin, see North Mtn. Trail, p. 297.

SOUTH PAWTUCKAWAY MTN., LONG LOOP

LP via Woronoco Trail, Split Rock Trail, Shaw Trail, South Ridge Trail, and Mountain Trail	7.3 mi.	1,000 ft.	4:10

Pass many natural features through the heart of Pawtuckaway State Park, en route to the summit, where you'll find excellent views. To begin, see Woronoco Trail, p. 303.

TRAIL DESCRIPTIONS

ODIORNE POINT STATE PARK

In the town of Rye, along the edge of the southern part of Portsmouth Harbor, in the area where the Piscataqua River merges into the Atlantic Ocean, Odiorne Point State Park contains the Seacoast Science Center (seacoastsciencecenter.org) and offers fine opportunities for walking along the shore in the transition zones between land and water. This is the largest undeveloped stretch of shore on New Hampshire's 18-mi. coast. Resident plants and animals regularly deal with significant fluctuations in the salt content of the water as tides rise and ebb. The U.S. military took over the once fine summer homes during World War II to provide protective fortification for the harbor; the land was given to the state after the war to be converted into the 330-acre park.

The park has two entrances from NH 1A. The main entrance is near the science center, and the second one is farther north, just before the bridge over Seavey Creek. An admission fee is charged from May through October, but the park is open for recreation year-round unless otherwise posted. Enjoyable walks abound on the shoreline and on the old roads and paths that crisscross the area; longer loops reach up to 2 mi., depending on the route chosen. Interesting features include Frost and Odiorne points, freshwater and saltwater marshes, a pond, and dense forest. Take care to avoid the plentiful poison ivy and ticks. A trail map is available at nhstateparks .org. Also, refer to the USGS Kittery quadrangle.

GREAT BAY

This 4,500-acre tidal estuary is the largest inland tidal bay on the East Coast of the United States, furnishing an ecosystem particularly notable for the constant, rhythmic changes in the conditions that confront resident plants and animals. At low tide much of the bay becomes exposed mud flats, while at high tide most of these flats are underwater. Numerous rivers and brooks continuously feed the bay with fresh water; the high tides of the Atlantic Ocean, coming twice each day, force salt water up the Piscataqua River and into the bay. The salinity of the water varies from place to place and fluctuates constantly with the tides. At low tide, minerals and organisms flow out of the bay and down the Piscataqua River to the coastal region. This constant bidirectional flow of nutrients and organisms contributes to the importance of Great Bay as a habitat that nurtures many forms of life, both resident and visitor, including the bald eagle.

SEC 5

Great Bay National Estuarine Research Reserve (greatbay.org), managed by the New Hampshire Fish and Game Department, encompasses several protected areas around the bay. Hiking opportunities include 4.6-mi. Sweet Trail and several casual interpretive walks. In addition to the areas described below, short, easy walks are available on several of Great Bay Reserve's properties: Spartina Point, Pickering Creek, Ellison Brook, Bunker Creek, Longe Marsh, Denbow's Brook, Crommet Creek, Turtle Quarry, and Chapman's Landing. (*Caution*: Poison ivy may be present in these areas; take care to avoid it.)

Great Bay National Wildlife Refuge

This area in Newington, on the northeast side of Great Bay, was occupied mainly by farms with pastures, orchards, and woodlots before it became part of Pease Air Force Base. After the base was closed in 1988, the 1,087-acre portion on and near Great Bay was turned into a national wildlife refuge. From US 4/NH 16, Exit 1 (the Spaulding Turnpike), follow Pease Blvd. into the Pease International Tradeport. After a stoplight, turn right at a stop sign onto Arboretum Dr. and follow Great Bay Refuge signs about 3 mi. to the parking area and refuge headquarters. The trails are open daily from dawn to dusk; pets are not allowed. Trail maps are usually available at the refuge headquarters, and a trail map is available at fws.gov. Also, refer to the USGS Portsmouth quadrangle. Most of the area is not open to the public; access is confined to designated trails, and this restriction is strictly enforced.

At present, there are two public trails: Ferry Way Trail, about 2.4-mi. round-trip on the west side of the parking area, runs past a former weapons-storage complex and a beaver pond to an old field and apple orchard and then makes a loop out to the edge of the bay and back to the field. Peverly Pond Trail, a wheelchair-accessible loop about 0.5 mi. long on the east side of the parking area, leads to the shore of Upper Peverly Pond. An interpretive brochure for Ferry Way Trail is available on the refuge website.

Adams Point

On the west shore of the north arm of Great Bay—known as Little Bay—Adams Point is almost directly opposite the less prominent point reached by William Furber Ferry Way Trail in the Great Bay National Wildlife Refuge. The large field and shoreline offer interesting views, including a photogenic scene across Great Bay with two small islands in the foreground. Adams Point, now almost reverted to nature except for the University of New Hampshire's Jackson Estuarine Laboratory, has at various times supported a farm, a hotel, a brickyard, and a shipyard. It is now part of the Great Bay National Estuarine Research Reserve.

Follow NH 108 south (toward Newmarket) from Durham. At 1.1 mi. from the intersection of NH 108 and Main St. in Durham, bear left onto Durham Point Rd. After 3.9 mi. on Durham Point Rd., turn left onto Adams Point Rd. and drive through a gate with a sign for the Jackson Estuarine Laboratory. Proceed for 1.2 mi. past a boat launch site to the parking area at the trailhead. Adams Point Rd. can also be reached by following Bay Rd. for 3.8 mi. from NH 108 in Newmarket. Refer to the USGS Portsmouth quadrangle. A trail map is usually available at the trailhead.

Evelyn Browne Trail, about 1 mi. long, makes a loop through the eastern part of the point; Adams Point Trail, also about 1 mi. long, circles the south and west perimeters of the point and connects back into Evelyn Browne Trail. The shoreline is reachable from this trail at several points. The two trails can be combined for a loop about 1.5 mi. long around the perimeter of the point.

SEC 5

Sandy Point

Sandy Point, at the southwest corner of Great Bay, offers two short interpretive trails and is home to the small but excellent Great Bay Discovery Center, where many exhibits help reveal the importance of Great Bay as a habitat and ecosystem. The center is open from May to October; the trails are open year-round. From NH 33, 0.3 mi. west of Stratham Hill Park and 1.5 mi. east of the rotary junction with NH 108, take Depot Rd. north for 1.0 mi. Turn left at a T intersection and continue 0.1 mi. to parking at the end of the road. Refer to the USGS Newmarket quadrangle.

Sandy Point Trail, about 0.6 mi. round-trip, starts behind the Discovery Center and follows a universally accessible boardwalk into a salt marsh, with a loop at the end offering open views across Great Bay. At the loop junction a spur called Woodland Trail diverges left and leads about 0.2 mi. through the forest to a partial view over the marsh.

SWEET TRAIL
(GBRPP/TNC; GBRPP TRAIL MAP, USGS NEWMARKET QUAD)

Cumulative from Longmarsh Rd. (70 ft.) to:	⥮	↗	○
First crossing of Dame Rd. (90 ft.)	1.2 mi.	50 ft. (rev. 50 ft.)	0:35
Parking area off Dame Rd. (110 ft.)	1.9 mi.	50 ft.	0:55

Rocky hogback between swamps (90 ft.)	2.8 mi.	50 ft.	1:25
Upper junction with Jeff's Hill Loop Trail (110 ft.)	3.7 mi.	100 ft.	1:55
Lower junction with Jeff's Hill Loop Trail (50 ft.)	4.2 mi.	100 ft. (rev. 50 ft.)	2:10
Shore of Great Bay (10 ft.)	4.6 mi.	100 ft. (rev. 50 ft.)	2:20

This 4.6-mi. trail leads through several parcels of conservation land, from the town of Durham's Longmarsh Preserve to The Nature Conservancy's Lubberland Creek Preserve in Newmarket on the shore of Great Bay. It also crosses land owned by the New Hampshire Fish and Game Department, the Society for the Protection of New Hampshire Forests (Forest Society), and private parties. The trail, opened in 2008, was developed as a collaborative effort by the Great Bay Resource Protection Partnership, which is composed of a number of government agencies and nonprofit conservation groups. AMC trail crew and numerous volunteers assisted with the construction of the trail. It was named for Cy and Bobbie Sweet, generous supporters of conservation efforts in the Great Bay area for many years. A brochure with map is available at greatbaypartnership.org.

The trail offers an unusual opportunity for an extended woodland hike, with minimal road walking, in one of the most heavily developed regions of New Hampshire. It passes numerous wetlands with many chances for wildlife observation. The terrain is mostly gentle, and the footing is good. The trail is well marked with white diamond-shaped GBRPP markers, though care must be taken to follow the main route at numerous intersections with side paths and woods roads. Trail signs posted at intersections provide direction and mileage information.

Reach the north end of the trail from Longmarsh Rd. in Durham, which leaves the east side of NH 108 1.5 mi. south of its junction with Main St. Longmarsh Rd. changes to gravel 0.9 mi. from NH 108. Trailhead parking for two or three cars is on the left at 1.3 mi., where the drivable road ends just beyond the last house. The trail can also be reached near its south end from the parking area for TNC's Lubberland Creek Preserve, on the north side of Bay Rd. 1.6 mi. from its junction with NH 108 in Newmarket, or 6.3 mi. from its junction with NH 108 in Durham (where it is named Durham Point Rd.). A short connecting path leads from the parking area to Sweet Trail, 0.4 mi. from its south terminus on Great Bay. A third access point is the New Hampshire Fish and Game Department parking area on the east side of Dame Rd. 1.5 mi. west of its junction with Durham Point Rd. and about 2 mi. east of its junction with NH 108.

From the parking area on Longmarsh Rd., walk ahead (east) on the extension of the road, passing a kiosk with a trail map on the right in 25 yd. (where a side path diverges right) and a gate just beyond. Sweet Trail (in this initial section marked with both GBRPP and yellow diamond markers) soon passes Colby Marsh, a large wetland on Crommet Creek, on the right. The trail descends gently, passing a diverging footpath on the right, and reaches the edge of a beaver pond on the left at 0.4 mi. Here, a wooden walkway continues ahead, providing a good view of the pond, while Sweet Trail turns right (south). Sweet Trail soon swings right around the corner of a wetland to pass a diverging path on the right; then it bears left to cross a brook on rocks and swings right again before climbing a short distance to higher ground. It meanders through the woods, with minor ups and downs, passing through a stone wall at 0.6 mi. and traveling along interesting ledges on the left at 0.9 mi. The trail passes through another stone wall and crosses gravel Dame Rd. at 1.2 mi. On the south side of the road, it follows a newer footway, passing a shrubby swamp on the left at 1.5 mi. and skirting private land on the right. After passing through some old pastureland, the trail swings right at 1.8 mi. near the edge of a swamp; a side path leads 15 yd. left to a good view.

At 1.9 mi. the trail emerges at the northeast corner of a gravel parking area on the east side of Dame Rd. Here, it turns left and follows a gravel spur road through a line of boulders. In 50 yd. the trail turns right off this road, passes through a patch of weeds, and reenters the woods. It crosses a stone wall and an old woods road, descends briefly, and swings right toward Dame Rd. at 2.2 mi. The trail turns left onto Dame Rd., follows it for 0.3 mi., and then turns left onto a woods road. (There are signs for Sweet Trail at both points where it intersects Dame Rd.) The route follows the woods road south between two swamps and then turns left off it at 2.7 mi. (Follow the road ahead for 40 yd. to a point just before it is submerged to reach rocks on the right with a good view of the swamp on the west side of the trail.)

After the trail turns left off the woods road, it climbs over a knoll and descends to a viewpoint on the eastern edge of the swamp. Here, it turns right, crosses a well-constructed bridge, and climbs over a rocky hogback between the swamps. The trail then swings right, crosses an inlet brook for the western swamp, and at 2.9 mi. turns left onto the woods road beyond the point where it is submerged. At 3.1 mi. Sweet Trail diverges left off the woods road onto a footpath and passes several views of a large wooded swamp on the left, where great blue herons may often be observed. (*Note*: Take care not to disturb these magnificent birds during summer nesting season.) Partway along this section there is a large glacial erratic—a glacially deposited rock that differs from the rest in the area—on the right. The footpath improves as the trail transitions into a woods road, passing

SEC 5

an unusually large oak on the right. At 3.6 mi. Sweet Trail diverges right off this road and meanders across a plateau on the side of Jeff's Hill. It soon passes through a stone wall, turns right, passes a TNC trail that diverges left, and makes a short loop over the wooded top of Jeff's Hill (150 ft.).

At 3.7 mi. Sweet Trail turns right at a T intersection with Jeff's Hill Loop Trail. (To the left, this TNC trail descends 0.1 mi. to a lower junction with Sweet Trail, a shortcut that saves 0.4 mi. in either direction.) Now coinciding with Jeff's Hill Loop Trail and marked with both GBRPP and TNC markers, Sweet Trail descends gradually north for 0.2 mi. before it swings sharply left and descends to the south. At 4.1 mi. it swings left and runs along the edge of a cattail swamp, coming to a four-way junction at 4.2 mi. To the left is the lower junction with Jeff's Hill Loop Trail; to the right is a short connecting path that leads to the parking area on Bay Rd. for TNC's Lubberland Creek Preserve. Sweet Trail continues ahead here, passing through an overgrown section (watch out for poison ivy) and dipping to cross Bay Rd. at 4.3 mi. The trail continues south through the woods, with gentle ups and downs, and passes a side path (left) to the edge of a private field with a glimpse of Great Bay at 4.5 mi. Sweet Trail meanders down through a pine grove and ends at an open spot at the edge of the Lubberland Creek salt marsh with granite benches, a monument, and an excellent view south across Great Bay.

PISCASSIC GREENWAY

This conservation area in Newfields and Newmarket, managed by Southeast Land Trust of New Hampshire, offers a network of multiuse trails, all with easy grades and good footing. Varied terrain includes open fields, ponds, wetland areas, and mature oak, pine, and hemlock forests. Parking is available at both trailheads. To reach the western trailhead from downtown Newfields, take NH 87 West for 3.3 mi., turn right onto Bald Hill Rd., and continue 0.5 mi. to a small parking area on the right. To reach the eastern trailhead from downtown Newfields, take NH 87 West for 1.5 mi., turn right onto Halls Mill Rd., and continue 0.9 mi. to a small parking area on the left. (Please do not block the gate or adjacent private driveways.) An AMC map is on p. 289, and a trail map is available at seltnh.org.

MRAZ TRAIL (SELT; SELT MAP, AMC PISCASSIC GREENWAY MAP)

Cumulative from Bald Hill Rd. (80 ft.) to:	⤊	↗	↻
Loop junction (120 ft.)	0.4 mi.	40 ft.	0:15
Starting point via complete loop	1.3 mi.	90 ft. (rev. 90 ft.)	0:40

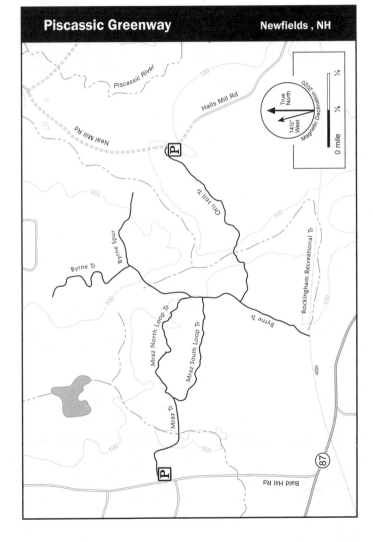

Piscassic Greenway

Newfields , NH

This white-blazed trail allows for a loop hike through the western section of the Greenway. The two loop branches are named Mraz North Loop Trail and Mraz South Loop Trail on the SELT map. The route is described in the counterclockwise direction. From the Bald Hill Rd. trailhead, the trail winds across two open fields, enters the woods and reaches a junction at 0.4 mi. where it splits into two branches.

Mraz South Loop Trail turns sharply right and heads south at first then southeast, ascending and then descending alongside an old stone wall. It crosses a footbridge over a small stream, passes through the stone wall, and bears left onto an old woods road at 0.3 mi. The road descends to a low wet area, climbs over a small rise, and then descends to meet Byrne Trail at 0.5 mi. Mraz South Loop Trail turns left and briefly coincides with Byrne Trail before diverging left, back into the woods, at 0.6 mi.

Mraz North Loop Trail now continues level at first and then descends. It bears left onto a relocated section, crosses a boardwalk, climbs over a small rise, and returns to the loop junction at 0.9 mi. Bear right here to return to the trailhead in 0.4 mi.

SEC 5

OTIS HILL TRAIL (SELT; SELT MAP, AMC PISCASSIC GREENWAY MAP)
From Halls Mill Rd.
(110 ft.) to:

	⥮	↗	○
Byrne Trail (130 ft.)	0.7 mi.	90 ft. (rev. 50 ft.)	0:25

This blue-blazed trail connects the unmaintained portion of Halls Mill Rd. with Byrne Trail. The easiest access is from the Halls Mill Rd. parking area. The trail begins 0.2 mi. farther along the road on the left. Heading generally southwest, Otis Hill Trail ascends briefly, continues level or at easy grades, and climbs easily to the height-of-land, 50 yd. north of the west knob of Otis Hill. The trail then descends gradually through dark pine forest to cross a footbridge over a small brook at 0.5 mi. It bears right onto an old woods road and continues level to meet Byrne Trail at 0.7 mi.

BYRNE TRAIL (SELT; SELT MAP, AMC PISCASSIC GREENWAY MAP)
From gate at start of trail
(110 ft.) to:

	⥮	↗	○
Gate at end of trail (130 ft.)	1.1 mi.	90 ft. (rev. 50 ft.)	0:35

This yellow-blazed trail follows an old woods road for its entire length, bisecting the Greenway from south to north. It also connects to other trails, making various loop hikes possible. The easiest access is via Rockingham Recreational Rail Trail and a short connector trail. Limited roadside parking is available where the rail-trail crosses NH 87 in Newfields,

3.1 mi. east of NH 125. From the parking area, walk 0.4 mi. east along the rail-trail to a four-way junction. Turn left and continue 0.1 mi. to a gate where Byrne Trail officially starts (the distances shown begin here). From the gate, Byrne Trail starts out level, crosses a clearing, and then passes a junction with Otis Hill Trail on the right at 0.2 mi. Byrne Trail then descends to a junction with the southern branch of Mraz Loop on the left at 0.4 mi., followed quickly by a junction with the northern branch. The trail ascends past an old cellar hole and at 0.7 mi. swings left at the junction with Byrne Spur Trail. (This short side trail descends 0.4 mi. and 50 ft. to meet Neal Mill Rd. In 2019, a boardwalk was constructed in a wetland area to make this trail, previously only accessible in winter, accessible year-round.) Byrne Trail heads northwest and traverses a logged area, turns right, climbs over a wooded hump, and descends through a series of switch-backs to a gate at 1.1 mi., where the trail officially ends.

SEC 5

STRATHAM HILL (286 FT.)

Stratham Hill, in Stratham, is a textbook example of a drumlin, a pile of gravel left by a continental glacier. It is about 150 ft. high and a half-mile long by a quarter-mile wide, oriented in the direction of the glacier's travel—northwest to southeast. The open, grassy summit has limited views, but the former fire tower, which has an observation deck built to replace the cab, offers good views in almost all directions. Mt. Washington is visible on a clear day. The 53-ft. steel tower is maintained by the town of Stratham. A trail map is available at strathamnh.gov. Also, refer to the USGS Newmarket quadrangle.

Access is from a large parking area at Stratham Hill Park (sign) on the south side of NH 33, opposite Sandy Point Rd. and 1.8 mi. east of the rotary junction with NH 108.

STRATHAM HILL TRAILS
(STRATHAM HILL PARK TRAIL MAP, USGS NEWMARKET QUAD)

Cumulative from Stratham Hill Park parking area (150 ft.) to:	⇕	↗	⟲
Stratham Hill summit (286 ft.) via Tuck Trail and Lincoln Trail	0.2 mi.	150 ft.	0:10
Parking area via return loop on Kitty Rock Trail and Old Tote Rd.	1.3 mi.	150 ft.	0:45

For the most direct route to the summit, follow Tuck Trail (sign), which starts between two boulders 20 yd. east of the parking area, near a picnic pavilion. After less than 0.1 mi. of steady climbing, Tuck Trail meets

Lincoln Trail opposite a plaque on a boulder marking the location where Robert T. Lincoln, Abraham Lincoln's son, read the Declaration of Independence on July 4, 1860. Turn left on the wider Lincoln Trail and follow it 0.1 mi. to the field and observation tower at the summit. (From the parking area, reach the bottom of Lincoln Trail by following a paved road south through a gate and past a park building on the left; 80 yd. from the gate the trail [sign] begins on the left. Distance to the summit is about the same as via the Tuck Trail route.)

Several other trails may be used for longer walks; they are shown on a trail sign at the entrance to the recreation area and on the map at strathamnh.gov. A pleasant loop can be made from the summit through the Gordon Barker Town Forest and back to the parking area. Follow Lincoln Trail 100 yd. east from the observation tower, and turn right at a sign for Kitty Rock Trail. In another 25 yd. bear left at an unsigned fork. Kitty Rock Trail descends easily through woods, swinging right where an unsigned trail diverges left. At a T junction 0.5 mi. from the tower, the loop route turns right onto Old Tote Rd. This level trail leads northwest between open fields on the left and swampy Stratham Hill Pond on the right, passing several diverging paths. At 0.9 mi. Old Tote Rd. reaches a parking area for the town forest, runs along its edge for 70 yd., and then turns right through a gate (sign for Stratham Hill). The trail follows a road past a house and then through the park, passing a junction on the right with Lincoln Trail 80 yd. before reaching the Stratham Hill Park parking area.

PAWTUCKAWAY STATE PARK

The Pawtuckaway Mtns. in Nottingham are a series of three parallel ridges—North Mtn. (996 ft.), Middle Mtn. (844 ft.), and South Mtn. (885 ft.)—all contained within 5,535-acre Pawtuckaway State Park, arguably the finest natural area in southeastern New Hampshire. The valley east of North Mtn. contains an extraordinary collection of huge boulders and several other unusual and interesting rock formations, designated as the Boulder Natural Area. While the mountains are small and provide only a few sweeping vistas, they offer a variety of surprisingly rugged, rocky scenery. Most of the trails in the park are marked with white blazes, rectangles, or diamonds. Use the AMC Pawtuckaway State Park trail maps (South and North) in this guide; there is a trail map at nhstateparks.org, and trail maps are available at the park office. Also, refer to the USGS Mt. Pawtuckaway quadrangle.

Reach the mountains from the west from NH 107 between Deerfield and Raymond by turning east onto Reservation Rd. (fire lookout sign) at a junction 3.1 mi. north of the junction of NH 107 with NH 27, and 0.7 mi. south of the southern junction of NH 107 with NH 43. Reservation Rd. bears right at 1.2 mi. from NH 107 and reaches a junction at 2.3 mi. From this point the roads create a loop through the heart of the Pawtuckaway Mtns.; Round Pond Rd., to the left at this junction, forms the western branch of the loop, which continues beyond the north end of the loop for some distance. Tower Rd. forms the eastern branch of the loop, which meets Reservation Rd. 0.2 mi. farther east. These roads are rough and eroded at times, but walking distances to most objectives from the loop are relatively short. Tower Rd. receives the majority of the traffic, since the southern part of Round Pond Rd. has sometimes been flooded by beaver activity near its midpoint. Reservation Rd. is plowed in winter to its junction with Tower Rd. and to the houses on the road that runs south from this junction, but parking may be limited.

For the trails to the three main mountains, continue on Reservation Rd. to the junction with Tower Rd. Turn left (sign: "Lookout Tower") on Tower Rd. and follow it for 0.8 mi. A tiny graveyard in the woods is on the left at the edge of a small clearing, which is the former site of the ranger's cabin. A few cars can park in the clearing. Middle Mtn. Trail begins about 50 yd. below (south of) the ranger's cabin site. An extension of Mtn. Trail (also called Tower Trail Connector) enters about 50 yd. beyond (north of) the clearing at a small parking area on the right, and South Mtn. Tower Trail leaves the same parking area on the right in another 50 yd. The trailhead where South Ridge Connector leads to South Ridge Trail is 0.2 mi. farther along the road beyond South Mtn. Tower Trail.

The north end of the road loop (the junction of Tower Rd. and Round Pond Rd.) is about 1.8 mi. (via Tower Rd.) from the junction of Tower Rd. and Reservation Rd. The north end of the loop can be reached more directly from Reservation Rd. by Round Pond Rd. in about 1.3 mi. when that road is passable. Boulder Trail to the Boulder Natural Area and North Mtn. begins on an extension of Round Pond Rd. 0.5 mi. north of the north loop junction. The other end of Boulder Trail, which provides access to the boulder area and North Mtn. via the Lower Slabs, begins at the edge of Round Pond 0.5 mi. farther along this road (this section may not be passable for many cars). Parking on Round Pond Rd. is limited to designated spots.

The easiest road access to the mountains (via NH 101, Exit 5) is on the south side of the main entrance to Pawtuckaway State Park, off NH 156,

SEC 5

SEC
5

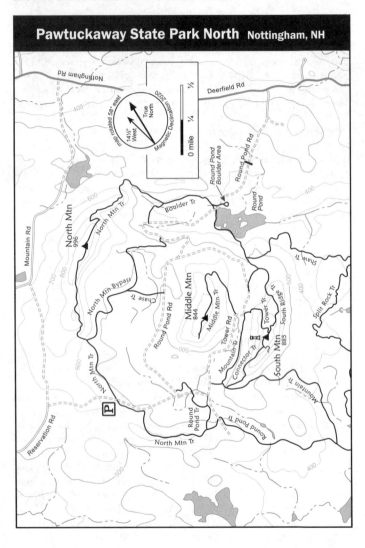

Pawtuckaway State Park North Nottingham, NH

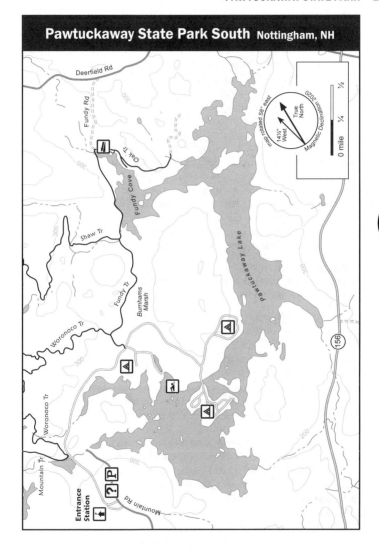

Pawtuckaway State Park South Nottingham, NH

SEC 5

but walking distances are much longer; in winter, however, some of the mountain trails may be more convenient to reach from this side. From NH 156, 1.4 mi. north of its junction with NH 107 in Raymond, turn west onto Mountain Rd. (sign for park). In 2.1 mi. turn left into the park entrance, and pass the park headquarters, visitor center, and a large parking area on the right. (Trail maps are usually available at the visitor center.) Follow the road north toward the swimming beach, passing a tollbooth (fee charged in summer) and then Mountain Pond on the left. The trailhead for Mountain Trail and Round Pond Trail, with limited roadside parking, is on the left at the north end of the pond, 0.4 mi. from the tollbooth; the trailhead for Fundy Trail is 1.0 mi. farther. Parking is not permitted on the pavement.

The trails in the eastern part of the park are favored by mountain bikers in summer and snowmobilers in winter; though they offer few long-range views, they frequently traverse interesting woodlands and pass near extensive wetlands. From early spring through late fall, the park's campground offers campsites and cabins near or on Pawtuckaway Lake. Make reservations through ReserveAmerica at reserveamerica.com or by calling 877-647-2757.

BOULDER TRAIL
(NHDP; AMC PAWTUCKAWAY STATE PARK NORTH MAP)

Cumulative from Round Pond Rd. (450 ft.) to:	�	↗	○
North Mtn. Trail (400 ft.)	0.2 mi.	0 ft. (rev. 50 ft.)	0:05
Round Pond Rd. at Round Pond (330 ft.)	0.7 mi.	0 ft. (rev. 50 ft.)	0:20

This scenic short trail runs through the principal boulder field and passes the Lower Slabs as well as several other interesting rock formations. It provides access to the northern terminus of North Mtn. Trail and to Round Pond Rd. at Round Pond (the northern terminus of South Ridge Trail). Boulder Trail also makes possible several interesting loops in the Round Pond and North Mtn. areas.

The white-blazed trail leaves Round Pond Rd. at a hairpin turn 0.5 mi. north of Tower Rd. and 0.5 mi. west of Round Pond. It descends on an old woods road through a dense hemlock forest, swings right and then left, and meets the northern terminus of North Mtn. Trail on the left at 0.2 mi. in the midst of an impressive field of large, moss-covered glacial erratics. Here, Boulder Trail bears right (east), becoming a footpath, and passes through a stone wall, then skirts the northern side of a marsh. At 0.5 mi. the trail reaches the base of nearly vertical ledges next to the marsh and passes beneath several overhanging boulders (arrow). It passes a number of slabs and ledges (popular with rock climbers) and soon reaches a junction where white-blazed Boulder Cutoff diverges left, leading about 100 yd. to an extension of Round Pond Rd. (which may be flooded). Across the road a short loop (sign: "Round Pond Boulder Area") leads through the Round Pond Boulders, another climbing area. From this junction Boulder Trail descends to cross a brook, passes a short path on the left connecting with the end of Round Pond Rd., and descends to Round Pond Rd. near the northwest corner of Round Pond, a short distance west of the northern terminus of South Ridge Trail.

NORTH MTN. TRAIL
(NHDP; AMC PAWTUCKAWAY STATE PARK NORTH MAP)

Cumulative from Boulder Trail (400 ft.) to:	⇅	⤢	↻
North Mtn. summit (996 ft.)	1.2 mi.	650 ft. (rev. 50 ft.)	0:55
North Mtn. Bypass (550 ft.)	2.2 mi.	750 ft. (rev. 550 ft.)	1:30
Reservation Rd. (530 ft.)	2.7 mi.	800 ft. (rev. 100 ft.)	1:45
Round Pond Trail (540 ft.)	3.6 mi.	900 ft. (rev. 100 ft.)	2:15

SEC 5

This trail, which traverses North Mtn. from north to south, is one of the longest and most scenic in the park, passing many interesting rock features and several vistas. The northern end of this route is on Boulder Trail near the principal boulder field 0.2 mi. from Round Pond Rd. via the boulder field and 0.5 mi. from Round Pond Rd. at Round Pond. The southern end is at a junction with Round Pond Trail 0.4 mi. south of that trail's crossing of Reservation Rd. The trail is described in the north-to-south direction.

From the junction with Boulder Trail, North Mtn. Trail climbs through a beautiful hemlock forest, passing large boulders and then impressive cliffs on the left. It swings right and dips near the swamp at Dead Pond at 0.3 mi.; then it turns left and climbs a steep boulder-strewn promontory with many boulder caves, soon reaching the Devil's Den (a crevice cave in the rocks to the left of the trail). North Mtn. Trail angles steeply up the north side of the ridge and turns sharply right on the ridge crest at 0.5 mi., where a side path leads 40 yd. left to a ledge with restricted views. Marked with cairns and white blazes, the route continues near the ridge crest, passing another side path left to a ledge with a restricted view; then it passes through a small notch below another set of boulder cliffs. The trail turns sharply left and climbs by a switchback to a side path leading 30 yd. left to an outlook to the east (including Middle Mtn. and South Mtn.) at 1.0 mi., on a bluff where there is a large green communications reflector. The trail then continues along the ridge to the ledgy, overgrown summit at 1.2 mi., marked by a cairn. Here, North Mtn. Trail drops steeply off the ledge; a short alternate path bypasses the summit on the left.

North Mtn. Trail continues along the ledgy ridge crest, descending easily with occasional short ascents. At 1.9 mi. it reaches the shoulder of the ridge; here, an open ledge 25 yd. to the left provides a good view south and east. Soon the trail begins a steeper descent over scattered ledges. At 2.2 mi., the foot of the steep section, the trail reaches a T intersection with a woods road. Here, North Mtn. Bypass diverges left, following the woods road in that direction. North Mtn. Trail turns right onto the woods road and in 25 yd. turns left onto another woods road just before reaching an orange gate. Snowmobile trail signs mark this turn. (In the reverse direction, turn right at these signs, and then in 25 yd. turn left off the woods road onto a footpath marked by a cairn.) Now coinciding with Snowmobile Corridor 17S, North Mtn. Trail descends gradually, passing an old road on the right. It crosses a stream and then ascends gradually, passing another old road on the right. At 2.7 mi. the trail reaches Reservation Rd. at a point 1.8 mi. east of NH 107 and 0.5 mi. west of Round Pond Rd. A small parking area is here.

Across Reservation Rd., North Mtn. Trail (sign) continues past a gate on an old road, still coinciding with Snowmobile Corridor 17S. It ascends past several stone walls, runs across a low ridge, and descends to a junction with Round Pond Trail, which continues ahead (east) and to the left (north).

NORTH MTN. BYPASS
(NHDP; AMC PAWTUCKAWAY STATE PARK NORTH MAP)

From Round Pond Rd. (470 ft.) to:	⇅	↗	↺
North Mtn. Trail (550 ft.)	1.4 mi.	200 ft. (rev. 100 ft.)	0:50
From Reservation Rd. (530 ft.) to:			
Starting point by complete loop via North Mtn. Trail, Boulder Trail, Round Pond Rd., and North Mtn. Bypass	5.0 mi.	1,000 ft.	3:00

This trail mostly follows woods roads, connecting Round Pond Rd. with North Mtn. Trail at the south end of North Mtn., and serves as a return route for a loop hike over North Mtn. It has good footing, with easy to moderate grades. Since the south end of the loop has the easiest vehicular access, this trail is described as a return route from north to south.

The trail leaves Round Pond Rd. 0.3 mi. north of its junction with Tower Rd. and 0.2 mi. south of the northern terminus of Boulder Trail. It ascends southwest on an old road, soon bears right onto another old road coming in from the left, and then swings sharply right to a viewpoint overlooking a clearing. It descends gradually, skirts the edge of a bog, swings left (south) at 0.4 mi., and ascends gradually. At 0.8 mi. the trail joins another old road and follows it to the right. (To the left, this road is named Chase Trail and leads in 0.3 mi. to Round Pond Rd., 0.4 mi. south of Tower Rd. and 0.9 mi. north of Reservation Rd.)

North Mtn. Bypass swings left, then right twice along a stone wall as it ascends gradually along the southeast slope of North Mtn. After two more bends, it meets North Mtn. Trail 0.5 mi. north of Reservation Rd. and 1.0 mi. south of the summit of North Mtn. Here, North Mtn. Trail leading south to Reservation Rd. continues ahead on the woods road and, in 25 yd., turns left (signs) onto another woods road, which is also Snowmobile Route 17S. For North Mtn. Trail leading to the summit of North Mtn., turn right onto a footpath at a cairn.

SEC 5

SOUTH MTN. TOWER TRAIL
(NHDP; AMC PAWTUCKAWAY STATE PARK NORTH MAP)

From Tower Rd. (540 ft.) to:	⇅	↗	↻
South Mtn. summit (885 ft.)	0.4 mi.	350 ft.	0:25

Probably the most popular hike in the park, this trail ascends South Mtn. directly from the north and provides access to fine vistas from the fire tower and nearby ledges for a modest effort. The extensive views include Mt. Wachusett, Mt. Monadnock, Mt. Sunapee, Lovewell Mtn., Mt. Kearsarge, Blue Job Mtn., and Fort Mtn. The trail begins on Tower Rd. 0.8 mi. north of Reservation Rd., just north of where an extension of Mtn. Trail (also called Tower Trail Connector) leaves Tower Rd. (The 0.6-mi. connector trail leads southwest to Mountain Trail; 0 ft., rev. 50 ft.) South Mtn. Tower Trail ascends by switchbacks through a pine grove on a white-blazed path; in the lower part there is a steep, direct route and a less steep, less direct route to the left. The trail passes several boulder caves (left) and the grade eases temporarily. Then the path ascends granite steps and climbs by switchbacks to the open ledges near the summit of South Mtn., where it reaches South Ridge Trail.

SOUTH RIDGE TRAIL
(NHDP; AMC PAWTUCKAWAY STATE PARK NORTH MAP)
Cumulative from Mtn. Trail
(500 ft.) to:

	⇅	↗	↻
South Mtn. summit (885 ft.)	0.6 mi.	400 ft.	0:30
South Ridge Connector (550 ft.)	1.3 mi.	400 ft. (rev. 350 ft.)	0:50
Shaw Trail (480 ft.)	1.4 mi.	400 ft. (rev. 50 ft.)	0:55
Round Pond Rd. (330 ft.)	2.0 mi.	400 ft. (rev. 150 ft.)	1:10

This white-blazed trail traverses South Mtn., providing access to its fire tower and far-reaching views. The southern terminus of South Ridge Trail is near the height-of-land on Mountain Trail, 1.8 mi. north of the park entrance road at Mountain Pond and 0.1 mi. south of Tower Rd. just north of its junction with Reservation Rd.

From its junction with Mountain Trail, South Ridge Trail ascends gradually along an old road for about 0.2 mi., passing several stone walls. Then it swings left, swings right, and climbs steeply through boulders and ledges. At 0.4 mi. an orange-blazed side path leads 60 yd. right to an open ledge with views south and east. (This path continues east from behind the ledge and ascends 0.2 mi. to rejoin the main trail 30 yd. west of the fire tower.) At 0.6 mi. South Ridge Trail emerges onto semi-open ledges with views to the west and soon arrives at the summit of South Mtn., where the fire tower provides extensive vistas. Here, South Mtn. Tower Trail comes up from the left (north).

From the summit, South Ridge Trail descends right (northeast) on a rocky ridge, with occasional minor ascents. Then it swings left across the ridge crest and descends sharply past interesting rock formations. At 1.1 mi. it swings right, past a beaver pond on the left, as the grade eases; a side path leads 15 yd. left to a ledge with a view of the pond. The trail crosses a small stream and ascends gradually to an old road at 1.3 mi. From here, the old road (South Ridge Connector) leads left 0.2 mi. (50-ft. ascent) to Tower Rd., 0.2 mi. north of the trailhead of South Mtn. Tower Trail. South Ridge Trail turns right onto this old road and descends along the stream past a cellar hole (right), soon reaching the junction with Shaw Trail on the right. South Ridge Trail continues straight and descends sharply by switchbacks to the southwest shore of Round Pond. Here, it swings left and follows the west shore of the attractive pond, passing a rock with an excellent view over the water. South Ridge Trail continues, with undulating grades, to the end of Round Pond Rd., a short distance east from the eastern terminus of Boulder Trail.

MIDDLE MTN. TRAIL
(NHDP; AMC PAWTUCKAWAY STATE PARK NORTH MAP)

From Tower Rd. (510 ft.) to:	⬇⬆	↗	⟳
Middle Mtn. outlook (820 ft.)	1.0 mi.	350 ft. (rev. 50 ft.)	0:40

The white-blazed trail to Middle Mtn. begins on an old woods road that leaves the west side of Tower Rd. just south of the site of the old fire warden's camp, a bit more than 100 yd. south of the trailhead for South Mtn. Tower Trail. Middle Mtn. Trail rises on the old road at a moderate grade along a stone wall; then it turns sharply left and climbs a steep, badly eroded section to the upper shoulder of the mountain. From there, the trail ascends gently over the almost imperceptible summit at 0.8 mi. and then descends gradually to a ledge with a view south.

MOUNTAIN TRAIL (NHDP; AMC PAWTUCKAWAY STATE PARK MAPS)

Cumulative from park entrance road (270 ft.) to:	⬇⬆	↗	⟳
Divergence of Round Pond Trail. (350 ft.)	0.5 mi.	100 ft.	0:20
South Ridge Trail (500 ft.)	1.8 mi.	350 ft. (rev. 100 ft.)	1:05
Tower Rd. (470 ft.)	1.9 mi.	350 ft. (rev. 50 ft.)	1:10
South Mtn. (885 ft.) via South Ridge Trail	2.4 mi.	750 ft.	1:35

This white-blazed trail, a wide woods road for most of its length, connects the park entrance road near the main south park entrance, off NH 156, with Tower Rd. just north of its junction with Reservation Rd. in the northwestern part of the park. It is a major access route from the southern and eastern park facilities to the hiking areas surrounding North, Middle, and South mtns.

Mountain Trail begins on the park entrance road 0.4 mi. north of the tollbooth and main parking area. Limited roadside parking is available at the trailhead; do not park on the pavement. The trail follows an old road along the northern shore of Mountain Pond, coinciding with Round Pond Trail. In 35 yd. Woronoco Trail diverges right (sign). Mountain Trail passes the west end of the pond, and at 0.5 mi. it turns right at an intersection where Round Pond Trail continues straight ahead.

Mountain Trail runs at easy grades, with minor ups and downs. It crosses a brook at 0.8 mi., swings left, crosses a small stream, and begins to ascend the south flank of South Mtn. The trail reaches the height-of-land at 1.6 mi. and then descends gradually to the junction with South Ridge Trail on the right at 1.8 mi. Mountain Trail then swings right, soon reaching an extension of this route on the right (also called Tower Trail Connector), which runs northeast for 0.6 mi. (50 ft.) to South Mtn. Tower Trail at its trailhead. Within another 0.1 mi., the main Mountain Trail reaches Tower Rd. just north of its intersection with Reservation Rd. (no sign, limited parking).

ROUND POND TRAIL
(NHDP; AMC PAWTUCKAWAY STATE PARK MAPS)

Cumulative from park entrance road (270 ft.) to:	↥↧	↗	↻
Divergence of Mountain Trail (350 ft.)	0.5 mi.	100 ft.	0:20
North Mtn. Trail (540 ft.)	1.6 mi.	300 ft.	0:55
Reservation Rd. (450 ft.)	2.0 mi.	300 ft. (rev. 100 ft.)	1:10
Round Pond Rd. (450 ft.)	2.2 mi.	300 ft.	1:15
Round Pond (330 ft.) via Round Pond Rd.	4.4 mi.	400 ft. (rev. 200 ft.)	2:25

This white-blazed trail, a wide woods road for most of its length, connects the park entrance road near the main south entrance with Round Pond Rd. just north of its junction with Reservation Rd., near the northwest entrance to the park. It is a major access route from the southern and eastern park facilities to the hiking areas surrounding North, Middle, and South mtns.

The trail begins at the park entrance road 0.4 mi. north of the tollbooth and main parking area. Limited roadside parking is available at the trailhead; do not park on the pavement. Coinciding with Mountain Trail, Round Pond Trail follows an old woods road along the northern shore of Mountain Pond. In 35 yd. Woronoco Trail diverges right (sign). Round Pond Trail passes the west end of the pond, and at 0.5 mi. it continues straight ahead where Mountain Trail turns right.

Round Pond Trail ascends 0.4 mi. to the height-of-land and then descends to a beaver pond on the right, where the footway may be flooded. It ascends through wooden gateposts to a point where an old road continues straight; here, Round Pond Trail turns right and emerges in an open area. The trail then descends and turns sharply left where another old road continues straight. After crossing the gravel southern extension of Tower Rd., next to a private home, Round Pond Trail passes yet another old road. At 1.6 mi. the trail reaches a junction marked by snowmobile signs. Here, North Mtn. Trail, coinciding with Snowmobile Route 17N, continues ahead on an old road, reaching Reservation Rd. in 0.9 mi.

Round Pond Trail turns right at this junction and descends to an intersection in a small clearing, where an old road continues straight 0.1 mi. to the intersection of Tower Rd. and Reservation Rd. Here, Round Pond

Trail swings left, swings right, descends past a beaver pond on the left, and crosses Reservation Rd. at 2.0 mi., 0.1 mi. west of its junction with Tower Rd. and 0.1 mi. east of its junction with Round Pond Rd. The trail ascends an old road, swings left past an old cellar hole, and ends at Round Pond Rd. about 75 yd. north of its junction with Reservation Rd. and 2.2 mi. south of Round Pond.

WORONOCO TRAIL
(NEMBA; AMC PAWTUCKAWAY STATE PARK MAPS)

Cumulative from Mountain Trail (270 ft.) to:	⏱	↗	⟳
Marsh overlook (370 ft.)	0.9 mi.	150 ft. (rev. 50 ft.)	0:30
Split Rock Trail (370 ft.)	1.5 mi.	150 ft.	0:50
Fundy Trail (280 ft.)	2.5 mi.	200 ft. (rev. 150 ft.)	1:20

This multiuse trail connects the south end of the coinciding Mountain and Round Pond trails with the south end of Fundy Trail and makes possible longer loop hikes with a minimum of road walking. The white-blazed trail follows a meandering course with good footing through the remote southern section of the park. (*Caution*: Be alert for mountain bikers.)

Woronoco Trail leaves the right (north) side of Mountain Trail/Round Pond Trail at a posted map 35 yd. from its trailhead on the park entrance road. It winds northward, ascending gradually, and then descends to cross a bridge over a brook draining from a swamp on the left at 0.4 mi. The route winds through boulders, and at 0.9 mi. it swings right. Here, a side path (sign: "Overlook") leads 10 yd. left to a fine view across a marsh to South Mtn. The main trail now heads northeast, crossing a bridge over a brook at 1.1 mi. and meandering over several knolls. At 1.5 mi. Split Rock Trail diverges left, and soon Woronoco Trail turns sharply right, heading east and southeast. It descends gradually through fine hemlock stands, leads between two boulders at 2.1 mi., passes an old cellar hole, and ends at Fundy Trail 0.2 mi. north of its southern trailhead on the park entrance road.

SPLIT ROCK TRAIL
(NEMBA; AMC PAWTUCKAWAY STATE PARK NORTH MAP)

From Woronoco Trail (370 ft.) to:	⏱	↗	⟳
Shaw Trail (390 ft.)	1.4 mi.	150 ft. (rev. 150 ft.)	0:45

This route connects Woronoco Trail with Shaw Trail. It leads through the center of Pawtuckaway State Park and makes possible an interesting 7.3-mi. loop hike over South Mtn. Marked with white diamonds, Split Rock

SEC 5

Trail diverges left from Woronoco Trail 1.5 mi. north of the Mountain Trail/Round Pond Trail trailhead on the park entrance road. It climbs briefly, swings right, and follows a meandering course at easy grades, passing to the left of a split boulder at 0.2 mi. It climbs over a knoll and swings right around a large glacial erratic (right) at 0.6 mi. The trail descends to cross a brook at 0.8 mi., ascends again, and then descends past a small swamp and more boulders. After passing to the left of a towering erratic, Split Rock Trail ends at Shaw Trail. Shaw Trail leads left 1.2 mi. to South Ridge Trail, and right 1.8 mi. to Fundy Trail.

FUNDY TRAIL
(NHDP; AMC PAWTUCKAWAY STATE PARK SOUTH MAP)
Cumulative from park entrance road
(250 ft.) to:

	⇅	↗	↻
Shaw Trail (270 ft.)	1.0 mi.	0 ft.	0:30
Boat launch (250 ft.)	1.7 mi.	0 ft.	0:50

This easy, scenic trail connects the park entrance road with the boat launch parking area at the northern tip of the northwest arm of Fundy Cove on Pawtuckaway Lake, reached in just a little more than 0.5 mi. by Fundy Rd., a good gravel road from Deerfield Rd. Fundy Trail has easy grades and mostly dry footing, and it passes interesting wetlands and historical sites. The white-blazed trail leaves the park entrance road 1.4 mi. north of the tollbooth and 1.0 mi. north of the Mountain Trail/Round Pond Trail trailhead. Parking is available across the road in the group picnic and camping area; do not block the trail entrance.

The trail follows a gravel road north between two wooden stakes, turns left onto an old road (arrow), and soon crosses a bridge over a small stream; on the far side, Woronoco Trail diverges left at 0.2 mi. Fundy Trail leads through the woods parallel to the western shore of Burnham's Marsh on the right, passing an open viewpoint at 0.5 mi. and a view over the northern part of the marsh at 0.7 mi.

At 1.0 mi. Fundy Trail crosses wooden planks over a brook next to a beaver bog on the left and immediately reaches the eastern terminus of Shaw Trail, also on the left, which affords access to the western trail network near Round Pond and South Mtn. Fundy Trail continues straight. At 1.2 mi. an opening 10 yd. to the right provides a fine view over Fundy Cove, an arm of Pawtuckaway Lake. Soon several old stone walls, cellar holes, and unmarked paths are visible on both sides of the trail, marking the site of a farming community that flourished more than 150 years ago.

The trail bears away from the lake, passes more stone walls and unmarked paths, crosses a bridge over an inlet to the north arm of Fundy Cove, and reaches the boat launch parking area.

SHAW TRAIL
(NEMBA; AMC PAWTUCKAWAY STATE PARK MAPS)

Cumulative from Fundy Trail (270 ft.) to:	⇅	↗	⟳
Split Rock Trail (390 ft.)	1.8 mi.	200 ft. (rev. 100 ft.)	1:00
South Ridge Trail (480 ft.)	3.0 mi.	400 ft. (rev. 100 ft.)	1:40

This route connects Fundy Trail near the southwest corner of Fundy Cove with South Ridge Trail south of Round Pond. It begins on Fundy Trail 1.0 mi. north of the park entrance road and 0.7 mi. south of the boat launch parking area. In the past Shaw Trail was often flooded near its eastern end, but a relocation now avoids the flooded area. In recent years the trail has been dry (with only an occasional muddy spot), has been well blazed in white, and is easily followed.

SEC 5

Shaw Trail follows an old road west alongside swamps and marshes. At 0.4 mi. it passes through a stone wall, bears right at a fork, and quickly descends to cross a brook that flows between two beaver ponds. It runs north along the east edge of a swamp, and at 0.7 mi. it makes a sharp turn left (south) and doubles back along the west side of the swamp. At 0.9 mi. Shaw Trail turns right into the woods at a double blaze and ascends easily, swinging left over a knoll where an older route of the trail leads into a swampy area on the right. (The older route rejoins the main route in 125 yd.) Shaw Trail continues on higher ground, with minor ups and downs, and at 1.4 mi. it turns sharply right (north) and ascends. At 1.8 mi. Split Rock Trail joins from the left. Here, Shaw Trail swings right and then swings left (west), with more ups and downs. At 2.3 mi. it descends to cross a small brook and soon runs across a stone wall and through a rocky area on a relocated section. At 2.5 mi. the trail turns left onto an old woods road. (In the reverse direction, turn right off the woods road.)

Shaw Trail follows the road at easy grades and then swings left and climbs moderately up a northern shoulder of South Mtn. It swings right and descends to cross a bridge over a small brook just before ending at a T intersection with South Ridge Trail. From here, it is 0.1 mi. to the left (south) to South Ridge Connector leading to Tower Rd. and 0.6 mi. to the right (north) to Round Pond Rd. and Boulder Trail at the northwestern end of Round Pond.

HOWARD SWAIN MEMORIAL FOREST

This 89-acre property in Deerfield and Nottingham provides access to a ledgy outcropping on the shore of Dead Pond with views up to the cliffs of Rocky Ridge, a section of the ancient ring dike that makes up the Pawtuckaway Mtns. The bouldery terrain around Dead Pond is very reminiscent of the neighboring peaks. (Additional trails are being considered to connect the forest to Pawtuckaway State Park.) Grades are mostly easy, and footing is good. A trail map is available at seltnh.org.

From NH 101, take Exit 3 and follow NH 43 north for 9.4 mi. then bear right onto Nottingham Rd. In 0.8 mi. bear right at the village of Deerfield Parade, and continue 2.5 mi. to a short access road on the right (the sign for the forest is set back from the road) that leads to a small parking area, kiosk, and gate.

HOWARD'S PATH (SELT; SELT MAP)
Cumulative from parking area (450 ft.) to:

	⇅	↗	○
Dead Pond outlook (500 ft.)	0.8 mi.	120 ft.	0:30
Starting point by loop via Quarry Trail	1.8 mi.	180 ft.	1:00

Howard's Path ascends easily along a woods road, heads straight through a clearing at 0.1 mi., and then dips to cross a causeway over a small inlet brook, with a view to a beaver pond on the right. The red-blazed trail swings right and makes a short, steep ascent to a lower junction with blue-blazed Quarry Trail at 0.3 mi. (This 0.4-mi. alternate loop trail passes high above the beaver pond, with an old quarry and a small cave on the left, and then ascends easily along the north side of a minor ridge to rejoin Howard's Path.)

Howard's Path bears left at the Quarry Trail junction, swings left through an area of boulders, and then meanders at easy grades, passing a vernal pool on the right at 0.4 mi. At 0.5 mi. it reaches the upper end of Quarry Trail. Here, Howard's Path bears left and narrows into a footpath. It runs on bog bridges through a wet area—passing a large glacial boulder—climbs over a small rise, and then descends gradually through boulders to a ledgy area and granite bench on the shore of Dead Pond.

STONEHOUSE FOREST

This multiuse trail system in Barrington, open to hikers, skiers, snowshoers and mountain bikers (with limited use by horses and snowmobiles; see SELT map for permitted uses) and maintained by Southeast Land Trust of New Hampshire, was opened in 2019 to connect with the existing trails

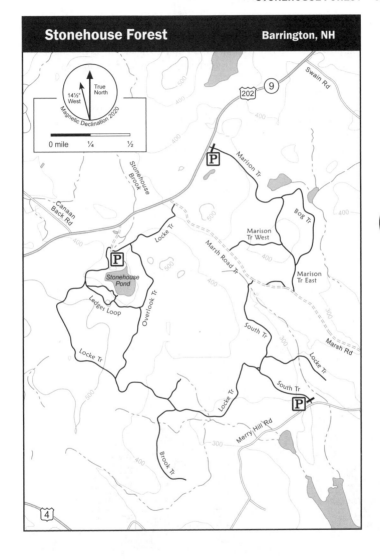

Stonehouse Forest — Barrington, NH

SEC 5

around Stonehouse Pond, a small, attractive pond dominated by a prow-like cliff that rises about 150 ft. from the water's edge on the southwest shore, forming an unusual and picturesque combination of rock and water. There are interesting views from the top of the cliff down to the pond and out across nearby hills.

Stonehouse Forest consists of more than 50 parcels of land that were once envisioned by a European investor as being a private exotic game hunting preserve, the evidence of which can still be seen in the form of old woods roads laid out with decorative stone walls and other architectural landscaping. While the project was ultimately abandoned, some of the property's nearly 11 mi. of trails follow this network of old roads. A map of the trail system is available at seltnh.org, or see the AMC map on p. 307.

The forest is served by three trailheads with parking and kiosks on the north, west and south (refer to map). The Marison trailhead (SELT sign: "Stonehouse Forest") is located along US 202, 3.7 mi. northeast of US 4 in Northwood (and 0.7 mi. northeast of the access road to the Stonehouse Pond trailhead). This trailhead is plowed in winter. To reach the Stonehouse Pond trailhead from US 202/NH 9—either 2.0 mi. west of the point where these routes divide west of Barrington village, or 3.0 mi. east of where they join US 4 in Northwood—a gravel side road (sign: "Stonehouse Pond") leads south 0.2 mi. to a kiosk and parking area. This access road is open to vehicles from April through October and may be gated at other times (SELT is planning to construct a winter parking area before the gate by winter 2020/2021). The Merry Hill Rd. trailhead (SELT sign: "Stonehouse Forest") is located along Merry Hill Rd., 1.6 mi. north of US 4 in Nottingham. This trailhead is also plowed in winter.

LOCKE TRAIL (SELT; SELT MAP)

Cumulative from Marsh Rd.

(410 ft.) to:	↧↥	↗	↻
Overlook Trail (390 ft.)	0.5 mi.	50 ft. (rev. 50 ft.)	0:15
Stonehouse Pond trailhead (370 ft.)	0.6 mi.	50 ft.	0:20
Ledges Loop (430 ft.)	1.0 mi.	130 ft.	0:35
Overlook Trail (485 ft.)	1.9 mi.	300 ft. (rev. 115 ft.)	1:05
Brook Trail (350 ft.)	2.4 mi.	300 ft. (rev. 135 ft.)	1:20
South Trail (360 ft.)	3.2 mi.	380 ft. (rev. 70 ft.)	1:45
SELT boundary (325 ft.)	3.8 mi.	410 ft. (rev. 70 ft.)	2:05
Starting point by loop via Locke Trail, South Trail, Marsh Road	4.7 mi.	550 ft. (rev. 370 ft.)	2:35

This trail, which follows a combination of snowmobile routes and is blazed in green, is the longest in the forest, stretching nearly 4 mi. from Marsh Rd. (an unmarked and unmaintained old town road that bisects the property and is used as a snowmobile trail and connecting route between trails; indicated as Longmarsh Rd. on some maps) to a SELT property boundary near the Merry Hill Rd. trailhead and runs mainly through the southwest section of the property, making various loop hikes possible. It also provides a portion of the main access routes to the Stonehouse Pond cliff. A section of this trail passes through private property; please stay on the marked trail and obey all posted signage.

From Marsh Rd., less than 0.1 mi. southeast of US 202 (no formal parking), Locke Trail heads southwest and descends easily, makes a gradual ascent, then dips to a junction on left with Overlook Trail at 0.5 mi. It reaches the Stonehouse Pond trailhead at 0.6 mi. and continues straight through a gate. It then ascends gradually on a winding route, swinging right at 0.8 mi. where beaten side paths lead left to the shore of Stonehouse Pond. At 1.0 mi. it bears right at a fork where Ledges Loop diverges left, climbs briefly, then turns right and enters private property (sign). For the next 0.6 mi. there are no SELT blazes, but in late 2019 the trail was well marked with blue flagging.

Locke Trail continues climbing easily, turns left onto another snowmobile trail at 1.2 mi. (in reverse, bear right here at arrow), continues straight through two unmarked junctions, then ascends gradually to the wooded summit of Bumfagging Hill (601 ft.; high point just off-trail on right) at 1.6 mi. The origin of this oddly named hill is uncertain, but there is some speculation it derives from "bumfeg," an obsolete sixteenth- and seventeenth-century term meaning to flog, beat, or thrash.

From the summit, Locke Trail soon reenters SELT property (sign), descends gradually to a junction with Overlook Trail on the left at 1.9 mi., followed by two junctions with Brook Trail—the northern branch at 2.4 mi. on the left and the southern branch less than 0.1 mi. farther on the right. It continues on a gentle descent past a wetland area on the right, runs level, then ascends again past an old warming hut. At 3.2 mi., Locke Trail bears left twice, briefly coincides with South Trail (green and blue blazes) and at 3.3 mi. diverges right off South Trail and descends to the property boundary (sign) at 3.8 mi.

SEC 5

LEDGES LOOP (SELT; SELT MAP)

Cumulative from Locke Trail
(430 ft.) to:

	⇕	⬈	⟳
Stonehouse Pond cliff (530 ft.)	0.3 mi.	100 ft.	0:10
Overlook Trail (480 ft.)	0.5 mi.	160 ft. (rev. 110 ft.)	0:20
Starting point by loop over cliff	0.6 mi.	100 ft. (rev. 100 ft.)	0:20

This loop trail leads to the spectacular cliff overlooking Stonehouse Pond where there are excellent views. Blazed in red, Ledges Loop diverges left from Locke Trail 0.4 mi. southwest of the Stonehouse Pond trailhead. It ascends easily 75 yds. to a junction where the loop splits into two branches. Turning left, Ledges Loop runs level along the base of a high rock wall on the right, climbs briefly, dips to cross a small brook, then ascends on a winding route to the main ledge overlooking the pond at 0.3 mi. Atop the ledge, the trail turns right and exits the back of it at a junction where a short branch on the left (also blazed in red) leads 0.2 mi. to Overlook Trail. At this junction, Ledges Loop bears right (despite no sign indicating this and no visible blaze ahead), descends easily, swings right around a rocky outcropping, and continues a gradual descent back to the loop junction at 0.6 mi. Continue straight and then turn right onto Locke Trail for 0.4 mi. to return to the trailhead.

OVERLOOK TRAIL (SELT; SELT MAP)

Cumulative from southern junction
with Locke Trail (485 ft.) to:

	⇕	⬈	⟳
Ledges Loop (480 ft.)	0.5 mi.	70 ft. (rev. 50 ft.)	0:15
Northern junction with Locke Trail (390 ft.)	1.0 mi.	120 ft. (rev. 60 ft.)	0:35

This trail connects two ends of Locke Trail and also provides access to the Stonehouse Pond cliff. From its southern junction with Locke Trail, 1.8 mi. from the Merry Hill Rd. trailhead, yellow-blazed Overlook Trail heads northeast, descends to cross a small stream, then ascends with several minor dips to T junction at 0.5 mi. with a short branch of Ledges Loop. Turn left here to reach the cliff in 0.2 mi. At this junction, Overlook Trail turns right (despite a sign pointing straight ahead), descends through two switchbacks, then swings left and makes a gradual descent to its northern junction with Locke Trail at 1.0 mi., 0.1 mi. east of the Stonehouse Pond trailhead.

BROOK TRAIL (SELT; SELT MAP)

Cumulative from SELT boundary
(380 ft.) to:

	⇕	⬈	⟳
Locke Trail (335 ft.)	0.7 mi.	30 ft. (rev. 80 ft.)	0:20
Scenic outlook (355 ft.)	0.8 mi.	40 ft. (rev. 80 ft.)	0:20

This white-blazed trail begins at a SELT property boundary near the southern corner of the forest 0.7 mi. south of Locke Trail and ends at a scenic outlook at a marsh. Sections of this trail can be wet at times. From the property boundary (sign), Brook Trail heads generally north at easy grades with several minor ascents and descents, crosses a small brook at 0.5 mi., then reaches a junction with Locke Trail at 0.7 mi. It turns left and both trails briefly coincide (marked with green and white blazes), then Brook Trail diverges right onto a footpath and continues to the outlook at 0.8 mi.

SOUTH TRAIL (SELT; SELT MAP)

Cumulative from Merry Hill Rd. (300 ft.) to:	⇅	↗	○
Locke Trail (360 ft.)	0.4 mi.	60 ft.	0:15
Marsh Rd. (320 ft.)	1.1 mi.	140 ft. (rev. 90 ft.)	0:35

This blue-blazed trail leaves from the Merry Hill Rd. trailhead and provides access to Locke Trail and Marsh Rd. From the trailhead, South Trail ascends along a wide woods road and at 0.4 mi. turns right onto an older road where Locke Trail continues ahead. Both trails briefly coincide (blazed in both blue and green), and at 0.5 mi. Locke Trail diverges right. South Trail continues ahead and descends on a winding route, crosses two small seasonal streams, and ends at Marsh Rd. at 1.1 mi.

MARISON TRAIL (SELT; SELT MAP)

Cumulative from Marison trailhead (450 ft.) to:	⇅	↗	○
Bog Trail (375 ft.)	0.7 mi.	30 ft. (rev. 100 ft.)	0:20
Branch junction (440 ft.)	1.0 mi.	90 ft.	0:30
Bog Trail via Marison East (365 ft.)	1.2 mi.	90 ft. (rev. 70 ft.)	0:40
Marsh Rd. via Marison East (350 ft.)	1.3 mi.	90 ft. (rev. 90 ft.)	0:40
Marsh Rd. via Marison West (350 ft.)	1.4 mi.	90 ft. (rev. 90 ft.)	0:45

This red-blazed trail is the main access route from the Marison trailhead. It ascends along a wide road to a clearing, then descends moderately at first then easily to a fork in a large clearing at 0.7 mi., where stone steps and an old foundation from the abandoned hunting preserve can be seen on the right. Here, Bog Trail diverges left and Marison Trail bears right and ascends to another large clearing at 1.0 mi. at the summit of an unnamed 440-ft. hill, site of an old warming hut, old cellar hole, and capped well. At a fork in the clearing (signs), Marison Trail splits off into two short red-blazed branches:

SEC 5

Marison East. Bearing left at the fork, this branch quickly swings right and descends to a junction with Bog Trail on the right at 0.2 mi., then ascends slightly to a junction with Marsh Rd. at 0.3 mi.

Marison West. Turning right at the fork, this branch passes in front of the hut in the clearing and descends along a small ridge, swings left, and then runs mostly level to junction with Marsh Rd. at 0.4 mi.

BOG TRAIL (SELT; SELT MAP)
From Marison Trail
(375 ft.) to:

	�???	↗	↻
Marison East (365 ft.)	0.7 mi.	30 ft.	0:20

This loop trail, blazed in white, begins on Marison Trail 0.7 mi. from the Marison trailhead. It diverges left at a fork in a clearing (sign) and ascends gradually along a wide road. It swings right and descends past a shelter and view down to the easternmost of the twin Round Ponds on the left at 0.2 mi., and at 0.4 mi. reaches another clearing. Bog Trail bears right here (arrow), enters the woods onto a footpath and continues mostly level with minor ups and downs to a junction with Marison East at 0.7 mi.

BLUE HILLS RANGE

The small but prominent Blue Hills Range, in the towns of Strafford and Farmington, consists of (from west to east) Evans Mtn. (1,232 ft.), Parker Mtn. (1,407 ft.), Mack Mtn. (1,145 ft.), Blue Job Mtn. (1,353 ft.), Nubble Mtn. (1,030 ft.), Hussey Mtn. (1,204 ft.), and Chesley Mtn. (1,035 ft.). Trails on Parker Mtn. and Blue Job Mtn. offer interesting walks; the best views are from the fire tower on Blue Job Mtn. and the open summit of Little Blue Job Mtn.

■ BLUE JOB MTN. (1,353 FT.)

Blue Job Mtn. is in Farmington, near the Strafford town line. There are excellent views from the fire tower on its summit as well as from its completely open lower subpeak, often called Little Blue Job Mtn. (1,250 ft.). In 2019 the trail system here was improved with new signage. A revised trail map should be available at nhdfl.org and at the main trailhead kiosk; also refer to the AMC map on p. 313 or the USGS Baxter Lake quadrangle.

The main trailhead is on First Crown Point Rd., which leaves NH 202A 3.9 mi. east of its junction with NH 126 in Center Strafford, or 4.5 mi. west of its junction with US 202 near Rochester. The trailhead is at a parking area (sign: "Blue Job State Forest") 4.8 mi. northwest from NH 202A (First Crown Point Rd. turns left at a stop sign 1.2 mi. from NH 202A.)

Blue Job Mtn.

Farmington, NH

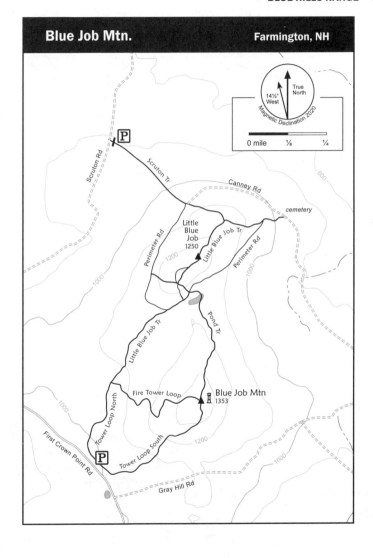

True North

14½° West

Magnetic Declination 2020

0 mile   ⅛   ¼

Scruton Rd

P

Scruton Tr

Canney Rd

800

cemetery

Perimeter Rd

Little Blue Job 1250

Little Blue Job Tr

1200

Perimeter Rd

1000

Little Blue Job Tr

Pond Tr

1000

Fire Tower Loop

Blue Job Mtn 1353

Tower Loop North

Tower Loop South

1200

1000

First Crown Point Rd

P

Gray Hill Rd

FIRE TOWER LOOP (NHDFL; NHDFL MAP, USGS BAXTER LAKE QUAD)

Cumulative from First Crown Point Rd. (970 ft.) to:	⇵	↗	↻
Blue Job Mtn. summit/Pond Trail (1,353 ft.)	0.5 mi.	400 ft.	0:25
Little Blue Job Trail (1,070 ft.)	1.0 mi.	400 ft. (rev. 300 ft.)	0:40
Starting point via complete loop	1.3 mi.	400 ft. (rev. 100 ft.)	0:50

This loop trail (faded orange blazes) over the summit of Blue Job Mtn. consists of the old fire warden's route and a newer route to the north of the old one, made up of a combination of woods roads and sections of footpath. In 2018, a 0.2-mi. relocation opened to bypass a new home that was constructed at the base of the mountain. The lower part of Fire Tower Loop is on private land whose owners have generously provided access; the upper part, including the summit, is in the Blue Job State Forest.

The loop is described here in the counterclockwise direction, because most hikers will probably find the footing on the steep and eroded fire warden's route easier for ascent. From the trailhead kiosk turn right, crossing an improved private road (which uses part of the fire warden's jeep road) in 75 yd. Fire Tower Loop soon joins the old fire warden's route, swings left at 0.1 mi., and ascends on a rough, rocky path—rather steeply at times—to a point just east of the summit and ledge with a restricted view 40 yd. down to the right. In another 80 yd. the trail swings left and ascends the last pitch to the summit and fire tower at 0.5 mi. (Climb the tower for the best views.)

From the summit, the loop trail descends northwest, then west, following a jeep road with fairly steep ledgy sections that are occasionally paved to minimize erosion. The road turns sharply left, and at 0.7 mi. it turns right just above the edge of an open field, with a communications tower visible through the trees. From this point downward, public use of the jeep road is prohibited; Fire Tower Loop turns right, off the road, and follows a footpath. It descends moderately through fine woods, crosses a small brook, and then turns left at a junction with Little Blue Job Trail, which leaves right at 1.0 mi. Fire Tower Loop recrosses the brook on a boardwalk and then bears right (the closed former route continues ahead and is now posted as no trespassing) onto a relocated section that descends easily to the trailhead and parking area at 1.3 mi.

LITTLE BLUE JOB TRAIL
(NHDFL MAP, USGS BAXTER LAKE QUAD)

Cumulative from Fire Tower Loop (1,070 ft.) to:	↓↑	↗	↺
Little Blue Job summit (1,250 ft.)	0.6 mi.	180 ft.	0:25
Scruton Trail (1,160 ft.)	0.7 mi.	180 ft. (rev. 90 ft.)	0:25
Canney Rd. (1,000 ft.)	0.9 mi.	180 ft. (rev. 160 ft.)	0:30

This unblazed trail leads to the open summit of the northern subpeak of Blue Job Mtn., often referred to as Little Blue Job, which provides excellent views in all directions. The lower section is on private land, and the upper section is within Blue Job State Forest. Footing is slightly rough, and the upper section is eroded from heavy use. This trail intersects many informal paths, so hikers must be careful to stay on the main route.

Little Blue Job Trail begins 0.3 mi. from the main trailhead along the northern section of Fire Tower Loop, where the mileages described below begin. From the junction where Fire Tower Loop turns right, Little Blue Job Trail continues straight and ascends at easy grades over a rooty footbed; at 0.3 mi. it crosses a newer skid road and descends to a muddy sag. Footing becomes more eroded as the trail climbs easily, bears right at a prominent fork, and then reaches a four-way junction at 0.4 mi. in the shallow col between Blue Job Mtn. and Little Blue Job. Little Blue Job Trail turns left here and ascends—easily at first, then steeply—an eroded pitch to reach the first open ledges. Grades ease as the trail breaks out into the open, clambers over ledges, and then makes a short traverse across the open ridge to the bare summit at 0.6 mi.

Little Blue Job Trail continues north over the summit and descends moderately over ledges marked with cairns to a junction with Scruton Trail on the left at 0.7 mi. It then swings right, passes through a stone wall, and descends easily through blueberry pastures with excellent views to end at Canney Rd., an abandoned town road, at 0.9 mi.

POND TRAIL (NHDFL MAP, USGS BAXTER LAKE QUAD)

Cumulative from Blue Job Mtn. summit (1,353 ft.) to:	↓↑	↗	↺
Little Blue Job Trail (1,220 ft.)	0.5 mi.	50 ft. (rev. 190 ft.)	0:15
Little Blue Job summit via Little Blue Job Trail (1,250 ft.)	0.7 mi.	80 ft. (rev. 190 ft.)	0:25

SEC 5

This trail connects Blue Job Mtn. and Little Blue Job. It is not blazed, but it is signed at both ends and is marked with cairns in ledgy areas. From the Blue Job Mtn. fire tower, Pond Trail leaves the north side of the summit and descends moderately over ledges, bearing right at a fork. At 0.2 mi. grades ease, and the trail slowly curves left, dips back into the woods, and then emerges on open ledges with a view back to the main summit. It soon levels and passes the small pond in the saddle between the peaks. At 0.4 mi. Pond Trail continues straight at a four-way junction with Perimeter Rd. (an old woods road that loops around the southern side of Little Blue Job). It then ascends easily to end at a junction with Little Blue Job Trail at 0.5 mi. Turn right (in the reverse direction, turn left at this junction for Pond Trail; Little Blue Job Trail continues straight) for an easy 0.2-mi. climb to the Little Blue Job summit.

SCRUTON TRAIL (NHDFL MAP, USGS BAXTER LAKE QUAD)

Cumulative from Scruton Rd.
(910 ft.) to:

	⇅	↗	↻
Little Blue Job Trail (1,160 ft.)	0.5 mi.	250 ft.	0:20
Little Blue Job summit via Little Blue Job Trail (1,250 ft.)	0.6 mi.	340 ft.	0:30

This signed but unblazed route ascends to Little Blue Job Trail just below the summit of Little Blue Job. It begins on Scruton Rd. in Farmington, 0.6 mi. south of Meaderboro Rd. The signed trailhead has a small parking area. Scruton Trail follows an old woods road at easy to moderate grades to a junction at 0.3 mi. where Canney Rd. turns left and Perimeter Rd. turns right. It continues straight ahead and climbs through a large blueberry pasture, with increasing views, to end at a junction with Little Blue Job Trail at 0.5 mi. Turn right here for a moderate 0.1 mi. ascent to the summit.

■ PARKER MTN. (1,407 FT.)

Parker Mtn., in the town of Strafford, is a long, fairly flat-topped ridge running southwest to northeast, with gentle slopes on the northwest but steep ones on the southeast. Refer to the USGS Parker Mtn. quadrangle. A small network of trails provides access on the northeast side of the mountain, which is in the Strafford Town Forest. A hand-drawn trail map is available at strafford.nh.gov.

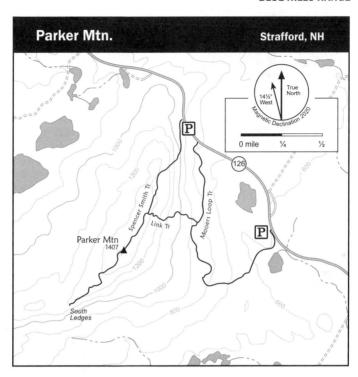

Parker Mtn.

Strafford, NH

Parker Mtn
1407

South
Ledges

SPENCER SMITH TRAIL (TSCC; TSCC MAP, USGS PARKER MTN. QUAD, AMC PARKER MTN. MAP)

Cumulative from NH 126 (910 ft.) to:	⇅	↗	↺
Parker Mtn. summit (1,407 ft.) via Spencer Smith Trail	1.1 mi.	500 ft.	0:50
South ledges (1,180 ft.)	1.8 mi.	500 ft. (rev. 250 ft.)	1:10
Starting point by loop via Link Trail and Mooers Loop Trail, including side trip to south ledges	4.2 mi.	850 ft.	2:30

Spencer Smith Trail, the main trail on Parker Mtn., ascends from the east (NH 126) and follows the ridge crest to the summit; then it continues down through private conservation land to open ledges with good views. Spencer Smith, Link, and Mooers Loop trails can make an attractive loop that is best hiked in the sequence described, because the eroded footing on Spencer Smith Trail is better tackled on the ascent. In addition to the trails mentioned here, there are others connected to the summer camps on the ponds at the northwest foot of the mountain.

Red-blazed Spencer Smith Trail (sign) begins at a wide turnout on the west side of NH 126 just south of its height-of-land, 7.4 mi. south of its junction with NH 28 in Center Barnstead and 2.5 mi. north of its northern junction with NH 202A in Center Strafford. The two trailheads for Mooers Loop Trail are 0.2 mi. and 1.1 mi. south of the trailhead for Spencer Smith Trail, respectively; the southern trailhead is in a field just south of a white farmhouse and opposite a brick house, marked by a Mooers Loop Trail signpost and a sign for the Strafford Town Forest.

From the turnout, Spencer Smith Trail passes a gate and follows a woods road uphill. At 0.3 mi. an unmarked but obvious side path leads 15 yd. left to a ledge with good views to the south, with nearby Blue Job Mtn. just barely visible to the far left. The badly eroded old woods road climbs fairly steeply, with rough footing; it reaches the shoulder of the ridge at 0.4 mi. and follows the ledgy ridge crest with generally easy grades. At 0.8 mi. it crosses an open ledgy area. Here, blue-blazed Link Trail comes up from the left (south) at a signed junction. At the junction, Spencer Smith Trail turns right and heads to the top of the ledge, where an arrow and "Bow" (for Bow Lake) are painted in red (very faded) on the rock. Limited views look back (east) over the trees; on the north side of the trail is a crudely built stone enclosure. The route soon swings left, descends slightly, and continues south along the ridge crest across ledges and through minor sags, passing a sparsely blazed path that runs off to the north. At 1.1 mi., after a short climb, the trail reaches the viewless true summit, where there is a large cairn under a pine tree that is intertwined with a small spruce. A ledge with old inscriptions is nearby. From here, Spencer Smith Trail descends gradually southwest down the ledgy ridge; at 1.8 mi. it ends at open ledges with excellent views south over Bow Lake.

To make a loop hike via Link Trail and Mooers Loop Trail in the recommended direction, follow Spencer Smith Trail back along the ridge to the junction on the right with Link Trail. Blue-blazed Link Trail descends east through a ledgy area, where the footway is obscured; follow the blazes carefully. It soon swings left for a rough sidehill traverse across the ledgy slope and then in about 50 yd. turns right and descends into the woods. It descends moderately through fine hemlock forest with good footing; follow the blazes carefully through the path's many twists and turns. At 0.6 mi. from Spencer Smith Trail, Link Trail ends at a T junction with red-blazed Mooers Loop Trail.

To complete the loop, turn left onto the northern section of Mooers Loop Trail, which follows an old woods road. The trail descends gradually north along the base of the steep southeast slope of Parker Mtn. for 0.6 mi., crossing several small brooks. It then swings right and ascends gradually to the northern trailhead for Mooers Loop Trail on NH 126. Turn left onto the road and walk 0.2 mi. up the gravel shoulder to the trailhead for Spencer Smith Trail. (From the junction with Link Trail, the southern section of Mooers Loop Trail, not described here, continues southeast to its southern trailhead on NH 126, 0.9 mi. south of its northern trailhead.)

MOOERS LOOP TRAIL (TSCC; TSCC MAP, USGS PARKER MTN. QUAD, AMC PARKER MTN. MAP)

Cumulative from southeastern trailhead (600 ft.) to:	⬆⬇	↗	↻
Link Trail (880 ft.)	1.3 mi.	280 ft.	0:45
Northwestern trailhead (820 ft.)	1.9 mi.	340 ft. (rev. 120 ft.)	1:05

This trail forms a partial loop between two trailheads located along NH 126 and in conjunction with Link Trail and Spencer Smith Trail, provides an alternative route to the summit of Parker Mtn. The southeastern trailhead is located 1.8 mi. northwest of Center Strafford in a large clearing on the south side of the road with plentiful parking (sign: "Strafford Town Forest"). The northwestern trailhead is 0.9 mi. farther west, also on the south side of the road, marked by a faded orange blaze and hard-to-see sign ("Mooers Loop Trail"). There is a pull-off here with room for a few cars.

From the southeastern trailhead, the orange-blazed trail leaves from the south side of the clearing at a white post ("Mooers Loop"), passes around a gate, then ascends at easy grades along an old logging road. In an unmarked clearing at 0.4 mi. it bears right (in reverse, bear left out of the clearing) and climbs moderately to a right turn at 0.8 mi., marked by a cairn and double blaze. Mooer's Loop Trail enters the woods here onto a footpath and ascends easily over rolling terrain. The trail is well-marked in this section, but requires some care to follow due to light use and lack of distinct treadway in areas. It crosses a small brook at 1.1 mi., climbs over a height-of-land then swings right then left to reach a junction with Link Trail on the left at 1.3 mi. Mooer's Loop Trail continues ahead along an old woods road, descends gradually, then ascends briefly to the northwestern trailhead at 1.9 mi.

APPENDIX

HELPFUL INFORMATION AND CONTACTS

Organization	Office	Phone Number
Appalachian Mountain Club (AMC)	Main Office	800-372-1758 (membership); 617-523-0636 (general info); 603-466-2727 (reservations)
AMC Berkshire Chapter		
AMC Cardigan Lodge		603-466-2727 (reservations)
AMC New Hampshire Chapter		
AMC Three Mile Island Camp		856-235-2210 (before June 15); 603-279-7626 (after June 15)
Ausbon Sargent Land Preservation Trust		603-526-6555
Bedford Conservation Commission		603-472-5242
Bedford Land Trust		603-228-1231
Belknap Range Conservation Coalition		
Belknap Range Trail Tenders		603-286-3506
Bow Open Spaces		603-225-3678
Bradford Conservation Commission		603-938-5900
Cardigan Highlanders Volunteer Trail Crew		603-727-2750
Chesterfield Conservation Commission		603-363-4624
City of Concord's Conservation Commission		603-225-8610
Crotched Mtn. Foundation		603-547-3311
Epsom Conservation Commission		603-736-9002

Address or Location	Website, Email
10 City Square, Boston, MA 02129	outdoors.org, AMCmembership@outdoors.org, AMCinformation@outdoors.org, AMClodging@outdoors.org
	amcberkshire.org
	outdoors.org/lodging/cardigan, AMClodging@outdoors.org
	amc-nh.org
P.O. Box 736, Moorestown, NJ 08057; AMC via U.S. Mail Boat, Laconia, NH 03246	3mile.org
P.O. Box 2040, New London, NH 03257	ausbonsargent.org
24 North Amherst Rd., Bedford, NH 03110	bedfordnh.org
53 Regional Dr, Suite 1, Concord, NH 03301	bedfordlandtrust.org, info@BedfordLandTrust.org
P.O. Box 151, Gilmanton, NH 03837	belknaprange.org, info@belknaprange.org
	facebook.com/belknaprangetrailtenders, halpeg76@metrocast.net
41 South Bow Rd., Bow, NH 03304	bowopenspaces.com
	bradfordnh.org , bcc@bradfordnh.org
P.O. Box 104, Enfield Center, NH 03749	cardiganhighlanders.com
P.O. Box 175, Chesterfield, NH 03443	chesterfieldoutdoors.com
41 Green St., Concord, NH 03301	concordnh.gov
1 Verney Dr., Greenfield, NH 03047	crotchedmountain.org, info@crotchedmountain.org
P.O. Box 10, Epsom, NH 03234	epsomnh.org

Organization	Office	Phone Number
Five Rivers Conservation Trust		603-225-7225
Francestown Conservation Commission		603-547-8773
Friends of Pisgah		
Friends of the Wapack		
Great Bay Resource Protection Partnership		
Griswold Scout Reservation (Daniel Webster Council, Boy Scouts of America)		603-625-6431
Hanover Conservancy		603-643-3433
Harris Center for Conservation Education		603-525-3394
Hebron Conservation Commission		603-744-2631
Lakes Region Conservation Trust		603-253-3301
Leave No Trace		800-332-4100
Monadnock Conservancy		603-357-0600
Monadnock–Sunapee Greenway Trail Club		
National Weather Service (Gray/Portland, ME)		207-688-3216 (office); 603-225-5191 (forecast)
The Nature Conservancy		603-224-5853
Nelson Trails Committee		603-847-0047
New England Mountain Bike Association		800-576-3622
New Hampshire Audubon		603-224-9909
New Hampshire Division of Forests and Lands		603-271-2214
New Hampshire Division of Parks and Recreation		603-271-3556
New Hampshire Outdoor Council		
New Hampshire State Parks campground reservations		877-647-2757

Address or Location	Website, Email
10 Ferry Street, Suite 311-A, Concord, NH 03301	5rct.org, info@5rct.org
P.O. Box 5, Francestown, NH 03043	francestownnh.org
P.O. Box 134, Chesterfield, NH 03443-0134	friendsofpisgah.org, friendsofpisgah@gmail.com
P.O. Box 115, West Peterborough, NH 03468	wapack.org, info@wapack.org
	greatbaypartnership.org, info@greatbaypartnership.org
571 Holt Ave., Manchester, NH 03109	nhscouting.org
71 Lyme Rd., Hanover, NH 03755	hanoverconservancy.org
83 Kings Highway, Hancock, NH 03449	harriscenter.org
P.O. Box 188, Hebron, NH 03241	hebronnh.org
P.O. Box 766, Center Harbor, NH 03226	lrct.org
P.O. Box 997, Boulder, CO 80306	lnt.org
P.O Box 337, Keene, NH 03431-0337	monadnockconservancy.org
P.O. Box 164, Marlow, NH 03456	msgtc.org, info@msgtc.org
P.O. Box 1208, Gray, ME 04039	weather.gov/gyx
22 Bridge St., 4th Floor, Concord, NH 03301	nature.org/newhampshire
7 Nelson Common Rd., Nelson, NH 03457	townofnelson.org
P.O. Box 2221, Acton, MA 01720	nemba.org, pk@nemba.org
84 Silk Farm Rd., Concord, NH 03301	nhaudubon.org, nha@nhaudubon.org
172 Pembroke Rd., Concord, NH 03301	nhdfl.org
172 Pembroke Rd., Concord, NH 03301	nhstateparks.org, nhparks@dncr.nh.gov
P.O. Box 157, Kearsarge, NH 03847-0157	nhoutdoorcouncil.org, nhocsecretary@nhoutdoorcouncil.org
	newhampshirestateparks. reserveamerica.com, nhocsecretary@nhoutdoorcouncil.org

Organization	Office	Phone Number
New Hampshire State Police		800-525-5555 (in-state emergency only); *77 (emergency cell in NH, ME, MA); 603-223-4381 (local)
New London Conservation Commission		
Plymouth Conservation Commission		603- 536-1731
Slim Baker Foundation for Outdoor Education		603-744-8094
Society for the Protection of New Hampshire Forests (Forest Society)		603-224-9945
Southeast Land Trust of New Hampshire		603-778-6088
Squam Lakes Association		603-968-7336
Sunapee–Ragged–Kearsarge Greenway Coalition		
Swanzey Conservation Commission		603-352-7411
Swanzey Open Space Committee		603-352-7411
Town of Hooksett's Conservation Commission		603-485-8471
Town of Strafford's Conservation Commission		603- 664-2192
United States Fish & Wildlife Service (Great Bay National Wildlife Reserve [NWR] and Wapack NWR, administered by Parker NWR)		978-465-5753
United States Geological Survey (New England Water Science Center - New Hampshire/Vermont Office)		888-275-8747
Wolfeboro Conservation Commission		603-569-5970

Address or Location	Website, Email
33 Hazen Dr., Concord, NH 03305	nh.gov
375 Main St., New London, NH 03257	nl-nhcc.com, nl_nhcc@yahoo.com
6 Post Office Sq., Plymouth, NH 03264	plymouth-nh.org/boards-committees/plymouth-conservation-commission, plyconcomm@gmail.com
Bristol, NH 03222	slimbaker.org
54 Portsmouth St., Concord, NH 03301	forestsociety.org, info@forestsociety.org
P.O. Box 675, Exeter, NH 03833	seltnh.org
534 U.S. Route 3, Holderness, NH 03245	squamlakes.org, info@squamlakes.org
P.O. Box 1684, New London, NH 03257	srkg.com, srkgc@srkg.com, trails@srkg.com (trail conditions)
P.O. Box 10009, Swanzey, NH 03446	swanzeynh.gov
P.O. Box 10009, Swanzey, NH 03446	swanzeynh.gov
35 Main St., Hooksett, NH 03106	hooksett.org
12 Mountain View Dr., Strafford, NH 03884	strafford.nh.gov, townclerk@strafford.nh.gov
Parker River NWR, 6 Plum Island Turnpike, Newburyport, MA, 01950	fws.gov, parkerriver@fws.gov
361 Commerce Way, Pembroke, NH 03275	store.usgs.gov, usgsstore@usgs.gov
P.O. Box 629, Wolfeboro, NH 03894	wolfeboronh.us

INDEX

Trail names in **bold type** indicate a detailed description in the text.

Where multiple page references appear, bold numbering indicates the main entry or entries for the trail.

[Bracketed information] indicates which of the four maps displays the features and where, by map section letter and number.

ABOUT AMC IN NEW HAMPSHIRE

The Appalachian Mountain Club's New Hampshire Chapter has more than 10,000 members and offers hundreds of trips each year. Well-trained and dedicated leaders guide hiking, paddling, skiing, and climbing excursions. The chapter is also active in trail work, conservation projects, and instructional programs. You can learn more about this chapter by visiting outdoors.org/chapters. To view a list of AMC activities in New Hampshire and other parts of the Northeast, visit trips.outdoors.org.

AMC BOOKS UPDATES

AMC Books strives to keep our guidebooks as up-to-date as possible to help you plan safe and enjoyable adventures. If we learn after publishing a book that relevant trails have been relocated or route or contact information has changed, we will post the updated information online. Before you hit the trail, visit outdoors.org/books-maps and click the "Book Updates" tab.

While hiking, if you notice discrepancies with the trip descriptions or maps, or if you find any other errors in this book, please let us know by submitting them to amcbookupdates@outdoors.org or to Books Editor, c/o AMC, 10 City Square, Boston, MA 02129. We will verify all submissions and post key updates each month. AMC Books is dedicated to being a recognized leader in outdoor publishing. Thank you for your participation.